THE NEW ENCYCLOPEDIA OF
AFRICAN, BRITISH &
EUROPEAN ANIMALS

THE NEW ENCYCLOPEDIA OF
AFRICAN, BRITISH &
EUROPEAN ANIMALS

TOM JACKSON

CONSULTANT: MICHAEL CHINERY

HERMES
HOUSE

This edition is published by Hermes House
an imprint of Anness Publishing Ltd
Hermes House
88–89 Blackfriars Road
London SE1 8HA
tel. 020 7401 2077
fax 020 7633 9499

www.hermeshouse.com; www.annesspublishing.com

If you like the images in this book and would like to investigate using
them for publishing, promotions or advertising, please visit our website
www.practicalpictures.com for more information.

Publisher: Joanna Lorenz
Senior Managing Editor: Conor Kilgallon
Senior Editor: Felicity Forster
Copy Editor: Alison Bolus
Designer: Nigel Partridge
Map Illustrator: Anthony Duke

Illustrators: Peter Barrett, Jim Channell, Rob Dyke,
John Francis, Rob Highton, Stuart Jackson-Carter,
Paul Jones, Stephen Lings, The Magic Group,
Shane Marsh, Robert Morton, Fiona Osbaldstone,
Mike Saunders and Sarah Smith
Production Controller: Wendy Lawson

ETHICAL TRADING POLICY

At Anness Publishing we believe that business should be conducted in an ethical and ecologically sustainable way, with respect for the environment and a proper regard to the replacement of the natural resources we employ. As a publisher, we use a lot of wood pulp to make high-quality paper for printing, and that wood commonly comes from spruce trees. We are therefore currently growing more than 500,000 trees in two Scottish forest plantations near Aberdeen – Berrymoss (130 hectares/320 acres) and West Touxhill (125 hectares/305 acres). The forests we manage contain twice the number of trees employed each year in paper-making for our books. Because of this ongoing ecological investment programme, you, as our customer, can have the pleasure and reassurance of knowing that a tree is being cultivated on your behalf to naturally replace the materials used to make the book you are holding. Our forestry programme is run in accordance with the UK Woodland Assurance Scheme (UKWAS) and will be certified by the internationally recognized Forest Stewardship Council (FSC). The FSC is a non-government organization dedicated to promoting responsible management of the world's forests. Certification ensures forests are managed in an environmentally sustainable and socially responsible way. For further information about this scheme, go to www.annesspublishing.com/trees.

A CIP catalogue record for this book
is available from the British Library.

Parts of this title also appear in *The World Encyclopedia of Animals*

1 3 5 7 9 10 8 6 4 2

PAGE 1: *Mountain gorilla.* PAGE 2: *Giraffe.* PAGE 3: *Reindeer.*
PAGE 4: *Loggerhead turtle; ruffed lemur.* PAGE 5: *Cheetah; fire salamanders.*

CONTENTS

INTRODUCTION

Africa, Britain and Europe are home to an extraordinary array of animal species. This book concentrates on amphibians, reptiles and mammals, with a section about understanding animals followed by a directory of animals across these continents.

The book opens with the question "what is an animal?" From very simple animals such as jellyfish and corals through to complex creatures such as birds and mammals, the first part of the book shows how animal bodies are organized, how they have evolved over time, and how their current forms survive and reproduce. The section focuses on the body forms of three main animal groups: amphibians, reptiles and mammals. This is followed by information about migration and hibernation, introduced and endangered species, and how ecologists are working to conserve wildlife. Finally, the section looks at the principal habitats, or biomes, in which animals live – oceans, fresh water, tropical forests, temperate forests, boreal forests, grasslands, polar regions, deserts, islands, mountains and human settlements – and explains how animals are able to survive in such varied environments, from the coldest Arctic landscapes to the hottest, driest deserts.

Below: Snakes are a large group of legless reptiles. Many, like this Natal green snake, live in warm parts of the world, such as Africa. This particular snake uses a venomous bite to kill prey, while other snakes squeeze the breath out of their prey with their muscular, coiled bodies.

Above: The world's islands are home to some of the most unusual animals in nature. For example, lemurs are found only in Madagascar. These animals live in the island's forests. Similar forests elsewhere in the world are populated by monkeys rather than lemurs.

The second part of the book consists of a directory sampling the many animals that populate African, British and European regions. Animals are displayed in related groups, beginning with amphibians such as salamanders, frogs and toads, then reptiles such as tortoises, lizards and crocodiles, and finally mammals such as big cats, hoofed animals and great apes.

Many of the world's most impressive beasts come from Africa, including the mighty rhinos, fierce lions and intelligent chimpanzees. The continent is also home to several giants: African elephants are the largest land animals on Earth, and the world's largest frog – the goliath bullfrog – lives in African rivers. Many of the continent's smaller animals may be harder to spot but are no less impressive. For example, naked mole rats inhabit tunnel networks in the semi-deserts of East Africa.

The animals of Britain and Europe have other claims to fame: for example, one of the world's smallest mammals, the tiny pygmy white-toothed shrew, is found across southern Europe. Also, many British and European animals are now very rare species: the chamois, once heavily hunted for its meat, lives in the steep alpine meadows of north-western Spain

Above: Not all mammals are furry and four-legged. Although dolphins have a few bristly hairs and are related to the land mammals, they never leave the water. Like whales and other sea mammals, a dolphin's limbs look more like a fish's fins than the legs of a land animal.

Above: Amphibians, such as this African bullfrog, were the first land animals. They have kept their close links to water, where their ancestors originated. Therefore amphibians are most common in damp places, such as riverbanks, where they can easily keep their bodies moist.

and central Italy, and is dependent on conservation efforts for its survival. Another example, the European bison, used to be very abundant at one time throughout Britain and Europe, but is now only found in eastern Europe.

As well as these indigenous examples, Europe is home to a wide range of introduced species. Many of them have been so successful in their new habitats that they are now seen as European animals in their own right. They include the cheeky barbary apes of

Gibraltar, originally from North Africa, the numerous grey squirrels that were brought to Europe from North America, and the raccoon dogs of eastern Asia, China and Japan, which were introduced to eastern Europe for fur-farming.

Last but not least, the book looks at sea mammals, from the common white-beaked dolphins of the Arctic Ocean to the critically endangered Mediterranean monk seals, discussing the unique adaptations that allow these aquatic animals to live in water.

Below: Cheetahs live in the grasslands of Africa. They are the fastest-running animals on Earth and can accelerate as quickly as a sports car. The cats use their speed to chase down nimble prey, such as gazelles, springbok, steenbok, impala, duiker and warthog.

Below: African elephants are the largest land animals in the world, weighing up to 7.5 tonnes (16,500lb) and living for 70 years. Their trunk functions as a nose, hand, extra foot and signalling device, as well as being a tool for gathering food, siphoning water and digging.

UNDERSTANDING ANIMALS

Animals can be defined in terms of their body organization, their place in evolution and their anatomy and key features, and this first part of the book examines how they see, hear, smell and taste, how they find food, how they defend their territories, and how they find mates and care for their offspring. It then examines amphibians, reptiles and placental mammals, describing and illustrating each type's body features and some of their behaviours. There are also discussions about ecology, migration and hibernation, introduced species, endangered species and conserving wildlife. The section then looks at Africa, Britain and Europe's principal life zones or biomes – oceans, fresh water, tropical forests, temperate forests, boreal forests, grasslands, polar regions, deserts, islands and mountains – and how animals have adapted to life there. For example, desert-dwelling animals are frequently only active at night when temperatures are cooler, and many of them do not need to drink liquid because they get all the moisture they need from plants. In contrast, animals from mountainous regions are often specially adapted for climbing and surviving windswept conditions, with sturdy legs and dense coats. The section concludes with an examination of the fastest growing habitat in the world – human settlements – with examples of the opportunistic animals that have learned to thrive in our cities.

Left: A young zebra and its mother take a drink at a watering hole in eastern Africa. Behind them a family of elephants plods past as they, too, head for the water. Some animals get all the moisture they need to survive from their food, but most need to drink water, so in dry regions watering holes are often crowded with wildlife.

WHAT IS AN ANIMAL?

More than two million animal species have been described by scientists, and there are probably millions more waiting to be discovered. They live in all corners of the world, and come in a huge range of shapes and sizes. The largest weighs over a hundred tonnes, while the smallest is just a fraction of a millimetre long.

Active feeders

The living world is divided into five kingdoms: animals, plants, fungi, protists and monerans, which include bacteria. The protists and monerans are micro-organisms. Each individual is just a single cell, and although they often form large masses or colonies – for example, yogurt contains a colony of bacteria – the micro-organisms do not form bodies. The plants, fungi and animals do grow bodies, which are made from millions of cells, all of which work together. These three types of macro-organism, as they are called, tackle the problems of life in different ways.

Plants are the basis of life on Earth, and without them animals would not exist. This is because plants get the energy they need from sunlight (because they do not have to feed actively they are called autotrophes, meaning self-feeders). The green pigments in the plants' leaves trap the energy found in light and convert carbon dioxide and water into glucose, a simple sugar, in a process of food production called photosynthesis. Its by-product is oxygen, which gradually drifts into the atmosphere.

Below: Anemones are members of the group of cnidarians, like jellyfish. Starfish belong to the group of echinoderms.

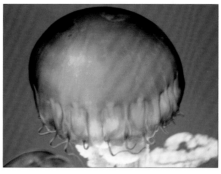
Above: Jellyfish are very simple animals, related to corals and sea anemones. They catch food by spearing prey with tiny cells called nematocysts.

Above: Snails belong to a large group of invertebrates called molluscs. Most live in water, but many snails, such as this giant land snail, survive on land.

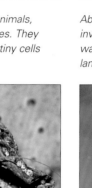
Above: Crabs, such as this hermit crab, are crustaceans. Other crustaceans include lobsters, prawns and krill. Their forelegs are armed with strong pincers.

Above: Spiders, scorpions and mites are arachnids. Many spiders build a sticky silk web to trap prey; others lie hidden and pounce on passing victims.

Fungi are largely invisible organisms that live in large masses of tiny fibres which run through the soil. They only pop up above the surface in the form of mushrooms and toadstools when they are ready to reproduce. Fungi do not photosynthesize, but they are valuable as decomposers. They grow over the dead bodies of other organisms, such as trees which have fallen to the ground, secreting digestive enzymes that break down the dead body from the outside. They thereby release valuable carbon, nitrogen, phosphorus and other elements which each tree locks up in itself over its lifetime.

Animals, on the other hand, could not be more different. They are active feeders (called heterotrophes or "other-eaters") which collect food from their surroundings. Unlike plants and fungi, animals have bodies that can swim, walk, burrow or fly during at least the early part of their lives.

Body organization

With the exception of primitive forms, such as sponges, all animal bodies are organized along the same lines. They process their food in a gut, a tube which passes through the body. In most cases the food enters the gut through an opening in the head, that is, the mouth. Once inside the body, the food is broken down into its constituent parts. The useful parts, such as proteins, fats and sugars – made by plants during photosynthesis – are absorbed into the body. The left-over waste material passes out of the gut through the anus, a hole at the other end of the body.

The useful substances absorbed from the food then need to be transported around the body to where they are needed. This job is done by the animal's circulatory system. The insides of many animals are simply bathed in a liquid containing everything required by the body. However, larger animals, including reptiles, amphibians and mammals, need to pump the useful substances around the body in the blood. The pump is the heart, a strong muscle that keeps the blood circulating through a system of vessels.

The blood carries food for the body and also oxygen, which reacts with the sugar from the food, releasing the energy that is essential for all living things to survive. Animals get their oxygen in a number of ways. Some simply absorb it through their skin, many that live in water extract it using gills, and those that live in air breathe it into their lungs.

Compared with other organisms, animals are more aware of their surroundings and certainly more responsive to them. This is because they have a nervous system which uses sensors to detect what is happening in their environment, such as changes in temperature, the amount of light and various sounds. This information is then transmitted by means of nerves to what could be called the central control. This might just be a dense cluster of nerves, of which the animal might possess several, or it may be a single controlling brain. The brain or nerve cluster then passes the information from the senses to the muscles so that the body can respond appropriately, for example either by running away to avoid being eaten or by attacking its prey.

Mammals, reptiles and amphibians share a similar body plan, having four limbs. They are members of the larger group of tetrapods, to which birds also belong. Almost all possess a visible tail. The brain and most of the sensors are positioned at the front of the body in the head. The vital organs, such as the heart and lungs (or gills), are located in the central thorax (chest area), while the gut and sex organs are found mainly in the abdomen at the rear of the body.

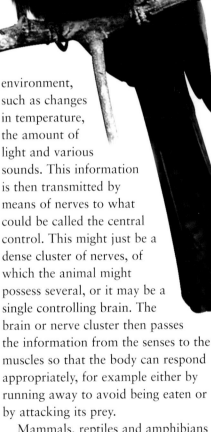

Left: Apart from bats, birds, such as this bee-eater, are the only flying vertebrates. Their forelimbs have evolved into wings that allow them to perform amazing feats of flight. Feathers are better than hair for keeping the body streamlined for flight.

Above: Fish live in all corners of the world's oceans. They also live in fresh water, where they are found everywhere from submerged caves to mountain lakes.

Above: Frogs are the most familiar of the amphibians. Others include salamanders and newts. This frog spends its life in trees, using suckers on its feet to cling to the branches.

Above: While a few other lizards can alter the shade of their scales slightly, chameleons can change colour completely. This may help them hide from predators or it may reflect their mood.

Above: Mammals, such as this ground squirrel, are the most widespread of vertebrates. They can survive in just about any habitat on Earth.

EVOLUTION

Animals and other forms of life did not just suddenly appear on the Earth. They evolved over billions of years into countless different forms. The mechanism by which they evolved is called natural selection. The process of natural selection was first proposed by British naturalist Charles Darwin.

Many biologists estimate that there are approximately 30 million species on Earth, but to date only about two million have been discovered and recorded by scientists. So where are the rest? They live in a staggering array of habitats, from the waters of the deep oceans where giant whales dive for food to the deserts of the Kalahari, inhabited by immense herds of wildebeest. The problems faced by animals in these and other habitats on Earth are very different, and so life has evolved in great variety. Each animal needs a body that can cope with its own environment.

Past evidence

At the turn of the 19th century, geologists began to realize that the world was extremely old. They studied animal fossils – usually the hard remains, such as shells and bones, which are preserved in stone – and measured the age of the exposed layers of rock found in cliffs and canyons. Today we accept that the Earth is about 4.5 billion years old, but in the early

1800s the idea that the world was unimaginably old was completely new to most people.

In addition, naturalists had always known that there was a fantastic variety of animals, but now they realized that many could be grouped into families, as if they were related. By the middle of the 19th century, two British biologists had independently formulated an idea that would change the way that people saw themselves and the natural world forever. Charles Darwin and Alfred Wallace thought that the world's different animal species had gradually evolved from extinct relatives, like the ones preserved as fossils.

Darwin was the first to publish his ideas, in 1859. He had formulated them while touring South America, where he studied the differences between varieties of finches and giant tortoises on the Galápagos Islands in the Pacific Ocean. Wallace came up with similar ideas about the same time, when studying different animals on the islands of South-east Asia and New Guinea.

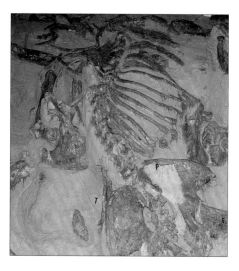

Above: Scientists know about extinct animals from studying fossils such as these mammoth bones. Fossils are the remains of dead plants or animals that have been turned to stone by natural processes over millions of years.

Survival of the fittest

Both came up with the same idea – natural selection. As breeders had known for generations, animals pass on their characteristics to their young. Darwin and Wallace suggested that wild animal species also gradually evolved through natural selection, a similar system to the artificial selection that people were using to breed prize cattle, sheep and pedigree dogs.

The theory of natural selection is often described as the survival of the fittest. This is because animals must compete with each other for limited resources including food, water, shelter and mates. But they are not all equal or exactly similar, and some members of a population of animals will have characteristics which make them "fitter" – better suited to the environment at that time.

The fitter animals will therefore be more successful at finding food and avoiding predators. Consequently, they will probably produce more offspring, many of which will also have the same characteristics as their fit parents. Because of this, the next generation

---

Jumping animals

Many animals can leap into the air, but thanks to natural selection this simple ability has been harnessed by different animals in different ways. For example, click beetles jump in somersaults to frighten off attackers, while blood-sucking fleas can leap enormous heights to move from host to host.

Above: The flying frog uses flaps of skin between its toes to glide. This allows these tree-living frogs to leap huge distances between branches.

Above: This Thomson's gazelle is pronking, that is, leaping in high arcs to escape a chasing predator. Pronking makes it harder for predators to bring the antelope down.

will contain more individuals with the "fit" trait. And after many generations, it is possible that the whole population will carry the fit trait, since those without it die out.

Variation and time

The environment is not fixed, and does not stay the same for long. Volcanoes, diseases and gradual climate changes, for example, alter the conditions which animals have to confront. Natural selection relies on the way in which different individual animals cope with these changes. Those individuals that were once fit may later die out, as others that have a different set of characteristics become more successful in the changed environment.

Darwin did not know it, but parents pass their features on to their young through their genes. During sexual reproduction, the genes of both parents are jumbled up to produce a new individual with a unique set of characteristics. Every so often the genes mutate into a new form, and these mutations are the source of all new variations.

As the process of natural selection continues for millions of years, so groups of animals can change radically, giving rise to a new species. Life is thought to have been evolving for 3.5 billion years. In that time natural selection has produced a staggering number of species, with everything from oak trees to otters and coral to cobras.

A species is a group of organisms that can produce offspring with each other. A new species occurs once animals have changed so much that they are unable to breed with their ancestors. And if the latter no longer exist, then they have become extinct.

New species may gradually arise out of a single group of animals. In fact the original species may be replaced by one or more new species. This can happen when two separate groups of one species are kept apart by an impassable geographical feature, such as an ocean or mountain range. Kept isolated from each other, both groups then evolve in different ways and end up becoming new species.

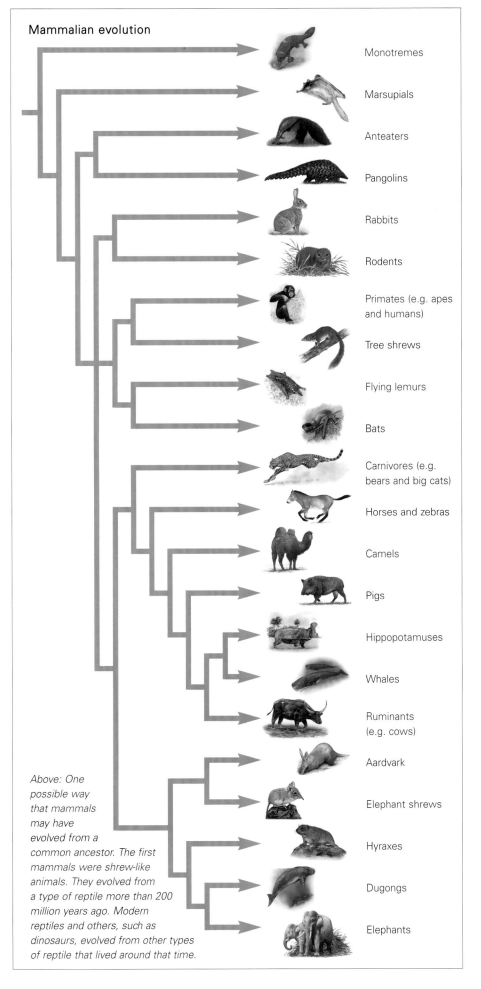

Mammalian evolution

- Monotremes
- Marsupials
- Anteaters
- Pangolins
- Rabbits
- Rodents
- Primates (e.g. apes and humans)
- Tree shrews
- Flying lemurs
- Bats
- Carnivores (e.g. bears and big cats)
- Horses and zebras
- Camels
- Pigs
- Hippopotamuses
- Whales
- Ruminants (e.g. cows)
- Aardvark
- Elephant shrews
- Hyraxes
- Dugongs
- Elephants

Above: One possible way that mammals may have evolved from a common ancestor. The first mammals were shrew-like animals. They evolved from a type of reptile more than 200 million years ago. Modern reptiles and others, such as dinosaurs, evolved from other types of reptile that lived around that time.

ANATOMY

Mammals, reptiles and amphibians (which are vertebrates, as are fish and birds), come in a mind-boggling array of shapes and sizes. However, all of them, from whales to bats and frogs to snakes, share a basic body plan, both inside and out.

Vertebrates are animals with a spine, generally made of bone. Bone, the hard tissues of which contain chalky substances, is also the main component of the rest of the vertebrate skeleton. The bones of the skeleton link together to form a rigid frame to protect organs and give the body its shape, while also allowing it to move. Cartilage, a softer, more flexible but tough tissue is found, for example, at the ends of bones in mobile joints, in the ears and the nose (forming the sides and the partition between the two nostrils). Some fish, including sharks and rays, have skeletons that consist entirely of cartilage.

Nerves and muscles

Vertebrates also have a spinal cord, a thick bundle of nerves extending from the brain through the spine, and down into the tail. The nerves in the spinal cord are used to control walking and other reflex movements by

co-ordinating blocks of muscle that work together. A vertebrate's skeleton is on the inside, in contrast to many invertebrates, which have an outer skeleton or exoskeleton. The vertebrate

skeleton provides a solid structure which the body's muscles pull against. Muscles are blocks of protein that can contract and relax when they get an electrical impulse from a nerve.

Invertebrates

The majority of animals are invertebrates. They are a much more varied group than the vertebrates and include creatures such as shrimps, slugs, butterflies and starfish. Although some squid are thought to reach the size of a small whale, and octopuses are at least as intelligent as cats and dogs, most invertebrates are much smaller and simpler animals than the vertebrates.

Below: The most successful invertebrates are the insects, including ants. This soldier army ant is defending workers as they collect food.

Reptile bodies

Reptiles have an internal skeleton made from bone and cartilage. Their skin is covered in scales, which are often toughened by a waxy protein called keratin. Turtles are quite different from other reptiles. They have a simpler skull and a shell that is joined to the animal's internal skeleton.

Below: Crocodiles have a very strong body, designed for life in and around shallow water.

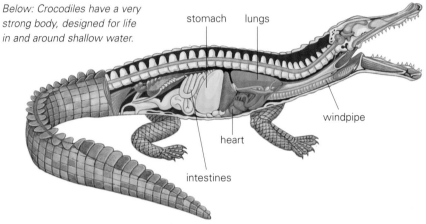

stomach   lungs

windpipe

heart

intestines

Below: Lizards have a similar body plan to crocodiles, although they are actually not very closely related.

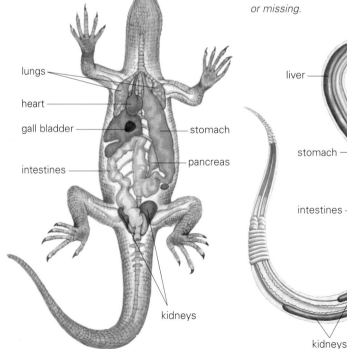

lungs

heart

gall bladder

intestines

stomach

pancreas

kidneys

Below: Snakes' internal organs are elongated so that they fit into their long, thin body. One of a pair of organs, such as the lungs, is often very small or missing.

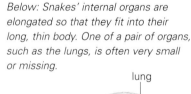

lung

liver

heart

stomach

intestines

kidneys

When on the move, the vertebrate body works like a system of pulleys, pivots and levers. The muscles are the engines of the body, and are attached to bones – the levers – by strong cables called tendons. The joint between two bones forms a pivot, and the muscles work in pairs to move a bone. For example, when an arm is bent at the elbow to raise the forearm, the bicep muscle on the front of the upper arm has to contract. This pulls the forearm up, while the tricep muscle attached to the back of the upper arm remains relaxed. To straighten the arm again, the tricep contracts and the bicep relaxes. If both muscles contract at the same time, they pull against each other, and the arm remains locked in whatever position it is in.

Vital organs

Muscles are not only attached to the skeleton. The gut – including the stomach and intestines – is surrounded by muscles. These muscles contract in rhythmic waves to push food and waste products through the body. The heart is a muscular organ made of a very strong muscle which keeps on contracting and relaxing, pumping blood around the body. The heart and other vital organs are found in the thorax, that part of the body which lies between the forelimbs. In reptiles and mammals the thorax is kept well protected, the rib cage surrounding the heart, lungs, liver and kidneys.

Vertebrates have a single liver consisting of a number of lobes. The liver has a varied role, making chemicals required by the body and storing food. Most vertebrates also have two kidneys. Their role is to clean the blood of any impurities and toxins, and to remove excess water. The main toxins that have to be removed are compounds containing nitrogen, the by-products of eating protein. Mammal and amphibian kidneys dissolve these toxins in water to make urine. However, since many reptiles live in very dry habitats, they cannot afford to use water to remove waste, and they instead get rid of it as a solid waste similar to bird excrement.

Mammalian bodies

Most mammals are four-limbed (exceptions being sea mammals such as whales). All have at least some hair on their bodies, and females produce milk. Mammals live in a wide range of habitats and their bodies are adapted in many ways to survive. Their internal organs vary depending on where they live and what they eat.

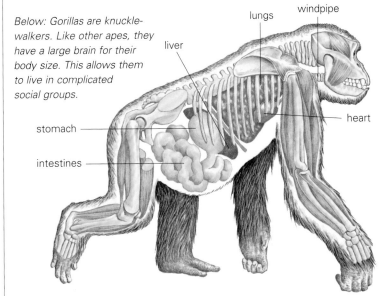

Below: Gorillas are knuckle-walkers. Like other apes, they have a large brain for their body size. This allows them to live in complicated social groups.

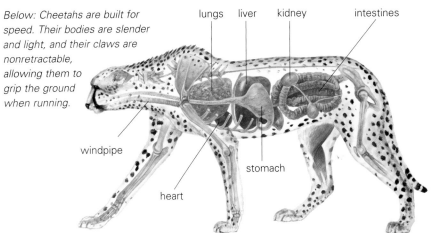

Below: Cheetahs are built for speed. Their bodies are slender and light, and their claws are nonretractable, allowing them to grip the ground when running.

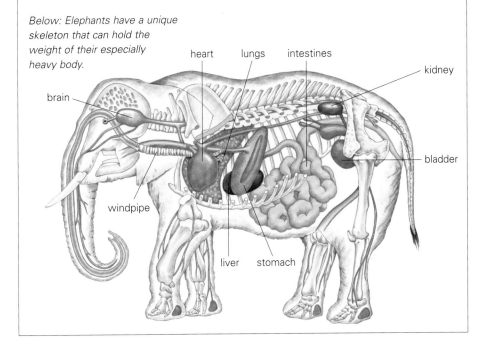

Below: Elephants have a unique skeleton that can hold the weight of their especially heavy body.

SENSES

To stay alive, animals must find food and shelter, and defend themselves against predators. To achieve these things, they are equipped with an array of senses for monitoring their surroundings. Different species have senses adapted to nocturnal or diurnal (day-active) life.

An animal's senses are its early-warning system. They alert it to changes in its surroundings – changes which may signal an opportunity to feed or mate, or the need to escape imminent danger. The ability to act quickly and appropriately is made possible because the senses are linked to the brain by a network of nerves which send messages as electric pulses. When the brain receives the information from the senses it co-ordinates its response.

In many cases, generally in response to something touching the body, the signal from the sensor does not reach the brain before action is taken. Instead, it produces a reflex response which is hardwired into the nervous system. For example, when you touch a very hot object, your hand automatically recoils; you don't need to think about it.

All animals have to be sensitive to their environment to survive. Even the simplest animals, such as jellyfish and roundworms, react to changes in their surroundings. Simple animals, however, have only a limited ability to move or defend themselves, and therefore generally have limited senses. Larger animals, such as vertebrates,

have a much more complex array of sense organs. Most vertebrates can hear, see, smell, taste and touch.

Vision

Invertebrates' eyes are generally designed to detect motion. Vertebrates' eyes, however, are better at forming clear images, often in colour. Vertebrates' eyes are balls of clear jelly which have an inner lining of light-sensitive cells. This lining, called the retina, is made up of one or two types of cell. The rod cells – named after their shape – are very sensitive to all types of light, but are only capable of forming black and white images. Animals which are active at night generally have (and need) only rods in their eyes.

Colour vision is important for just a few animals, such as monkeys, which need, for example, to see the brightest and therefore ripest fruits. Colour images are made by the cone cells – so named because of their shape – in the retina. There are three types of cone, each of which is sensitive to a particular wavelength of light. Low wavelengths appear as reds, high wavelengths as blues, with green colours being detected in between.

Above: Frogs have large eyes positioned on the upper side of the head so that the animals can lie mainly submerged in water with just their eyes poking out.

The light is focused on the retina by a lens to produce a clear image. Muscles change the shape of the lens so that it can focus the light arriving from different distances. While invertebrates may have several eyes, all vertebrates have just two, and they are always positioned on the head. Animals such as rabbits, which are constantly looking out for danger, have eyes on the side of the head to give a wide field of vision. But while they can see in almost all directions, rabbits have difficulty judging distances and speeds. Animals that have eyes pointing forward are better at doing this because each eye's field of vision overlaps with the other. This binocular vision helps hunting animals and others, such as tree-living primates, to judge distances more accurately.

Eyes can also detect radiation in a small band of wavelengths, and some animals detect radiation that is invisible to our eyes. Flying insects and birds can see ultraviolet light, which extends the range of their colour vision. At the other end of the spectrum many snakes can detect radiation with a lower wavelength. They sense infrared, or heat, through pits on the face which enables them to track their warm-blooded prey in pitch darkness.

Below: The lion's golden eyes are able to reflect light back through the retina, giving the animal excellent night vision because the retina has two chances to catch the light.

Below: Like other hunters, a seal has eyes positioned on the front of its head. Forward-looking eyes are useful for judging distances, making it easier to chase down prey.

Hearing

An animal's brain interprets waves of pressure travelling through the air, and detected by the ears, as sound. Many animals do not hear these waves with ears but detect them in other ways instead. For example, although snakes can hear, they are much more sensitive to vibrations through the lower jaw, travelling through the ground. Long facial whiskers sported by many mammals, from cats to dugongs, are very sensitive touch receptors. They can be so sensitive that they will even respond to currents in the air.

In many ways, hearing is a sensitive extension of the sense of touch. The ears of amphibians, reptiles and mammals have an eardrum which is sensitive to tiny changes in pressure. An eardrum is a thin membrane of skin which vibrates as the air waves hit it. A tiny bone (or in the case of mammals, three bones) attached to the drum transmit the vibrations to a shell-shaped structure called a cochlea. The cochlea is filled with a liquid which picks up the vibrations. As the liquid moves inside the cochlea, tiny hair-like structures lining it wave back and forth. Nerves stimulated by this wave motion send the information to the brain, which interprets it as sound.

A mammal's ear is divided into three sections. The cochlea forms the inner ear and the middle ear consists of the bones between the cochlea and eardrum. The outer ear is the tube joining the outside world and the

Below: Hares have very large outer ears which they use like satellite dishes to pick up sound waves. They can rotate each ear separately to detect sound from all directions.

auricle – the fleshy structure on the side of the head that collects the sound waves – to the middle ear. Amphibians and reptiles do not possess auricles. Instead their eardrums are either on the side of the head – easily visible on many frogs and lizards – or under the skin, as in snakes.

Smell and taste

These two senses are so closely related as to form a single sense. Snakes and lizards, for example, taste the air with their forked tongues. However, it is perhaps the most complex sense. Noses, tongues and other smelling

Below: Lizards do not have outer ears at all. Their hearing organs are contained inside the head and joined to the outside world through an eardrum membrane.

Above: Snakes have forked tongues that they use to taste the air. The tips of the fork are slotted into an organ in the roof of the mouth. This organ is linked to the nose, and chemicals picked up by the tongue are identified with great sensitivity.

organs are lined with sensitive cells which can analyse a huge range of chemicals that float in the air or exist in food. Animals such as dogs, which rely on their sense of smell, have long noses packed with odour-sensitive cells. Monkeys, on the other hand, are less reliant on a sense of smell, and consequently have short noses capable only of detecting stronger odours.

Below: Aardwolves have an excellent sense of smell and taste. They communicate with pack members and rival packs by smell, as part of a complex set of social behaviours.

SURVIVAL

In order to stay alive, animals must not only find enough food, but also avoid becoming a predator's meal. To achieve this, animals have evolved many strategies to feed on a wide range of foods, and an array of weapons and defensive tactics to keep safe.

An animal must keep feeding in order to replace the energy used in staying alive. Substances in the food, such as sugars, are burned by the body, and the subsequent release of energy is used to heat the body and power its movements. Food is also essential for growth. Although most growth takes place during the early period of an animal's life, it never really stops because injuries need to heal and worn-out tissues need replacing. Some animals continue growing throughout life. Proteins in the food are the main building blocks of living bodies.

Plant food

Some animals will eat just about anything, while others are much more fussy. As a group, vertebrates get their energy from a wide range of sources – as diverse as shellfish, wood, honey and blood. Animals are often classified according to how they feed, forming several large groups filled with many otherwise unrelated animals.

Animals that eat plants are generally grouped together as herbivores. But this term is not very descriptive because there is such a wide range of plant foods. Animals that eat grass are known as grazers. However, this term can also apply to any animal which eats any plant that covers the ground

Above: Impala are grazers. They eat grass and plants that grow close to the ground. Because their food is all around them, grazers spend a long time out in the open. They feed together in large herds since there is safety in numbers.

in large amounts, such as seaweed or sedge. Typical grazers include bison and wildebeest but some, such as the gelada baboon, are not so typical. Animals such as giraffes or antelopes, which pick off the tastiest leaves, buds and fruit from bushes and trees, are called browsers. Other browsing animals include many monkeys, but some monkeys eat only leaves (the folivores) or fruit (the frugivores).

Many monkeys have a much broader diet, eating everything from insects to the sap which seeps out from the bark of tropical trees. Animals that eat both plant and animal foods are called omnivores. Bears are omnivorous, as are humans, but the most catholic of tastes belong to scavenging animals, such as rats and some other rodents, which eat anything they can get their teeth into. Omnivores in general, and scavengers in particular, are very curious animals. They will investigate anything that looks or smells like food, and if it also tastes like food, then it probably is.

A taste for flesh

The term carnivore is often applied to any animal that eats flesh, but it is more correctly used to refer to an order of mammals which includes cats, dogs, bears and many smaller animals, such as weasels and mongooses. These animals are the kings of killing, armed with razor-sharp claws and powerful jaws crammed full of chisel-like teeth. They use their strength and speed to overpower their prey, either by running them down or taking them by surprise with an ambush.

Below: Zebras are browsers, not grazers. They will eat some grass but also pick tastier leaves, buds and fruit off trees and shrubs. They often live in herds to stay safe from attack.

Below: Lions are unusual cats because they live together in prides. The members of the pride co-operate to catch food. They hunt as a team and share the food between them.

Above: African elephants have few predators. Younger elephants are at risk of leopard attacks, and the adults defend them by trumpeting, stamping and flapping their large ears. If that fails, they will charge.

However, land-dwelling carnivores are not the only expert killers. The largest meat-eater is the orca, or killer whale, which is at least three times the size of the brown bear, the largest killer on land.

While snakes are much smaller in comparison, they are just as deadly, if not more so. They kill in one of two ways, either suffocating their prey by wrapping their coils tightly around them, or by injecting them with a poison through their fangs.

Arms race

Ironically, the same weapons used by predators are often used by their prey to defend themselves. For example, several species of frog, toad and salamander secrete poisons on to their skin. In some cases, such as the poison-dart frog, this poison is enough to kill any predator that tries to eat it, thus making sure that the killer won't repeat its performance. More often, though, a predator finds that its meal tastes horrible and remembers not to eat another one again. To remind the predators to keep away, many poisonous amphibians are brightly

coloured, which ensures that they are easily recognized.

Many predators rely on stealth to catch their prey, and staying hidden is part of the plan. A camouflaged coat, such as a tiger's stripes, helps animals blend into their surroundings. Many species also use this technique to ensure that they do not get eaten. Most freeze when danger approaches, and then scurry to safety as quickly as possible. Chameleons have taken camouflage to an even more sophisticated level as they can change the colour of their scaly skins, which helps them to blend in with their surrounding environment.

Plant-eating animals that live in the open cannot hide from predators that are armed with sharp teeth and claws. And the plant-eaters cannot rely on similar weapons to defend themselves. They are outgunned

Right: Chameleons have skin cells that can be opened and closed to make their skin colour change.

Filter-feeders
Some animals filter their food from water. The giant baleen whales do this, sieving tiny shrimp-like animals called krill out of great gulps of sea water. Some tadpoles and larval salamanders filter-feed as well, extracting tiny plant-like animals which float in fresh water. However, after becoming adults, all amphibians become hunters and eat other animals. All snakes and most lizards are meat-eaters, or carnivores, as well.

Below: The largest animals of all, baleen whales, are filter-feeders. They do not have teeth. Instead, their gums are lined with a thick curtain of baleen that filters out tiny shrimp-like krill from sea water.

because they do not possess sharp, pointed teeth but flattened ones to grind up their plant food. The best chance they have of avoiding danger is to run away. Animals such as antelopes or deer consequently have long, hoofed feet that lengthen their legs considerably; they are, in fact, standing on their toenails. These long legs allow them to run faster and leap high into the air to escape an attacker's jaws.

Animals that do not flee must stand and fight. Most large herbivores are armed with horns or antlers. Although used chiefly for display, the horns are the last line of defence when cornered.

REPRODUCTION

All animals share the urge to produce offspring which will survive after the parents die. The process of heredity is determined by genes, through which characteristics are passed from parents to offspring. Reproduction presents several problems, and animals have adopted different strategies for tackling them.

Animals have two main goals: to find food and a mate. To achieve these goals, they must survive everything that the environment throws at them, from extremes of the weather, such as floods and droughts, to hungry predators. They have to find sufficient supplies of food, and on top of that locate a mate before their competitors. If they find sufficient food but fail to produce any offspring, their genes will not be passed on.

One parent or two?

There are two ways in which an animal can reproduce, asexually or sexually. Animals that are produced by asexual reproduction, or parthenogenesis, have only one parent, a mother. The offspring are identical to their mother and to each other. Sexual reproduction involves two parents of the opposite sex. The offspring are hybrids of the two parents, with a mixture of their parents' characteristics.

The offspring inherit their parents' traits through their genes. Genes can be defined in various ways. One simple definition is that they are the unit of inheritance – a single inherited

Above: Many male frogs croak by pumping air into an expandable throat sac. The croak is intended to attract females. The deeper the croak, the more attractive it is. However, some males lurk silently and mate with females as they approach the croaking males.

characteristic which cannot be subdivided any further. Genes are also segments of DNA (deoxyribonucleic acid), a complex chemical that forms long chains. It is found at the heart of every living cell. Each link in the DNA chain forms part of a code that controls how an animal's body develops and survives. And every cell in the body contains a full set of DNA which could be used to build a whole new body.

Animals produced through sexual reproduction receive half their DNA, or half their genes, from each parent. The male parent provides half the supply of genes, contained in a sperm. Each sperm's only role is to find its

Above: In deer and many other grazing animals, the males fight each other for the right to mate with the females in the herd. The deer with the largest antlers often wins without fighting, and real fights only break out if two males appear equally well-endowed.

way to, and fertilize, an egg, its female equivalent. Besides containing the other half of the DNA, the egg also holds a supply of food for the offspring as it develops into a new individual. Animals created through parthenogenesis get all their genes from their mother, and all of them are therefore the same sex – female.

Pros and cons

All mammals reproduce sexually, as do most reptiles and amphibians. However, there are a substantial number of amphibians and reptiles, especially lizards, that reproduce by parthenogenesis. There are benefits and disadvantages to both types of reproduction. Parthenogenesis is quick and convenient. The mother does not need to find a mate, and can devote all of her energy to producing huge numbers of young. This strategy is ideal for populating as yet unexploited territory. However, being identical, these animals are vulnerable to attack. If, for example, one is killed by a disease or outwitted by a predator, it is likely that they will all suffer the same fate. Consequently, whole communities of animals produced through parthenogenesis can be wiped out.

Below: Crocodiles bury their eggs in a nest. The temperature of the nest determines the sex of the young reptiles. Hot nests produce more males than cool ones. Crocodile mothers are very gentle when it comes to raising young.

Sexual animals, on the other hand, are much more varied. Each one is unique, formed by a mixture of genes from both parents. This variation means that a group of animals produced by sexual reproduction is more likely to triumph over adversity than a group of asexual ones. However, sexual reproduction takes up a great deal of time and effort.

Attracting mates

Since females produce only a limited number of eggs, they are keen to make sure that they are fertilized by a male with good genes. If a male is fit and healthy, this is a sign that he has good genes. Good genes will ensure that the offspring will be able to compete with other animals for food and mates of their own. Because the females have the final say in agreeing to mate, the

Above: Lions live in prides, in which one or two males father all the children. When a new adult takes control of the pride, he kills the cubs of his deposed rival so that the pride's females will be ready to mate with him sooner.

Below: Rhinoceroses are generally solitary animals, but offspring stay with their mother for at least a year while they grow big enough to look after themselves.

males have to put a lot of effort into getting noticed. Many are brightly coloured, make loud noises, and they are often larger than the females. In many species the males even compete with each other for the right to display to the females. Winning that right is a good sign that they have the best genes.

Parental care

The amount of care that the offspring receive from their parents varies considerably. There is a necessary trade-off between the amount of useful care parents can give to each offspring, the number of offspring they can produce and how regularly they can breed. Mammals invest heavily in parental care, suckling their young after giving birth, while most young amphibians and reptiles never meet their parents at all.

By suckling, mammals ensure that their young grow to a size where they

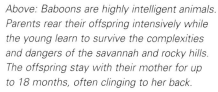

Above: Baboons are highly intelligent animals. Parents rear their offspring intensively while the young learn to survive the complexities and dangers of the savannah and rocky hills. The offspring stay with their mother for up to 18 months, often clinging to her back.

can look after themselves. Generally, the young stay with the mother until it is time for her to give birth to the next litter – at least one or two months. However, in many species, including humans, the young stay with their parents for many years.

Other types of animals pursue the opposite strategy, producing large numbers of young that are left to fend for themselves. The vast majority in each batch of eggs – consisting of hundreds or even thousands – die before reaching adulthood, and many never even hatch. The survival rates, for example of frogs, are very low.

Animals that live in complicated societies, such as elephants, apes and humans, tend to produce a single offspring every few years. The parents direct their energies into protecting and rearing the young, giving them a good chance of survival. Animals which live for a only a short time, such as mice, rabbits, and reptiles and amphibians in general, need to reproduce quickly to make the most of their short lives. They produce high numbers of young, and do not waste time on anything more than the bare minimum of parental care. If successful, these animals can reproduce at an alarming pace.

CLASSIFICATION

Scientists classify all living things into categories. Members of each category share features with each other – traits that set them apart from other animals. Over the years, a tree of categories and subcategories has been pieced together, showing how all living things seem to be related to each other.

Taxonomy, the scientific discipline of categorizing organisms, aims to classify and order the millions of animals on Earth so that we can better understand them and their relationship to each other. The Greek philosopher Aristotle was among the first people to do this for animals in the 4th century BC. In the 18th century, Swedish naturalist Carolus Linnaeus formulated the system that we use today.

By the end of the 17th century, naturalists had noticed that many animals seemed to have several close relatives that resembled one another. For example lions, lynxes and domestic cats all seemed more similar to each other than they did to dogs or horses. However, all of these animals shared common features that they did not share with frogs, slugs or wasps.

Linnaeus devised a way of classifying these observations. The system he set up – known as the Linnaean system – orders animals in a hierarchy of divisions. From the largest division to the smallest, this system is as follows: kingdom, phylum, class, order, family, genus, species.

Each species is given a two-word scientific name, derived from Latin and Greek. For example, *Panthera leo* is the scientific name of the lion. The first word is the genus name, while the second is the species name. Therefore *Panthera leo* means the *"leo"* species in the genus *"Panthera"*. This system of two-word classification is known as binomial nomenclature.

Lions, lynxes and other genera of cats belong to the Felidae family. The Felidae are included in the order Carnivora, along with dogs and other similar predators. The Carnivora, in

*Above: Like the lion, the leopard (*Panthera pardus*) belongs to the cat family, Felidae. This is divided into two main groups, the big and small cats. The group of small cats includes wildcats and domestic cats.*

turn, belong to the class Mammalia, which also includes horses and all other mammals.

Mammals belong to the phylum Chordata, the major group which contains all vertebrates, including reptiles, amphibians, birds, fish and some other small animals called tunicates and lancelets. In their turn, Chordata belong to the kingdom Animalia, comprising around 31 living phyla, including Mollusca, which contains the slugs, and Arthropoda, which contains wasps and other insects.

Although we still use Linnaean grouping, modern taxonomy is worked out in very different ways from the ones Linnaeus used. Linnaeus and others after him classified animals by their outward appearance. Although they were generally correct when it came

*Left: The lion (*Panthera leo*) belongs to the genus Panthera, the big cats, to which tigers also belong. All cats are members of the large order of Carnivora (carnivores) within the class of Mammalia (mammals).*

Close relations

Cheetahs, caracals and servals all belong to the cat family Felidae, which also includes lions, tigers, wildcats, lynxes and jaguars. Within this family there are two groups: big and small cats. These can generally be distinguished by their size, with a few exceptions.

For example, the cheetah is often classed as a big cat, but it is actually smaller than the cougar, a small cat. One of the main differences between the two groups is that big cats can roar but not purr continuously, while small cats are able to purr but not roar.

Above: The cheetah (Acinonyx jubatus) differs from all other cats in possessing nonretractable claws without sheaths. This species is classed in a group of its own, but is often included within the group of big cats.

Above: The caracal (Caracal caracal) is included in the group of small cats (subfamily Felinae), but most scientists place it in a genus of its own, Caracal, rather than in the main genus, Felis.

Above: The serval (Felis serval) is a medium-sized member of the Felis or small cat genus. This cat has very large ears, which are used to detect the sounds of prey hidden among tall grasses.

Distant relations

All vertebrates (backboned animals), including birds, reptiles and mammals such as seals and dolphins, are thought to have evolved from common fish ancestors that swam in the oceans some 400 million years ago. Later, one group of fish developed limb-like organs and came on to the land, where they slowly evolved into amphibians and later reptiles, which in turn gave rise to mammals. Later, seals and dolphins returned to the oceans and their limbs evolved into paddle-like flippers.

Above: Fish are an ancient group of aquatic animals that mainly propel themselves by thrashing their vertically aligned caudal fin, or tail, and steer using their fins.

Above: In seals, the four limbs have evolved into flippers that make highly effective paddles in water but are less useful on land, where seals are ungainly in their movements.

Above: Whales and dolphins never come on land, and their ancestors' hind limbs have all but disappeared. They resemble fish but the tail is horizontally – not vertically – aligned.

to the large divisions, this method was not foolproof. For example, some early scientists believed that whales and dolphins, with their fins and streamlined bodies, were types of fish and not mammals at all. Today, accurate classification of the various genera is achieved through a field of study called cladistics. This uses genetic analysis to check how animals are related by evolutionary change. So animals are grouped according to how they evolved, with each division sharing a common ancestor somewhere in the past. As the classification of living organims improves, so does our understanding of the evolution of life on Earth and our place within this process.

AMPHIBIANS

Amphibians are the link between fish and land animals. One in eight of all vertebrate animals are amphibians. This group includes frogs, toads and newts as well as rarer types, such as giant sirens, hellbenders and worm-like caecilians. Amphibians are equally at home in water and on land.

Amphibians live on every continent except for Antarctica. None can survive in salt water, although a few species live close to the sea in the brackish water at river mouths. Being cold-blooded – their body temperature is always about the same as the temperature of their surroundings – most amphibians are found in the warmer regions of the world.

Unlike other land vertebrates, most amphibians spend the early part of their lives in a different form from that of the adults. As they grow, the young gradually metamorphose into the adult body. Having a larval form means that the adults and their offspring live and feed in different places. In general the larvae are aquatic, while the adults spend most of their time on land.

The adults are hunters, feeding on other animals, while the young are generally plant eaters, filtering tiny plants from the water or grazing on aquatic plants which line the bottom of ponds and rivers.

Below: Amphibians must lay their eggs near a source of water. In most cases, such as this frog spawn, the eggs are laid straight into a pond or swamp. The tadpoles develop inside the jelly-like egg and then hatch out after the food supply in the egg's yolk runs out.

Life changing

Most amphibians hatch from eggs laid in water or, in a few cases, in moist soil or nests made of hardened mucus. Once hatched, the young amphibians, or larvae, nearly all live as completely aquatic animals. Those born on land wriggle to the nearest pool of water or drop from their nest into a river.

The larvae of frogs and toads are called tadpoles. Like the young of salamanders – a group that includes all other amphibians except caecilians – tadpoles do not have any legs at first. They swim using a long tail that has a fish-like fin extending along its length. As they grow, the larvae sprout legs. In general the back legs begin to grow first, followed by the front pair. Adult frogs do not have tails, and after the first few months a tadpole's tail begins to be reabsorbed into the body – it does not just fall away.

All adult salamanders keep their tails, and those species that spend their entire lives in water often retain the fin along the tail, along with other parts, such as external gills, a feature that is more commonly seen in the larval stage.

Above: Amphibians begin life looking very different from the adult form. Most of the time these larval forms, such as this frog tadpole, live in water as they slowly develop into the adult form, growing legs and lungs so that they can survive on land.

Body form

Amphibian larvae hatch with external gills but, as they grow, many (including all frogs and the many salamanders which live on land) develop internal gills. In most land-living species these internal gills are eventually replaced by lungs. Amphibians are also able to absorb oxygen directly through the skin, especially through the thin and moist tissues inside the mouth. A large number of land-living salamanders get all their oxygen in this way because they do not have lungs.

All adult frogs and toads return to the water to breed and lay their eggs, which are often deposited in a jelly-like mass called frog spawn. Several types of salamander do not lay eggs, and instead the females keep the fertilized eggs inside their bodies. The larvae develop inside the eggs, fed by a supply of rich yolk, and do not hatch until they have reached adult form.

Above: After the first few weeks, a tadpole acquires tiny back legs. As the legs grow, the long tail is gradually reabsorbed into the body. The front legs appear after the back ones have formed.

Adult form

Most adult amphibians have four limbs, with four digits on the front pair and five on the rear. Unlike other land-living animals, such as reptiles or mammals, their skin is naked and soft. Frogs' skin is smooth and moist, while toads generally have a warty appearance.

The skins of many salamanders are brightly coloured, with patterns that often change throughout the year. Colour change prior to the mating season signals the salamander's readiness to mate. Many frogs also have bright skin colours. Although their skin shades can change considerably in different light levels, these colours are generally not mating signals to fellow frogs. Instead they are warnings to predators that the frog's skin is laced with deadly poison. While toads tend to be drab in colour, many also secrete toxic chemicals to keep predators away. These substances are often stored in swollen warts which burst when the toad is attacked.

Below: Adult frogs may live in water or on land. Aquatic ones have webbed feet, while those on land have powerful legs for jumping and climbing. All frogs must return to a source of water to mate.

Forever young

Salamanders which have changed into adults, but which have not yet reached adult size, are called efts. The time it takes for an amphibian to grow from a newly hatched larva to an adult varies considerably, and the chief factor is the temperature of the water in which it is developing. Most frogs and toads develop in shallow waters, warmed by the summer sun, and they generally reach adulthood within three to four months. However, salamanders, especially the largest ones, can take much longer, and at the northern and southern limits of their geographical spread some salamanders stay as larvae for many years. It appears that the trigger for the change into adult form is linked to the temperature, and in cold climates this change happens only every few years. In fact it may not happen during a salamander's lifetime, and consequently several species have evolved the ability to develop sexual organs even when they still look like larvae.

Below: The olm is a highly unusual blind amphibian that lives in caves in the western Balkans. Olms never make the change to a fully adult form. Instead they resemble a larva, with external gills and an aquatic lifestyle, for their whole lives.

REPTILES

Reptiles include lizards, snakes, alligators, crocodiles, turtles and tortoises, as well as now-extinct creatures such as dinosaurs and the ancestors of birds. Crocodiles have roamed the Earth for 200 million years and are still highly successful hunters.

Reptiles are a large and diverse group of animals containing about 6,500 species. Many of these animals look very different from each other and live in a large number of habitats, from the deep ocean to the scorching desert. Despite their great diversity, all reptiles share certain characteristics.

Most reptiles lay eggs, but these are different from those of an amphibian because they have a hard, thin shell rather than a soft, jelly-like one. This protects the developing young inside and, more importantly, stops them from drying out. Shelled eggs were an evolutionary breakthrough because they meant that adult reptiles did not have to return to the water to breed. Their waterproof eggs could be laid anywhere, even in the driest places. Reptiles were also the first group of land-living animals to develop into an adult form inside the egg. They did not emerge as under-developed larvae like the young of most amphibians.

Below: Crocodiles are an ancient group of reptiles that have no close living relatives. They are archosaurs, a group of reptiles that included the dinosaurs. Other living reptiles belong to a different group.

Released from their ties to water, the reptiles developed new ways of retaining moisture. Their skins are covered by hardened plates or scales to stop water being lost. The scales are coated with the protein keratin, the same substance used to make fingernails and hair.

All reptiles breathe using lungs; if they were to absorb air through the skin it would involve too much water loss. Like amphibians, reptiles are cold-blooded and cannot heat their bodies from within as mammals can. Consequently, reptiles are most commonly found in warm climates.

Ancient killers

Being such a diverse group, reptiles share few defining characteristics besides their shelled eggs, scaly skin and lungs. They broadly divide into four orders. The first contains the crocodiles, alligators and caimans; these are contemporaries of the dinosaurs, both groups being related to a common ancestor.

In fact today's crocodiles have changed little since the age when dinosaurs ruled the world over 200

Above: Turtles and their relatives, such as this terrapin, are unusual reptiles. Not only do they have bony shells fused around their bodies, but they also have skulls that are quite different from other reptiles. Turtles are also unusual because many of them live in the ocean, while most reptiles live on land.

million years ago. Unlike the dinosaurs, which disappeared 65 million years ago, the crocodiles are still going strong. Technically speaking, the dinosaurs never actually died out; their direct descendants, the birds, are still thriving. Although birds are now grouped separately from reptiles, scientists know that they all evolved from ancestors which lived about 400 million years ago. Mammals, on the other hand, broke away from this group about 300 million years ago.

Above: Most reptiles, including this royal python, lay eggs. The young hatch looking like small versions of the adults. However, several snakes and lizards give birth to live young, which emerge from their mother fully formed.

Distant relatives

The second reptile order includes turtles, terrapins and tortoises. These are only distantly related to other reptiles, and it shows. Turtles are also the oldest group of reptiles, evolving their bony shells and clumsy bodies before crocodiles, dinosaurs or any other living reptile group existed. Although turtles evolved on land, many have since returned to water. However, they still breathe air, and all must return to land to lay their eggs.

The third group of reptiles is the largest. Collectively called the squamates, this group includes snakes and lizards. Snakes, with their legless bodies and formidable reputations, are perhaps the most familiar reptiles. They evolved from animals that did have legs, and many retain tiny vestiges of legs. The squamates include other legless members such as the amphisbaenians (or worm lizards). These are more closely related to lizards than snakes, despite looking more like the latter. Lizards are not a simple group of reptiles, and many biologists refer to them as several different groups, including the skinks, monitors, geckos and iguanas.

Below: Lizards, such as this savannah monitor, are the largest group of reptiles. Most are hunters that live in hot places, and they are especially successful in dry areas where other types of animal are not so common.

The squamates are so diverse in their lifestyles and body forms that it is hard to find factors which they have in common. One feature not found in other reptile orders is the Jacobson's organ. It is positioned in the roof of the mouth and is closely associated with the nose. All snakes and most lizards use this organ to "taste" the air and detect prey. The long forked tongue of most of these animals flicks out into the air, picking up tiny particles on its moist surface. Once back inside the mouth, each fork slots into the Jacobson's organ which then analyses the substances.

The final order of reptiles is very small: the tuataras. These include just two species, which cling to life on a few New Zealand islands. To most people a tuatura looks like a large iguana. However, scientists believe that it is only a distant relative of lizards and other squamates.

Legless lizards

Snakes are not the only reptiles without any legs. A small group of legless squamates is called the amphisbaenians. These are worm-like reptiles that live underground. They are sometimes called worm lizards. This name is misleading because they are only distantly related to lizards. However, there are also several species of lizard that have also lost their legs. At first glance these animals also look like snakes. Legless lizards are related to alligator lizards, which are known for having long, thin bodies and short legs.

Below: Looking more like a snake than a lizard, the slow worm is a burrowing legless lizard that eats slugs.

MAMMALS

Mammals are the most familiar of all vertebrates. This is because not only are human beings mammals, but also most domestic animals and pets belong in this category. Mammals are also more widespread than other types of animal, being found in all parts of the world.

Mammals are grouped together because they share a number of characteristics. However, these common features do not come close to describing the huge diversity within the mammal class. For example, the largest animal that has ever existed on Earth – the blue whale – is a mammal, and so this monster of the deep shares several crucial traits with even the smallest mammals, such as the tiniest of shrews. Other mammals include elephants and moles, monkeys and hippopotamuses, and bats and camels. To add to this great diversity, mammals live in more places on Earth than any other group of animals, from the frozen ice fields of the Arctic to the humid treetops of the Congo rainforest, and even under the sandy soil of the Sahara Desert.

Mammal bodies
The most obvious mammalian feature is hair. All mammals have hair made of keratin protein and, in most cases, it forms a thick coat of fur, though many

Below: Although they are often mistaken for fish, dolphins are mammals: they breathe air and suckle their young. However, life under water requires flippers and fins, not legs.

Above: The African wildcat has successfully adapted to its surroundings by blending in with the background: wildcats found in arid areas tend to have lighter, sandy-coloured coats, while those found in forested regions are darker, with an overlaying tabby pattern.

mammals are relatively naked, not least humans. Unlike reptiles and amphibians, all mammals are warm-blooded, which means that they can keep their body temperature at a constant level. While this requires quite a lot of energy, it means that mammals are not totally dependent on the temperature of their surroundings. In places where other vertebrates would be frozen solid, mammals can survive by seeking out food and keeping themselves warm. Many mammals,

including humans, can also cool their bodies using sweat. The water secreted on the skin cools the body efficiently, but it does mean that these animals need to drink more replacement water than do other groups.

Incidentally, the name mammal comes from the mammary glands. These glands are the means by which all female mammals provide milk (or liquid food) to their developing young. The young suck the milk through teats or nipples for the first few weeks or months of life.

Reproduction
Mammals reproduce in a number of ways. Monotremes, such as the duck-billed platypus, lay eggs, but all other mammals give birth to their young. Marsupials, a small group of animals which includes kangaroos, give birth to very undeveloped young which then continue to grow inside a fold or pouch on the mother's skin.

The majority of mammals, called the placental mammals or eutherians, do not give birth to their young until they are fully formed and resemble the adults. (All European and African mammals are eutherians.)

The developing young, or foetus, grows inside a womb or uterus where it is fed by the mother through a placenta. This large organ allows the young to stay inside the mother for a lot longer than in most other animals. It forms the interface between the mother's blood supply and that of the foetus, where oxygen and food pass from the parent to her offspring. The placenta is attached to the foetus by an umbilical cord which drops off after birth.

Widespread range

Mammals are found in a wider variety of habitats than any other group of animals. While mammals all breathe air with their

Right: One factor that makes mammals unique is that the females have mammary glands. These glands produce milk for the young animals to drink, as this fallow deer fawn is doing. The milk is a mixture of water, fat, protein and sugars.

Above: Elephants are the largest land mammals in the world. They are most closely related to rabbit-like hyraxes and walrus-like dugongs and manatees.

lungs, this has not prevented many from making their homes in water. In many ways the streamlined bodies of whales and dolphins, for example, resemble those of sharks and other large fish. However, they are very much mammals, breathing air through a large nostril or blowhole in the top of the head, but their body hair has been reduced to just a few thick bristles.

Above: Plenty of mammals can glide, but only bats join birds and insects in true flight. A bat wing is made from skin that is stretched between long finger bones.

At the other end of the spectrum, some mammals even fly. Bats darting through the gloom of a summer evening may appear to be small birds, but they too are mammals with furry bodies and wings made from stretched skin instead of feathers. Although most other mammals have a more conventional body plan, with four legs and a tail, they too have evolved to survive in a startling range of habitats. They have achieved this not just by adapting their bodies but by changing their behaviour. In general, mammals have larger brains than reptiles and amphibians, and this allows them to understand their environment more fully. Many mammals, such as monkeys and dogs, survive by living in complex social groups in which individuals co-operate with each other when hunting food, protecting the group from danger and even finding mates.

ECOLOGY

Ecology is the study of how groups of organisms interact with members of their own species, other organisms and the environment. All types of animals live in a community of interdependent organisms called an ecosystem, in which they have their own particular role.

The natural world is filled with a wealth of opportunities for animals to feed and breed. Every animal species has evolved to take advantage of a certain set of these opportunities, called a niche. A niche is not just a physical place but also a lifestyle exploited by that single species. For example, even though they live in the same rainforest habitat, sloths and tapirs occupy very different niches.

To understand how different organisms interrelate, ecologists combine all the niches in an area into a community, called an ecosystem. Ecosystems are hard to define because it is impossible to know where one ends and another begins, but the system is a useful tool when learning more about the natural world.

Food chains

One way of understanding how an ecosystem works is to follow the food chains within it. A food chain is made up of a series of organisms that prey on each other. Each habitat is filled with them, and since they often merge into and converge from each other, they are often combined into food webs.

Below: The lion is at the top of a very simple food chain: lions eat zebras, and zebras eat grass. Energy is lost at each stage of the food chain, so there are fewer lions than there are zebras, and fewer zebras than there is grass.

Ecologists use food chains to see how energy and nutrients flow through natural communities. Food chains always begin with plants. Plants are the only organisms on Earth that do not need to feed actively, deriving their energy from sunlight, whereas all other organisms, including animals, get theirs from food. At the next level up the food chain come the plant-eaters. They eat the plants, and extract the sugar and other useful substances made by them. And, like the plants, they use these substances to power their bodies and stay alive. The predators occupy the next level up, and they eat the bodies of the plant-eating animals.

At each stage of the food chain, energy is lost, mainly as heat given out by the animals' bodies. Because of this, less energy is available at each level up the food chain. This means that in a healthy ecosystem there are always fewer predators than prey, and always more plants than plant-eaters.

Nutrient cycles

A very simple food chain would be as follows: grass, wildebeest and lion. However, the reality of most ecosystems is much more complex, with many more layers, including certain animals that eat both plants and animals. Every food chain ends with a top predator, in our example, the lion. Nothing preys on the lion, at least when it is alive, but once it dies the food chain continues as insects, fungi and other decomposers feed on the carcass. Eventually nothing is left of the lion's body. All the energy stored in it is removed by the decomposers, and the chemicals which made up its body have returned to the environment as carbon dioxide gas, water and minerals in the soil. And these are the very same substances needed by a growing plant. The cycle is complete.

Above: Nothing is wasted in nature. The dung beetle uses the droppings of larger grazing animals as a supply of food for its developing young. Since the beetles clear away all the dung, the soil is not damaged by it, the grass continues to grow, and the grazers have plenty of food.

Living together

As food chains show, the lives of different animals in an ecosystem are closely related. If all the plants died for some reason, it would not just be the plant-eaters that would go hungry. As all of them began to die, the predators would starve too. Only the decomposers might benefit temporarily. Put another way, the other species living alongside an animal are just as integral to that animal's environment as the weather and landscape. This is yet another way of saying that animal species have not evolved isolated from each another.

The result is that as predators have evolved new ways of catching their prey, the prey has had to evolve new ways of escaping. On many occasions this process of co-evolution has created symbiotic relationships between two different species. For example, honeyguide birds lead badgers to bees' nests.

Some niches are very simple, and the animals that occupy them live simple, solitary lives. Others, especially those occupied by mammals, are much more complex and require members of a species to live closely together. These aggregations of animals may be simple herds or more structured social groups.

Food chain

Food chains show how the energy needed for life passes through an ecosystem. The energy originates in the sun. This makes plants grow, which are then eaten by animals. The plant-eating animals then become meals themselves.

Below: This food chain shows what animals eat in a temperate country, such as Britain. Herbivores eat only plants, while carnivores eat mainly other animals. Animals that eat both plants and animals are omnivores – for example, humans.

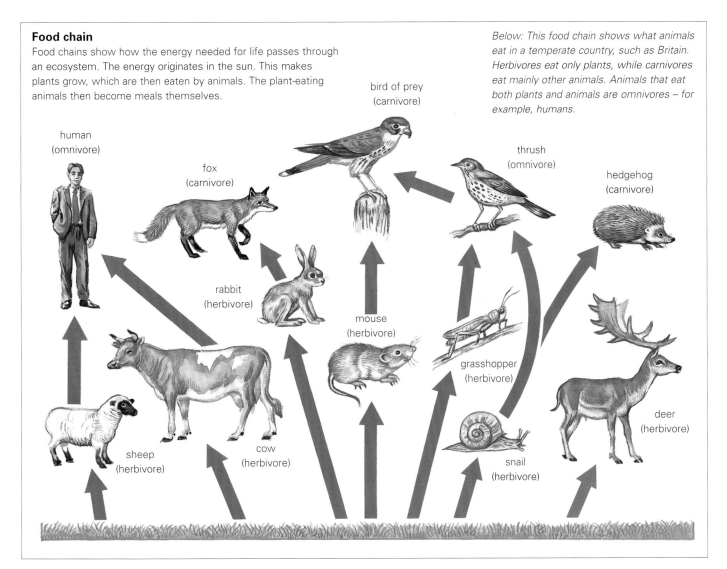

human
(omnivore)

fox
(carnivore)

bird of prey
(carnivore)

thrush
(omnivore)

hedgehog
(carnivore)

rabbit
(herbivore)

mouse
(herbivore)

grasshopper
(herbivore)

deer
(herbivore)

sheep
(herbivore)

cow
(herbivore)

snail
(herbivore)

Group living

A herd, flock or shoal is a group of animals which gathers together for safety. Each member operates as an individual, but is physically safest in the centre of the group, the danger of attack being greatest on the edge. Herd members do not actively communicate dangers to each other. When one is startled by something and bolts, the rest will probably follow.

Members of a social group, on the other hand, work together to find food, raise their young and defend themselves. Many mammals, for example apes, monkeys, dogs, dolphins and elephants, form social groups, and these groups exist in many forms. At one end of the spectrum are highly ordered societies, such as lion prides and baboon troops, which are often controlled by one dominant male, the other members often having their own ranking in a strict hierarchical structure. At the other end of the spectrum are leaderless gangs of animals, such as squirrel monkeys, which merge and split with no real guiding purpose.

There are many advantages of living in social groups, with members finding more food and being warned of danger, for example. However, in many societies only a handful of high-ranking members are allowed to breed. In these cases, the groups are held together by a complex fusion of family ties in which brothers and sisters help to raise nephews and nieces. Politics also plays its cohesive part, with members forming and breaking alliances in order to rise to the top.

Below: Meerkats live in family groups called bands. They need to live together because they live in a dry habitat where they must co-operate to find food, raise young and avoid being eaten by predators.

MIGRATION AND HIBERNATION

Migration and hibernation are two ways in which animals cope with the changing seasons and fluctuations in the supply of food. By hibernating, they sleep through periods of bad weather when food is hard to find, and by migrating, they reach places where food is more readily available.

Everywhere on Earth, the climate changes throughout the year with the cycle of seasons. In some places these changes are hardly noticeable from month to month, while in others each new season brings extremes of weather from blistering hot summers to freezing winters, or torrential rains followed by drought.

Change of lifestyle

In temperate regions, such as Europe, the year is generally divided into four seasons. By contrast, in the Arctic and Antarctic, the change between summer and winter is so quick that, in effect, there are only two seasons. Other regions experience a different annual cycle of changes. For example, tropical regions do not really have fluctuating temperatures, but many areas do experience periods of relative dry and at least one period of heavier rains each year.

Hibernating heart rate

The hibernating animal's heart rate slows to just a few beats per minute. It breathes more slowly and its body temperature drops to just a few degrees above the surrounding air temperature.

Below: The bodies of true hibernators, such as the dormouse, shut down almost completely during hibernation. Other hibernators, such as bears, may be out of sight for most of the winter, but they do not become completely dormant and their temperature does not fall drastically.

Above: Reptiles that live in cooler parts of the world – adders, for example – spend a long time lying dormant. They do not hibernate like mammals, but because they are cold-blooded and do not need lots of energy to function, they can go for long periods without food.

Animals must, of course, react to these changes if they are to survive the harshest weather and make the most of clement conditions. Monkeys, for example, build up a mental map of their patch of forest so that they know where the fresh leaves will be after the rains, and where to find the hardier forest fruits during a drought. Wolves living in chilly northern forests hunt together in packs during the cold winter, working together to kill animals which are much larger than they are. However, when the summer arrives they tend to forage alone, picking off the many smaller animals, such as rodents and rabbits, which appear when the snow melts.

Hibernation

The reason the wolves find these smaller animals in the summer is that they suddenly emerge, having passed the winter in cosy burrows or nests. This behaviour is commonly called hibernating, but there is a distinction between true hibernation and simply being inactive over winter.

Animals such as bears and tree squirrels are not true hibernators. Although they generally sleep for long periods during the coldest parts of winter, hunkered down in a den or drey, they do not enter the deep, unconscious state of hibernation. Unable to feed while asleep, these animals rely on their bodily reserves of fat to stay alive. However, they often wake up during breaks in the harshest weather and venture outside to urinate or snatch a meal. Because tree squirrels have less fat reserves than bears, they frequently visit caches (stores) of food which they filled in the autumn.

On the other hand, the true hibernators, such as dormice, do not stir at all over winter. They rely completely on their reserves of fat to stay alive, and to save energy their metabolism slows to a fraction of its normal pace.

Only warm-blooded animals hibernate because they are the main types of animals which can survive in places where hibernation is necessary. However, snakes often pass the winter in rocky crevices and burrows. Reptiles and amphibians which live in very hot, dry places have their own form of hibernation, called aestivation. They

become dormant when their habitat becomes too dry. Most bury themselves in moist sand or under rocks, only becoming active again when rain brings the habitat back to life. Some aestivating frogs even grow a skin cocoon which traps moisture and keeps their bodies moist while they wait for the rains to return.

Migration

Another way of coping with bad conditions is to migrate. Migrations are not just random wanderings, but involve following a set route each year. In general they are two-way trips, with animals returning to where they started once conditions back home become favourable again.

All sorts of animals migrate, from insects to whales, and there are many reasons for doing so. Most migrators are looking for supplies of food, or for a safe place to rear their young. For example, once their home territory becomes too crowded, young lemmings stampede over wide areas looking for new places to live, sometimes dying in the process. Herds of reindeer leave the barren tundra as winter approaches, and head for the relative warmth of the forest. Mountain goats act in a similar way: having spent the summer grazing in high alpine meadows, they descend below the treeline when winter snow begins to cover their pastures.

Other migrations are on a much grander scale, and in some cases an animal's whole life can be a continual migration. Wildebeest travel in huge

Above: Whales make the longest migrations of all mammals. They move from their warm breeding grounds near the Equator to feeding areas in cooler waters near the poles.

herds across southern Africa in search of fresh pastures. They follow age-old routes but may take a detour if grass is growing in unusual places. Among the greatest migrants are the giant whales, which travel thousands of miles from their breeding grounds in the tropics to their feeding grounds near the poles. The cool waters around the poles teem with plankton food, while the warmer tropical waters are a better place for giving birth.

Day length

How do animals know that it is time to hibernate or migrate? The answer is often that they respond to changing day lengths as the seasons change.

All animals are sensitive to daylight, and use it to set their body clocks or circadian rhythms. These rhythms

Above: Bats spend long periods hibernating. They mate before winter, and the females store the sperm inside their body, only releasing it on the eggs as spring approaches.

affect all bodily processes, including the build-up to the breeding season. The hibernators begin to put on weight or store food as the days shorten, and many migrants start to get restless before setting off on their journey. However, not all migrations are controlled by the number of hours of daylight. Some migrators, such as wildebeest and lemmings, move because of other environmental factors, such as the lack of food caused by drought or overcrowding.

Below: The migration of enormous herds of wildebeest across the huge grasslands of Africa is one of the natural wonders of the world. These large antelopes travel in search of watering holes and new areas of fresh grass. The migrations do not follow the same route each year, but the herds generally do stay on tried and tested trails.

INTRODUCED SPECIES

Centuries ago, as people started exploring and conquering new lands, many animals travelled with them. In fact, that's the only way many animals could travel such long distances, often crossing seas. Many introduced species then thrived in their new habitats, often at the expense of the native wildlife.

Looking around the European countryside, you would be forgiven for thinking that cows, sheep and other farm animals are naturally occurring species. In fact, all come from distant parts of the world. Over the centuries, livestock animals have been selectively bred to develop desirable characteristics, such as lean meat or high milk production. Despite this, they can be traced back to ancestral species.

For example, goats – a domestic breed of an Asian ibex – were introduced to North Africa about 3,000 years ago. These goats, with their voracious appetites, did well feeding on dry scrubland. In fact they did too well, and had soon stripped the earth almost bare of plants. Without plant roots to hold water in the soil, the soil dried out, turned to sand and blew away. Although the climate plays an important role, it could be said that introducing goats helped make North

Below: Grey squirrels are one of the most common wild mammals in Europe. They were introduced to Britain from North America in the early 1900s, and later to Italy and South Africa. In Europe, especially Britain, grey squirrels have wiped out many of the endemic red squirrels.

Africa's Sahara the largest desert in the world. Similarly, horses introduced to Europe and Africa by invading armies from Asia had a marked effect on that continent.

Rodent invaders

While many animals were introduced to new areas on purpose as livestock or pets, other animals hitched a lift. For example, some animals were more or less stowaways on ships, but only those that could fend for themselves at their new destination were successfully introduced. These species tended to be generalist feeders, and none was more successful than rodents, such as mice and rats. In fact the house mouse is the second most widespread mammal of all, after humans. It lives almost everywhere that people do, except in the icy polar regions, although it is very likely that rodents did reach these places but then failed to thrive in the cold.

The black rat – also known as the ship rat – has spread right around the world from India over the last 2,000 years. On several occasions it has brought diseases with it, including bubonic plague, or the Black Death, which has killed millions. Bubonic

Cows and sheep
European cows are believed to be descendants of a now-extinct species of ox called the auroch, while modern sheep are descended from the mouflon. From their beginnings in the Middle East, new breeds were introduced to all corners of the world, where they had a huge effect on the native animals and wildlife.

Above: Cattle have been bred to look and behave very differently from their wild ancestors. Few breeds have horns, and they are generally docile animals. Some breeds produce a good supply of milk, while others are bred for their meat.

Below: Sheep were among the first domestic animals. They are kept for their meat and sometimes milk, which is used for cheese. The thick coat or fleece that kept their ancestors warm on mountain slopes is now used to make woollen garments.

Above: Rabbits and hares have long been seen as natural members of British wildlife. However, the hare was introduced by the Romans about 2,000 years ago. It is likely that rabbits arrived at this time as well, but some evidence suggests that they were introduced by the Normans in the 12th century.

plague was caused by bacteria living in the stomachs of rat fleas. The bacteria built up in the flea's stomach until there was no room for any food. The blood-sucking flea became ravenous and began biting all living things, including humans, in hope of a meal. As a result the flea infected its victims with the deadly bacteria. In the plague pandemic of the mid-14th century, nearly half of the population of western Europe was killed.

Another prolific travelling rodent is the brown rat, which is thought to have spread from China, and now exists everywhere except the poles.

Rodents are so successful because they will eat almost anything and can reproduce at a prolific rate. These two characteristics have meant that mice and rats have become pests wherever they breed.

Going wild

When a domestic or captive animal escapes and lives in the wild, it is described as being feral. There are many feral animals in Europe and Africa. For example, American minks were brought to Europe to stock fur farms. Many of these carnivores escaped, and feral American mink are now more common than European mink in some places.

Horses were introduced from Central Asia. There are no wild horses left in the world, although several feral populations still exist. For example, Shetland ponies were bred as small but sturdy work horses. Today they live wild on Dartmoor in Devon, England.

A third example is the feral pig, which lives wild across Europe, sometimes forming large herds of up to 100 individuals.

Below: With their sharp and ever-growing teeth, rodents are very adaptable animals. Rats and mice have spread alongside humans, and wherever people go, these little gnawing beasts soon become established, breeding very quickly and spreading into new areas.

ENDANGERED SPECIES

Many animals are threatened with extinction because they cannot survive in a world which is constantly being changed by human intervention. Many species have already become extinct, and if people do nothing to save them, a great many more will follow.

Ever since life began on Earth, species have become extinct from time to time – it is a natural part of the evolutionary process. As the climate and landscape have changed in a given area over millions of years, the animals that live there have also changed. And as a new species evolves, so another is forced out of its habitat and becomes extinct. All that remains, if we are lucky, are a few fossilized bones – a record in stone.

Mass extinction?

Biologists estimate that there are at least several million species alive today, and possibly as many as 30 million. Whatever the figure, there are probably more species on Earth right now than at any other time. However, because of the habitat destruction caused by people, more species are becoming extinct or are being threatened with extinction than ever before.

Geologists and biologists know that every now and then there are mass extinctions, in which great

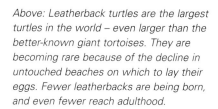

Below: Okapis are mammals whose closest living relatives are giraffes, despite the zebra-stripes on their hindquarters and forelegs. They live in the forest of the Congo in central Africa. This forest has been ravaged by war and deforestation, and okapis and other forest-dwellers are now very rare.

Above: Leatherback turtles are the largest turtles in the world – even larger than the better-known giant tortoises. They are becoming rare because of the decline in untouched beaches on which to lay their eggs. Fewer leatherbacks are being born, and even fewer reach adulthood.

numbers of the world's animals die out forever. For example, it is widely believed that the dinosaurs and many other reptiles were wiped out after a meteorite smashed into Mexico 65 million years ago. But the questions are now: are we witnessing the natural world's latest mass extinction? And are humans the cause?

Most of the world's animal species are insects – especially beetles – and other invertebrates. It is likely that many of these species, especially those living in tropical forests, are becoming extinct. However, since scientists may never have had a chance to describe many of them, nobody knows the true number.

Life list

With vertebrate animals, it is a different story. Because there are only a few thousand species of animals with backbones, most of which have been recognized for hundreds of years, we know a great deal more about the plight of each species. Many species, for example mice, dogs and horses, thrive in a world dominated by people. However, a great many more species have suffered as people have changed their habitats, either destroying them completely or upsetting the balance of nature by introducing species from other parts of the world.

The International Union for the Conservation of Nature and Natural Resources (IUCN) produces a Red List of animals which are in danger of extinction. There are currently about 15,500 animals listed in a number of categories, including extinct in the wild, endangered and vulnerable. Nearly one-quarter of all mammals are

included on the list, and about four per cent of reptiles and three of amphibians. However, while the status of all mammals has been assessed by the IUCN, only a fraction of reptiles and amphibians have been as thoroughly checked, and it is very likely that many more species are much closer to extinction than was previously thought.

Below: Over the past century, cheetah populations have declined rapidly. One of the main reasons for this is that humans have hunted them for their pelts, reducing their genetic diversity and making them more vulnerable to disease. In addition, much of their grassland habitat has been used for farming.

Above: Gorillas are endangered because their forest habitats are being destroyed. They are not able to thrive anywhere else. Also, these great apes are hunted for meat. Although illegal, the bush-meat trade is highly profitable, but soon there may be no gorillas left.

Wiped out

As the forests of Europe were cleared over the past thousand years, forest animals had increasingly fewer places to live. And as they inevitably came into increasingly close contact with people, wild animals, such as boars, bears and wolves, became persecuted and were eventually wiped out in many areas.

Above: All five species of rhinoceros are dangerously close to extinction in the wild. During the 1970s half of the world's population disappeared, and today less than 15 per cent of the 1970s population remains, an estimated 10,000 to 11,000 individuals.

As the world's human population soared in the 20th century, a similar process took place elsewhere. Another major habitat being destroyed was, and still is, the tropical rainforest. The number of species living in these areas is much higher than elsewhere, and a proportionately huge number of species are finding it harder to survive.

Although few animals on the Red List have actually become extinct, the situation is becoming graver for most species. The monkeys and apes of the tropical rainforests are among the worst affected, with nearly one in four species being very close to extinction. This is because rainforests are complicated places, and many primate species there have evolved a specialized lifestyle, for example feeding on fruit in the tallest trees. These species are very badly affected by sudden changes in their environment, for example when a logging team cuts down all the tall trees leaving just the shorter ones behind.

CONSERVING WILDLIFE

With so many species facing extinction, conservationists have their work cut out. Conservationists try to protect habitats and provide safe places for threatened animals to thrive, but the activities of ordinary people can often also have an adverse effect on the future of natural habitats.

People give many reasons why wildlife should be conserved. Some argue that if all the forests were cleared and the oceans polluted, the delicate balance of nature would be so ruined that Earth would not be able to support any life, including humans. Others suggest that if vulnerable species were allowed to die, the natural world would not be sufficiently diverse to cope with future changes in the environment. Another reason to save diversity is that we have not yet fully recorded it. Also, there are undoubtedly many as yet unknown species – especially of plants – which could be useful to humankind, for example in the field of medicine. But perhaps the strongest argument for the conservation of wildlife is that it would be totally irresponsible to let it disappear.

Habitat protection

Whatever the reasons, the best way to protect species in danger of being wiped out is to protect their habitats so that the complex communities of plants and animals can continue to live. However, with the human population growing so rapidly, people are often forced to choose between promoting their own interests and protecting wildlife. Of course, people invariably put themselves first, which means that the conservationists have to employ a range of techniques in order to save wildlife.

In many countries it has now become illegal to hunt certain endangered animals, or to trade in any products made from their bodies. Whales, gorillas and elephants are protected in this way. Many governments and charitable organizations have also set up wildlife reserves, where the animals stand a good chance of thriving. The oldest

Below: One of the main causes of deforestation is people clearing the trees and burning them to make way for farmland. The ash makes good soil for a few years, but eventually the nutrients needed by the crops run out and so the farmers often begin to clear more forest.

Above: If logging is done properly, it can make enough money to pay to protect the rest of the rainforest. Only selected trees are cut down and they are removed without damaging younger growth. Forests can be used to grow crops, such as coffee and nuts, without cutting down all the trees.

protected areas are in North America and Europe, where it is illegal to ruin areas of forest wilderness and wetland. Consequently, these places have become wildlife havens. Other protected areas include semi-natural landscapes which double as beauty spots and tourist attractions. Although these areas often have to be extensively altered and managed to meet the needs of the visitors, most still support wildlife communities.

In the developing world, wildlife refuges are a newer phenomenon. Huge areas of Africa's savannahs are protected and populated with many amazing animals. However, the enormous size of these parks makes it very hard to protect the animals, especially elephants and rhinoceroses, from poachers.

Reintroduction

Large areas of tropical forests are now protected in countries such as Congo and Cameroon, but often conservation efforts come too late because many animals have either become rare or are completely absent after years of human

Zoo animals

Once zoos were places where exotic animals were merely put on display. Such establishments were increasingly regarded as cruel. Today, the world's best zoos are an integral part of conservation. Several animals, which are classified as extinct in the wild, can only be found in zoos where they are being bred. These breeding programmes are heavily controlled to make sure that closely related animals do not breed with each other. Later, individual animals may be sent around the world to mate in different zoos to avoid in-breeding.

Below: Giraffes are just one example of the many animals that have been bred successfully in zoos. Many of the world's rarest species are kept in zoos, partly so that people can see them, since they are too rare to be spotted in the wild.

damage. However, several conservation programmes have reintroduced animals bred in zoos into the wild.

To reintroduce a group of zoo-bred animals successfully into the wild, conservationists need to know how the animal fits into the habitat and interacts with the other animals living there. In addition, for example when trying to reintroduce chimpanzees to the forests of the Congo, people have to teach the young animals how to find food and fend for themselves.

Below: Breeding centres are an important way of increasing the number of rare animals. Most, such as this giant panda centre in China, are in the natural habitat. If the animals kept there are treated properly, they should be able to fend for themselves when released back into the wild.

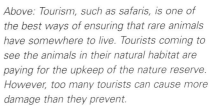

Above: Tourism, such as safaris, is one of the best ways of ensuring that rare animals have somewhere to live. Tourists coming to see the animals in their natural habitat are paying for the upkeep of the nature reserve. However, too many tourists can cause more damage than they prevent.

Understanding habitats

A full understanding of how animals live in the wild is also vitally important when conservationists are working in a habitat that has been damaged by human activity. For example, in areas of rainforest which are being heavily logged, the trees are often divided into isolated islands of growth surrounded by cleared ground. This altered habitat is no good for monkeys, which need large areas of forest to swing through throughout the year. The solution is to plant strips of forest to connect the islands of untouched habitat, creating a continuous mass again.

Another example of beneficial human intervention involves protecting rare frogs in the process of migrating to a breeding pond. If their migration necessitates crossing a busy road, it is likely that many of them will be run over. Conservationists now dig little tunnels under the roads so that the frogs can travel in safety. Similar protection schemes have been set up for hedgehogs and ducks, to allow them safe passageways.

BIOMES

The Earth is not a uniform place but has a complex patchwork of habitats covering its surface from the Equator to the poles. Biologists have simplified this patchwork by dividing it into zones called biomes, each of which has a particular climate and a distinct community of animals.

The places where animal communities live can be radically different. So, for example, vipers slither along the tops of sand dunes in the middle of the Sahara Desert while sperm whales live hundreds of metres down in the gloomy, ice-cold depths of the ocean. The environmental conditions determine what kind of animals and plants are able to survive there.

Climate control

The world's habitats are generally divided into 11 biomes: oceans, freshwater rivers and wetlands, tropical forests, temperate forests, boreal forests, tropical grasslands or savannahs, temperate grasslands or prairies, tundra, polar ice caps, deserts and mountains.

The overriding factor that determines whether an area belongs to one biome or another is its climate – chiefly the rainfall and temperature.

Understanding the climate of a place is a complicated business because the factors involved – including rainfall, temperature and light levels – vary from day to night and throughout the year. The latitude is probably the best place to start. In general terms, regions close to the Equator, at a latitude of 0°, are hot. The coldest places are the poles, with a latitude of 90°. The territory in between generally cools as you travel to higher latitudes.

However, other factors also affect climate. For example, during the hot days of summer, the land at certain latitudes warms up more quickly than the ocean. Six months later, in the depths of winter, the land cools down more quickly than the ocean. This means that the oceans and the areas of land bordering them tend to enjoy a mild climate with smaller fluctuations

of temperature each year, while the interiors of large continental landmasses experience very hot summers and extremely chilly winters.

Animal communities

Other geographical factors – ocean currents, mountains and depressions in the Earth's surface – also have a major influence on climate and biomes. The climate defines which plants can grow in any particular spot and how quickly. And since the plants form the basis of all food webs and ecosystems, each biome has a particular community of animals which have evolved to exploit the plant life.

Below: This map shows how the world can be divided into biomes. The climate of a region has the greatest effect on the sorts of plants and animals that can survive there. Some animals may live across an entire biome, while others are found only in particular habitats.

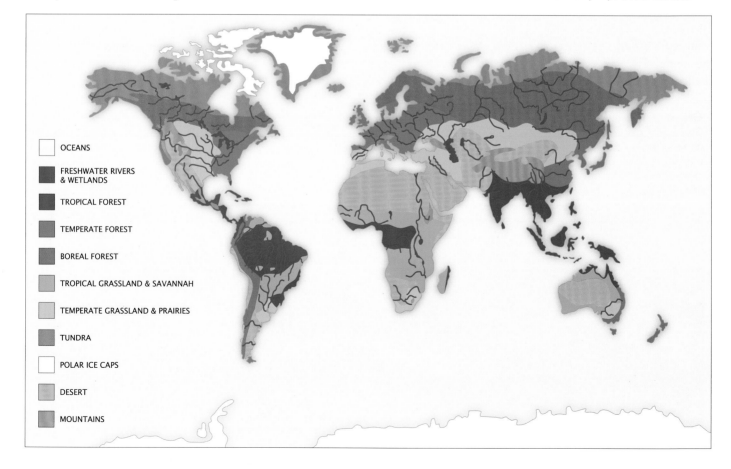

OCEANS

FRESHWATER RIVERS & WETLANDS

TROPICAL FOREST

TEMPERATE FOREST

BOREAL FOREST

TROPICAL GRASSLAND & SAVANNAH

TEMPERATE GRASSLAND & PRAIRIES

TUNDRA

POLAR ICE CAPS

DESERT

MOUNTAINS

Biomes and ear size

Closely related animals that live in different biomes have different features that help them function under different conditions. For example, foxes live in similar ways across the world. However, the Arctic fox, which lives in cold polar areas, has very small outer ears. The red fox that lives in the mild temperate biome of Europe has medium-sized ears, while the bat-eared fox and other species that live in hot areas have very large ears. Ear size is linked to the control of body heat. The small size of the Arctic fox's ears prevents heat wastage, while the large ears of the bat-eared fox are useful for radiating away unwanted heat, helping the animal keep cool. The red fox's ears are a compromise: large enough to hear very clearly, but small enough to conserve heat in the winter.

Arctic fox

Red fox

Bat-eared fox

Rainfall has a major influence on biomes. It is generally heaviest in tropical regions, resulting in lush rainforests. In colder regions, rainfall may be almost as high but it results in a different type of forest. In areas with less rain, deserts or grasslands appear.

The animals in different biomes face the same challenges: finding enough food and water, and finding a mate to raise offspring. However, the different conditions in each biome mean that the animals have to meet these challenges in very different ways.

In all biomes, the animal communities have a similar structure. Grazers and other plant-eating animals survive by eating any plants which have evolved to make the most of the climatic conditions. These grazers are, in turn, preyed upon by a series of hunters. In the most productive biomes, such as forests, many of these hunting animals might be hunted in turn by larger, fiercer predators.

However, the plant-eaters of grasslands, such as bison and antelopes, live a very different life from their counterparts in tropical forests, such as monkeys and tapirs. Similarly, ocean hunters, such as mighty orcas (killer whales), have a body adapted to swimming at great speed through the water; the predators in a boreal forest, such as wolves, have very different bodies for covering long distances quickly and bringing down animals more than twice their size. One of the main purposes of biology is to understand how communities of plants and animals have evolved to survive in the world's different biomes.

Grassland animals

Grasslands are unusual habitats because food is everywhere. While animals that live in other biomes must seek out and defend a source of food, grazing animals are surrounded by it, and no single animal can control it. Instead of competing for food, they compete for mates, and many grazers are tough fighters. Grass and other plant foods are not very nutritious, so animals have to eat a lot of them. Since they have plenty of food, many grassland animals, such as buffalos and elephants, are big. Being large also helps defence against predators. Grassland predators such as lions tend to hunt in groups so that they can work together to bring down powerful animals.

Buffalo

Elephant

Lion

OCEANS

The oceans cover nearly three-quarters of the Earth's surface and create by far the largest and most complex biome. They contain the world's largest and smallest animals, from tiny zooplankton to the mighty blue whale. Between these two extremes, the oceans contain an incredible wealth of life.

The oceans are not a simple biome because they consist of countless habitats, including everything from colourful coral reefs to mysterious, deep-sea hydrothermal vents. The depth of the ocean obviously has a marked effect on the conditions.

The first few hundred metres (yards) below the surface is called the photic zone, where the water is bathed in sunlight during the day. This upper layer is the limit of plant growth in the ocean because below this depth the light fades, unable to penetrate any deeper, and plants rely on light to make their food.

As on land, many ocean animals graze on plants, which means that they have to live in the photic zone. Ocean plants tend to be simple algae, known as phytoplankton, which float in the current. These plants do not have complicated body structures, and many are just single cells. Consequently, many of the ocean plant-eaters are also tiny floating organisms, known collectively as zooplankton.

Leatherback turtles have long front flippers that allow them to swim long distances each day.

Yellow-bellied sea snakes have flattened tails that work as paddles to help them swim through water.

Common seals have large, sensitive eyes that help them to see their fish prey underwater.

South African fur seals spend most of the year at sea, surviving on a diet of fish and squid.

Zooplankton – largely shrimp-like crustaceans – is a very important part of the ocean food chain, being the main food for toothless baleen whales. These ocean giants filter out the zooplankton from gulps of seawater.

Deeper down, in the dark depths, life continues without plants. Despite conditions being too dark for plants, most deep-sea animals still get their energy from them indirectly by feeding on marine "snow". This consists of the waste products of the organisms higher up.

These food chains provide the basis of animal life in the ocean, feeding many types of larger vertebrate animals including fish, turtles and sea mammals. While fish evolved in the sea, the sea-living reptiles, such as turtles and sea snakes, and the sea mammals, such as seals and whales, actually evolved from animals which once lived on land.

A great deal of this evolution must have taken place in shallow coastal waters, and while whales and dolphins have become completely independent of land, other sea mammals and most reptiles must return to land at some point during the year to breed.

Seals and sea lions make their homes in coastal waters where the ocean meets the land. Coral reefs, sometimes described as the rainforests of the ocean because they support so much life, are a feature of coastal waters in the tropics. In shallow seas, tall kelps and other kinds of seaweed can grow into thick underwater forests, providing habitats for a whole range of animals, such as sea otters.

Although many marine mammals and reptiles spend some time on land, true amphibians are found only in fresh water, and relatively few animals can survive in both salty and fresh water.

White-beaked dolphins live in coastal waters. They are famed for leaping and somersaulting.

Harbour porpoises rarely jump out of the sea like dolphins. Instead, they rise to the surface to breathe.

Humpback whales live in deep waters, spending the summer in cold waters near the poles.

Sperm whales are the largest hunting predators in the world. Their preferred food is squid.

FRESH WATER

Only three per cent of the world's water is fresh, but experts estimate that this covers a total of over 100,000sq km (40,000sq miles), including the polar icecaps. The rivers, lakes and wetlands supplied by fresh water are some of the best places to see wildlife. But where does fresh water come from?

The Earth's atmosphere is a huge water pump that transfers water from the oceans to the land. The heat from the sun makes water evaporate from the surface of the ocean, and the water vapour produced becomes part of the atmosphere. The warm water vapour in the air may then cool down for various reasons. As it cools, the vapour begins to turn back into a liquid, forming tiny droplets on the surface of particles of dust carried in the wind. These moist dust particles gather to form the clouds that often obscure clear skies. If the air cools even more, the amount of water condensing in cloud becomes too much for it to hold, and the water falls to the surface as rain.

Since most of the Earth's surface is covered by oceans, most of the rain falls back into the sea. However, some falls on to land where it forms rivers, lakes and waterlogged ground, such as swamps and marshes, known collectively as wetlands. Mountain ranges receive high rainfall because they force the moist air to rise up

European pond turtles have webbed feet which help them to move quickly through water.

Nile crocodiles are excellent at fishing, herding fish into shallow waters before catching them.

Green water snakes actively patrol shallow swamps and backwaters for their favourite food of frogs.

Aquatic genets live alone, spending most of their time in or near water, feeding on fish.

over them and cool. The rain then flows down the mountainsides in torrents and waterfalls. Down on the lowlands, these fast-flowing streams join together to make larger, deeper rivers which move more slowly across the landscape. Nearly all the fresh water falling on land eventually makes its way back to the oceans via rivers. Some fresh water does seep into rocks under the ground, but it reappears as springs which feed yet more rivers.

All the rivers in the world combined contain just a fraction of the Earth's water, though some of them form huge freshwater systems. The largest river system in Europe and Africa is the Congo. This Central African network of rivers is second only in size to the Amazon of South America. Africa also has the world's longest river, the Nile, which flows from East Africa to the Mediterranean Sea.

Rainwater and other forms of precipitation provide fresh water. When water evaporates from the oceans, the salt is left behind and only the water molecules rise into the atmosphere. Although fresh water acquires small amounts of dissolved salts as it flows over rocks on its journey to the sea, it is much less salty than sea water, and this has an effect on the animals that live in it. Sea water is saltier than animal body fluids. Fresh water is less salty, which means that water tends to flow into the animal from outside. If the animal does not get rid of some moisture, it will become swollen, and its body fluids will be too diluted.

Freshwater fish and amphibians tackle this problem by urinating all their excess water. Semi-aquatic mammals and reptiles, such as otters and anacondas, rely on their skin to act as a barrier to the influx of water.

European otters have webbed feet for swimming and sensitive whiskers to help them detect prey.

Aquatic tenrecs have sleek fur resembling that of an otter. They live in fast-running streams.

Hippopotamuses keep cool in water, with only their nostrils, eyes and ears above the surface.

Sitatungas are semi-aquatic antelopes that live in swamps. They can swim to avoid predators.

TROPICAL FORESTS

Tropical forests are the oldest and most complex forests on Earth. They contain a greater variety of animal species than anywhere else, from the great apes, such as gorillas, and big cats, such as leopards, to tiny frogs and pencil-thin snakes.

The lush, steamy jungles of tropical forest grow in a band around the Earth's Equator. These forests are packed with wildlife, more so than any other biome. The total number of animal species living in tropical forests is unknown because most have never been identified, but it probably adds up to several million. The majority of these species are insects, such as beetles and bugs, but tropical forests also contain the greatest diversity of vertebrate animals. Unfortunately, large tracts of these forests are now under threat from human activities such as logging.

Tropical forests are among the wettest places on Earth. Most receive about 2.5m (8ft) of rain every year, while forests that grow on ocean islands often receive over 6m (19ft). The tropics receive so much rain because near the Equator the sun is always high in the sky, keeping temperatures elevated. Consequently, a great deal of water evaporates from the oceans and rises into the sky here. The water vapour cools as it rises and

Foam-nesting frogs lay their eggs over water. The hatched tadpoles then drop into the water below.

Gaboon vipers are covered in diamond and zigzag patterns, which camouflage them in leaf litter.

Leopards are well adapted to climbing trees, and often hide their kills in branches for eating later.

Hammer-headed fruit bats fly through the tropical forest at night in search of ripened fruit.

condenses into vast rain clouds. Generally, towards the end of the day, these clouds release their load of water.

Rainfall defines the two main types of tropical forest – rainforest and monsoon forest. Rainforests grow in places where rainfall is heavy all year round, although there are often drier spells throughout the year. There are no rainforests in Europe. The main African rainforest is in the Congo Basin. Monsoon forests grow in tropical areas where most rain falls during an annual wet season. The largest African monsoon forests are in Madagascar and West Africa.

With so much water and warmth, plants grow larger and more quickly than just about anywhere else on land. Most trees reach at least 50m (150ft) tall and form a dense network of branches, or canopy, high above the ground. The canopy is so thick in places that underneath it is very gloomy and humid. Taller trees poke their crowns out above the canopy. The tallest of these emergent trees grow over 100m (300ft) high.

Tropical forest plants grow more thickly than elsewhere, too. Some plants, known as air plants or epiphytes, do not grow in the ground but attach themselves on to the trunks or branches of larger plants. Within this complex framework of plant life, there are countless places for all types of animal to thrive. For example, amphibians need to live in water during the early stages of their life. And with so much rain falling, tropical forests are rarely short of water. Some epiphytes have bowl-shaped leaves to catch the rain, and several amphibian species use these aerial ponds as breeding sites. Down on the ground some frogs and salamanders just lay their eggs in damp soil, which is wet enough for their young to develop in.

Chimpanzees are able to make tools for extracting termites by stripping the leaves from twigs.

Mandrills cover 8km (5 miles) of forest per day, foraging for fruit, nuts and other vegetable material.

Pottos have wide, sensitive eyes, which help them locate fruit at the tops of trees at night.

Okapi live in dense tropical forests, communicating with vocalizations and mutual grooming.

TEMPERATE FORESTS

Before the rise of agriculture, temperate forests covered most of the northern hemisphere. Today, however, nearly all of these wild woodlands have been replaced by meadows and farmland. After tropical forests, temperate forests contain the greatest diversity of animal life.

Temperate forests grow in mild regions that receive a lot of rain but do not get very hot or cold. The largest temperate forests are in the northern hemisphere, in a belt north of subtropical regions.

The main difference between the temperate forests and other forest biomes is that most temperate trees are deciduous, dropping their leaves in the autumn, and growing new ones in spring. Although there are a few deciduous trees, such as paper birch, growing in the southern zones of northern boreal forests, there are many more evergreen conifers.

The reason why temperate forests lose their leaves is to save energy during the winter. Because it is rarely very bright over winter, the leaves would not be able to photosynthesize food from sunlight. And because the cold and frosts would damage the redundant leaves during winter, it is best that they are dropped. As autumn progresses, the leaves' valuable green pigments, which trap the sun's energy, withdraw back into the tree. Then, as

Adders bask in sunshine by day and hunt by night. In winter they hibernate in underground burrows.

Beech martens are well adapted to forest life, making their dens in hollow trees, burrows and crevices.

Badgers eat anything they can find on the forest floor: worms, berries, fungi and carrion.

Red squirrels live high up in the trees. They bury nuts in autumn, to feed on during the winter.

the green disappears, so the less important red and brown pigments are revealed, giving the forest its beautiful autumn colours.

As with a few other land biomes, temperate forests are poorly represented in the southern hemisphere, with only a few patches in South Africa, because there is very little southern land with an appropriate climate. The temperate forests that grow in slightly warmer and drier regions, such as the Mediterranean and South Africa, are not deciduous. They are populated with evergreen trees with toughened leaves that keep the moisture in with a coating of oily resin.

Ten thousand years ago much of Europe was covered in temperate forest. These forests were a mixture of oak, ash, beech and cherry trees. Nearly all of Europe's forest has been cut down over the years to make way for farms and towns. Today only a fraction of Europe is covered by forest. Much of this forest is not wholly natural because it is managed by people to produce timber or other products. Only a fraction of land is covered in so-called ancient forest. These forests have been relatively untouched by human activities for hundreds if not thousands of years. Perhaps the most spectacular temperate

forest in Europe is the Bialowieza Forest in Poland and Belarus. This forest is one of the few places where European bison lives wild.

During winter, with the leaves fallen, temperate forests become desolate places with little food available. Larger animals may migrate to warmer, more productive areas to spend the winter, or scratch out a living while depending on their body fat reserves. Smaller animals, such as dormice and ground squirrels, hibernate to save energy until the spring, while others, such as most tree-living squirrels, rely on food caches that they built up in the autumn.

European rabbits live in large colonies, inhabiting complex mazes of burrows, or warrens.

Noctule bats roost in hollow trees or old woodpecker holes, and forage for insects at dusk.

Wild boars construct forest shelters from grass, and look after their young in crude nests.

European bison congregate around good feeding grounds, eating leaves, twigs and grass.

BOREAL FORESTS

Boreal forest, or taiga as it is also known, grows in the icy conditions of the far north. This biome is dominated by conifers, which are the only trees that can survive the harsh conditions. Boreal forests form the largest swathes of continuous forest and cover about ten per cent of the Earth's land.

Boreal forest gets its name from the Greek god of the north wind, Boreas. The name is apt because this type of forest only grows in the northern hemisphere – not because the climatic conditions for boreal forest do not exist in the southern hemisphere, but because there is little land down there where such forests can grow. The alternative name, taiga, is a Russian word meaning marshy pine forest. This name is also apt because boreal forests often grow around moss-filled bogs, the actual bogs being too wet for tree growth.

Boreal forests grow in huge unbroken swathes in Siberia and Scandinavia. A few small patches have survived in Scotland and a few areas of Central Europe. These parts of the far north have very long days in summer and very short ones in winter, with the sun rising for only a few hours. Winter temperatures regularly plunge to −25°C (−13°F).

Compared to other forests, boreal ones are very simple because they contain far fewer species; in fact,

Eurasian lynxes have furred feet that give them a good grip as well as warmth on frozen ground.

Raccoon dogs vary their diet according to the seasons, eating whatever they can find.

Grey wolves are strong runners, and can cover vast distances of their boreal habitat in one night.

Sables build dens on the forest floor. When weather is extreme, they store their prey in the dens.

almost all the trees in these forests are conifers. Because of the cold and dark, boreal forests appear frozen in time for much of the year; when summer comes, it takes a long time to warm up enough for plant growth and animal activity, and never becomes warm enough for most cold-blooded animals, such as amphibians and reptiles. Adders do survive in the southern fringes of conifer forests, but amphibians are uncommon on land and only a few survive in the often-frozen water. Mammals such as marmots and bears, and also the rattlesnakes, hibernate or become inactive during the coldest months of the year. Incredibly, wood frogs endure the winter frozen inside river ice, becoming active again after the thaw.

Mammals that do not hibernate often adopt a very different lifestyle to survive the winter months. For example, herds of reindeer migrate into the forests, only heading back to the barren tundra in summer. Small rodents, such as mice or shrews, construct tunnels in the snow during winter, and moose survive by eating strips of bark.

Because their growth is so slow and intermittent, boreal forests are relatively free of animals compared to other forests. However, many of the animals that do live there are much larger than their relatives living farther south. For example, the moose is the world's largest deer and wolverines are the size of a dog, much larger than most mustelids.

The reason for this is that larger animals need to eat less food per unit of weight than smaller ones. They lose heat more slowly, and do not have to burn food at a such a high rate. Scientists have noticed that even animals of the same species tend to be bigger if they are living further north.

Eurasian beavers are powerful swimmers, with their large flipper-like tail and webbed feet.

Siberian flying squirrels are able to glide from tree to tree, rarely coming down to the ground.

Elk plod through forests and marshes, browsing on a variety of leaves, mosses and lichens.

Red deer graze on grasses, but when food is scarce they will also eat heather and dwarf shrubs.

GRASSLANDS

Although a lot of wild countryside is covered in different grasses – not to mention the many acres of garden lawns – little of it is true grassland. If left alone, these habitats would eventually become thick woodland. True grasslands, from prairies to the savannah, have very few trees but contain many creatures.

Grasslands appear in areas where there is some rain, but not enough to support the growth of large numbers of trees. These conditions exist on all continents, and consequently grasslands come in many forms, growing in both tropical and more temperate regions.

The world's grasslands have many different names. The temperate grasslands of North America are called prairies, in South America they are known as the pampas, and in Europe and Asia they are the steppes. The tropical grasslands of East Africa and Australia are called savannah, and in southern Africa they are the veldt.

Temperate grasslands tend to be located in so-called rain shadows. For example, many of the savannahs of East Africa are in the rain shadow of the Ruwenzori Mountains of Congo and Uganda. A rain shadow is an area that rarely gets rain because the wind bringing it must first travel over a range of mountains.

The European steppes, which run into the grasslands of Central Asia,

Black mambas live in permanent savannah lairs, actively hunting small mammals and birds.

Cheetahs are the fastest land animals in the world, hunting a range of hoofed grassland animals.

Spotted hyenas hunt antelope, buffalo and zebra, and scavenge from other grassland carnivores.

Springhares bound rapidly across the savannah. Their back feet can sense vibrations from predators.

form because they are located so far from the sea. Most of the rain carried on the wind falls to Earth long before it arrives above the steppeland.

The main plant food in grasslands is, of course, grass. Grass is an unusual type of plant because its growing points are near to the ground rather than at the tip of the stem, as with most other plants. This means that it can keep growing despite having its juicy blades eaten by grazing animals.

Grazing animals are commonly found in grasslands, as are the browsers which pick the leaves and fruit of small shrubs which often grow in the area. With few places to hide in the wide-open spaces, grazing animals group together into herds for safety. Fortunately, grass and other plant foods are virtually omnipresent, which means that members of these herds only need to compete when it comes to choosing a mate. This has led them, especially the males, to evolve elaborate weapons and display structures, such as horns or tusks. Grazing animals are large anyway because they have to survive on huge meals of tough grass which is low in nutrition, while the pressure to compete with each other has made them even larger.

Without trees to hide in, smaller animals, such as ground squirrels and marmots, take refuge under the ground in burrow complexes. Many, such as moles and mole rats, have adapted to a totally subterranean lifestyle.

Much of the world's temperate grassland has been turned into farmland for growing cereal crops and raising livestock. Cereals, such as wheat and rye, are actually domestic breeds of grass which would naturally grow in these regions anyway. Most of the animals once found on grasslands have suffered badly because of the rise of agriculture.

African elephants are able to feed on tall trees in the grassland by using their trunks as tools.

Zebras' black and white stripes help them to blend in with natural patterns of light and shade.

Black rhinoceroses enjoy mud baths in wallowing sites, which help to keep their skin healthy.

Warthogs kneel down to eat grass and roots. When threatened, they flee to the nearest available hole.

POLAR REGIONS

Despite being freezing cold and largely covered with ice, polar regions can be characterized as deserts. Although there is solid water almost everywhere, the few plants and animals which do live there often have great difficulty in obtaining liquid water, just like the wildlife in scorching deserts.

The polar regions – the Arctic in the north and Antarctic in the south – begin at 66° North and 66° South. These positions on the globe are marked as the Arctic and Antarctic Circles. Within these imaginary circles, something very strange happens on at least one day every summer: the sun does not set. Similarly, for at least a single 24 hours in winter, it does not rise. The wildlife of the Arctic is not similar to that around the Antarctic. This is not just because they are at opposite ends of the world, but also because the geography of the two areas is very different. The Antarctic is dominated by Antarctica, a mountainous landmass which is a significantly sized continent, larger than Australia. Meanwhile the Arctic has the Arctic Ocean – the world's smallest ocean – at its centre.

The wildernesses of ice and rock in the Antarctic are the coldest places on Earth, and are too inhospitable for any completely terrestrial animals. Antarctic animals, such as seals,

Arctic foxes have thick fur to keep them warm. They also have hair on their paw pads to grip the ice.

Lemmings construct tunnel systems under the snow. These protect them from predators.

Reindeer have broad, flat hooves which help them to walk over soft ground and deep snow.

Muskoxen survive by eating hardy grasses, mosses and sedges within the Arctic Circle.

penguins and whales, rely on the sea for their survival. No reptiles or amphibians survive there, and even warm-blooded animals leave in winter, with the exception of the hardy emperor penguin.

In the Arctic, seals, whales and other sea creatures also thrive, while the lands and islands of the Arctic Ocean provide a home for many animals dependent on land, such as muskoxen and reindeer. Animals such as polar bears spend their time on the thick shelves of sea ice which extend from the frozen coastlines for much of the year.

While Antarctica is almost entirely covered in snow and ice, the ground in lands around the Arctic circle is mainly ice-free during the summer and so has periods of frenzied growth and breeding. North of the boreal forests it is too cold and dark for trees to grow, and treeless tundra takes over. Plants – mainly tough grass and sedges, mosses and lichens (not actually plants but a symbiotic relationship between fungi and tiny algae) – must be able to survive the long and desolate winters. When the warm weather – which generally lasts little more than six weeks – arrives, they must be ready to reproduce.

While the summer sun thaws the snow and ice, it never heats the soil for more than a few centimetres below the surface. The deep layer of soil remains frozen and is called permafrost. It forms a solid barrier which prevents the melt waters from seeping away. The trapped water forms shallow pools and bogs, which are a haven for insects.

Billions of insects, which spent the winter underground as inactive pupae, emerge from hiding in the spring. They swarm across the tundra, mating and laying eggs in the water as they race against time to produce the next generation before winter arrives again.

Harp seals congregate in huge numbers to give birth on ice floes. Pups have very thick fur.

Walruses spend most of their life in water. They have a thick coat of blubber to help keep them warm.

Narwhals use a sophisticated system of ultrasonic clicks to find food in coastal Arctic waters.

Bowhead whales live among the ice floes of the Arctic Ocean, feeding on plankton and krill.

DESERTS

Deserts make up the largest terrestrial biome, covering about one-fifth of the world's dry land.
The popular image of a desert is a parched wilderness with towering sand dunes and no sign of life.
However, deserts can also be very cold places and most contain a surprising amount of wildlife.

A desert forms wherever less than 25cm (10in) of rain falls in a year. Areas that get less than about 40cm (16in) of rain per year are semi-deserts. The largest desert is the Sahara in North Africa, which covers about the same area as the United States. Other desert regions are found in southern Africa. There are no hot deserts in Europe. However, parts of Iceland are classed as desert. Although these areas are very cold, they are still very dry and receive only small amounts of rain or snow.

Desert life is tough. The wildlife has to contend with lack of water and also survive extremes of temperature. With little or no cloud cover for most of the year, land temperatures rocket during the day to over 40°C (104°F) but can plunge to below freezing at night. Plants are the basis for all life in this biome, being the food for grazing animals. Some plants have to extend enormously long underground roots to collect enough water to live. Other plants, such as cacti and other succulents, store water inside their

Armadillo lizards are able to roll themselves into armoured balls to protect themselves from predators.

Namib web-footed geckos have webbed feet to stop them from sinking into desert sands.

Fennec foxes have large ears filled with blood vessels, which are used to radiate body heat away.

Golden spiny mice do not need to drink, extracting all the moisture they need from their food.

fleshy stems and leaves, and have a thick, waxy covering to stop the water from evaporating.

Deserts are not completely dry, because rain does eventually arrive. True to the extremes of a desert, rainstorms are so violent that they often cause devastating flash floods which gush down temporary rivers, known as wadis or arroyos. Then the desert plants bloom and breed for a few short weeks before withering and waiting for the next supply of water.

Many desert animals, such as blind snakes and several types of frog, follow a similar pattern. They only come to the surface during and after the rains, preferring to stay moist underground during the hot and dry parts of the year. Desert frogs prevent themselves from drying out by growing a thin, fluid-filled skin bag around their bodies.

Even the more active desert animals remain hidden during the day, sheltering from the scorching sun among rocks or in burrows. When night falls, plant-eaters, such as the addax and ass, begin to pick at the dried leaves, fruit and twigs of scrawny desert plants, while smaller jerboas and ground squirrels collect seeds and insects.

Other insect-eaters include geckos and other lizards. Many have wide, webbed feet to help them walk across the loose sand and burrow into it when danger approaches. Larger meat-eaters include vipers, which patrol in search of small rodents, and jackals, which scavenge for the carcasses of dead animals.

Most of these animals never drink liquid water. They get all the moisture they need from their food. Camels' humps store fat, which keeps them alive when there is no food. Lizards and several desert rodents store fat in their tails, while other desert animals build up food stores in their burrows.

Fat sand rats eat succulent plants that store water. Their black skin protects them from the sun.

Lesser mouse-tailed bats have a valve inside their nostrils, which closes to keep out desert dust.

Camels can endure very hot, dry conditions. They can survive for long periods without drinking.

Addaxes rarely drink, obtaining most of the moisture they need from the plants they eat.

ISLANDS

Because they have been isolated from the rest of the world for so long, islands tend to contain species which have evolved independently of their relatives on the mainland. Consequently, islands are good places to observe the process of natural selection at work.

Islands do not really constitute a biome because they exist in all parts of the world and come in all shapes and sizes. For example, Greenland, the world's largest island, is a place of vast ice fields edged with tundra, while Great Britain, Europe's largest island, contains a mixture of biomes. Most islands are much smaller and are little more than rocks or reefs poking a few centimetres above the surrounding surf.

Small islands and coasts generally are unusual places to live because they are regularly transformed by tides washing in and out. While life in a desert or on an icy mountain may have its challenges, coastal plants and animals must cope with being immersed in salt water twice a day and then being dried by the sun and wind.

While island edges are a haven for coastal wildlife, many of the animals found inland are rather unusual. This is because islands are populated by animals which were there before the land became an island, or by those which have flown or swum from the

Atlantic lizards inhabit the Canary Islands, living on insects and plants around sand dunes and lava flows.

Malagasy leaf-nosed snakes blend perfectly into the background of their Madagascan habitat.

Fossas are the largest carnivores in Madagascar, preying on lemurs, rodents, birds and frogs.

Malagasy giant rats are highly endangered, surviving only on the west coast of Madagascar.

mainland. On continents, an animal that is successful in a particular habitat will eventually spread across the land until it lives in all areas where that habitat is found. For example, brown bears live in conifer forests across the world. They did not evolve in all these places at the same time but spread out from a single location. But because brown bears and many other continental animals cannot get to islands, their place is filled by the animals that were originally there.

Madagascar is an excellent example of an island populated by animals that came from the mainland before the island became separate. It is associated with the African continent, and became an island about 175 million years ago. Madagascar is 400km (250 miles) east of Mozambique and more than 4,800km (3,000 miles) from Indonesia to the east. Humans only arrived on the island about 2,000 years ago.

Being isolated for so long, many of the animals that were on Madagascar when it became an island have evolved in different ways from their relatives that live elsewhere. The island is home to several very unusual habitats, such as spiny forest and highland meadows.

There are more than 1,000 Malagasy species that have evolved to survive in this island's unique environment.

Perhaps the most familiar examples of this are the lemurs. These are primates and are therefore relatives of monkeys and apes. While the ancestors of monkeys came to dominate Africa, Asia and South America, the primates on Madagascar evolved into lemurs, which are more cat-like and less intelligent than their more widespread cousins. Madagascar is also home to a range of unusual insectivores, mongooses and bats, as well as many reptiles and amphibians.

Rodrigues flying foxes are very rare bats, only found on the island of Rodrigues, east of Madagascar.

Tailless tenrecs inhabit the forests of Madagascar, foraging for fruit, insects and small vertebrates.

Ruffed lemurs live in eastern Madagascar, using scent markings to signal their home territory.

European mouflons are small wild sheep found on the Mediterranean islands of Corsica and Sardinia.

MOUNTAINS

Mountains form an unusual biome because they encapsulate a number of climate zones within a small geographical area. This variation defines the lives of the inhabitants. Some animals are highly evolved for mountain life; others have extended their lowland ranges into high altitudes.

A mountainside is like several biomes stacked on top of one another. As the mountain rises out of the surrounding lowlands, the air temperature, wind speed, light levels, water supply and, on the highest peaks, even the amount of oxygen begin to change. Most of the largest mountain ranges, such as the Alps of Europe, rise out of temperate or boreal biomes. Therefore the foothills of these ranges are generally covered in temperate forest or woodland. As the altitude increases, the weather conditions become colder and harsher and the trees of the temperate forest find it increasingly hard to grow. They eventually become smaller and more gnarled, and then conifer trees take over. Like their relatives in boreal forests, mountain conifers are better at surviving in colder conditions than broad-leaved trees.

As the journey up the mountain continues, the conditions get worse. Rain that falls on the mountain runs through or over the surface before joining a torrential mountain stream

Alpine salamanders live at high altitudes, sometimes remaining dormant for up to eight months.

Ethiopian wolves can be found in pockets of alpine grassland, living on rodents, hares and calves.

Rock hyraxes have rubber-like soles on their feet, enabling them to climb steep surfaces with ease.

Mountain gorillas live in cold high-altitude rainforests, foraging for bamboo shoots and leaves.

and being carried swiftly down. With all the water sluicing rapidly down the mountain, territory nearer the top has less water for the plants to draw on, and eventually there is not enough moisture in the soil for trees to grow. The point where conditions become just too tough for even conifer trees to grow is called the timberline.

Above the timberline, small, hardy alpine plants grow in regions which resemble a cold desert. Alpine plants share features with desert species because they, too, must hang on to any water they can get before it is evaporated by the strong mountain wind. At even higher altitudes, as in the polar regions, the conditions become too harsh and plant life gives way to snow and ice at the snowline. From here upwards very little plant life survives and animals are infrequent visitors, except for the birds of prey soaring on the thermals of warmer air high above the peaks.

The story is different in tropical regions. Here the mountain slopes are clothed in so-called cloud forests which are similar to other tropical forests, but with shorter trees and a thinner canopy. In the humid tropics, these mountain forests are often shrouded in cloud, and this extra moisture makes them ideal places for epiphytes (plants which grow on other plants rather than in the ground).

Many mountain forests have populations or subspecies which are distinct from lowland populations, but they are still fundamentally the same species. However, many mountain species are specially adapted to living on steep slopes. A large proportion of these are small animals, such as rock hyraxes. Large species, including wild sheep and mountain antelopes such as the nyala, are sure-footed animals that can move safely around rocky slopes.

Geladas prefer to sleep high up on rocky cliffs, where they are relatively safe from predators.

Barbary apes forage for food in mountain clearings by day and sleep high up in trees by night.

Chamois are well adapted to their mountainous habitat, able to bound straight up steep slopes.

Barbary sheep inhabit desert mountains where water is scarce. They can survive without drinking.

HUMAN SETTLEMENTS

The fastest growing habitats are those made by humans, which are generally expanding at the expense of natural ones. Fortunately, many animals (as well as pets) do thrive with people. Animals that feed on a wide range of foods are the most successful species in human settlements.

Human beings have a huge effect on their environment. Since the dawn of agriculture, people have been clearing natural landscapes to make way for their livestock and crops. Agriculture began in the Middle East 14,000 years ago, and is now so extensive that nearly all the world's grasslands and temperate forests have been replaced by fields. More recently, tropical and boreal forests have also been cut back to make room for agriculture. In evolutionary terms, this change has been very fast, and the natural world is reeling in shock, unable to respond to the changes quickly enough.

Building cities

Several thousand years ago, people began to learn how to farm more efficiently, and farmers began to produce more than they could consume themselves. With a surplus of food, farmers began to trade it for other items. In the fertile river valleys of the Middle East, India and China, agricultural communities were so successful that the first cities grew up. Uniquely among mammals, some members of these large human communities did not find any of their own food. Instead, they bought what they needed with other products.

But while agriculture creates a habitat that mirrors the grassland in some ways, cities were a brand new type of habitat. In 1500, the world population was about 500 million. Only 500 years later, this figure had increased 12-fold, topping six billion in 2000. By this time there were over 200 cities containing over one million

Above: Red foxes are extremely adaptable animals. They have become very common in suburban and more built-up areas, where they make their homes in gardens and wasteland, and feed on rubbish.

Below: Barbary macaques on Gibraltar are the only monkeys living in Europe. They were introduced to the rock by the Romans, and those that survive there rely on being fed by tourists or stealing food from people's homes.

Above: Roe deer have lived in Britain since prehistoric times. Despite being shy, they often feed on the edges of agricultural land, bringing them close to human activity.

people each. Huge sprawling urban centres, such as Cairo and London, now contain more than 7 million people each – and, of course, also millions of animals.

Opportunists

Although changes to the environment caused by humans are happening at a lightning pace, many animals have made the most of the opportunity presented. The destruction of natural habitats has had a terrible effect on those animals which live in particular places. For example, leaf-eating monkeys cannot survive without trees bearing plentiful leaves. However, animals which make the most of any feeding opportunity can survive anywhere, including cities. These so-called generalist feeders have thrived alongside humans for many thousands of years. The most familiar generalists are rodents such as mice and rats. They are typical generalist feeders because they will investigate anything for its food potential and are not fussy about what they eat. Other generalists are monkeys, such as macaques and vervets, which are a common sight in many tropical cities. Here and elsewhere, suburban areas with gardens are the perfect environment for many other adaptable animals, such as squirrels, rats and foxes.

Although some people enjoy sharing their cities with wildlife, others regard wild creatures in cities as dirty and dangerous. Several diseases, such as typhus and plague, are associated with rats and other city animals. These animals are so successful that their populations have to be controlled. On the whole, however, as cities mature, their wildlife communities stabilize into a sustainable ecosystem, just as they do in the wild.

Prized pets

Another group of animals live in our cities – pets. People have kept pets for thousands of years. Typical pets, such as cats and dogs, are not generalist feeders and rely on their owners to provide food and shelter. Unlike scavenging city animals, pets live in partnership with people and have done well out of this relationship in which almost every facet of their lives, including their reproduction, is often controlled. Without their human masters, many of these species would now be close to extinction.

Below: The domestic cat is a very popular pet. Like most wild cats, domestic ones are solitary animals and spend their time patrolling their territory looking for mates and rivals.

Below: Domestic guinea pigs, or cavies, are related to wild forms that live in South America. Selective breeding has resulted in individuals that have long, colourful fur.

Below: Perhaps the most popular pet reptiles are tortoises, which can live for many years if properly looked after. Trade in tortoises is heavily controlled to protect wild populations.

DIRECTORY
OF ANIMALS

Africa and Europe are separated by the Mediterranean Sea, and although the divide is only a few miles in some places, the two continents are very different, both in terms of climate and their animal life. This section of the book focuses on the most significant amphibians, reptiles and mammals that live in these continents. The animal species are organized into a number of related groups: salamanders, frogs and toads, turtles and tortoises, lizards, crocodiles, non-venomous snakes, venomous snakes, cats, hyenas, civets and genets, dogs, small carnivores, mongooses, rodents, rabbits, bats, aardvark and pangolins, insectivores, elephant shrews, apes, monkeys, lemurs, indri and sifakas, bushbabies, elephant and hyrax, hoofed animals, deer, antelopes, seals, dolphins, toothed whales, other whales and sirenians. Each entry is accompanied by a fact box containing a map that shows where the animal lives, and details about the animal's distribution, habitat, food, size, maturity, breeding, life span and conservation status. This last category gives a broad indication of each species' population size, as recorded by the International Union for the Conservation of Nature and Natural Resources (IUCN). At one end of the scale a species might be described as common or lower risk, then vulnerable, threatened, endangered or critically endangered. In addition to the main animal entries, the directory also contains lists of related animals, with short summaries indicating their distribution, main characteristics and behaviour.

Left: A herd of springboks rest on an African grassland. These wild grasslands host the largest populations of grazing beasts on Earth. The springboks are known for "pronking" – leaping high into the air – when predators attack.

SALAMANDERS AND RELATIVES

Of the living amphibians, salamanders and newts are the most similar to ancestral amphibians, known from fossils. Salamanders typically have rougher skin than newts and are better able to survive out of water because they have glands to keep their skins moist. They are also frequently brightly coloured and armed with toxins to repel predators.

Olm

Proteus anguinus

Olms have elongated bodies, pinkish skin, external gills and tiny eyes that can only perceive light and shadow. Olms were once more common, but numbers have dropped because of water pollution.

The olm is the world's largest cave-dwelling vertebrate. It lives in the dark, in bodies of cold, underground water. The olm has dull white, sometimes pinkish skin and three tufted, bright red gills on each side of its neck. Its tail is long and eel-like. The olm's gills are filled with blood, allowing the animal to breathe underwater. Oxygen in the water is transferred to the blood via the surface of the gills. The olm's eyes are reduced to tiny black dots under the skin, leaving it virtually blind. Newly born young can see better than the adults, but their eyes degenerate after a year. The olm has a powerful sense of smell. It can also find food and communicate by detecting weak electric signals emitted by fish and other olms. Olms have tiny legs for the size of their bodies, with only three stumpy toes on their front legs and two on their back legs. Their snouts are broad and help them to burrow into mud to find shellfish.

Distribution: Slovenia through to Bosnia-Herzegovina.
Habitat: Underground lakes and streams.
Food: Freshwater crustaceans.
Size: 25–30cm (10–12in).
Maturity: Very little information. Thought to be 16–18 years.
Breeding: Females normally give birth to 2 larvae. If the water is warm enough up to 80 eggs may be laid instead.
Life span: 100 years.
Status: Rare.

Fire salamander

Salamandra salamandra

Fire salamanders have poison glands in their skins that are surrounded by special muscles. These are particularly concentrated on their backs. When the muscles contract, they squeeze toxins from the glands. The salamanders can squirt their poison up to 2m (6.5ft). The poison irritates the skin and may affect the nervous systems of any animals that it touches. It can even kill certain predators by paralyzing their lungs, thus stopping them from breathing.

Females are able to store sperm from males for up to two years. They carry 10–40 live young around in their bodies. These are born with their legs well developed, but they still possess larval gills. Some females have been found carrying only four or five young, but these were born fully developed, without gills. By having fewer young, a female is able to provide her offspring with more food. Being so far developed means the young can continue to grow and survive on land, where it is relatively safe.

The fire salamander has a bright yellow and black pattern that warns all would-be predators that it carries toxins. The underside is dark grey with fewer markings. When adult, females are larger than males.

Distribution: Central and southern Europe, Middle East and north-west Africa.
Habitat: Forested, hilly or mountainous country, not far from water.
Food: Invertebrates such as slugs, worms, flies, beetles and centipedes.
Size: 14–17cm (5.5–6.75in).
Maturity: Change into adults 2 or 3 months after birth.
Breeding: 10–40 young develop inside female and born after 8 months.
Life span: 20 years.
Status: Common.

Alpine salamander

Salamandra atra

The alpine salamander lives in the mountains and meadows of the southern Alps and neighbouring mountain ranges in the southern Balkans. Although it shares a geographical range with the fire salamander, the two species rarely meet. The fire salamander is found at low altitudes, while this species is rarely found below an altitude of about 800m (2,620ft).

Within its range, the salamander can be seen in large numbers. The species is most active at night. It hides by day under stones and logs but may emerge into shady places during daylight hours. Direct sunlight would dry its skin. Alpine salamanders hibernate to avoid colder winter weather. Those that live at high altitudes may stay dormant for eight months.

Alpine salamanders do not lay eggs. Instead the eggs develop inside the female's body and the young hatch while still inside. Once out of the egg, the young eat the wall of their mother's egg chamber. They grow to a third of adult size before being born. In most cases two young are born in each litter.

Distribution: Switzerland, Austria, southern Germany, northern Italy, Slovenia and Croatia; separate population in southern Bosnia and northern Albania.
Habitat: Mountain woodlands and meadows.
Food: Invertebrates.
Size: 15cm (6in).
Maturity: 2–3 years.
Breeding: 2–4 young born live.
Life span: 10 years.
Status: Common.

Most alpine salamanders are totally black, though the populations that live in northern Italy have a varying amount of pale yellow on their heads, backs and tails. This colour may show as several spots or as a solid band.

Corsican fire salamander (*Salamandra corsica*): 20cm (8in)
This species is similar to the fire salamander found on the European mainland. Like its more common neighbour, it has yellow or orange patches on a black background. However, the Corsican species is plumper and has smaller parotid glands (the lumps behind the eyes). The Corsican fire salamanders live in most habitats and are most common on the slopes of the island's mountains. These mountains are clothed in beech and chestnut woodlands. Females do not lay eggs. During wet periods, the female will give birth to larvae (gilled swimming forms) into shallow pools of stagnant water, where their development continues. During dry periods when there is no standing water, the young will metamorphose inside their mothers into the land-living adult body form before being born.

Lanza's alpine salamander (*Salamandra lanzai*): 17cm (6.75in)
This species is a large version of the alpine salamander. However, the adults have a considerably flatter head. It lives at higher altitudes on two mountain ranges, one in western Switzerland and the other in the southern French Alps. It occupies alpine meadows and rock fields, where it searches out slow-moving invertebrates to eat. The flat head enables the salamander to search the rocky crevices that are common in its habitat. It is most active in rainy conditions and emerges into the open by both day and night. At these times it can be seen standing in the open. During dry periods the salamander hides under rocks.

Luschan's salamander

Mertensiella luschani

The Luschan's salamander is the only species of tailed amphibian to live in the south of the Aegean. Its main range is three small islands between Crete and Rhodes, but there are reports of it living on the Turkish coast.

The salamander is most active at night. It may be seen during daylight hours when the weather is wet, but on dry days it lies in shaded nooks, such as under flat stones. Luschan's salamander becomes dormant during the hot summer, when it lies in crevices.

If threatened, Luschan's salamanders rear up on their hind legs and squeak. If attacked, the salamander may drop its tail to buy time for it to escape. The tail quickly re-grows.

The male's spur is used in mating. The male wriggles underneath the female and tickles her cloaca (rear opening) with his spur to stimulate her into mating. The male drops a large sac of sperm, which the female picks up with her cloaca. The eggs hatch inside the mother, and develop for several months before two 7cm (2.75in) young are born fully formed.

Distribution: Islands of southern Aegean Sea.
Habitat: Dry woodlands and rocky fields.
Food: Invertebrates.
Size: 14cm (5.5in).
Maturity: 2 years.
Breeding: 2 young born live.
Life span: About 6 years.
Status: Common.

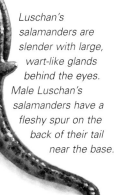

Luschan's salamanders are slender with large, wart-like glands behind the eyes. Male Luschan's salamanders have a fleshy spur on the back of their tail near the base.

Spectacled salamander

Salamandrina terdigitata

The spectacled salamander is the only European salamander to have four toes on all four feet. Most others have four on their front feet and five on their back feet. It is found in the mountains of central and southern Italy and has a very particular habitat, living on north-facing slopes in mixed forests that have a thick covering of shrubs. It is often found near to fast-flowing rocky streams.

The spectacled salamander is nocturnal and is most active during spring and autumn. In these warmer periods the salamanders may be seen in the early morning and at dusk. The salamander becomes dormant during extremes of weather. It finds its way deep underground in winter to avoid any frosts that penetrate the upper layers of soil and leaf litter. When it is attacked, the salamander pretends to be dead by rolling on to its back and exposing its bright red underside. Predators are suspicious of dead animals and this is compounded by the startling red colouring.

The females stores sperm from the males, enabling them to produce young as soon as spring arrives, giving them the best chance of survival. They find mates when there is more time later in the year. Mating takes place on land. The male follows the female in a circle as both of them wave their tails in the air.

Distribution: Italy.
Habitat: North-facing mountain woodlands and forests with clear streams and rocky beds. More common in the west than east.
Food: Ground-living invertebrates.
Size: 9–11.5cm (3.5–4.5in).
Maturity: Able to breed at a length of 7cm (2.75in).
Breeding: 30–60 eggs laid in slow-moving water.
Life span: 10 years.
Status: Common.

Spectacled salamanders have prominent eyes with an orange patch on the top of the head between them. The upper body is black with a ridge running down the spine, while the undersides of the legs and tail are red.

Golden-striped salamander

Chioglossa lusticanica

The golden-striped salamander lives in mountainous regions that receive more than 100cm (39.5in) of rain each year. This rain supports thick forests of pine and broad-leaved trees. In the south of its range in central Portugal it reaches altitudes of 1,300m (4,270ft). Mostly it lives lower down, especially in northern and colder areas. The salamander occupies low-growing undergrowth such as moss and is seldom found far from clear rocky streams. It sometimes lives in caves.

In the right conditions, the salamanders occur in large numbers, with a 10m (33ft) stretch of water hosting more than 40 individuals. Golden-striped salamanders are fast-moving and can travel half a mile in one night. This species of salamander is nocturnal. It aestivates (becomes dormant in summer) to avoid the dry conditions. Mating takes place on rocky stream beds. Females lay about 20 eggs in shallow water attached to stones and roots; these hatch after about eight weeks. The larvae live in the water for at least a year before changing into the land-living adult form. Those that live in cold water take up to three years to develop into adults.

Distribution: North-west Spain and northern Portugal as far south as the River Tajo.
Habitat: Mountains forests with high rainfall and clear fast-flowing streams surrounded by thick moss.
Food: Slow-moving invertebrates caught using long and sticky tongue.
Size: 13cm (5in).
Maturity: 4 years or at a length of 4 cm (1.5in).
Breeding: 12–20 eggs laid in shallow water.
Life span: 8 years in the wild and more than 10 years when kept in captivity.
Status: Common.

The golden-striped salamander is a long and slender species. The tail may be more than twice as long as the head and body section. A golden stripe runs from behind the head to the tip of the tail. A groove also runs along the centre of this stripe.

Great crested newt

Triturus cristatus cristatus

Distribution: England, Scotland, central Europe from France to Urals, and southern Scandinavia to Alps.
Habitat: Spend most of the year in weedy ponds.
Food: Small aquatic invertebrates and vertebrates, including other amphibians.
Size: 11–16cm (4.5–6.25in).
Maturity: Tadpoles change into newts after 8–16 weeks. Reach adult size after 2 years.
Breeding: 200–300 eggs laid between April and mid-July.
Life span: 27 years.
Status: Vulnerable.

During the breeding season, male great crested newts become brightly coloured, particularly on their bellies. They also develop high toothed crests along their backs and white bands along the sides of their tails. The newts hibernate on land during the winter. They return to the water in March, and the males develop their breeding livery two weeks later. Once the breeding season is over, their crests and outer skins are absorbed into their bodies.

Young great crested newts hatch in water as tadpoles. They feed on fish, tadpoles, worms and aquatic insects. The adults feed on larger prey, including newts and frogs. They locate their prey in the mud using smell and sight.

Great crested newts are afforded protection by their skins. If threatened, their skins release a white, creamy fluid, which is an irritant to the eyes, nose and mouth of predators.

Great crested newts have dark backs, while their bellies are orange or red with large black blotches or spots. The males are more colourful than the females, with tall crests along their backs during the breeding season.

Pyrenean brook newt (*Euproctus asper*): 16cm (6.25in)
This species of newt is found only in the Pyrenees and other mountains in northern Spain. It has very rough grey-green skin and the paratoid glands (bumps behind the head) that are common in other species are absent in this newt. Females have a pointed opening to their cloaca (rear opening) and the males have a rounded opening. Females also have yellow stripes and patches on their upper side. This newt lives in cold mountain streams and lakes. It rarely comes out of water by day but in the cool of the night ventures on to the land.

Corsican brook newt (*Euproctus montanus*): 13cm (5in)
Apart from the Corsican fire salamander, this is the only other tailed amphibian to live in the mountains of Corsica. It has dull colouring, with a mottled pattern of black and yellow patches. The males have blunt spurs on their hind legs and a cone-shaped swelling at the cloaca (rear opening). It lurks beneath stones in streams or along the bank. This species has small lungs because oxygen is absorbed through the skin.

Sardinian brook newt (*Euproctus platycephalus*): 15cm (6in)
The Sardinian brook newt is one of just two tailed amphibians to live on Sardinia, the other being the supramonte cave salamander. Sardianian brook newts exhibit a range of colour patterns on their pale green skin. The main feature is the orange or red stripe along their back. The males have spurs on their hind legs.

Sharp-ribbed newt

Pleurodeles waltl

The sharp-ribbed newt has special rib bones that are able to inject poison into a predator by protruding through pores in its skin. When the poison enters the skin of a predator, it causes a great deal of pain. The newt will also head-butt a predator, exposing glands at the back of its head that exude a toxic fluid. It has similar glands on its tail, which it lashes to release the toxin.

This species lives permanently in water and only leaves if the water level falls. Sharp-ribbed newts breed twice in a year, in early spring and again in midsummer. The males have much longer tails than the females, and during the mating season they develop special pads under their front legs to help grasp the females when transferring their sperm.

Distribution: Spain, Portugal and Morocco.
Habitat: Entirely aquatic, in standing water such as ponds, lagoons, dams and irrigation systems.
Food: Invertebrates, small fish and carrion.
Size: 15–30cm (6–12in).
Maturity: 4 years.
Breeding: Female lays between 100 and 1,000 eggs depending on her size. Breeding takes place twice: once in the spring and again in midsummer.
Life span: Not known.
Status: Common.

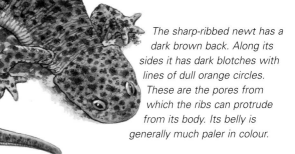

The sharp-ribbed newt has a dark brown back. Along its sides it has dark blotches with lines of dull orange circles. These are the pores from which the ribs can protrude from its body. Its belly is generally much paler in colour.

Northern crested newt

Triturus cristatus carnifex

The northern crested newt, also known as the warty newt, lives across Europe to the north of the Alps. It ranges from Britain (but not Ireland) to the Ukraine. It also lives in southern Scandinavia, where individuals have a solid black underside in place of the orange belly of other members of the species.

Being a newt, this species is more closely associated with water than salamanders. Mating takes place in or close to deep streams. The newt occasionally returns to water outside the breeding season, but it is also common far from water in damp woodlands. Northern crested newts are nocturnal. When it is under threat, the newt plays dead and produces an offensive-smelling white liquid from its skin.

During the breeding season in spring, the males are adorned with crests and gather in groups to display to females. After mating, females lay 200–400 eggs. However, due to a genetic anomaly, only half of these eggs develop. The eggs hatch after three weeks and the larvae live in water for about four months before changing into the adult form. In cold areas, the larvae may never metamorphose, instead living their whole lives in water. They retain the larval body form but grow adult sex organs to allow them to breed. This phenomenon is called neoteny.

Distribution: Northern and central Europe. Absent from Ireland and from all but southern Scandinavia. Also occurs in central Asia.
Habitat: Broad-leafed woodlands with plenty of pools and streams.
Food: Water and land invertebrates as well as fish and other amphibians.
Size: 15cm (6in).
Maturity: At the age of 3 years or at the length of 12cm (4.75in).
Breeding: 300 eggs laid in water. Hatch with 3 weeks.
Life span: 8 years.
Status: Common.

Crested newts are named after the jagged ridge that grows from a male newt's back prior to the mating season. Its tail also develops a white stripe. Females lack these crests. The newts' underside is orange with black spots.

Alpine newt

Triturus alpestris

Despite its name, this species is found in lowland as well as highland regions across much of mainland Europe, from the Atlantic coast to Romania and from Denmark in the north to northern Spain and Greece in the south.

This species of newt is always in or close to water. They prefer cold and clear pools and slow-flowing streams. In southern Europe, the newt is found only at higher altitudes where the water is cold enough. For example, an isolated population lives in the Guadarrama Mountains of central Spain. The alpine newt prefers pools with few plants in them, and therefore is most common above the tree line, sometimes surviving as high as 2,500m (8,200ft). Farther north, where the climate is cooler, water that is cold enough for the newts is located in lowland areas.

Mating takes place in water in spring. At the highest altitudes, the newts may breed only every two years. Females lay about 250 eggs, which hatch between two and four weeks later. The larvae take about three years to mature into adults. In especially cold habitats, the aquatic larvae will never metamorphose, but become sexually mature while still having the swimming body form of larvae.

Distribution: Most of central Europe. There are isolated populations in central Spain and southern Italy.
Habitat: Ponds and other pools of water.
Food: Large invertebrates, tadpoles and fish.
Size: 12cm (4.75in).
Maturity: 2–4 years.
Breeding: 250 eggs laid in spring.
Life span: 11 years in the wild and up to 20 years when kept in captivity.
Status: Common.

Alpine newts have grey bodies with black spots on the snout and flanks. The spots extend on to the legs. The underside is solid orange, but there may be spots on the throat. Males grow a smooth crest during the mating season.

Common newt

Triturus vulgaris

Distribution: Northern Europe and western Asia.
Habitat: Damp woodlands, gardens and fields.
Food: Invertebrates.
Size: 11cm (4.25in).
Maturity: 3 years.
Breeding: Up to 300 eggs laid on water plants.
Life span: 7 years.
Status: Common.

The common newt, or smooth newt as it is sometimes called, lives across northern Europe from the British Isles to Russia and western Asia. It is less reliant on water than most newts and is seen on the ground in damp habitats. Like other newts, however, the common newt must return to water to breed.

The males develop a large crest prior to the spring breeding season. Females are attracted to males with larger crests. After mating, the female will lay up to 300 eggs on water plants. The eggs hatch after about two weeks. The larvae stay close to the bottom of the pool, which keeps them out of the way of the adults, which are more common near to the surface. This divide prevents the two generations competing for food. A larva will metamorphose into the adult form once it reaches 4cm (1.5in) long. This might take a year or even longer. In cold waters the larvae may never take the adult form.

The common newt exhibits a variety of colour patterns. The common form is grey-green skin on the upper side and an orange belly with black spots. The male has large spots on the back and grows a jagged crest for the breeding season.

Marbled newt (*Triturus marmoratus*):
9–11cm (3.5–4.25in)
The marbled newt is found in south-west France, Spain and Portugal. It has a green back, interrupted by black marbling, and a grey belly. Both males and females develop orange-red stripes along their backs, from neck to tail. The females keep this stripe when they return to water to breed. During this time, the males lose their red stripes and develop crests, along with silver bands on their tails. When threatened, they raise their tails and sway from side to side.

Danube crested newt (*Triturus dobrogicus*):
13cm (5in)
The Danube crested newt lives in the vast wetlands formed by the Danube Delta in Romania and is also found upstream as far west as Austria. This newt is red-brown on top with an orange underbelly speckled with black spots. It spends long periods in slow-flowing water, often among thick growths of water plants. Both adult and larval Danube crested newts eat invertebrates such as insect larvae.

Italian crested newt (*Triturus carnifex*):
15cm (6in)
This crested newt lives in northern Italy. It resembles the northern crested newt but has a more orange belly. Adult members of this species travel far from water outside the breeding season but must return to water to reproduce. At high altitudes, where the water is cold, the aquatic larvae never develop into the adult form but become neotenous (sexually mature while retaining the body of larvae).

Palmate newt

Triturus helveticus

The palmate newt lives in western Europe, from Britain to north-west Spain and Portugal and Switzerland. This species is often mistaken for the common newt, but is generally smaller and has fewer spots on the belly, which is also a pale yellow rather than a dark orange. Like the common newt, the palmate newt is regularly found out of water but never strays out of moist habitats.

The newts hibernate under logs and stones from November through to March, when they return to water to breed. The males grow a low smooth crest to attract females and their hind feet become webbed. After mating, the females lay 290–460 eggs on aquatic plants. The eggs hatch within a fortnight. The larvae that emerge have gills for breathing exclusively underwater. Once they reach about 3cm (1.25in) long, their gills are absorbed into the body and they take on the four-legged adult form that is capable of surviving out of water. The adults breathe with small lungs but they can also take oxygen from the air or water in through their damp skin.

Distribution: Western Europe.
Habitat: Shallow water and damp land habitats.
Food: Invertebrates.
Size: 9cm (3.5in).
Maturity: 2 years.
Breeding: 400 eggs laid in water.
Life span: 12 years.
Status: Common.

Male palmate newts have webbed feet, yellow bellies and thin filaments of skin that extend 5mm (0.25in) from the tips of their tails. The females are much duller and lack the tail filaments.

Carpathian newt

Triturus montandoni

As its name suggests, the Carpathian newt lives in the Carpathian Mountains of Romania, southern Poland and Slovakia. It is a relatively small species, with males being the smaller sex. Montandon's newt, as it is also known, lives in conifer forests that grow mainly above 500m (1,640ft). The maximum altitude the newts survive at is 2,000m (6,560ft). The newts prefer cold and clear streams that are rich in acidic minerals. However, they also inhabit muddier watercourses at lower altitudes.

Montandon's newt occasionally ventures on to land but rarely moves far from the water's edge. The nocturnal amphibians avoid drying out in the sunlight by lurking under stones and fallen leaves and bark.

Breeding takes place in spring. The females lay 30–250 eggs in water. Older females tend to produce more eggs than less-mature individuals. The eggs may hatch in as few as ten days, but in high locations, where the water stays cold all year around, the larvae can take up to a month to emerge. The larvae metamorphose into tiny adult forms when they reach the length of just 1cm (0.4in), which is considerably smaller than the size for other newts. In many places, the larvae stay in the juvenile form through the winter.

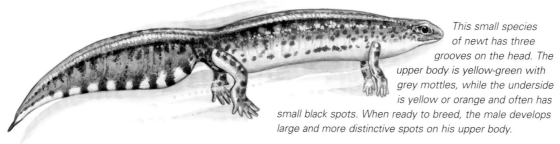

This small species of newt has three grooves on the head. The upper body is yellow-green with grey mottles, while the underside is yellow or orange and often has small black spots. When ready to breed, the male develops large and more distinctive spots on his upper body.

Distribution: The Carpathian Mountains of eastern Europe, which extend from Romania through Ukraine to western Poland and Slovakia.
Habitat: Areas of mountain conifer forests with many ponds and streams.
Food: Invertebrates, tadpoles and spawn (eggs).
Size: 10cm (4in).
Maturity: 3 years.
Breeding: Up to 250 eggs laid in later spring.
Life span: Unknown.
Status: Common.

Bosca's newt

Triturus boscai

Bosca's newts live in ponds and streams in the western part of the Iberian Peninsula. Although this species is often confused with the palmate and common newt species, it is the only newt to be found in this part of the world. Only in the north of its range does this species live alongside similar newts. However, there are some obvious differences between them all. For example, Bosca's newt has a single groove on its snout, while the other two species have three grooves.

Bosca's newts prefer clean, cold and still water, although they also occupy muddier water that is thick with vegetation if that is all that is available. They even survive in animal troughs, caves and brackish lagoons. In warmer spots the newts are completely aquatic and have no reason to leave the water. In damper habitats, however, such as alpine ones, the newts may make forays on to dry land in search of food.

They are most active at night, but during the breeding season the newts are also seen during the day. Female newts lay up to 250 eggs in the water, which hatch within three weeks. The larvae metamorphose into adult forms once they reach 3cm (1.25in) long. This development is delayed in individuals living in cold water. Despite having an adult form, the young newts do not mature sexually for several months.

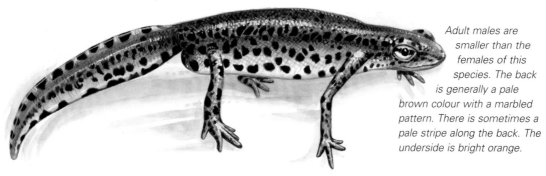

Adult males are smaller than the females of this species. The back is generally a pale brown colour with a marbled pattern. There is sometimes a pale stripe along the back. The underside is bright orange.

Distribution: Portugal and western and central Spain.
Habitat: Clear ponds and streams in both lowland and highland areas. Also lives in brackish lagoons close to the seashore and in underground lakes inside caverns.
Food: Land and water invertebrates, tadpoles, frog's spawn and small fish.
Size: 10cm (4in).
Maturity: 2–4 years.
Breeding: 100–250 eggs laid underwater in spring. Eggs hatch within 3 weeks.
Life span: 7 years in the wild, longer in captivity.
Status: Common.

Kirk's caecilian

Scolecomorphus kirkii

Distribution: Southern Tanzania.
Habitat: Soil.
Food: Insects and worms.
Size: 20–35cm (8–13.75in).
Maturity: Unknown.
Breeding: Eggs laid underground.
Life span: Unknown.
Status: Lower risk.

Kirk's caecilian is rarely seen on the surface. It spends its days burrowing through the loose soil of moist savannahs near to Lake Tanganyika and Lake Nyasa. Caecilians are all burrowing amphibians. Like snakes, which also first evolved as burrowers, caecilians have no legs, which helps them to slither through the soil. They move by lifting some of their body off the ground, and pushing back with the parts that remain touching the ground. Grooves around the body, known as annuli, give the animal some purchase on the ground.

Kirk's caecilian has small eyes located on small tentacles. These tentacles can lift the eyes slightly above the head. Little is known about the caecilian's other senses.

When mates do find each other, they copulate underground. The female then lays a clutch of sticky eggs underground. There is no larval stage, as with many amphibians; instead, the young hatch out as small versions of the adults.

With its apparently segmented body, this bizarre amphibian looks like a giant earthworm. On closer inspection, the head, jaw and teeth show that it is a vertebrate with bones and a spine.

Ambrosi's cave salamander (*Speleomantes ambrosii*): 12.5cm (5in)
Like all cave salamanders, this species is a member of a much larger group of salamanders called the lungless salamanders. Most of these species live in the Americas. As their name suggests, lungless salamanders do not breathe using lungs; instead, they absorb all the oxygen they need through their skin. The most active gas-exchange surface is the moist lining of the mouth. Cave salamanders are closely associated with regions of limestone where caves are common. However, they are also found on the surface. Ambrosi's cave salamander lives in southern France and northern Italy. It is nocturnal and often climbs up vegetation to find food.

Italian cave salamander (*Speleomantes italicus*): 12.5cm (5in)
The Italian cave salamander is very similar to Ambrosi's cave salamander but lives farther south, in the northern Apennines. It is nocturnal and therefore not often seen. It can exist in large numbers and is most likely to be spotted on a limestone rock.

Supramontane cave salamander (*Speleomantes supramontis*): 13.5cm (5.25in)
The supramontane cave salamander is one of only two salamanders living on the island of Sardinia. This rare salamander lives in the east of the island inland from the Gulf of Orosei. It spends a lot of its time underground in damp caves. When on the surface, the nocturnal salamander does most of its foraging among lush mosses.

Boulenger's caecilian

Boulengerula boulengerina

Boulenger's caecilian lives in the loose soils of the lush and humid forests that clothe the Usambaras Mountains of southern Tanzania. Most caecilians are opportunist feeders: they sit underground and wait for prey to come within their grasp. They will eat almost anything, using a strong bite and two rows of backward-curving teeth to hang on to their prey. Many of the muscles used for swallowing in other amphibians are employed to close the mouth in caecilians, which results in a powerful bite for such a small animal. Boulenger's caecilian, however, is something of a specialist feeder and is seldom far from a source of termites.

Like the other East African caecilians, Boulenger's caecilian lays eggs. Little is known about how Boulenger's caecilians breed. It is thought that the female lays her eggs in an underground chamber and guards them until they hatch.

Distribution: South-eastern Tanzania.
Habitat: Soil.
Food: Termites.
Size: 20–28cm (8–11in).
Maturity: Unknown.
Breeding: Eggs laid in underground chamber.
Life span: Unknown.
Status: Common.

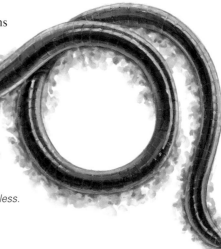

Boulenger's caecilian is a slender species with a striking blue-grey body with more than 100 rings around it. The throat is pinkish, and the eyes are covered by skin and so rendered useless. Juveniles of this species are pinkish.

FROGS AND TOADS

Throughout the world, there are over 4,000 species of frog and toad – more than ten times the number of salamanders and newts. Frogs are often recognized by their long legs, hopping motion and smooth, often brightly coloured skins. Toads, on the other hand, are often dark brown, warty amphibians that walk rather than hop. However, many frogs and toads are difficult to distinguish from one another.

Common toad

Bufo bufo

The common toad lives away from water for most of the year. Its thick, loose skin and nocturnal habits help to protect it from drying out. Toads protect themselves with foul-tasting chemicals released by warty glands in their skins. If threatened, the common toad also inflates its body and rises up on its legs, to intimidate predators.

Toads use their sticky tongues to catch ants, their favourite prey. They have a good sense of smell, which helps them to find their way to breeding sites each year. They hibernate until February and March – usually a few weeks later than common frogs.

Rather than laying clumps of spawn, as frogs do, common toads release a strand of spawn that hangs on weeds. In warm weather, tadpoles metamorphose in about eight weeks.

Common toads are olive brown and covered in warts. They walk rather than hop like frogs. The males are smaller and have fewer warts than the females, and only the males croak.

Distribution: Europe, north-west Africa, and Asia.
Habitat: Woodland, gardens, and fields. In the breeding season, they live in ponds and slow-moving rivers.
Food: Insects, spiders, slugs and worms.
Size: 8–15cm (3–6in).
Maturity: 4 years.
Breeding: Lays up to 4,000 eggs.
Life span: 40 years.
Status: Common.

European common frog

Rana temporaria

European common frogs are found in a variety of habitats, including fields and woodland close to water. Their diet is eclectic, including insects, molluscs and worms. Male common frogs have swellings on their first fingers to help them grasp the females when mating. Sometimes two or three males may try to mate with one female. Occasionally she will die in this situation through drowning or being squashed by their combined weight.

Spawning can take place as early as December or January but it is more usual in late February, March or April. Frogs flock to a traditional breeding pond, lake or ditch, where hundreds or thousands may be swimming around. Males emit quiet croaks and can be seen jostling for the best females. While a female is releasing her 1,000–4,000 eggs, the male, directly on top, will spread his sperm over them.

After spawning, the ponds become quiet again, as the frogs leave to live on land. They do so until the autumn, when they hibernate under logs and rocks. When it is very cold, they will rest in the water, usually in amongst thick vegetation.

Common frogs are variable in colour, but generally have a greenish-brown body colour with darker blotches and dark masks on their faces.

Distribution: Widespread throughout Europe, including Turkey and Russia.
Habitat: Live in meadows, gardens and woodland. Breed in puddles, ponds, lakes and canals. Prefer areas of shallow water.
Food: Insects, snails, slugs and worms, caught with long, sticky tongues. Tadpoles are herbivorous and feed on algae.
Size: 6–10cm (2.5–4in).
Maturity: 3 years.
Breeding: 1,000–4,000 eggs laid.
Life span: 12 years.
Status: Common in most of range.

Marsh frog (*Rana ridibunda*): Females 7.5–14cm (3–5.5in); males 6.5–10cm (2.5–4in)
The marsh frog lives in the rivers and other waterways that cross the plains of eastern Europe. It also occurs in parts of France, the Rhine Valley and southern England. The species was originally introduced to western Europe by humans. Marsh frogs also live in central Asia. Its loud croaking can be heard from pools during the day and night. When calling, special sacs are inflated and bulge out on either side of the head. The frogs make a number of loud calls to attract mates throughout May and June. It is the largest European frog and usually remains in the water for most of the year.

Iberian water frog (*Rana perezi*): 8.5cm (3.25in)
This species of water frog lives in the south of France, Spain and Portugal. It has also been introduced to the Canaries, Balearics and Madeira. The Iberian water frog is seldom out of water. It lives in all types of water, even stagnant and brackish water. It is most often seen by day, sunbathing in warm shallow water. When disturbed the frog ducks into deeper water. The females of this species lay more than 1,000 eggs. The tadpoles have to cope with the temperature of the water rising in the summer and the amount of oxygen in it dropping. Tadpoles in pools that are likely to dry up will metamorphose into adults more quickly than usual so that they can escape on to land. As a result, these newly emerged frogs are much smaller than normal.

European tree frog

Hyla arborea

European tree frogs are bright green frogs. They are able to change colour, and when they first come out from hibernation, in the spring, they are grey-brown. They are good climbers, living in trees throughout Europe. They have suckers on the ends of their toes to help them grasp branches. The green skin helps to keep them hidden among the leaves.

Tree frogs are most active during the night, particularly if it has been raining. They leap around, catching a variety of night-flying flies and moths. In late spring, the males sit by the edges of ponds or on plants overhanging the water, croaking to attract females. When the males call, they inflate vocal sacs, which produce their distinctive sound. When full of air, the sacs are as big as the frogs. The song produced is a mixture of barks and quacks. When a number of males croak together, they can be heard several kilometres away.

The European tree frog is lime green on top and white underneath. It has a somewhat contorted appearance because the skin on its head is fused to its skull.

Distribution: Europe, below 800m (2,640ft) above sea level.
Habitat: Scrub and open woodland with shrubs.
Food: Flies and moths.
Size: 3–4.5cm (1.25–1.75in).
Maturity: Not known.
Breeding: 800–1,000 eggs laid in small clumps during late April or May.
Life span: 20 years.
Status: Declining.

Midwife toad

Alytes obstetricans

Distribution: West and south-west Europe.
Habitat: Quarries, scree slopes and uncultivated land. Sand dunes and gardens are inhabited in France.
Food: Small insects.
Size: 5cm (2in).
Maturity: 2 years.
Breeding: Female lays several batches of 20–60 eggs in strings between April and June, which are carried on the male's back legs. Tadpoles are released into water between 2 and 6 weeks later.
Life span: Not known.
Status: Locally common.

The midwife toad looks very similar to the common toad. However, it has vertical pupils instead of horizontal ones, a more pointed snout, and does not have the protective glands behind the head. Midwife toads are night-active and spend the day hidden in crevices in rocks, under logs or in burrows.

In late spring, the males give out short peeping calls to attract females. Mating occurs on land. As the females produce strings of 20–60 eggs, the males catch them with their legs. They then position the strings of spawn between their thighs and waists. The females play no part in looking after the eggs. The eggs remain embedded in a whitish-yellow mass of mucus that keeps them moist.

The male secretes antibiotics over the eggs to protect them from fungus and bacteria. After two to six weeks, the eggs develop into tadpoles. The males travel to ponds where the young release themselves into the water. Some males attract two or more females, and therefore look after a larger number of eggs.

The midwife toad is dull grey, olive or brown in colour, occasionally with green spots and often with darker markings. The belly is whitish with grey blotches. Females sometimes have red spots running down their flanks. This toad is particularly proficient at leaping.

Fire-bellied toad

Bombina bombina

Fire-bellied toads are named after the bright red and yellow markings on their undersides; these form a unique pattern, rather like human fingerprints. When adults call, they inflate their throats and show off their bright colours. This species of toad produces a melancholy triple "oop" call, which is sometimes confused with that of a small owl. A chorus of toads can evoke the sound of distant bells.

Fire-bellied toads live across central and eastern Europe. They also occur in Denmark and southern Sweden and appear as far east as Turkey. They live exclusively in lowland habitats, preferring shallow water that is not too clogged with plant growth. This species often makes forays away from the water, especially after rain. In colder areas, the toad hibernates under logs and stones.

In late spring the toad always returns to water to breed. Mating takes place at night, after rain has cooled the water. There is no tadpole stage in this species; instead, tiny baby toads just 1cm (0.4in) long emerge from the eggs after a few weeks. These toadlets are able to survive on land.

From above, fire-bellied toads are well camouflaged by their dull, mottled colours. They have black or dark brown warty skins, covered in dark spots with green patches on their shoulders and broad, green central lines. By contrast, the bellies are black with bright red or yellow patches.

Distribution: Eastern and central Europe from Denmark and southern Sweden to Russia and Serbia to Turkey.
Habitat: Always close to shallow pools, marshes, and streams in lowland areas. Hibernates under logs and flat stones
Food: Insects, spiders, slugs and worms.
Size: 5cm (2in).
Maturity: 1–2 years.
Breeding: 150 eggs laid in 5–6 clumps on water plants. Eggs hatch into toadlets.
Life span: 20 years.
Status: Common.

Painted frog

Discoglossus pictus

The painted frog lives in Mediterranean habitats, including coastal dunes, meadows, vineyards and forests. They like to live in thickets of dense vegetation and are seldom far from shallow water, either still or slow flowing. The frog can also survive in brackish waters (a mixture of sea water and freshwater) in tidal zones.

The frog is probably African in origin. Those on the mainland were probably introduced from the Maghreb (north-west Africa) in prehistoric times. The frogs that live on Mediterranean islands are a separate subspecies. In Sicily, where the species is one of the few frogs on the island, painted frogs are often found in manmade cisterns and watercourses.

Painted frogs breed several times in winter and early spring. The males attract mates with a "rar-rar-rar" call. Females mate with several males, each time laying about 50 eggs. In total each female can lay 5,000 eggs in a year over several breeding periods. The eggs hatch in about a week.

Despite their colourful name, the painted frogs have a grey-green colour, typical of many European frogs. The name applies to the dark blotches on the back, which are framed by a pale yellow border. Some members of this species also have a pale brown stripe running along the back from the snout to the rump.

Distribution: Sicily, Malta, Gozo, eastern Pyrenees of southern France, Gerona in north-east Spain, and parts of north-west Africa.
Habitat: Fields, woodland, sandy areas, and marshes close to hallow water.
Food: Catches invertebrates using a disc-shaped tongue.
Size: 8cm (3.25in).
Maturity: 3–5 years.
Breeding: Eggs scattered on lake or river bed.
Life span: 10 years.
Status: Common.

Common spadefoot

Pelobates fuscus

Distribution: Central and eastern Europe from the Baltic to northern Italy and Bulgaria.
Habitat: Woodlands, fields and heaths in lowland areas.
Food: Invertebrates.
Size: 8cm (3.25in).
Maturity: 2 years.
Breeding: Up to 3,500 eggs laid in long bands.
Life span: 10 years.
Status: Common.

Spadefoots are a widespread group of frogs. A few species live in Europe and north-west Africa, but most are found in southern Asia and North America. The common spadefoot lives across central and eastern Europe to the edge of Asia, from northern France and Denmark in the west to the Urals and the Aral Sea in the east.

Common spadefoots are active only at night, apart from in the spring breeding season, when they attempt to mate during both night and day. Spadefoots are generally found in areas of sandy soil that are easy to dig through. They dig with their hind feet and use their wide head to barge through loose soil.

The frogs mate in deep pools with thick vegetation growing along the edge. Males attract females with a triple "clock" call. Females lay many hundreds of eggs in strings that can be 1m (3.25ft) long. Tadpoles often spend the winter in the water before developing into the adult form.

Like all spadefoots, this species has spade-like growths on its hind feet. They are an extension of a foot bone next to the inside toe used for burrowing in soil. The "spade" of common spadefoots is black. The hind feet are also heavily webbed.

Iberian frog (*Rana iberica*): 7cm (2.75in)
The Iberian frog is found only in the western Iberian Peninsula, mostly Portugal and north-western Spain. It is a close relative of the common frog, which is found in the European hinterland to the east. The Iberian species is easily mistaken for this more widespread relative. However, Iberian frogs have extensive webbing on their hind feet, while common frogs do not. Iberian frogs are most common in the mountains and prefer cold, fast-flowing streams that have plenty of shaded areas nearby. In the northern parts of their range, the climate can be cool enough for the frogs to live at lower altitudes. Iberian frogs are active during both the day and night. They breed in the autumn.

Balkan stream frog (*Rana graeca*): 8cm (3.25in)
The Balkan stream frog lives across the eastern Balkan Peninsula from Serbia to Greece. It is always found close to or swimming in cold running water and is most common on the middle slopes of mountains, about 1,200m (3,940ft) up. It prefers clear streams without too much vegetation clogging the flow over a rocky bed. By day the frog basks on the bank, only to leap into the water if disturbed. After rain, the frog also makes night-time trips into woodland, but seldom travels far from the water.

Pyrenean frog (*Rana pyrenaica*): 5cm (2in)
This species lives in the central region of the Spanish Pyrenees Mountains. It is one of the smallest species of frog in Europe. Pyrenean frogs are good swimmers and live in streams.

Parsley frog

Pelodytes punctatus

Parsley frogs live in a range of habitats in eastern Spain. They are found in swamps and streams but outside the spring breeding season often venture to quite dry habitats. In the south of their range, where the weather is consistently warmer, the frogs live on the slopes of mountains. Farther north, they are limited to lowland habitats.

These frogs are nocturnal. By day they rest under stones and logs and are frequent visitors to caves. During the breeding season, the frogs become more active and can be seen during the day as well.

The frogs' breeding is stimulated by the spring rains. The frogs gather in waters to mate. The females mate several times, and after each mating they wrap strings of up to 350 eggs around stems. In a single season one female may lay up to 1,600 eggs. Tadpoles develop into froglets in late autumn. These young frogs mature the following spring.

This little frog has long legs with very long toes on its hind feet. Its name comes from the bright green spots on its upper back, which resemble sprigs of parsley. Males are slightly smaller and have shorter limbs than females.

Distribution: Eastern Spain.
Habitat: Swamps, woodlands and meadows.
Food: Invertebrates.
Size: 5cm (2in).
Maturity: 1 year.
Breeding: Several strings of eggs twisted around stems.
Life span: 15 years.
Status: Common.

Natterjack toad

Bufo calamita

The natterjack toad has dark, warty skin like the common toad and a yellow line all the way from the head to the end of the spine. During the breeding season, the males develop purple-violet throats, while the females' throats remain white. Males have large throat sacs, which are used to make loud calls.

The natterjack toad is found throughout western and central Europe and is the smallest of all the European toads. In northern Europe, including Britain, the toads are restricted to lowland habitats such as heaths and dunes, although they are also often found in broken habitats, such as a quarry. Farther south the toads are able to survive in a wider range of habitats, including the slopes of mountains.

Natterjack toads are nocturnal. They live away from water outside the breeding season and will travel large distances if necessary, using their sense of the Earth's magnetic field as a means of navigating. The toads hibernate under stones and in other sheltered spots during the worst of the winter weather. If alarmed, the toads inflate their bodies and exude an unpleasant-smelling liquid through their skin to scare off predators. The breeding season lasts for most of the spring and summer. Males position themselves in or near to shallow water and attract mates with their croaks. The toads are thought to be Europe's noisiest toads because the male's croaking can be heard up to 3km (2 miles) away. Eggs are laid in ponds. They hatch in about a week.

Distribution: Western and central Europe as far east as the Baltic states, Belarus and western Ukraine.
Habitat: Meadows, dunes, quarries and woodlands in the north, and also mountains in the south.
Food: Invertebrates.
Size: 7cm (2.75in).
Maturity: 2 years.
Breeding: Single and double strings of eggs laid in shallow water. A female can lay 7,000 eggs in one season.
Life span: 10 years in the wild; 17 years in captivity.
Status: Common.

Green toad

Bufo viridis

Female green toads are larger than the males. They look similar to the natterjack toad but the females have a more contrasted speckled colouring on their backs. Green toads also generally lack the yellow stripe commonly seen in their western neighbours. The green toads' back legs are also longer than the those of the natterjacks. Green toads hop in a typical frog-like way, while the natterjack crawls on all fours.

Green toads are an eastern European species. They occur as far west as eastern France and Denmark, but their main range is Russia and on into central Asia. This species is also found on several Mediterranean islands, such as Corsica and Mallorca, and occurs in North Africa. These southern populations are thought to be the result of people introducing (by accident or design) the frogs to these regions in the Bronze Age.

The green toad is nocturnal. It is better able to survive dry conditions than many other toad species and is often found far from water. It is especially common in sandy soils, where it digs itself a burrow to hide out in during the day. Inside the damp burrow, the toad is protected from the dryness and heat.

In most parts of the range, the green toad hibernates, seeking refuge in a damp place. It awakes in spring in time for the breeding season. Green toads will lay their eggs in a range of waters, including stagnant and brackish bodies. Eggs hatch within a week of being laid, and the tadpoles metamorphose into the tailless adult form when they reach 1cm (0.4in) in length.

Distribution: Eastern and central Europe, western Mediterranean islands, North Africa, Middle East and central Asia.
Habitat: Dry habitats, such as sandy and rocky areas. Common close to human settlements.
Food: Insects, spiders, worms and slugs.
Size: 10cm (4in).
Maturity: 3 years.
Breeding: Strings of thousands of eggs are laid among water plants.
Life span: 10 years.
Status: Common.

Moor frog

Rana arvalis

Distribution: Scandinavia, central and eastern Europe and northern Asia.
Habitat: Moors, bogs, floodplains and tundra.
Food: Insects and worms.
Size: 8cm (3.25in).
Maturity: 2–3 years.
Breeding: Up to 4,000 eggs laid in 2–3 clumps.
Life span: 10 years.
Status: Common.

Moor frogs live in the extreme east of France and Belgium and extend northwards to northern Sweden and Finland and south to the foothills of the Alps. The frog's range extends as far east as the Lake Baikal region in Siberia.

The frog is found at mainly low altitudes and occupies habitats such as moors and bogs. In the south, where the climate is often wet, they occur on mountains. In the north, they live on tundra close to river banks.

Moor frogs have a short breeding season in spring. The frogs gather at pools and mate intensively. Males stay in one location, calling female mates, who come and go. Once mated, the females lay a total of 4,000 eggs in large clumps. Collectively the eggs make up a third of the female's weight. The eggs hatch after a few weeks, or more slowly in cold areas. Tadpoles change into the adult form when they grow to 1cm (0.4in) long.

Moor frogs are robust frogs with a pointed snout and short legs. When the hind legs are extended, their heels do not reach past the snout. When ready to breed, the males develop a violet colouring (seen here) and grow nuptial pads on their forelimbs for gripping females during mating.

Italian stream frog (*Rana italica*): 6cm (2.25in)
This species lives in western Italy and is very similar to the Balkan stream frog. It was classified as a separate species to its eastern neighbour only in 1985. The Italian stream frog is found mainly in mountain habitats, close to fast-flowing streams with rocky bottoms. It may follow these streams to lower altitudes if the water remains clear and free of thick vegetation. The females lay spawn under stones to prevent them being washed away by the current.

Italian agile frog (*Rana latastei*): 7.5cm (3in)
This species is found in northern Italy, though it also crosses into southern Switzerland, Slovenia and Croatia. Male Italian agile frogs are smaller than females. The species looks similar to the agile frog but has a pale stripe on the dark background of the throat. Males have pinkish tinges to their throats and legs during the breeding season. Italian agile frogs are a lowland species. They live in woodlands and meadows for most of the year and seek out swampy areas in which to breed.

Agile frog

Rana dalmatina

Agile frogs are found across central Europe as far east as Romania. The range extends south to Turkey and northern Iran. They are absent from northern areas, such as Denmark and the Rhine Valley, and do not occur in Portugal or much of Spain.

When not breeding, agile frogs live in woodlands. Their colouring helps them blend in with the leaves that cover the ground. They hide by day and emerge at dusk to feed. When close to water, the agile frog dives in when danger is near. However, the species is often far from water and instead uses its long legs to bound away from a threat. This behaviour is what gives the species its name.

Agile frogs can be heard during the spring breeding season producing a "quar-quar" call. Choruses gather in still water. The frog prefers to breed in open habitats. Females stick clumps of eggs around twigs in deep water. As the eggs develop, the clumps float to the surface, where the tadpoles hatch after about three weeks. Tadpoles become froglets once they grow to 2cm (0.75in).

Distribution: Central Europe.
Habitat: Woodlands.
Food: Invertebrates.
Size: 9cm (3.5in).
Maturity: 2–3 years.
Breeding: Spawn contains about 1,000 eggs.
Life span: 10 years.
Status: Common.

Female agile frogs tend to be larger than the males, but both sexes have a strongly contrasting colour pattern. The back is pinkish-brown and is often described as resembling the colours of dead leaves. Some individuals have a faint stripe down the back and an A-shaped mark between the shoulders. The legs are conspicuously banded and the groin area is bright yellow.

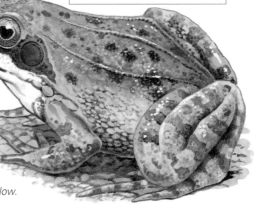

Foam-nesting frog

Chiromantis xerampelina

Foam-nesting frogs are found in tropical and subtropical parts of Africa, where they inhabit trees and shrubs of savannahs. When mating, pairs of foam-nesting frogs produce large amounts of foam in which the eggs are laid. The foam masses are attached to branches, overhanging temporary pools of water. The foam stops the eggs from drying out in the hot climate where the frogs live, and females occasionally remoisten it with water.

The tadpoles hatch after two days and survive in the foam as it dries out. After about a week, when the nests become very crowded, the tadpoles drop from the foam into the water below. In most matings, two or three males will be involved with each female. All the males help in beating mucus to produce the foam nests. Male foam-nesting frogs have large testicles to produce copious amounts of sperm. This increases their chances of success in fertilizing the eggs.

Foam-nesting frogs live in areas that reach very high temperatures, and they can be found sitting in direct sunlight. Compared to other types of frogs, they lose very little water from their bodies. The frogs have special skin that turns white in the sunshine. This stops the frogs from heating up and losing water through evaporation. To avoid overheating, they also produce a watery mucus from glands in their waterproof skins.

The foam-nesting frog is a light-coloured, grainy, pale green frog with light brown lines on its legs and irregular spots across its body. Many individuals are darker with several brown areas on the body.

Distribution: Tropical and southern subtropical parts of Africa, in the south and east of these areas.
Habitat: Bushes and trees that grow in dry African grasslands.
Food: Large flying insects, such as moths, butterflies, ants, plant bugs and beetles.
Size: 6cm (2.5in).
Maturity: Not known.
Breeding: During the rainy season. Eggs laid in ball of foam on branches. Tadpoles drop into pools.
Life span: 2.5 years.
Status: Common.

Bushveld rain frog

Breviceps adspersus

The Bushveld rain frog has a very rounded body. The neck is almost absent completely. It is brown with rows of light yellow or orange patches along its spine and sides. It also has a broad black stripe from each eye to its armpit. Females have a speckled throat, while the throat is black in males.

The Bushveld rain frog is a rather rotund burrowing frog with a short head and blunt snout. It spends most of its life underground in the soft soils of low hills and grasslands. The frog only comes up to the surface to feed and breed after heavy rains create the right damp conditions. The frog's globular shape makes burrowing through soft sandy soil easier, but it also makes mating difficult. To help the male stay on top of the female, he secretes a sticky substance from glands around his rear. This acts like a glue and binds him to his mate.

The fertilized eggs are laid in an underground chamber. When mating and egg-laying is over, the glue either breaks down or the female sheds her skin to release the male. The tadpoles are unable to feed while underground and have to develop quickly into tailless froglets before they have their first meal.

The males attract female mates by giving short, blurred whistles, which are emitted in a continuous series of single calls. Two or more males may call together in a chorus.

Distribution: South Africa and Swaziland, Mozambique, Botswana and Namibia.
Habitat: Hot, dry foothills. Dry bushveld, and areas of scrub and grassland, in northern part of southern African range. Breeds in open and closed woodland with sandy soils.
Food: Insects.
Size: 3–6cm (1.25–2.5in).
Maturity: Not known.
Breeding: After rains.
Life span: Not known.
Status: Common.

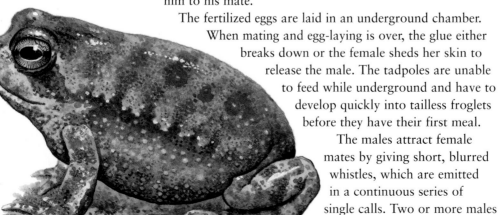

Red-legged pan frog (*Kassina maculata*):
6.5cm (2.5in)
The red-legged pan frog is grey with black oval
spots, outlined with thin, light-coloured lines.
The parts of the legs that are less visible, such
as the rear and armpits, are bright red with
black spots. This species is active at night in
the lowlands of eastern Africa, when males
congregate to call while floating in the water.

Trilling reed frog (*Hyperolius parkeri*):
2.5cm (1in)
This African tree frog is pale lime green in colour
with broad, whitish bands on the sides of its
body, running from its snout to its tail. It lives in
low-lying grasslands in East Africa, where it is
active at night. Males send out high-pitched
bird-like trills to attract females. The frogs live
in trees, reeds and grasses and breed by ponds,
where the females lay their 70–110 eggs on
vegetation, usually grasses growing over the
water. After hatching, the tadpoles drop into
the water to complete their development.
This is the only African tree frog of which the
male is larger than the female.

Kihansi spray toad (*Nectophrynoides
asperginis*): 1.5cm (0.6in)
This tiny, mustard-yellow toad lives in the forest
that grows in the spray of the Kihansi waterfall
in southern Tanzania. Surviving in just this tiny
habitat, the spray toad is consequently critically
endangered. This problem is compounded by
the toads' low breeding rates compared to other
amphibians. Females do not lay eggs but give
birth to a few fully formed toadlets.

Greater leaf-folding frog

Afrixalus fornasinii

Greater leaf-folding frogs inhabit savannah
country in eastern and southern Africa. The
female lays her eggs on grass overhanging
water. She folds the edges over, gluing them
together with secretions from a gland on her
rear. These leaf nests protect the eggs from
predators and from drying out in the sun.

The eggs are pale in colour, lacking
pigment. This is common with frogs and
toads that lay their eggs in burrows or fold
them in leaves. As they are not exposed, the
eggs do not need to be coloured or have
disruption patterns to camouflage them and
help them blend into the surroundings. When
the tadpoles have developed, their leaf nests
break up and they fall into water, where
they continue their development.

Distribution: Eastern and
southern Africa.
Habitat: Grasslands,
particularly with large bushes
and trees. Also found in
coastal lowlands and up to
1,300m (4,260ft) above sea
level in Malawi.
Food: Eggs and developing
larvae of other frogs that
breed earlier.
Size: 3–4cm (1.25–1.5in).
Maturity: Not known.
Breeding: 80 pale eggs laid
on a grass leaf. The tadpoles
hatch and drop into water
Life span: Not known.
Status: Common.

*Greater leaf-folding frogs have
a dark reddish-brown body
colour. They have black
warts on their backs and
broad silver bands
running along their
sides from their snouts
to their rear. These frogs
feed on the spawn and
tadpoles of other frogs that
breed earlier than they do.*

Banded rubber frog

Phrynomerus bifasciatus

Distribution: Southern and
East Africa.
Habitat: Savannah and
scrubland.
Food: Ants and other insects.
Size: 7.25cm (2.75in)
Maturity: Not known.
Breeding: Eggs laid in shallow
pools of water.
Life span: Not known.
Status: Common.

The banded rubber frog is pear-shaped, with shiny smooth
skin. It is nocturnal and breeds early in the season in
floodwaters. The males issue melodious trills, lasting several
seconds, from the banks or on floating vegetation. The eggs
are laid in large masses on the water's
surface or attached to aquatic plants.

The frog has a bright black and
red skin, signalling to predators
that it is poisonous. The skin,
which becomes paler in bright
light, contains toxins that can
harm any animal that attempts to eat
it. During the dry season the banded
rubber frog seeks cover in tree
hollows and burrows, away from
the heat and dryness. This species is
also known as the African snake-
necked frog, because it is able to bend
its neck much more than typical frogs.

*The banded rubber frog is a shiny
black frog with red spots on its
legs and thick red-orange bands
running from its eyes, right along
the sides of its body. The belly is
grey with white blotches.*

African clawed toad

Xenopus laevis

Today, chemical tests are used to tell whether women are pregnant. However, African clawed toads were once commonly used in hospitals as pregnancy tests. Pregnant women produce a particular hormone, which is released into their urine. If this hormone is present in the urine when injected into female toads, then the toads spontaneously lay eggs. In nature, the toad's eggs are laid singly and are attached to water plants or rocks.

From the head along the toad's sides there are a few rows of small stitch-like lines. Each line is a little depression containing minute hairs. Currents and vibrations in the water waft these hairs, and so the frog can detect them. This helps to tell the toad where it is and the location of other toads or predators and occasionally of food.

African clawed toads like to hang just below the water surface, waiting for food to swim by. They are the only South African amphibians to feed and breed in the water for their whole lives. If their pools dry up, they bury themselves in the mud and wait for the rainy season to arrive.

The African clawed toad is very flat, with small upward-facing eyes. Its skin is very slimy and generally coloured brown, green or grey, with darker spots or blotches on its back. Its belly is a yellowish-white colour. Females are generally larger than males.

Distribution: Southern and Central Africa. The species has been introduced as pets to Britain, Europe and North America. Escaped frogs now live wild in these places.
Habitat: Muddy water in permanent pools.
Food: Small worms, crustaceans, fly larvae and tadpoles of own species.
Size: 6–9cm (2.5–3.5in).
Maturity: Females 15–18 months; males 12 months.
Breeding: Spawn from August–December.
Life span: Over 20 years.
Status: Common.

Cape ghost frog

Heleophryne purcelli

Cape ghost frogs live in very fast-flowing mountain streams in the mountains of South Africa. They have well-developed toe pads that act like suckers for clinging to wet rocks in these torrential habitats. Their large hind feet are also heavily webbed, to help them swim against the current. Male Cape ghost frogs also have pads along the insides of their front legs and, prior to the mating season, they develop small spines around the rims of their lower jaws. These modifications help them grasp females and prevent them from being washed away while mating.

The females lay their large eggs under stones or in gravel in shallow backwaters, alongside the main channels of streams. The eggs are protected from the current by a tough capsule of jelly. The tadpoles of ghost frogs are long and flat. They, too, must cling on to rocks to avoid being washed away by the torrents. They attach themselves to smooth rocks with their large sucker-like mouths. The tadpoles feed on microscopic algae that grow on the surfaces of the rocks. They use their long, muscular tails to swim against the currents for long periods while grazing.

Distribution: Western South Africa.
Habitat: Fast-flowing streams in forested mountain areas. The adults leave the water during damp periods.
Food: Tadpoles eat algae while the adult prey on insects and other invertebrates.
Size: 3.5–5cm (1.5–2in).
Maturity: 2 years.
Breeding: Late summer after rain. The rain deepens streams and slows currents.
Life span: Not known.
Status: Common.

The Cape ghost frog is a small frog with dull green skin, covered in black-brown spots bordered with yellow. Its eyes are a coppery colour. The body is flatter than those of most frogs.

Tomato frog (*Dyscophus antongilii*): 5–10cm (2–4in)
Tomato frogs have orange-red backs, yellowish undersides, green eyes and sometimes black spots on their throats. The females are a brighter red than the males. They live in the lowlands of Madagascar, in swamps and shallow pools. Breeding occurs during the rainy season in stagnant or very slow-moving water. Females lay 1,000–1,500 small black and white eggs on the water's surface. The tadpoles are very quick to hatch and do so only 36 hours later, changing into adults after about 45 days.

Mountain ghost frog (*Heleophryne rosei*): 3.5–5cm (1.5–2in)
The mountain ghost frog is extremely rare and restricted to an area only 7–8sq km (1.5sq miles) in size on Table Mountain in South Africa. It has specific breeding requirements and needs areas that have water all year round. The tadpoles take a long time to grow and need at least two seasons before they change into adults.

African "hairy" frog (*Trichobatrachus robustus*): 9–13cm (3.5–5in)
The African "hairy" frog lives in western Africa. It gets its name from special hair-like filaments that develop on the male frog's legs and sides. The filaments are full of blood vessels and grow when the frog needs more oxygen to breathe. The species has lungs that are much smaller than the lungs of other frogs of a similar size. This means that when the males become very active as they jostle over females to mate with, they require more oxygen. The filaments act as external lungs, providing them with extra oxygen.

African bullfrog
Pyxicephalus adspersus

To avoid drying up, the African bullfrog can wrap itself in a cocoon. This is made from many layers of dead skin, and looks like plastic film. The frog can survive in this cocoon for two or three months, getting all the moisture it needs by absorbing water from its bladder. When the rains finally arrive, the cocoon softens and splits open. The frog scrambles out and eats the cocoon.

The male guards its eggs and tadpoles in a shallow puddle. Sharp upper teeth and two horny spikes at the tip of the lower jaw help ward off intruders. If the puddle is in danger of drying out, the male digs an escape channel for transferring the tadpoles to water. When the tadpoles develop, they can be aggressive and cannibalistic.

Distribution: Tropical areas across central Africa.
Habitat: Temporary bodies of water and small lakes in open or bush country.
Food: Insects and other invertebrates, reptiles, amphibians, birds and rodents.
Size: Up to 20cm (8in); 2kg (4.5lb).
Maturity: 1–2 years.
Breeding: Female lays up to 4,000 eggs in temporary pools. Tadpoles change into striped froglets but lose their stripes over time.
Life span: More than 20 years.
Status: Not known.

African bullfrogs are generally olive-green, with lighter coloured throats and bellies to help them blend in with their surroundings. Juveniles have obvious stripes, which later fade as the bullfrogs get older.

Goliath bullfrog
Conraua goliath

Distribution: Cameroon and Equatorial Guinea.
Habitat: Swiftly flowing rivers in dense rainforests.
Food: Small freshwater invertebrates, fish and other amphibians. Tadpoles eat plants.
Size: 30cm (12in); 3.3kg (7.25lb).
Maturity: Not known.
Breeding: Eggs laid in water.
Life span: Not known.
Status: Vulnerable.

Goliath bullfrogs are the largest frogs in the world, and can grow to more than 30cm (12in) in length. They live in only a few rivers in western Africa and are at risk from disappearing altogether because their rainforest home is being cleared for farmland. The species is also collected to be sold as pets.

Adult Goliath bullfrogs eat insects, crustaceans, fish and other frogs. The tadpoles, however, are plant eaters and will only feed on certain species of water plant that are found near rapids.

The Goliath bullfrog is silent, not having a vocal sac in its throat to make any sound. It is a shy species that is hunted by local people, who eat them and keep the thigh bones as good-luck charms.

The Goliath bullfrog is a very dark coloured frog, mainly a blackish-green. The belly is a lighter pinkish-orange and the eyes are a coppery brown.

White-lipped river frog

Amnirana albolabris

Like many of its close relatives found along the western edge of Africa, the white-lipped river frog has a pale stripe along its upper lip. The males have larger eardrums than the females.

The white-lipped river frog is a widespread and common species. It lives in forests along the coastal strip of West Africa between Sierra Leone and Gabon. Its range also extends inland into the Congo Basin as far east as Uganda. The frog has several common names across this large range, including the Congolo frog and Parker's white-lipped frog.

White-lipped river frogs live in gallery forest – a forest type that grows beside rivers and in flooded areas – and they are also common in deforested areas that have grown a layer of shrubs among the widely spaced trees that remain.

This species belongs to a genus of ten other frogs. All of them have suction discs on their toes, which help them to climb up smooth surfaces such as leaves or tree trunks. However, despite this climbing adaptation, the frogs are classified as belonging to the Ranidae (true frog) family rather than being included with the tree frogs.

Distribution: West and Central Africa from Sierra Leone and the Great Lakes of Uganda. Also lives on the island of Bioko.
Habitat: Forest rivers, mainly associated with the Niger and Congo River system.
Food: Tree-living insects, such as beetles and ants.
Size: 10cm (4in).
Maturity: Unknown.
Breeding: Breeding takes place in water.
Life span: Unknown.
Status: Common.

Tropical platanna

Xenopus muelleri

The tropical platanna belongs to a small group of seemingly primitive frogs. Most of them live in South America, but a few are found in Africa. They are all highly aquatic species, and the tropical platanna rarely comes out of water. In the dry season, the platannas' pools begin to evaporate and become shallower or may disappear completely. The frogs bury themselves in mud to stay moist during these dry periods.

As well as having long toes and claws, the frog's other unusual features include having no tongue and having lateral-line sense organs, which are more common in fish, such as sharks. These organs are a series of depressions along the frog's flanks that contain minute hairs. These hairs are sensitive to movements in the water and can detect currents produced by the frog's prey. Tropical platannas eat aquatic invertebrates and small river fish. They will also consume their own tadpoles.

Mating takes place underwater. The females lay tiny eggs. Each one is attached to a rock or stem on the river bed. The frogs have ears adapted to hearing mating calls underwater. The tadpoles hatch within a few days. They have flimsy and transparent bodies. The tadpoles are filter feeders. They have only thin tails and do not swim well, so instead they hang with their heads down and filter plankton from the water.

Distribution: East Africa from southern Kenya to Mozambique and South Africa. The platanna is also found on Zanzibar and Mafia islands in the Indian Ocean.
Habitat: Freshwater.
Food: Fish and invertebrates.
Size: 9cm (3.5in).
Maturity: 1–2 years.
Breeding: Tiny eggs deposited in stagnant water attached to stems and rocks on the river bed.
Life span: 15 years.
Status: Common.

The tropical platanna is a smooth-skinned frog with long toes on its forelimbs. The hind feet are webbed to help with swimming. Three of the hind toes have claws. It is one of only 30 frog species that have these claws.

Marbled snout-burrower

Hemisus marmoratus

Distribution: Africa south of the Sahara Desert.
Habitat: Savannah.
Food: Insects.
Size: 4cm (1.5in).
Maturity: 1 year.
Breeding: Eggs laid in underground chamber.
Life span: Unknown.
Status: Common.

The marbled snout burrower, also known as the pig-nosed frog and mottled shovel-nosed frog, lives across most of Africa south of the Sahara Desert. It is a savannah species and is not found in rainforests, although it does live along the edges of forests near rivers.

The frog survives in open country by digging into loose soil. As their name implies, snout burrowers burrow head first, and they are the only frogs to do so. (Other burrowing frogs use their hind legs to do most of the digging.) By day the marbled snout burrower rests about 15cm (6in) underground. At night it comes up to the surface to feed on insects.

The female digs an egg chamber near to a pond. She lays eggs in the chamber, which are then fertilized by a male. After the tadpoles hatch, the mother carries them to the pond.

Snout burrowers are also called shovel-nosed frogs because the small and pointed snout is used for digging. The short forelegs are also used for burrowing. The skin is smooth and covered in a mottled brown pattern, which gives it the look of marble.

West African live-bearing toad
(*Nimbaphrynoides occidentalis*): 2.5cm (1in)
This small and critically endangered frog is also known as the western Nimba toad because one of the few places in which it survives is the Mount Nimba reserve in Côte d'Ivoire and Guinea. They live in grasses and thickets and lie dormant in rocky crevices during droughts. Females of this species do not lay eggs. Instead the eggs are held inside the body, where the young develop for up to nine months. While inside the mother, the tadpoles are first nourished by the contents of the egg; once that is used up, they are fed by their mother. At birth the young have metamorphosed into tiny toadlets. During the birth, the mother inflates her body with air and uses it to push the toadlets (up to 16 in each litter) out.

African tree frog (*Leptopelis modestus*): 4.5cm (1.75in)
The African tree frog lives in two populations. The larger one is located in the forests of Cameroon while the smaller population survives in a pocket of forest in western Kenya. Like all tree frogs, this species has disc-shaped suction pads on the tips of its toes to aid with grip while climbing. The African tree frog is rarely seen and is most easily located by the deep "clack" call that males make to attract females.

Dwarf-ridged frog (*Ptychadena taenioscelis*): 2.5–4cm (1–1.5in)
A small savannah frog with a dark band running between each knee under the body. Breeds after rains in temporary pools.

Sharp-nosed ridge frog

Ptychadena oxyrhynchus

The sharp-nosed ridge frog is also known as the rocket frog because of its pointed snout and its ability to make leaps of up to 3m (10ft). It can make such huge jumps thanks to its long hind legs. The frog's leaping is a survival tactic used to escape predators on the open savannah, where there are few places to hide. The species lives across Africa south of the Sahara Desert. In most places the species avoids dense forests, but in East Africa one subspecies lives in mountain forests.

The frogs spend dry periods of the year in or close to rivers. When the rains come, the frogs hop off into open country and prepare to breed. The males position themselves beside a puddle or other temporary pool and attract mates with a short and shrill call. After mating, females lay long strings of eggs on the bottom of the pools. The strings each contain up to 3,500 eggs. These strings slowly break apart, and the eggs float in small groups to the surface, where the tadpoles emerge after a few days.

Distribution: Africa south of the Sahara Desert.
Habitat: Savannah.
Food: Invertebrates.
Size: 6cm (2.25in).
Maturity: 9 months.
Breeding: Eggs laid in temporary pools after rains.
Life span: 2 years.
Status: Common.

The sharp-nosed ridge frog is relatively large. The skin is grey-green with brown spots in several rows along the back. The belly is smooth and white, although the groin areas may be yellow.

Common squeaker

Arthroleptis stenodactylus

The common squeaker is a plump frog with short legs. The third finger on the forefeet is elongated, especially in males. The body is largely brown, sometimes with a light stripe down the back. There is also a darker swathe of skin curving from behind the eye to the shoulder.

Common squeakers live among the leaf litter of forests. They are often seen in clearings and appear to be able to survive in many human-influenced habitats. This adaptability is partly due to the fact that this species is not reliant on water to breed. There is no water-based tadpole stage in their development; instead, fully formed froglets that are capable of life on land emerge from the eggs.

These frogs live across much of Central and southern Africa from the coast of Kenya to Angola and South Africa. During the dry season, they lie dormant buried in damp soil. During wet periods, the frogs move around on the forest floor often hidden beneath leaf litter.

The males attract females with a high-pitched call that earns the species its common name. The males hide themselves under leaf litter when calling to make it harder for predators to locate them.

The female buries her eggs in a shallow hole in damp soil most often located under a bush or among tree roots, where the earth is unlikely to dry out. The froglets hatch after a few weeks and dig themselves out once the conditions are damp enough.

Distribution: Southern and Central Africa from northern Kenya and Angola to South Africa.
Habitat: Forests and forest clearings.
Food: Insects, worms and other invertebrates.
Size: 4.25cm (1.75in).
Maturity: 2 years.
Breeding: Froglets grow directly from eggs. There is no tadpole stage.
Life span: Unknown.
Status: Common.

Guttural toad

Bufo gutturalis

The guttural toad is one of the most common amphibians in southern Africa. It regularly hops into houses and survives in a mixture of habitats, including many manmade ones, ranging from agricultural fields to gardens. It is also a common resident of savannahs, shrublands and wetlands. The toad's range extends as far north as the southern tip of Somalia in the arid region of eastern Africa. However, the species is more common on the western side of the continent from the Democratic Republic of Congo to Namibia and the central region of South Africa. This species of toad is one of the few to be expanding its range. The toad is an insect eater and often snatches flying insects from the air. However, it also feeds on other invertebrates, such as spiders and worms.

The toad is named after its deep "kwaak" call, which is often likened to a snore. The males produce this call to attract mates during periods of rain, when pools begin to fill with fresh water. The toads always lay their eggs in permanent water sources, although many of these pools shrink considerably during the dry season. The females produce eggs in huge numbers because most tadpoles will not survive for long enough to metamorphose into the adult form and leave the water.

Like other toads, this species is a stocky amphibian with rough, warty skin. Behind the eyes there are bumps called parotid glands, which secrete unpleasant-smelling toxins when the toad is threatened.

Distribution: Across southern Africa from Somalia and Congo in the north to central South Africa.
Habitat: Grasslands, thickets, shrublands, marshes, gardens and fields. Not found in tropical forests.
Food: Insects and other invertebrates.
Size: 10cm (4in).
Maturity: 1–2 years.
Breeding: Females lay strings containing up to 25,000 eggs in permanent pools of water. The tadpoles hatch out within a few days.
Life span: Unknown.
Status: Common.

Woodland toad

Mertensophryne micranotis

Distribution: Coast of Kenya, Zanzibar and mountains of southern Tanzania.
Habitat: Woodland.
Food: Invertebrates.
Size: 2.5cm (1in).
Maturity: 1 year.
Breeding: About eight eggs laid in puddles formed in fallen logs and stumps.
Life span: Unknown.
Status: Common.

The woodland toad lives on the floor of East African forests. East Africa is a dry region and any forests that do grow are associated with microclimates, such as those around mountains and gorges, where enough rain falls to support tree growth. In Kenya, in the north of the range, woodland frogs are found close to the coast. The species also lives on the island of Zanzibar. On the Tanzanian mainland the toad is in the Udzungwa Mountains.

These toads need just a puddle of water in which to lay their eggs. Males call for mates while buried in leaf litter. The females respond to their chirping calls, and after mating the females lay a few eggs in tiny puddles. They have even been known to lay eggs inside a flooded snail's shell or broken coconut. Small pools such as these have limited oxygen, so the tadpoles have small fleshy crowns with a large surface area. They poke these crowns above the surface of the water to absorb oxygen from the air.

This species has very small, toxin-filled, parotid glands unlike most toad species. The outer toes of the hind feet are also very short, though it is unclear why this is. Males have rough patches on their thumbs to help grip on to females while mating.

Golden mantella (*Mantella aurantiaca*): 3cm (1.25in)
This striking frog is found only on the western slopes of Madagascar's spine of mountains. Like most Malagasy species, the golden mantella is vulnerable to extinction due to the loss of its habitat. Many of Madagascar's forests are being cut down for firewood and to make way for farmland. Adult golden mantellas are completely terrestrial and never enter pools of standing water, not even to breed. The frogs mate during the rainy season. The female lays eggs among moist leaf litter on the forest floor. This location is damp enough for the eggs to develop and for tadpoles to hatch out. The young amphibians then rely upon the torrential tropical rain to wash them into the nearest stream or pond, where they can continue their development.

Senegal kassina (*Kassina senegalensis*): 4cm (1.5in)
This burrowing frog occurs across sub-Saharan Africa, from Senegal in West Africa to northern Kenya and south to the Cape province of South Africa. The largest individuals in the species live in South Africa, where a few can reach 5cm (2in) long. The Senegal kassina is a striking animal, with its broad brown stripes on a paler, tan background running down its back. The kassina is found mainly in savannah habitats. It spends most of the day underground, emerging on damp nights to eat termites and other insects. The frogs travel to standing water to mate. The males call to females hidden in bankside plants. The females lay eggs underwater.

Red toad

Schismaderma carens

The red toad lives across much of southern Africa, from northern Kenya to the East Cape of South Africa. It is a savannah species and spends most of the year on land. However, like most toads, this species needs water to breed in.

Outside the breeding season, the red toad forages for slugs and insects out in the open. It hunts under the cover of darkness. As day approaches, the toad buries itself in fallen leaves or hides under a stone. As a result of this lifestyle, this species is rarely seen outside the mating season.

The breeding season begins with the rainy season. The males give a low, booming call while floating in deep water. The toads are unfussy about their breeding pools and often gather around dirty water. Females lay up to 20,000 eggs in double strings. Once hatched, the tadpoles crowd the pools and many are eaten before they get the chance to metamorphose into adults.

Distribution: Southern Africa.
Habitat: Grasslands and woodlands.
Food: Invertebrates.
Size: 9cm (3.5in).
Maturity: 1–2 years.
Breeding: 20,000 eggs laid in deep water.
Life span: Unknown.
Status: Common.

The red toad gets its name from its rusty-coloured back. This section of its body is demarcated from the pale and mottled flanks by a ridge of warts.

Common reed frog

Hyperolius viridiflavus

The common reed frog is found in a vast array of colours and patterns. Each pattern is strongly associated with one location. For example, the frogs in coastal Kenya are cream all over; in Uganda they are green; while in Tanzania they are yellow with dark stripes.

The common reed frog is found across the tropical region of Africa. It lives in the grasslands and small areas of woodland that make up African savannah. The frogs have small suction discs on all their toes and this makes them able to climb well, even on smooth surfaces such as leaves.

There are currently 28 subspecies of common reed frog that have been described. Many of these subspecies themselves have two or three colour forms. Biologists are currently attempting to work out how each group is related. The frogs are described as a species complex and that may actually turn out to be a collection of different species.

Each colour pattern, or morph, is found at a certain location and there are almost no places where two morphs live alongside each other in the whole of Africa. Instead, individuals that live at the boundary between morphs display a transitional hybrid pattern. To add to the confusion, the colour patterns of individual frogs can become bleached by long exposure to sunlight.

Distribution: 28 subspecies live across Africa south of the Sahara Desert. Some biologists suggest that the species is actually comprised of several species, which do not interbreed.
Habitat: Savannah, grassland and woodlands.
Food: Insects and other invertebrates.
Size: 4cm (1.5in).
Maturity: Unknown.
Breeding: Males call to females with clicks. Females lay 300 eggs in open water.
Life span: Unknown.
Status: Common.

Tinker reed frog

Hyperolius tuberilinguis

The tinker reed frog is relatively nondescript with its uniform colouring, which can be anything from pale green to brown. However, it is easily recognizable by its pointed snout, a backward-pointing triangle between the eyes and its toe pads. No other frog in the lowlands of East Africa shares all these features.

The tinker reed frog lives in the lowlands of eastern Africa from the southern coastal region of Kenya through Mozambique and Malawi to South Africa and Zimbabwe. It is most common in the wooded savannahs in this region, where it breeds in watering holes and temporary pools that are surrounded by thick vegetation.

The males climb up the stems of tall waterside plants to call for mates from a high vantage point. They produce a series of slow clicks to attract mates. After mating, the females lay small white eggs on vegetation that hangs above the water. The eggs are surrounded by a clear, sticky jelly, which keeps them in place. After a few days, the tadpoles emerge from the eggs and drop into the water below.

The tadpoles feed in the pool for several weeks, preying on aquatic insect larvae. Once they grow to a length of 4.5cm (1.75in), they begin to change into the adult form. Paradoxically, the tadpole is longer than the tailless adult form into which it metamorphoses.

Distribution: Eastern Africa from Kenya to northern parts of South Africa.
Habitat: Savannahs and woodlands.
Food: Insect larvae and other invertebrates.
Size: 3.5cm (1.5in).
Maturity: Unknown.
Breeding: Sticky masses of eggs are fixed to plants that hang above the water's surface. When tadpoles emerge they fall into water below to continue their development.
Life span: Unknown.
Status: Common.

Natal puddle frog

Phrynobatrachus natalensis

Distribution: Whole of the south of the Sahara Desert.
Habitat: Savannahs.
Food: Termites, other insects and spiders.
Size: 4cm (1.5in).
Maturity: 1–2 years.
Breeding: Mat of eggs laid on surface of temporary pool of water.
Life span: Unknown.
Status: Common.

The Natal puddle frog's name tells two stories. Firstly, the species is indeed found living in the savannahs of South Africa's Natal, but, as one of Africa's most widespread frog species, it also lives in most other parts of the continent as far north as the Sahara. Secondly, the frog does not need permanent flowing water to lay its eggs in; instead, it relies on shallow puddles that form after rains.

Puddle frogs live on the African savannah. In rainy periods most of their diet is made up of termites. In drier times they eat other insects, such as crickets, and spiders. The frogs can be seen by night or day.

They are most active during the rainy season, when males gather beside puddles and call to attract mates with a snore-like call. The female floats her small white eggs on to the surface of the puddle, forming a thin mat.

The Natal puddle frog exhibits a bewildering number of colour types across the continent. The species can be identified by its pointed snout and short, webbed toes, which, unlike those of many frogs, have fleshy tips.

Spotted reed frog (*Hyperolius puncticulatus*): 3cm (1.25in)
This relatively large orange-brown reed frog is named after the large yellow spots fringed with black that appear on its snout and back. The spotted reed frog is a forest species found in East Africa. It spends most of its year among leaf litter and undergrowth on the ground and breeds in temporary pools after heavy rains. The males attract mates by climbing into low vegetation beside the pool and giving out a series of high-pitched clicks. The female lays eggs on leaves that overhang the water so that hatching tadpoles can fall into the pool.

de Witte's frog (*Afrana wittei*): 6cm (2.25in)
This small frog lives in three separate populations in the highlands of Ethiopia, Kenya and Uganda, where it is found in marshy areas. These habitats form the watershed of the Nile and are often fed by heavy rains. The frog is active during the day and seldom strays too far from water, where it escapes to when danger approaches. The eggs are laid in the water, where the tadpoles develop only slowly compared to other tropical species.

Boettger's dainty frog (*Cacosternum boettgeri*): 2cm (0.75in)
This tiny frog is another highland species. Outside the breeding season it lives in meadows, sheltering by day in burrows abandoned by rodents or in other crevices. In the breeding season, males call for mates from thick vegetation beside marshy pools.

Ornate frog

Hildebrandtia ornata

The ornate frog is a burrowing species. It prefers dry habitats, such as savannahs, but is also seen along forest edges. The frogs avoid hot weather by resting in burrows. They emerge at night or on damp, cloudy days to feed on ground insects.

The frog's breeding season begins as soon as the rains arrive. As the rains replenish the savannah's water holes, the male frogs begin to call for mates with a harsh bellow. The calls come from beside the water, but the frogs are nowhere to be seen. This is because they are calling from underground.

After mating, the eggs are laid in masses of up to 200 eggs that float on the surface of the water. The colour of the tadpoles matches that of the bottom of the pool. This adaptation may make the tadpoles harder to spot and so save them from predators.

This small fat frog has smooth skin and a bright pattern. The back is bright green with black blotches. Dark broken bands run along the sides of the snout and through the eyes. The throat has a pair of marks in the shape of a Y. The hind feet have short toes and are only slightly webbed.

Distribution: Sub-Saharan Africa.
Habitat: Savannah and dry forest.
Food: Invertebrates.
Size: 7cm (2.75in).
Maturity: Unknown.
Breeding: Large egg masses laid in marshes.
Life span: Unknown.
Status: Common.

Cryptic sand frog

Tomopterna cryptotis

This burrowing frog has a large, spade-like structure on the heel of each hind foot. The back has a mottled pattern of grey, rusty brown and tan blobs. The flanks continue this pattern but with smaller markings. A pale line down the back is sometimes present.

The cryptic sand frog's colouring helps it to remain hidden against the dry sandy soil of its savannah habitat. (The word "cryptic" is used by biologists to refer to this and other adaptations that help an animal to hide.)

The sand frog is found in most of Africa south of the Sahara Desert. It lives far from running water, relying instead on seasonal rains to produce temporary pools for its tadpoles. For much of the rest of the year the frog lies dormant deep underground. The frog burrows into loose sandy soil to a depth of about 50cm (20in), where the soil remains damp and cool all year round.

When the rains arrive, the sand frogs have no time to waste. A male will find a raised mud bank near a pool to call a mate from. He produces a rapid "bing bing" call that sounds like a telephone ringing. After mating, the female scatters the dark eggs one by one into shallow, muddy water. One female may produce as many 3,000 eggs in a season. The eggs hatch into tadpoles after a few days. The tadpoles metamorphose into froglets after about a month in the water.

Distribution: The whole of Africa south of the Sahara Desert.
Habitat: Dry grassland areas with rainfall between June and October. Also found in woodlands in a few areas.
Food: Termites and beetles.
Size: 6cm (2.25in).
Maturity: 1 year.
Breeding: Eggs laid at night in temporary pools. Tadpoles stay in the water for 30 days.
Life span: Unknown.
Status: Common.

Angola river frog

Afrana angolensis

The Angola river frog spends most of its time in shallow parts of permanent bodies of water. It has long legs with highly webbed toes, which are used to paddle through the water. The frog does sometimes climb out of a pond or stream either in pursuit of prey or to call for a mate. It prefers to do this at places where the bank is covered by thick vegetation for it to hide among. The river frog cannot survive out of water for long.

Despite its name, the Angola river frog is found across most of the southern half of Africa, from Eritrea and the Democratic Republic of Congo to South Africa. It occurs in most habitats where there are sufficient bodies of water. As long as there is a pond or river, this species is just as happy in the middle of tropical rainforest as it is in an arid grassland.

The Angola river frog hunts in and out of water. It feeds on insects, especially aquatic larvae, and it also preys on smaller frogs. As the breeding season approaches, males develop swollen thumbs with dark areas. These swellings, called nuptial pads, are used to grip on to females during mating. Competition for partners is stiff, so males must hang on tightly to avoid being knocked off by a rival. The males call to females either floating in shallow water or from along the bank. The call is a complex one and ends in a long rattle and croak. After mating, the females lay the eggs in a shallow area of still water.

The Angola river frog is relatively large. It has an olive back with dark spots. There are heavy folds of skin behind the forelegs on the flanks. The belly is pale with a mottled brown pattern that is strongest at the throat.

Distribution: Much of equatorial and southern Africa, from Eritrea and the Congo in the north to South Africa. Absent from Namibia. The species is likely to be comprised of several separate species.
Habitat: Rivers, ponds and permanent bodies of water. Prefers water with thick plant growth on the banks.
Food: Large insects and small frogs.
Size: 9cm (3.5in).
Maturity: Unknown.
Breeding: Eggs laid in large numbers in shallow water.
Life span: Unknown.
Status: Common.

Bocage's tree frog

Leptopelis bocagii

Distribution: Most of southern Africa from Ethiopia and the Congo to the Transvaal of South Africa.
Habitat: Savannah.
Food: Invertebrates.
Size: 5cm (2in).
Maturity: Unknown.
Breeding: Eggs laid in holes.
Life span: Unknown.
Status: Common.

Bocage's tree frog may never climb a tree in its life. This species has evolved to survive on grasslands, where it exists as a burrower rather than a climber. It is found across southern Africa. It also appears likely that the frogs identified as Bocage's tree frog in fact belong to a number of different species, some of which look indistinguishable. However, evidence suggests that they will breed with only a certain subgroup of frogs. A species is a group of animals that can breed successfully with each other. Since some Bocage's tree frogs will not breed with others, they must by definition belong to a different species, irrespective of the fact that they all look and behave in the same way.

The frogs spend hot periods underground. Breeding begins as heavy rain soaks into the ground. Males take up a position on low vegetation and call with a low "quaak" call. Females lay their eggs in deep holes. The soil around these holes is waterlogged enough for tadpoles to develop quickly into froglets.

Being a tree frog by name only, this species lacks the round sucker-like pads on the tips of the toes as used by climbing frogs to grip on to flat surfaces. It also lacks webbing between its feet, since it rarely enters water.

Dwarf bullfrog (*Pyxicephalus edulis*): 10cm (4in)
Despite being a dwarf, this species is still a large frog compared to most other frogs. Males are a mottled brown while females are a dull grey-green. It lives across Central and southern Africa, from Nigeria and Somalia in the north to South Africa. The dwarf bullfrog is found in a range of habitats from marshy ground to dry savannahs. For nine months of each year, the frog lives underground. It conserves water by surrounding itself in a bag-like cocoon of dead skin. During the breeding season, the males position themselves in a flooded thicket and produce a barking call to attract females. The females lay eggs in shallow water. The tadpoles develop very quickly to avoid predation. The dwarf frog is also called the edible bullfrog, and it is hunted by people across Africa for its meat.

Mababe puddle frog (*Phrynobatrachus mababiensis*): 2cm (0.75in)
This tiny frog lives in woodlands across eastern and southern Africa. They are very common and often seen in huge numbers as they gather to breed in temporary pools. Males produce a long buzzing sound to attract females. The males stay hidden in leaf litter until a female approaches, at which time there is fierce competition to mate with her. Once the eggs are fertilized, they are floated on to the surface of the water.

Eastern puddle frog (*Phrynobatrachus acridoides*): 2cm (0.75in)
A species that lives alongside the Mababe puddle frog. It is distinguished by its pale grey-green skin and its creaking call.

Yellow-spotted tree frog

Leptopelis flavomaculatus

Distribution: Eastern region of Africa.
Habitat: Forests.
Food: Invertebrates.
Size: 6cm (2.25in).
Maturity: Unknown.
Breeding: Eggs laid on floating vegetation.
Life span: Unknown.
Status: Common.

The yellow-spotted tree frogs live in the dry deciduous forests of eastern Africa. Their range runs from the southern coast of Kenya to the Save River in Mozambique and southern Zimbabwe. By contrast, their close relative, *L. vermiculatus*, lives in the damp evergreen forests that grow in this region.

The species is a relatively large tree frog. It has webbed feet and large toe pads. These pads help the frog to grip while climbing.

The frog's forest habitat experiences long periods without rain. The trees drop their leaves during dry periods. The frogs sit out the drought crammed into damp hollows.

When the rains return, the frogs prepare to breed. The males climb up into a tree to a high point 4m (13ft) above the ground to attract females with a "clack" call. They may even call from underground burrows in dangerously exposed locations. The females lay eggs on floating vegetation.

Despite their name, many adult yellow-spotted tree frogs are grey-brown in colour. They often have a darker brown triangle between the eyes. Younger frogs tend to be paler, with yellow spots on their backs.

TURTLES AND TORTOISES

Tortoises, terrapins and turtles appeared on Earth around 200 million years ago. Tortoises are the land form of the three and generally have dome-shaped shells. Terrapins tend to live in fresh water while turtles live in the sea. Tortoises are most common in warm regions and are therefore uncommon in northern Europe. However, turtles and terrapins are found right across both Europe and Africa.

European pond turtle

Emys orbicularis

European pond turtles used to be common in Britain when the weather warmed after the last Ice Age, but they disappeared around 5,000 years ago when temperatures fell once more. Today the species is found across the rest of Europe, including northern France. Although the adult turtle can survive the British climate, it is too cool for the eggs to hatch successfully. During warm weather, European pond turtles can be found basking on exposed rocks. They can be quite shy and if disturbed will quickly dive back into the water where their webbed feet allow them to move around rapidly.

Males can mate with females throughout a seven-month period from March to October, although most activity is seen during March and April. Two or three months after mating the females lay 3–16 eggs in burrows. The young turtles hatch in August and September before the onset of autumn and winter.

The European pond turtle has a smooth, oval shell. Younger individuals have lighter, sometimes yellowish, spots and streaks on their shells, necks and heads. Older individuals are entirely dark. They hibernate in winter, burying themselves in mud.

Distribution: Europe, North Africa and western Asia.
Habitat: Ponds, lakes and slow-moving streams.
Food: Fish, amphibians, insects, molluscs, young snakes and small mammals.
Size: 18–35cm (7–14in); 5–10kg (11–22lb). Female larger.
Maturity: Females 15 years; males 12 years.
Breeding: Females lay eggs in soil during June.
Life span: Up to 120 years.
Status: Common.

Marsh terrapin

Pelomedusa subrufa

The marsh terrapin is one of Africa's most common freshwater reptiles. Also known as the African helmeted turtle, the marsh terrapin is found in still waters across most of central and southern Africa. The north-western limit of its range is Ghana, and the species is found all the way down to South Africa's Cape Province. The terrapin is even found on the island of Madagascar and across the Red Sea in Yemen.

Marsh terrapins are side-necked turtles, which means that, when threatened, they tuck their head under the shell to one side. They do not pull it backwards like other species. Perhaps surprisingly, marsh terrapins are voracious hunters. They eat waterborne insect larvae, freshwater crabs and other crustaceans, and other shellfish, such as water snails and mussels. They also catch fish underwater and have even been known to drag birds into the water when they come to drink.

The breeding season begins in spring. The male courts the female by following her with his head on her back. He gives her back legs regular nips. After mating, the female buries her eggs in a nest in soft sand.

The marsh terrapin is small by turtle standards, but one of the larger terrapin species. The flat green shell is often discoloured by mud and slime. The neck is long and there are two soft sensory tentacles on the chin.

Distribution: Central and southern Africa, Madagascar and Yemen.
Habitat: Rivers, lakes and marshes.
Food: Insects, crustaceans, small birds, snails and worms.
Size: 20–32cm (8–12.5in).
Maturity: Unknown.
Breeding: 30 soft eggs laid in sand. Hatch after 75 days.
Life span: Unknown.
Status: Common.

Leatherback turtle

Dermochelys coriacea

The leatherback turtle is the world's largest marine turtle. Its shell has a leathery texture and is semi-rigid; it is made from thousands of individual tiny bony plates connected together. Each plate can move a little, making the shell more flexible than if it were completely solid. The turtles have long front flippers that enable them to swim up to 30km (20 miles) per day.

Leatherback turtles are very unusual reptiles because they are able to generate body heat through the movement of their muscles. The heat is maintained by the turtle's huge size, layers of fat under the skin and also by a long oesophagus, which coils back before reaching the stomach, helping to heat up swallowed food.

The turtles also have special blood vessels that stop heat being lost to cold water. Heat is transferred from arteries entering the flippers to veins carrying blood away from the flippers, keeping the limbs colder than the rest of the body. Mating takes place at sea and the females nest on tropical beaches, where they lay eggs in pits dug into sand.

Distribution: Atlantic, Pacific and Indian Oceans.
Habitat: Marine water.
Food: Jellyfish.
Size: 2–3m (6.5–10ft); up to 900kg (1,980lb).
Maturity: 30–50 years.
Breeding: 80–100 eggs laid on beaches every other year, hatching after 60 days.
Life span: Over 50 years.
Status: Critically endangered.

The leatherback turtle has a dark grey or black upper surface with additional spotting. Ridges run from the front end of the shell down to the tail. The span of the flippers is equal to the length of the animal.

Loggerhead turtle

Caretta caretta

Loggerhead turtles live in all the world's oceans and seas. They avoid the cold polar waters, but have been spotted as far north as Norway and eastern Russia.

Like other large chelonians (turtles and tortoises), loggerheads grow slowly and have a long life. Adults may travel across thousands of kilometres of ocean in a lifetime, although these sea turtles tend to stay in shallow waters close to the shore, and they are often spotted in river mouths and in bays.

Adult loggerheads forage for much of their food on the sea bed, although they can survive perfectly well in very deep waters by hunting for fish. Very young loggerheads cannot dive to the bottom to find food. Instead they foraging near to the surface and often hide from predators in mats of floating seaweed.

Like other sea turtles, loggerheads are endangered with extinction, the main reason for which is the scarcity of suitable nesting sites. Mating takes place at sea. Female loggerheads must come ashore to bury their eggs high on gently sloping sandy beaches. These same habitats are also attractive to tourists, who scare the laying turtles away. Along developed coasts today, loggerheads and other sea turtles nest in large numbers at only the few protected sites.

Females lay up to 120 eggs in a deep hole at night. The hatchlings dig themselves out about 50 days later and make a perilous dash for the ocean. Sea birds pick off many of them even before they get wet. The lights from beachside buildings also affect the hatchlings. The young turtles use the moon to orientate themselves so they can find the water. However, after reaching the surface the confused loggerheads can head off up the beach, away from the sea.

Distribution: Worldwide including the Atlantic Ocean, Black Sea, Mediterranean Sea and Indian Ocean.
Habitat: Warm sea water.
Food: Sponges, jellyfish, crabs, clams, fish and squid.
Size: 1.25m (4ft); 100–150kg (220–330lb).
Maturity: 12 years.
Breeding: Clutches of eggs laid every 2–3 years.
Life span: 60 years.
Status: Endangered.

Loggerheads are so called because of their large heads and powerful jaws. Unlike larger sea turtles, loggerheads have a hard shell. They are the largest hard-shell turtle in the world – larger even than the giant tortoises of the Galápagos.

Leopard tortoise

Geochelone pardalis

The leopard tortoise is a very distinctive tortoise, with obvious black and yellowish markings on its shell. The shell patterns are variable; indeed, each pattern is unique, like human fingerprints. Leopard tortoises from Ethiopia are paler than most, while those from South Africa are exceptionally large.

A musk gland near the tail emits a powerful and distinctive smell, which is used by the tortoises to attract partners for mating or to drive away predators. When it becomes hot, the leopard tortoise digs a hole and remains underground to avoid overheating or dehydrating. It stays in the burrow until the temperatures fall and the rains come again. If food becomes hard to find, the tortoises travel long distances to seek more. To continue growing healthy shells and to ensure their bones remain strong, they eat old bones found when they forage.

The leopard tortoise is straw-coloured, with black blotches evenly spread over the shell. Shell markings are reminiscent of the pelt of a leopard cat, hence the tortoise's name.

Distribution: South and East Africa, south of the Sahara.
Habitat: Semi-arid, thorny and dry grassland habitats.
Food: Grasses, fruit of the prickly pear, thistles and other plants.
Size: 40–65cm (15.75–25.5in); 10–40kg (22–88lb).
Maturity: 6–10 years.
Breeding: Eggs laid in autumn.
Life span: 50–150 years.
Status: Vulnerable.

Radiated tortoise (*Geochelone radiata*): 40cm (15.75in)
The radiated tortoise is a very colourful tortoise with streaks radiating out from each section of its shell. It lives on the island of Madagascar and is less common than it used to be because the Chinese prize it as a purported aphrodisiac. The vegetation where it lives is disappearing, including a type of spiny cactus, which provides important cover for the tortoise. Males and females encounter each other during late afternoon sorties, but they only mate if it is dry.

Atlantic or **Kemp's ridley turtle** (*Lepidochelys kempii*): 50–70cm (19.5–27.5in)
The Atlantic ridley turtle is the smallest marine turtle and the most endangered. The turtles live in sheltered areas such as large estuaries, bays and lagoons where they feed on crabs, jellyfish, squid, snails, starfish and a variety of other marine invertebrates, as well as some seaweeds. They have distinctive heart-shaped shells that may be black, grey-brown or olive in colour.

East African side-necked turtle (*Pelusios subniger*): 20cm (8in)
The East African side-necked turtle lives in shallow ponds and streams with muddy bottoms. When the pools dry out or it gets too hot or cold, the turtle burrows into the mud and remains protected until the rains come. When threatened, this species pulls its neck to one side rather than bringing it back into the shell like typical tortoises and turtles. They have dark – often black – domed shells with yellow undersides. They are found in East Africa, below the Sahara Desert and throughout Madagascar.

Pancake tortoise

Malacochersus tornieri

The pancake tortoise is very rare and suffered from illegal pet trade in the 1960s and 70s. Its tiny size meant it could be smuggled out of Kenya and Tanzania in very large numbers. The tortoise lives in rocky cliffs, hidden in crevices during the day. Grasses are very important for feeding and breeding. These grassy areas around the cliffs are disappearing through human activity, which prevents the species from increasing its population.

The pancake tortoise has a lightweight shell, which helps it scurry along and escape from predators more quickly. The bony plates that make up the shell are reduced in this species, leaving spaces where the bones would be, making it less heavy and more flexible. The shell is also flattened, which helps the tortoise to rest or escape under very low rocks. The tortoise can wedge itself into crevices by inflating its lungs with air and pushing down with its legs. If the tortoise falls and lands on its back, it can right itself quite easily.

The pancake tortoise has a brown shell, marked with pale yellow and black. It has a more pronounced hook to its beak than other species. The males have longer, thicker tails than the females.

Distribution: Kenya and Tanzania.
Habitat: Small rocky cliffs called "kopjes", over 1,000m (3,280ft) above sea level.
Food: Dry grasses and vegetation.
Size: 15cm (6in).
Maturity: Not known.
Breeding: Single eggs laid 3 or 4 times a year.
Life span: 25 years.
Status: Endangered.

Spanish terrapin (*Mauremys leprosa*): 20cm (8in)
The Spanish terrapin is found across southern Spain and Portugal. The species also lives in north-west Africa, between Morocco and Libya. The Spanish terrapin resembles the European pond terrapin but is lighter in colour and often has stripes on the neck. The shell is also slightly more elongated. The terrapin lives in shallow pools and can tolerate high salt contents as the water slowly evaporates away in the heat. If the pools dry out completely, the terrapin burrows into the damp mud until the pool refills.

Yellow-bellied hinged terrapin (*Pelusios castanoides*): 23cm (9in)
The yellow-bellied hinged terrapin lives along the eastern coast of Africa from Kenya to Kwazulu in South Africa. It is also found on several offshore islands. The shell is olive-coloured and the plastron (bottom shell) is yellow with black markings. The skin on the legs and neck is also yellow. The terrapin lives in shallow pools and aestivates (becomes dormant in hot weather) in damp mud when the pools dry out.

Forest hinged terrapin (*Pelosios gabonensis*): 20cm (8in)
This species is one of the few terrapins to live in the rainforests of Central America. It lives in swamps and pools on the forest floor. It is a favourite food of forest people, despite producing a foul-smelling liquid from its anus when threatened.

Marginated tortoise

Testudo marginata

Marginated tortoises live in the rocky hills of southern Greece. They are also found on many Greek islands. A large population lives in Sardinia after being introduced to the island in Roman times. These tortoises have become rare in the wild because large numbers are collected for the pet trade.

The tortoise's diet consists of thin leaves, such as rocket, radish and clover, as well as grass and fruits. In winter, when food is in short supply in the exposed highland habitat, the tortoises dig long burrows in which to hibernate until spring.

After the tortoises emerge from hibernation, the breeding season begins. During mating the male sticks out his bright red tongue as he produces loud barks. The female buries about 10 eggs in soft soil. They incubate for 100 days before hatching.

The marginated tortoise is the largest land tortoise in Europe. As with other European tortoises, the tail of the male is considerably longer than that of the female. The rear of the shell is very distinctive, with thick scales flared outwards with orange markings.

Distribution: Southern Greece.
Habitat: Rocky hillsides.
Food: Leaves and shoots.
Size: 38cm (15in); 5kg (11lb).
Maturity: Several years.
Breeding: About 10 eggs laid in spring.
Life span: 100 years.
Status: Lower risk.

Zambezi soft-shelled terrapin

Cycloderma frenatum

Distribution: Lower watershed of the Zambezi River.
Habitat: Lakes, rivers and ponds.
Food: Snails and other molluscs.
Size: 51cm (20in); 14kg (30.75lb).
Maturity: Unknown.
Breeding: 20 eggs laid in sand banks.
Life span: Unknown.
Status: Lower risk.

This species is one of just five soft-shelled terrapins living in Africa. Zambezi soft-shelled terrapins live in the lakes and tributaries that are associated with the Zambezi River system. These terrapins are also known as flap-shell turtles after the flaps of skin at the rear of their shell. The terrapin is more common in the lower areas of the watershed, between Zambia and the delta in Mozambique, where the river flows more slowly. Many lakes, natural and manmade, also feed the river and are good habitats for the terrapin.

The terrapins are hunters, eating mainly shelled molluscs, such as snails and mussels. They use their forelimbs to dig food out of the mud. They then crush their prey's shells with powerful jaws to get at the soft body inside.

The Zambezi soft-shelled terrapin often hides itself by digging into soft sand, so only its snout is visible. The females also dig a hole for their eggs, which are buried in sand banks, often close to a similar nest built by a crocodile.

This terrapin has a long neck and a pointed snout, which can be poked out of the water to breath like a snorkel. The forelimbs are powerful and used for digging. When the hind legs are pulled into the shell they are covered by flaps of skin.

LIZARDS

Eighty per cent of all the world's reptiles are lizards and snakes. Lizards are able to move their upper jaws as well as their lower jaws, helping them to tackle large prey and swallow them more easily. Many also possess the ability to lose their tails if attacked by predators; special bones in the tail are pulled apart by muscles and the tail is released from the body. This is called autotomy.

Panther chameleon

Furcifer pardalis

Throughout the range of the panther chameleon, males and females vary in colour. There are at least 25 different forms, with each one occurring in a different region. Males from north-west Madagascar are bright turquoise and green, with red and gold colours radiating from their eyes and heads. Another type of male from a different region has up to six different body colours with white streaks around its eyes. Breeding females become brighter too, developing black and red-orange colouring. Their black markings vary in pattern. The panther chameleon is able to change colour very quickly when it moves into different vegetation – as camouflage – or when being approached by other chameleons – as communication. They can be very aggressive with one another, and changing colour can warn other individuals to keep away.

Males have white stripes along their bodies and can display a variety of colours. Females are grey or brown, but turn red-orange when breeding.

Distribution: North and east Madagascar. Introduced to Reunion and Mauritius and neighbouring islands.
Habitat: Lowland coastal areas.
Food: Small insects.
Size: Females 18–23cm (7–9in); males: 30–45cm (12–17.75in).
Maturity: Females 5 months; males 12 months.
Breeding: 4–6 clutches of 12–30 eggs are laid per year.
Life span: Not known.
Status: Vulnerable.

Mediterranean chameleon

Chamaeleo chamaeleon

The Mediterranean chameleon is the only species of these appealing lizards to live wild in Europe. They are restricted to the extreme south of the mainland and are most common on islands such as Malta, Crete and Sicily.

The lizard is found in dry habitats and is generally seen climbing slowly through bushes. As it moves, the chameleon's eyes scan its surroundings; each eye can move independently. If the chameleon spots danger, it inflates its body and turns dark.

As well as looking out for danger, the chameleon is looking for insects. Once it spots a suitable victim it unleashes its long tongue, which is almost as long as the lizard's body and has a sticky tip that clings to prey.

Mediterranean chameleons put a lot of energy into reproduction. The males defend a territory and each female mates with several before climbing to the ground. They dig a trench and lay 30 eggs in it; the eggs might make up half of the female's weight. About a third of females die from exhaustion after their first breeding season.

This species' leaf-shaped body is flattened laterally. This makes the lizard difficult to see except from side on. However, the chameleon's ability to change colour to match its surroundings, allows the lizard to hide in plain sight.

Distribution: Southern Europe, North Africa and the Middle East.
Habitat: Bushes in dry habitats.
Food: Insects.
Size: 30cm (12in).
Maturity: 1 year.
Breeding: 30 eggs buried in soil. Hatch after 2–3 months.
Life span: 3 years.
Status: Common.

Usambara two-horned chameleon (*Chameleo fischeri*): 40cm (15.75in)

A large chameleon found only in the forested Usambara Mountains on the border between Kenya and Tanzania. It has two very striking horns pointing straight out of its face. These horns are not present at hatching but develop as the chameleon grows.

Kenya leaf chameleon (*Rieppleleon kertseni*): 6cm (2.25in)

This tiny chameleon species lives in the leaf litter of woodlands and thickets in East Africa. It is unusual for its small size but also because it lives on the ground, not in the branches like its cousins. However, this species is well served by its camouflaging ability among the fallen leaves. When not on the move the leaf chameleon rests in termite burrows.

Giant one-horned chameleon (*Chamaeleo melleri*): 50cm (19.75in)

The giant one-horned chameleon is the largest chameleon species in Africa. It lives in woodlands and forests that grow beside rivers in southern Tanzania. Its large size is given a boost by a crest of scales running down its back. Males also have a blade-like horn on their noses. This species is found high in the tops of trees, reaching heights of 10m (33ft), where it feeds on large insects. As with other chameleon species, the giant chameleon climbs to the ground only to bury its eggs. This species finds a warm, sunny gap between the trees in which to build its nest. Each female lays 90 eggs in a hole, where they are incubated for several months.

Slow worm

Anguis fragilis

The slow worm has a long, smooth body and lacks legs. Although it is often mistaken for a snake, it is a legless lizard. Unlike snakes, it has movable eyelids so that it can blink. It also has a broader, flatter tongue with a notch at the tip rather than a deep fork.

Slow worms hibernate between October and March. The males appear before the females, and when they come out in the spring, they warm themselves up by resting under rocks and logs. Slow worms are secretive creatures and spend most of their time underground. If they are attacked, they can shed their tails, which continue to wriggle for about 15 minutes. This distracts a predator while the slow worm escapes.

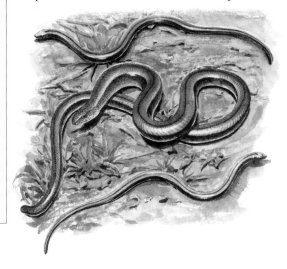

Distribution: Europe, South-west Asia and western Siberia.
Habitat: Rough grassland, hedgerows, heathland, woodland edges, downs and moorland. Also found in gardens and along railway or motorway embankments.
Food: Molluscs and earthworms, and also insects and spiders.
Size: 30–50cm (12–19.75in).
Maturity: Females 4–5 years; males 3–4 years.
Breeding: Mate in summer; eggs incubated inside body.
Life span: 10–15 years.
Status: Common.

Females are brown with coppery or reddish-coloured backs. Dark stripes run down each side of the body. Males are brown and lack the dark stripes. Both sexes have whitish or reddish bellies and throats, with copper-red eyes.

Savannah monitor

Varanus albigularis

The savannah monitor lizard is a large lizard with a sandy-coloured skin, patterned with lines of small black spots. The amount of black can vary and may be quite extensive. The head is darker on top and the tail has black bands. These lizards inhabit dry savannah or rocky terrain, and feed mostly on invertebrates.

The savannah monitor lives in very hot, grassy habitats, feeding on small mammals and insects. During the breeding season, males will search for females. In the Namib Desert, they have been known to travel up to 6km (3.75 miles) per day looking for females ready to mate. Their territories may be up to 18sq km (7sq miles) in size. Females ready to breed will climb trees to make themselves more obvious to males, and release a pheromone into the air.

During very hot weather, savannah monitors help to keep themselves cool by sitting with their mouths open and vibrating their throats very quickly. This is known as gular fluttering and allows water to evaporate from the throat, thus cooling the blood passing through this area. They are unable to sweat, and their covering of tough, waterproof scales means they can lose little heat through their skin.

Distribution: Eastern and southern Africa.
Habitat: Dry grassland or rocky areas.
Food: Mainly invertebrates plus reptiles, birds, mammals, eggs and carrion.
Size: 1–1.9m (3.25–6.25ft); 6–10kg (13.25–22lb).
Maturity: 2 years.
Breeding: Up to 50–60 eggs laid in burrows during the spring.
Life span: Not known.
Status: Vulnerable.

Water monitor

Varanus niloticus

Distribution: Africa.
Habitat: Rivers.
Food: Crabs, fish and eggs.
Size: 2.2m (7.25ft).
Maturity: At about 1m (3.25ft) in length for males, and half that for females.
Breeding: 60 eggs laid in termite nests and under logs.
Life span: Unknown.
Status: Common.

Water monitors are among the largest lizards in Africa; only the African forest monitor is larger, and that species is classified by some as a subspecies of its more common relative anyway. Water monitors are sometimes called Nile monitors because they have historically been common along the Nile. In the past they were also found in the Middle East. Today, however, the lizards are a purely African species. They live across the continent wherever there is enough flowing water to supply them with food.

Water monitors catch fish and freshwater crabs, but above all they are predators of egg-filled nests. They dig their way into egg mounds left by crocodiles and river turtles. In return, the monitors are frequent victims of crocodiles, who are protecting their nests as well as looking for something to eat.

The lizards themselves sometimes protect their own eggs by burying them in the nests of a termite colony. Water monitors are large enough to be unaffected by the termites' bites and stings, but an attack from termites defending their nest is enough to keep all but the most determined predators away from the monitors' eggs. Otherwise monitors bury eggs beside rotting logs. Eggs hatch after several weeks. Newly hatched monitors are tiny versions of adults. They prey on frogs and insects.

Like all monitors, the water monitor has a long body and an elongated head. The thick tail is also longer than the body. The tail is used to support the monitor when it rears up on its hind legs when threatened or fighting over breeding partners.

Starred agama

Laudakia stellio

A lizard of many names, the starred agama is also known as the hardun, painted dragon and sling-tailed agama. It is the only agama species to live in Europe. All the others live in Africa, Australia and Asia. This species is restricted to warm and dry areas. It is found in southern Greece and on several islands in the eastern Mediterranean, including the Cyclades and Rhodes. It is also a resident of Turkey and other parts of south-west Asia and is also found in north-east Africa.

The starred agama can change colour, becoming darker when cold and lighter when warm. This makes it less visible at different light levels.

Distribution: Greece, Aegean Islands, Malta, Turkey, Middle East and Egypt.
Habitat: Rocky areas, roofs and walls.
Food: Insects, small lizards and small amounts of plants.
Size: 20–30cm (8–12in).
Maturity: Unknown.
Breeding: 2 clutches of 8 eggs produced each year.
Life span: 10–15 years.
Status: Common.

Starred agamas prefer rocky habitats where there are plenty of places to bask in the sunshine. As a result they are well suited to life in and around human settlement. They are often seen basking on stone walls and roofs. The lizards remain motionless apart from the odd bob of the head. The lizards are quite shy and are ever ready to dive into cracks to hide from potential predators.

Like all reptiles, the agamas must warm themselves before they have the energy to move quickly enough to hunt. The colour of their scales become slightly paler as the lizards warm up. Once warmed enough, starred agamas look for food, often climbing into trees. Like all agamas, the starred agama is an insect-eater. This species also eats smaller lizards and nibbles on fruits and flowers.

Starred agamas breed two or three times a year. Females lay between six and ten eggs in each clutch. The eggs hatch after about 60 days. As they hatch out, the young agamas are about 3.5cm (1.5in) long.

Mozambique agama

Agama mossambica

Distribution: Southern Tanzania and Mozambique.
Habitat: Woodlands.
Food: Ants.
Size: 20–31cm (8–12.25in).
Maturity: Unknown.
Breeding: About a dozen eggs laid in decaying leaves in damp locations.
Life span: Unknown.
Status: Common.

The Mozambique agama lives on the floor of woodlands in southern Tanzania and parts of Mozambique. They forage among leaf litter looking for insects. Although they do eat other insects, this species is something of a specialist and searches out columns of ants on the move through the decaying leaves. The agama is also a good climber and often follows its prey into the branches.

The Mozambique agama is not shy of people and it often searches for food on the outskirts of villages. It feeds on ants and other insects also attracted there by the promise of food waste.

After the males take on their vibrant breeding colours, they defend a territory as they attempt to attract females. Fights between males are frequent and bloody. After mating, females lay up to 14 eggs in a rotting stump or under a log. They choose a location with plenty of damp soil containing a lot of decaying plant matter in which to bury the eggs.

Mozambique agamas are more slender than other agamas. The females and young are a mottled grey, which helps them blend in to their leaf-litter habitat. The males, on the other hand, take on a vibrant colouring during the breeding season, with a blue head and a pale line on the back.

Grass lizard (*Chamaesaura miopropus*): 35–55cm (13.75–21.75in)
This species lives in the marshy savannahs of southern Tanzania and western Zambia. At first glance the lizard looks more like a snake. The forelimbs are tiny and very hard to see, while the hind limbs are longer and have a single toe equipped with a claw. The grass lizard moves over the ground with a curving motion like a snake's. This locomotion allows the grass lizard to chase its insect prey through the grass. This species is viviparous (it does not lay eggs but gives birth to its young instead). Births occur during the rainy season. Most females produce about six offspring each year.

Long-tailed seps (*Tetradactylus ellenbergeri*): 20–30cm (8–12in)
Ellenberger's long-tailed seps is a lizard, but it is often mistaken for a snake. It lives in just a few pockets of damp savannah across southern Africa. The forelimbs are absent altogether and the back legs are little more than spikes. From above the seps is a brown-green colour, making it hard to spot among the low-growing plants.

Tree agama

Acanthocercus atricollis

Tree agamas are found across Central and eastern Africa. They occupy woodland habitats, which are increasingly becoming fragmented, as a result of which the tree agama population is split into small pockets. They eat mainly flying insects, plucking them from the air with their large mouths. However, the lizards also eat insects crawling along branches and in some cases they will take small frogs and other lizards.

If threatened, the lizard opens its mouth to display a startling orange lining. Many humans have suffered painful bites from this otherwise harmless agama.

Male agamas are easy to see among the branches with their bright breeding coloration. They display to females by clinging to vertical trunks and nodding their bright blue heads continuously. Once a female has mated and is no longer receptive to the males, she develops orange spots along the spine. When the rainy season arrives, these gravid (egg-carrying) females climb to the ground to lay their dozen eggs in a small hole.

Distribution: Eastern and Central Africa.
Habitat: Woodlands.
Food: Flying insects.
Size: 20–35cm (8–13.75in).
Maturity: Unknown.
Breeding: Eggs laid underground during rainy season.
Life span: Unknown.
Status: Common.

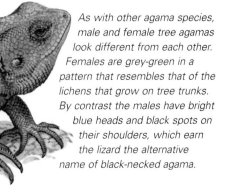

As with other agama species, male and female tree agamas look different from each other. Females are grey-green in a pattern that resembles that of the lichens that grow on tree trunks. By contrast the males have bright blue heads and black spots on their shoulders, which earn the lizard the alternative name of black-necked agama.

Boulenger's scrub lizard

Nucrus boulengeri

Boulenger's scrub lizard lives in broken, rocky habitats in Kenya, Tanzania and Mozambique. As the lizard's name suggests, these dry areas support scrub – a mixture of brush and grass. The tail, which is twice as long as the body, is the lizard's most striking feature. There is also a collar of enlarged scales around the neck.

Boulenger's scrub lizard is a ground-living animal, sheltering in burrows at night and during the hottest parts of the day. This species is also described as a wall lizard because it substitutes rocky areas for stone walls and roofs. The scrub lizard may stay out of sight for long periods and emerges on to the surface only when there are plenty of insects to eat. The lizard is especially active when winged termites emerge from their underground nests in search of new mates and to set up new colonies.

Little is known about the reproductive behaviour of Boulenger's scrub lizards. They lay eggs rather than give birth to their young, although the size of the clutch is unclear. Juvenile lizards have red tails and a pale stripe along the back. These colours fade as the lizard matures.

Distribution: Eastern Africa from Kenya to Mozambique.
Habitat: Rocks and grasslands. Also seen in walls and roofs.
Food: Termites in their winged dispersal form and other insects.
Size: 12–18cm (4.75–7in).
Maturity: Unknown.
Breeding: Lays eggs but clutch size is uncertain.
Life span: Unknown.
Status: Common.

Boulenger's scrub lizard lives in and on the ground among rocks, dead leaves and soil. Its brown back has cream and black blotches that break up the outline of its body, making it hard to spot while it forages.

Jackson's forest lizard

Adolfus jacksoni

Jackson's forest lizards live in forest clearings and edges within East Africa in Kenya, Uganda, Rwanda and the extreme east of the Democratic Republic of Congo. They are most common in the outer regions of the colourfully named Bwindi Impenetrable Forest, the largest area of pristine forest in East Africa. Most of the Impenetrable Forest, which is also known as The Place of Darkness, is located in the southern habitat where it forms a large protected reserve. The forest is home to one of the greatest diversities of wildlife in Africa. A population of mountain gorillas is perhaps its most famous residents.

The forest is a rugged highland region which receives a lot of rain throughout the year. Jackson's forest lizards are often seen on rocks and fallen trunks in sunny places between the trees. They hunt for small insects while clambering over obstacles and over the ground. Members of the species that live outside of the dense forest sometimes forage for food in living trees. However, this behaviour is not seen in forested areas, presumably because other species already exploit that niche.

Little is known about the breeding behaviour of Jackson's forest lizards. The females lay a few eggs (about five) in rocky crevices. Often many females will select the same location in which to lay their eggs, and so a large collection of eggs develops, sometimes numbering in the hundreds. The eggs are of different ages so hatchlings crawl over recently laid eggs to leave the nest. The eggs take about two months to hatch.

Distribution: Mainly southern Uganda, but also Kenya, Burundi, Rwanda and eastern fringe of Democratic Republic of Congo.
Habitat: Forest edges and clearings.
Food: Small insects and other invertebrates.
Size: 15–25cm (6–9.75in).
Maturity: Unknown.
Breeding: Several females lay their eggs in communal nests thoughout the year.
Life span: Unknown.
Status: Common.

This small lizard has a large head and long snout. The tail is longer than the body. Dozens of rows of small scales form a speckled pattern on the back and flanks. The belly is yellow.

Angolan rough-scaled lizard

Ichnotropis bivittata

Distribution: Southern Africa.
Habitat: Dry savannah.
Food: Small insects.
Size: 17–20cm (6.75–8in).
Maturity: 8 months.
Breeding: A dozen eggs laid between April and June.
Life span: Unknown, probably less than 3 years.
Status: Common.

The Angolan rough-scaled lizard is found across southern Africa from Angola and Namibia in the west to the southern region of Tanzania. It lives in dry grassland areas.

The lizard is active during the day and hunts down small insects among the short grasses. They are fast-moving creatures and rush their prey before they can escape.

Living in such an open and exposed habitat means that life is short for these lizards. They mature within eight months in time for the start of the breeding season in April and May. Many will die soon after that from the stress of competing for mates or producing eggs. Females bury their eggs in soft sand beneath bushes.

Few members of this species will survive beyond two years. Predation is also a major threat, especially for displaying males. Jackals, long-legged secretary birds and airborne birds of prey pick the lizards off as they attempt to attract the attention of females.

As its name implies, the scales of this lizard are strongly keeled: that is, they have a central ridge. The lizard also has distinctive stripes running down its flanks. The neck is a rich yellow. Juveniles are less brightly coloured.

Dalmatian algyroides (*Algyroides nigropunctatus*): 14cm (5.5in)
This small lizard lives on the Dalmatian coast of the Adriatic Sea in south-eastern Europe. Its range runs from Slovenia to northern Greece. The lizards are red-brown and have long, thin tails. The males are longer than the females and also have vibrant blue throats and eyes. The belly of both sexes is orange. The Dalmatian algyroides lives in a range of habitats. It is a good climber and is often found in trees and on walls. It tends to prefer shaded areas.

Steppe runner (*Eremias arguta*): 15cm (6in)
A plump lizard with a pointed snout, it lives in dry areas with sparse vegetation. It is a frequent visitor to sand dunes. Its range runs from the Danube Delta area in eastern Romania around the Black Sea to southern Ukraine. The steppe runner is capable of crossing the ground at a high speed, often to get out of sight as quickly as possible. The lizard hides under stones or in the burrows of rodents and also digs its own burrows at the base of small bushes.

Large psammodromus (*Psammodromus algirus*): 24cm (9.5in)
This lizard from Portugal, Spain and southern France has a tail that is at least twice as long as its body. It lives in bushy areas and hunts in the leaf litter. This species has pockets on the sides of the neck that fill with mites and other tiny skin parasites. The function of the pockets is believed to be to attract these parasites away from other parts of the lizard's body, where they might do more damage.

Spiny-footed lizard

Acanthodactylus erythrurus

Spiny-footed lizards live in the southern Iberian Peninsula and the Mahgreb region of north-west Africa. Although they are absent from full-blown desert areas, the lizards occupy very dry sandy areas on which there is a thin covering of scrub. The species is often found in large numbers, with 200 individuals crowding together in certain places.

The lizards sometimes come into completely open habitats, such as beaches or rocky areas, which is where people are most likely to come across them. The lizards are not particularly shy, but if one feels threatened it leaves the area with a series of short sprints in a straight line, pausing several times with its tail raised during its retreat. It takes refuge under bushes and may retreat farther into a spiny bush or short burrow. When resting, the spiny-footed lizards raise their forefeet. They also raise their feet in turn while basking in an attempt to reduce the heat their body absorbs from the ground.

Distribution: Southern Spain and Portugal and north-western Africa.
Habitat: Dry sandy areas.
Food: Ants, beetles and bugs.
Size: 24cm (9.5in).
Maturity: 18 months.
Breeding: Single clutch of 8 eggs.
Life span: 3 years.
Status: Common.

Adult spiny-footed lizards have pale stripes running along their back. The under parts are white. Juvenile lizards have black and white striped backs and a red tail. The red tail may remain even when the lizard matures. The lizard is named after a comb of spines on its hind legs.

Tropical girdled lizard

Cordylus tropidosternum

This little lizard is named after the way its scales are arranged in overlapping rings, or girdles, resembling in some ways the tiles on a roof. The arrangement of the scales makes the lizard very rough to the touch. Most individuals have a wide dark band running from the top of the head and along each side to the groin.

The tropical girdled lizard lives in dry woodland areas of Central and southern Africa. The most northerly part of its range is the coastal forests of southern Kenya.

The lizards spend most of their time clambering through trees looking for food. Their diet consists of large insects, such as moths, and spiders. They are also partial to the winged termites that swarm through the forests from time to time.

By night, the tropical girdled lizard rests in a tree hollow. It rarely moves too far from this den when feeding during the day. In dry spells, it may stay in the den for days on end. The lizard also becomes dormant during the short winter in southern Africa. The breeding season follows this dormancy.

The females do not lay eggs. Instead, they keep the eggs inside their body, and the young hatch out inside. The young look like miniature versions of adults.

The tropical girdled lizard's armoured and prehistoric appearance makes the species a favourite among reptile enthusiasts. As a result, the wild population is being reduced by people collecting them for sale as pets. Many die before they even arrive at the pet shop.

Distribution: Central, eastern and southern Africa. Its most northern occurence is southern Kenya, the most southerly is South Africa.
Habitat: Dry woodlands.
Food: Spiders and insects.
Size: 13–16cm (5–6.25in).
Maturity: About 3 years but longer in areas with less food.
Breeding: Mating season occurs after winter dormancy. Up to 4 young born in rainy season between 4 and 8 months after mating. Young are born over several days.
Life span: Unknown.
Status: Vulnerable.

Rough-scaled plated lizard

Gerrhosaurus major

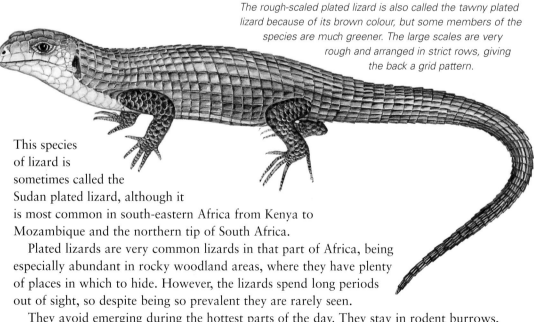

The rough-scaled plated lizard is also called the tawny plated lizard because of its brown colour, but some members of the species are much greener. The large scales are very rough and arranged in strict rows, giving the back a grid pattern.

This species of lizard is sometimes called the Sudan plated lizard, although it is most common in south-eastern Africa from Kenya to Mozambique and the northern tip of South Africa.

Plated lizards are very common lizards in that part of Africa, being especially abundant in rocky woodland areas, where they have plenty of places in which to hide. However, the lizards spend long periods out of sight, so despite being so prevalent they are rarely seen.

They avoid emerging during the hottest parts of the day. They stay in rodent burrows, termite mounds or rocky crevices. The lizards are well protected from predators by their rough scales. They rarely bite, but whip attackers with their jagged tails.

These reptiles are omnivorous: they eat both plant and animal foods. They prefer larger insects but also eat worms, smaller lizards and soft fruits. The rough-scaled plated lizard is a popular pet because it is relatively large yet docile and easy to maintain.

Distribution: Eastern Africa from eastern Kenya to northern South Africa.
Habitat: Rocky hills and areas of semi-desert and scrublands.
Food: Insects, worms, fruits and flowers.
Size: 30–40cm (12–15.75in).
Maturity: Unknown.
Breeding: Up to 6 eggs, each 12cm (4.75in) wide, are buried in a shallow hole that is dug underneath a rock or log. Hatchlings are 10cm (4in) long.
Life span: Unknown.
Status: Common.

Sand lizard

Lacerta agilis

Distribution: Central and eastern Europe.
Habitat: Meadows, steppe, dunes and hedgerows.
Food: Insects.
Size: 18–19cm (7–7.5in).
Maturity: 2–3 years.
Breeding: A dozen eggs buried in a sunny area.
Life span: 12 years.
Status: Common.

The sand lizard is found throughout much of Europe and central Asia. It is one of the few reptiles to live in Britain. It survives in two tiny pockets, one on the south coast and the other in the north-west. In both places, the lizards live in sandy heathlands. Elsewhere in the lizard's range, which extends from southern Sweden to the Middle East, the lizards are found in similar dry habitats.

During courtship, male sand lizards fight over access to the biggest and most fertile females. Both males and females will mate with several partners during a season, as a result of which the eggs laid by a female will have been fertilized by more than one male. Females lay up to 14 eggs in a nest dug in dry, sandy soil close to vegetation. In the northern parts of the lizard's range these nests are located in sunlit areas to ensure that the eggs do not get too cold. In warmer parts, females may be able to produce two clutches in a single year.

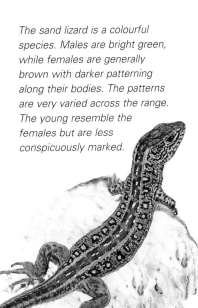

The sand lizard is a colourful species. Males are bright green, while females are generally brown with darker patterning along their bodies. The patterns are very varied across the range. The young resemble the females but are less conspicuously marked.

Giant plated lizard (*Gerrhosaurus validus*): 69cm (27in)
This huge species of plated lizard lives on the rocky hills in southern Africa and uses the crevices between rocks as places to hide. During midsummer, four or five large, oval eggs are laid between rocks and covered with soil. Giant plated lizards are dark brown or black, with yellow spots and shields on their heads. Their throats are whitish and their bellies are light brown. Males develop a pinkish-purple hue on their throats, chins and the sides of their heads during the breeding season.

Ocellated lizard (*Lacerta lepida*): 50cm (19.75in)
This is one of the largest lizards living in Europe. Rare sightings of individuals 80cm (31.5in) long have been recorded. About two-thirds of the lizard's length is made up by its tail. Ocellated lizards live in Portugal, Spain, the south of France and northern Italy. Adults have blue spots on their flanks against a grey-brown background. In the south of their range members of this lizard live in highland habitats. Farther north they are common residents of olive groves and vineyards. They spend most their time on the ground and often climb wall crevices to escape notice.

Balkan green lizard (*Lacerta trilineata*): 45cm (17.5in)
This species is very similar to the more widespread green lizard. However, it tends to be slightly larger and is found in drier areas of south-east Europe and Turkey. The two species often occur in the same areas, each one being specialized to either arid or damp habitats.

Green lizard

Lacerta bilineata

The green lizard is found across most of southern Europe as far north as the Channel Islands and east through Austria to southern Ukraine. It also lives on a few of the Mediterranean islands.

The lizard is found in the dense vegetation that grows on the edges of fields and in disturbed areas of woodland. In the southern portion of their range, where the climate is dry, the lizards are confined to damp areas, such as highland meadows.

The green lizard hunts among the branches of low bushes, looking for insects and spiders. It is most active in the cool of early morning and evening. In the middle of hot days and at night the lizards retreat to shadier parts of the bush or into crevices or disused rodent burrows.

Female green lizards lay about 20 eggs. These hatch out after between 7 and 15 weeks, depending on the climate. The eggs take longer to develop in colder areas.

Distribution: Southern and eastern Europe.
Habitat: Thickets and hedges.
Food: Insects.
Size: 40cm (15.75in).
Maturity: 18 months.
Breeding: Two dozen eggs laid.
Life span: Unknown.
Status: Common.

This large, slender lizard has a tail that is more than twice the length of its body. As the name suggests, the males of this lizard are a bright emerald-green. The females may also be green but less vibrantly so. Other females are brown with a blotchy pattern.

Viviparous lizard

Lacerta vivipara

One of the most common European reptiles, the viviparous lizard is found across northern and central Europe and into northern parts of Asia. It is the only reptile found in Ireland. This indicates that it was the fastest reptile to broaden its range back northwards when temperatures increased following the last Ice Age, reaching Ireland before the Irish Sea rose up and engulfed the land-bridge connecting it with mainland Britain and the rest of Europe.

Viviparous means "live birth" – viviparous lizards don't lay eggs, but give birth to fully formed young. These miniatures of their parents are completely independent from birth, receiving no help from their mothers. However, by keeping the eggs within their bodies until they have hatched, the female viviparous lizards have already given their progeny a head-start, since they don't have to lie prone and defenceless as eggs.

The viviparous lizard is a common sight in the UK, for those that look closely enough. Up close they are striking animals, with delicate patterns of coloured scales. However, from a distance they blend easily into the background, making life difficult for kestrels and other predators.

The skin of the viviparous lizard is patterned with a mosaic of brown, dark green and bronze scales.

Distribution: Northern and central Europe and northern Asia.
Habitat: Wide-ranging habitats including woodland, marshland, heath, sand dunes, hedgerows, bogs and rubbish dumps.
Food: Insects, spiders, snails and earthworms.
Size: 10–16cm (4–6.5in).
Maturity: Not known.
Breeding: 3–10 live young born between June and September.
Life span: 8 years.
Status: Common.

European glass lizard

Ophisaurus apodus

Distribution: South-east Europe and south-west Asia.
Habitat: Open woodland and fields.
Food: Molluscs, insects and small vertebrates.
Size: Up to 1.2m (4ft).
Maturity: 2–3 years.
Breeding: 8–10 eggs.
Life span: 60 years.
Status: Common.

European glass lizards belong to a family of lizards that have given up the pedestrian way of life, preferring instead to crawl around on their bellies in the manner of snakes. Indeed, having lost their legs almost entirely, glass lizards are often mistaken for snakes. Nevertheless, they can be identified as lizards due to their having ears and eyelids, features which snakes do not possess.

Their body also differs from that of a snake by the length of its tail. The tail of a snake – the portion of the body behind the anus and genitals – usually only makes up a small proportion of its body length, whereas two-thirds of a glass lizard's body is made up of tail. The tail also gives rise to the glass lizard's name. Like other lizards, this species is able to shed its tail when threatened – a process called autotomy. However, unlike those of other lizards, the tail then breaks up into lots of small pieces, as though it were shattering like glass. As the actual body of the snake is not much bigger than one of the pieces of tail, people used to believe that these lizards were entirely made from glass.

Not a snake but a lizard with no legs, the European glass lizard has a groove down each side of its body. These legless reptiles are fairly common in fields and highly wooded areas, where they hunt hard-shelled snails and insects.

African fire skink

Lygosoma fernandi

The fire skink really lives up to its name, with its shiny scales of many colours – from black and blue to red and gold, including stripes that look like fire on their sides. These fiercely territorial lizards dart among the dead leaves of the forest floor, looking like living flames.

The African fire skink is a medium-sized member of the varied and widespread skink family. It is also one of the most spectacular-looking members of that group. When not in breeding coloration, the male's sides are bright red, merging into the copper colour on its back. This is very impressive in its own right. However, come the breeding season, the red colours extend up on to the back, becoming suffused with the copper and resulting in a brilliant orange. Meanwhile, both pairs of legs darken to near black, with a few light spots, and pearlescent stripes extend from the throat right down the lizard's body. Even juveniles are brightly coloured, having intense light blue tails, which slowly fade as they grow older.

Adult fire skinks are territorial, defending their burrows in the leaf litter on the forest floor from invaders. Their bright colours make them highly visible to predators, so they really need handy bolt holes for when trouble appears.

Distribution: West Africa.
Habitat: Tropical forest.
Food: Invertebrates.
Size: 30cm (12in).
Maturity: 1 year.
Breeding: Female fire skinks lay 6 clutches of 4–9 eggs per year.
Life span: 10 years.
Status: Threatened.

Four-toed burrowing skink (*Sepsina tetradactyla*): 10–15cm (4–6in)
This species of skink lives in the decaying leaves that litter the forest floors of Tanzania and Burundi. These habitats are most common in highland areas. The four-toed burrowing skink has an elongated body, even for a skink. The tip of the tail is blunt and round and of similar dimensions to the head. This feature ensures that a predator will be easily confused as to which end to attack first. The limbs are tiny and barely used as the skink writhes through the deep leaves in search of insects.

Peter's writhing skink (*Lygosoma afrum*): 16–23cm (6.25–9in)
This long, sausage-shaped skink lives in the savannah regions of East Africa. It has very short forelegs and moves by wriggling its body. It eats termites and other insects living in the rotting wood. The tube-shaped body is an adaptation to burrowing. When weather is inclement or when danger is near, the skink worms its way into sandy soil. Its body is a pale red-brown to match the colour of the ground. Unusually for a skink, this species has movable eyelids.

Fat-tailed gecko (*Hemitheconyx caudicinctus*): Females 20cm (8in); males 25cm (9.75in)
Fat-tailed geckos are striking in appearance, with alternating thick bands of colour. They live in dry grassland and woodland in western Africa. If the lizard re-grows its tail following an attack, the tail is much shorter and fatter than before, resembling its head. Again, this is a defence mechanism, designed to fool predators.

Moorish gecko

Tarentola mauritanica

Moorish geckos are Europe's most common geckos. They are also found throughout North Africa. Like many of the world's most successful animals, they have learned to live alongside people and even benefit from their presence. They spend most of their time literally hanging around houses. Geckos are fantastic climbers, even able to climb up panes of glass and hang from ceilings. They are able to do this because of their toes, which have many tiny suction pads on their undersides. The pads actually comprise thousands of micro-hairs, which form a temporary molecular bond with the surface being walked over.

These geckos are usually easy to spot, since they tend to congregate at night around wall lights, waiting for their favourite food – moths – to arrive. As the moths are drawn in by the light, they become easy prey.

These are the only lizards to possess voiceboxes, which allow them to produce the "gecko" calls from which they get their name. They also produce a "tutting" noise, used between rival males.

Distribution: Mediterranean regions.
Habitat: Dry, rocky areas.
Food: Mainly insects.
Size: 15cm (6in).
Maturity: 2 years.
Breeding: Up to 6 clutches of 1–6 eggs per year.
Life span: Not known.
Status: Common, but declining due to collection for the pet trade.

The Moorish gecko is also known as the crocodile gecko because of its rough scales.

Armadillo lizard

Cordylus cataphractus

The armadillo lizard lives in groups of up to 30 animals. Small groups, with nine lizards or fewer, are usually all females with just one adult male. Larger groups contain more males. They are active during the day, searching for insects in the dry desert areas in which they live. Their sandy colour keeps them hidden from birds and other reptiles, and their spines act as a protective armour.

If they are out in the open, away from cover, and are threatened by a predator, these lizards will roll themselves into balls like armadillos, keeping a tight hold of their tails with their mouths. This exposes their tough, horny skin and spines, making it difficult for a predator to eat the lizard. If the lizard has enough time, or is close to cover, it will squeeze into a small crevice in nearby rocks. Because it has a flattened body, few predators are able to follow it into its hideaway.

Armadillo lizards have flattened bodies and broad heads. The body is sandy yellow or brown and covered with spiny scales. They have either yellow or violet throats, embellished with brown blotches. When threatened, these lizards roll into a tight ball, creating a spiny ring.

Distribution: Southern tip of Africa.
Habitat: Dry, desert areas with plants able to withstand drought and high temperatures.
Food: Insects, spiders and other invertebrates.
Size: 7.5–16.5cm (3–6.5in); 400–800g (0.9–1.75lb).
Maturity: Not known.
Breeding: Females give birth to 1 or 2 young lizards towards the end of summer.
Life span: Not known.
Status: Uncommon.

Atlantic lizard

Gallotia atlantica

The Atlantic lizard is one of the seven lizard species living on the Canary Islands, which are located off the coast of north-west Africa. This particular species lives on Lanzarote, Fuerteventura and several of the smaller islands. It is found in a range of habitats, from sand dunes and cultivated fields and gardens to the barren malpaís or lava fields that scar the islands.

In vegetated areas, the lizards forage for insects. They also pick over the remains of small birds and other warm-blooded prey that have been discarded by the islands' falcons and other hunting birds. However, in more barren areas, most notably on the lava flows that cover the islands, insects are very rare. Those insects that do live there are very hard to catch. In these places the lizards survive by eating only plant food, mainly fruits and flowers.

Lizards that survive on a diet of insects are smaller than those that eat plants. The reason for this size difference is the quality of the animals' diet. Plants contain a lot less nutrition than insects. As a result the lizards must eat more of them. Being larger allows the plant-eating lizards to consume enough food. The larger reptiles also lose heat more slowly than smaller ones and so they require less food to function efficiently.

Males court females by approaching them slowly, nodding their heads, with their throats inflated. About a month after mating, the females lay two or three clutches of eggs, each containing a few eggs. Babies hatch out between seven and ten weeks later.

The Atlantic lizard is a medium-sized species. The males are larger than the females. Males have blue blobs on their flanks, while the colouring of females and young males is a more muted green and brown. This species and the other Canary Island lizards are most closely related to the psammodromus species of Spain and Portugal.

Distribution: Eastern Canary Islands including Lanzarote, Fuerteventura, Lobos, Graciosa, Alegranza, Monte Clara and Roque del Este.
Habitat: Sand dunes and lava flows.
Food: Insects, carrion and plants.
Size: 22cm (8.75in).
Maturity: 1 year.
Breeding: 10–15 eggs produced in 2–3 clutches per year.
Life span: 5 years.
Status: Common.

Snake-eyed skink

Ablepharus kitaibelii

Distribution: South-eastern Europe.
Habitat: Oak and chestnut woodlands.
Food: Insects.
Size: 13cm (5in).
Maturity: 2 years.
Breeding: Up to 6 eggs buried in soil.
Life span: 3 years.
Status: Common.

Snake-eyed skinks live in south-eastern Europe. The northern limit of their range is Slovakia. To the south they are found throughout the Balkans as far east as the mouth of the Danube.

In most places, the snake-eyed skink lives in dry woodland habitats, where it hides among fallen leaves and under logs and stones. In southern areas of its range, however, it is also found in grasslands. In these habitats the skink appears to aestivate (become dormant in the high summer). Adult snake-eyed skinks use their forelimbs to pull themselves along, but most of their locomotion is through slithering in a manner similar to snakes.

During mating, a male bites the flanks of his mate. She produces between about four eggs shortly afterwards, which are buried in soil. The eggs double in size over their nine-week development, at which point the young hatch.

The snake-eyed skink is a tiny lizard. As with all skinks, it has a small head and a thick, rounded body. The legs are very short, and almost useless in larger individuals. The eyes have transparent eyelids, which are always closed, so the skink is unable to blink. This is a feature shared with snakes and other skink species.

Ibiza wall lizard (*Podarcis pityusensis*):
20cm (8in)
Native to the Balearic Islands, this is a slim, agile and very hardy lizard, mainly inhabiting barren, sun-baked rocks, often by the seashore. It can also be found combing neglected gardens, rubbish dumps and waste ground for scraps to complement its usual diet of insects and some plant matter. The colouring of this lizard is variable but there seem to be two predominant forms: those from Formentera have green backs with grey-brown sides, while those from Ibiza have brown backs and reddish sides.

Hierro giant lizard (*Gallotia simonyi*):
60cm (23.55in)
Once believed to be extinct but rediscovered in 1975, the Hierro giant lizard has at present only a small population of 150 individuals, living on the island of El Hierro in the Canary Islands. It is Europe's most endangered reptile. It feeds almost exclusively on only two types of plant. It is a large, stocky lizard with a broad head and pronounced jowls. The lizard has not coped well with the expansion of tourism in the Canaries.

Tenerife lizard (*Gallotia galloti*):
30cm (11.75in)
This species occupies the western Canary Islands. It resembles the Atlantic lizard in colouring and sexual differences, but members of this species are longer and more robust. Like large Atlantic lizards, this species has a mainly plant diet. The lizard forages in a range of habitats but is less common in damper areas such as woodland or heathland.

Namib web-footed gecko

Palmatogecko rangei

As their name suggests, the Namib web-footed geckos have webbed toes on their long, spindly legs. The webbing is not for swimming, not in water anyway: the wide feet stop the lizard from sinking into soft sand. They are also used for digging burrows. The webs are not simply flaps of skin: they contain tiny muscles and can be formed into a scoop for shovelling fine sand. As with other geckos, the toes of this species have intricately folded pads, which are used to grip while climbing over rocks.

Namib web-footed geckos are nocturnal. By day they keep cool in deep burrows in the sand but at night, when the conditions on the surface have cooled, the geckos emerge to hunt. Their diet consists of insects and spiders.

Breeding takes place between April and May. The females lay hard-shelled eggs, which are buried in pairs or singly on occasion, over the next few months. The eggs' hard shell is made from chalky calcium compounds like those in a bird's egg. The shell stops the eggs drying out in the desert heat. A total of about ten eggs is laid. They take eight weeks to hatch.

Distribution: Namibia.
Habitat: Desert sand dunes.
Food: Insects and spiders.
Size: 10–15cm (4–6in).
Maturity: 1 year.
Breeding: About 10 eggs laid in May–August.
Life span: 5 years.
Status: Common.

Namib web-footed geckos have almost transparent skin. The only colourful features are the eyes. These are covered in clear and fixed eyelids, which have to be cleaned regularly with the tongue.

Mediterranean gecko

Hemidactylus turcicus

This species is typical of Old World geckos (those living in Europe, Asia and Africa): it has eyes with a vertical pupil, no movable eyelids and pads on the tips of its toes. The pads do not extend to the very end of the toes. The vertical pupil is a more efficient system than a circular pupil for controlling the amount of light getting into the eye. Many nocturnal animals have vertical pupils.

Mediterranean geckos are found all the way around the sea of the same name. They are generally found close to the coast, where the habitats are less arid, although the geckos do follow river valleys a long way inland in certain areas.

The geckos are nocturnal and are often seen in the evening and at night, scurrying up walls and across other rocky surfaces. On cooler days they can also be spotted sunning themselves. They are able to scale vertical surfaces, even glass and other smooth materials, by gripping with the pads on their toes. These pads feel sticky but, contrary to popular belief, they do not exude any adhesive liquids. The grip is due to hundreds of minute folds on the pad's lower surfaces. These increase the pad's surface area hugely and allow the toe to grip on to the slightest deformity.

Mediterranean geckos communicate with each other using a series of calls, and during the breeding season males call females to their territories. The females lay up to six eggs in two or three clutches each year. The eggs are laid under dead leaves or in crevices. They all hatch within three months.

Distribution: All parts of the Mediterranean coast and introduced to the Canary Islands and the Americas.
Habitat: Rocky areas, walls, roofs and inside houses in coastal areas. Only found inland close to a river.
Food: Insects such as moths, cockroaches and beetles.
Size: 15cm (6in).
Maturity: 6 months.
Breeding: 2–3 small clutches of eggs laid under stones.
Life span: 3 years.
Status: Common.

European leaf-toed gecko

Euleptes europaea

This tiny species of gecko lives mainly on Corsica, Sardinia and a few other islands in the western Mediterranean. The lizards are also found in tiny pockets of mainland along the French and Italian coasts.

Leaf-toed geckos are nocturnal and are rarely seen. They hunt for prey on rocky surfaces but avoid places associated with people. They also avoid cultivated areas. Being an island species, they are at risk from disruption to their habitat, which causes concern for conservationists. Nevertheless, these geckos are present in large numbers in rocky places with plenty of crevices in which to hide.

The gecko stalks its insect prey, at first slowly creeping up on its prey and then making a dash for the kill. The lizard is also capable of making mighty leaps for an animal of its size.

Like other geckos, the leaf-toed gecko calls to attract mates. Males of this species use a "tsi tsi tsi" call to lure females. The females lay small clutches of eggs, numbering just one or two eggs at a time. In warmer parts of their range they may manage three clutches a year, but a single clutch is the norm in highland areas. The eggs take between 8 and 13 weeks to hatch. The hatchlings are about 3cm (1.25in) long. They look like miniature adults.

This is the smallest species of gecko in Europe. It has relatively short legs compared to the size of its body and tail. Climbing pads are located at the tips of its toes. Females have thicker tails than males.

Distribution: Corsica, Sardinia and smaller Mediterranean islands, including those near the North African coast
Habitat: Rocky areas, such as drystone walls. Appears most common in areas with a lot of granite outcrops.
Food: Insects.
Size: 6cm (2.25in).
Maturity: 2–3 years.
Breeding: 1–2 eggs laid in rock crevices. Several geckos may use the same site and return to it each year.
Life span: 10 years, but double that when in captivity.
Status: Lower risk.

Tropical house gecko

Hemidactylus mabouia

Distribution: Sub-Saharan Africa; introduced to North and South America.
Habitat: Forests and human settlements.
Food: Insects.
Size: 10cm (4in).
Maturity: 1 year.
Breeding: Several clutches laid throughout year.
Life span: Unknown.
Status: Common.

This is one of the most common and widespread species of gecko in Africa. This species is now also common in tropical and subtropical parts of the Americas, having been introduced to the Amazon from Africa by human migrations. In the wilds of Africa these geckos live in forests, where they shelter out of sight under loose flaps of bark. However, as their name suggests, they have also become common in human settlements including even the largest cities.

House geckos are nocturnal hunters. They have wide toe pads, which make the toes sticky so that they can grip on to even very flat surfaces. House geckos often rest on tree trunks and on walls in a head-down position. This allows them to head for the safety of the forest floor (or another hiding place) should danger approach.

By day the geckos sleep on a leaf. Their skin is darker at these times and becomes lighter as they forage. Geckos that are hunting on whitewashed walls have been known to become very pale in response to the white background.

This common gecko has wide pads on its toes, which help them cling to vertical surfaces such as tree trunks and walls. The body is pale grey with several dark crossbars on the back. These markings begin to fade in bright light so the gecko becomes more difficult to see.

Gran Canaria gecko (*Tarentola boettgeri*): 12cm (4.75in)
This gecko species lives on Gran Canaria and El Hierro, two of the Canary Islands. A population also lives on the Selvages (tiny islands uninhabited by people to the north of the Canaries). The individuals on Gran Canaria are yellow, while those living elsewhere tend to be smaller and grey. Like the Tenerife gecko and the two other gecko species on the Canary Islands, this is a coastal animal. It is most often found when people turn over flat stones.

Eastern Canary gecko (*Tarentola angustimentalis*): 8cm (3in)
This gecko resembles the Moorish gecko more than the other species living on the other Canary Islands. It is very common on Fuerteventura, Lanzarote, Lobos and the small islands north of Lanzarote.

Kotschy's gecko (*Cyrtopodion kotschyi*): 10cm (4in)
Kotschy's gecko ranges from Albania and Greece to the Crimean Peninsula and southern Bulgaria. It lives in dry rocky areas. It is less of a climber than other European geckos and lacks the adhesive pads of other species. Nevertheless, it is very agile and darts over and around rough ground and is often found on walls. Males call females with a "chick" sound. The females lay just two eggs in cracks or under stones. These hatch after three or four months. The baby geckos are a fifth of their adult size, which they reach after two or three years.

Flat-headed gecko

Hemidactylus platycephalus

Flat-headed geckos live in East Africa. This part of the continent is also populated by the more widespread tropical house gecko. The two species are similar and are often found at the same location. Flat-headed geckos are also known as tree geckos (not to be confused with other tree geckos from other continents). The animal's wild habitat is dry forest, where its mottled colouring helps it to blend in with the lichen-covered trees. However, like its close relative the house gecko, the flat-headed species is also a common visitor to houses. It is more aggressive than the house gecko and will eat smaller geckos if provoked.

Males call females with a clicking sound. Females lay their eggs under bark or in tree hollows. They prefer to lay their eggs on baobab trees. Many choose the same places to deposit their eggs, and large communal nests are formed as a result.

This species has body colouring that looks very similar to the tropical house gecko. This poses a problem for observers, since the two live in the same habitats. However, the flat-headed gecko is larger and more robustly built.

Distribution: Eastern Africa.
Habitat: Woodlands.
Food: Moths and other large insects, also other lizards.
Size: 12–18cm (4.75–7in).
Maturity: 1 year.
Breeding: Eggs laid in communal nests.
Life span: Unknown.
Status: Common.

Yellow-headed dwarf day gecko

Lygodactylus picturatus

The yellow-headed dwarf day gecko's common name says it all: the males have a vibrant yellow head and neck. The species is small compared to other geckos; and it is one of the few African species to be active during the day. The species lives in the woodlands and coastal savannahs of East Africa.

Originally a tree-living lizard, the gecko is now a common resident of huts and other rural buildings. It is equipped with toe pads, which help it to grip as it scurries up trunks and walls and through the branches in search of insects. As well as insect food, the yellow-headed dwarf day gecko also laps nectar from flowers.

Being a diurnal species puts the yellow-headed dwarf day gecko at risk of being attacked by a bird of prey or small carnivore. The lizard employs a very simple strategy to avoid predators. When danger threatens, the gecko races around to the blind side of a tree trunk. It keeps the trunk between itself and the threat, often racing around several times before the predator gives up.

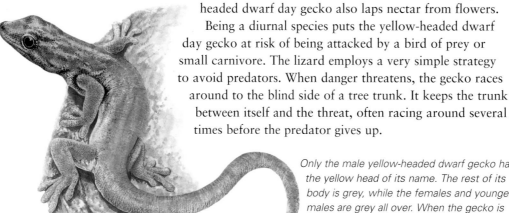

Only the male yellow-headed dwarf gecko has the yellow head of its name. The rest of its body is grey, while the females and younger males are grey all over. When the gecko is cool and resting, the grey background is covered by darker blotches and lines. These fade when the gecko is active.

Distribution: Southern Kenya and eastern Tanzania.
Habitat: Woodlands, coastal grasslands and villages.
Food: Ground- and tree-living insects and nectar from large flowers.
Size: 4–9cm (1.5–3.5in).
Maturity: Unknown.
Breeding: Clutches of two hard-shelled eggs laid at several times throughout the year.
Life span: Unknown.
Status: Common.

Common barking gecko

Ptenopus garrulus

The common barking gecko is known for the loud calls made by males as they stand at the entrance to their burrows at dusk. The males call as they prepare to set off to forage for food. The function of the call is to advertise the male's presence and so warn off rival males and attract females to the area.

The common barking gecko is a desert species. It lives in the Namib and Kalahari Deserts of Namibia and western Botswana. During the heat of the day the gecko rests in a deep burrow. It uses its long toes and blunt head to dig into the sand. The toes are fringed with flat scales, which make them a more useful shovel.

The wide feet also prevent the lizard from sinking into soft sand as it looks for food during the night. The gecko moves slowly, looking for insects such as beetles, ants and bugs. If it senses danger, the gecko freezes and relies on its camouflaged skin to hide it from a predator. If the threat remains close by the gecko will dash to its burrow or scurry into another nearby hiding place.

Common barking geckos mate at all times of the year. To save water the females lay just one or two eggs a year. These take from two to six months to hatch. The hatchlings are already large and look very similar to the adults.

This little gecko is a burrowing species and has a large round head to help it push through soft sandy soil. Its upper body is covered by a mottled red-brown pattern, which keeps it camouflaged while moving across sand.

Distribution: Namibia and Botswana.
Habitat: Areas of desert with loose sandy soil.
Food: Insects and other invertebrates.
Size: 6–10cm (2.25–4in).
Maturity: Unknown.
Breeding: Males bark at dusk to attract female mates. The female lays a single egg after each mating. Most females will mate once or twice a year, generally with different mates each time.
Life span: Unknown.
Status: Common.

East African lidded gecko

Holodactylus africanus

Distribution: Somalia, Kenya and Tanzania.
Habitat: Bush and scrub in dry areas.
Food: Insects and other invertebrates.
Size: 8–11cm (3.25–4.25in).
Maturity: 1 year.
Breeding: 2 hard-shelled eggs laid in soil.
Life span: Unknown.
Status: Common.

The East African lidded gecko lives in a few pockets of bush land in Somalia, Kenya and the extreme north of Tanzania. It is most common in the Masai Mara region. The lidded gecko is a burrowing species, using the claws on its large forefeet to dig into the ground. The gecko stays underground during the day to avoid the heat. It has retained movable eyelids as an adaptation to life in soft soil. The eyelids clean soil away from the eyes and can be shut completely if needed. The gecko also has a short and swollen tail, which might also aid its movement underground.

By night the gecko comes to the surface and creeps slowly through the bushes in search of its insect food. It is a ground-living species and does not climb into the bushes. Female East African lidded geckos lay just two hard-shelled eggs during each breeding season. These eggs are buried in sandy soil, protected from drying out by the shell. After laying, the females have no further dealings with their young. The hatchlings emerge after several weeks and look like small versions of the adults.

The East African lidded gecko is a stout lizard. It is different from most other African and European geckos in that it has movable eyelids, hence its common name. The species is also often referred to as the African clawed gecko due to the long claws on its forefeet.

Malagasy day gecko (*Phelsuma madagascariensis*): 22–30cm (8.75–12in)
This robust gecko lives in the forests of northern Madagascar. It is a vivid green with red-orange spots on its back. Males have a swelling at the base of the tail. The geckos cling to tree trunks and branches with large toe pads. They are also common visitors to homes, where they prey on insects. Like many geckos, members of this species stand with their head down when resting on a trunk or wall.

Elegant sand gecko (*Stenodactylus sthenodactylus*): 9–10.5cm (3.5–4.25in)
This small, slender gecko lives in the Sahara Desert of North Africa. It has a sand-coloured body speckled with grey. The gecko spends most of its life underground in a burrow, which it digs with its long toes. The gecko emerges on to the ground surface only at night, and during the hottest parts of the year it will stay in the cool of its burrow even at night.

Forest dwarf day gecko (*Lygodactylus gutturalis*): 5–9cm (2–3.5in)
Despite its name, this is a medium-sized gecko. It lives in the mountain forests on the western side of the Rift Valley and across Central Africa. It is a diurnal species and lacks the toe pads seen in most African geckos. It forages in leaf litter and on rotting logs. It eats insects especially ants. Breeding takes places at all times of the year, and females may produce several clutches each year. Each clutch contains two eggs with a hard shell.

Tete thick-toed gecko

Pachydactylus tetensis

Distribution: Southern Tanzania.
Habitat: Baobab trees.
Food: Insects.
Size: 13–18cm (5–7in).
Maturity: Unknown.
Breeding: Several pairs of eggs laid in wet season.
Life span: Unknown.
Status: Common.

The Tete thick-toed gecko lives in moist savannahs of southern Tanzania. It is one of several thick-toed geckos living in Africa. These velvety-skinned geckos are named after their extra-large toe pads.

The geckos are nocturnal and are chiefly arboreal lizards, that is they hunt for food in trees. The lizard is closely associated with the giant baobab trees that grow in this region. They shelter during the day in hollow areas inside the massive trunk and branches. In areas where trees are unavailable, the geckos use their large toe pads to scale rocky outcrops. They are often to be found resting in rocky crevices.

Breeding takes place at the start of the rains. Males attract females with calls made at dusk. The females lay several pairs of eggs over the following weeks. They take between two and three months to hatch.

As its named suggests, the Tete thick-toed gecko is noted for its large toe pads, or scansors. These are even larger than those of most geckos. The scansors are covered in bristled ridges, which make the toes excellent at gripping on to surfaces.

CROCODILES

The last living members of an ancient group known as the archosaurs, crocodiles are little changed from the days of the dinosaurs. The 25 surviving species stand as testament to the success of the crocodilian body design. Thick, scaly skin keeps predators at bay, a special respiratory system allows them to keep hidden underwater for up to five hours at a time, and powerful jaws make them fearsome predators.

Nile crocodile

Crocodylus niloticus

Nile crocodiles were once widespread in eastern and southern Africa, but are now scarcer. With powerful jaws, strong tails, a terrifying turn of speed and stealth belying their enormous size, these crocodiles are efficient killing machines. Nile crocodiles have evolved to be very good at fishing, and during the times of the year when fish migrate along the rivers they hunt cooperatively. Forming cordons across rivers, they herd the fish into shallow waters, where they can be picked off with ease.

Nile crocodiles are ecologically important as predators. They help to keep the environment in balance by eating catfish, which are predators themselves. By keeping the catfish numbers in check, Nile crocodiles allow the smaller fish, which are eaten by catfish, to thrive, providing food for more than 40 species of bird. In turn, bird droppings fertilize the waters, keeping them rich enough to support a large diversity of life.

The Nile crocodile's powerful body is covered in greyish plate-like scales. The powerful tail is ridged with two keels of scales.

Distribution: Africa (not in the north-west or Sahara region) and Madagascar.
Habitat: Rivers, freshwater marshes, estuaries and mangrove swamps.
Food: Fish, water birds and land mammals.
Size: 3.5–6m (11.5–19.75ft); up to 225kg (496lb).
Maturity: 10 years.
Breeding: 25–100 eggs laid in nest.
Life span: 45 years.
Status: Common.

Dwarf crocodile

Osteolaemus tetraspis

Distribution: West Africa.
Habitat: Freshwater lakes, swamps and slow-moving rivers.
Food: Fish, birds, crustaceans and occasionally small mammals.
Size: 1.8m (6ft).
Maturity: 6 years.
Breeding: Clutches of up to 20 eggs.
Life span: 40 years.
Status: Vulnerable.

Like other crocodilians, female dwarf crocodiles make very attentive mothers. Laying their eggs in mounds of rotting vegetation on the shore, the females guard them fiercely for the three months it takes for them to incubate. As hatching time arrives, they dig the eggs out of the nests to help the hatchlings escape. They may even roll the eggs gently around in their mouth to break the shells open.

Once out of their eggs, the young face a journey fraught with danger down to the water, but the mothers are there to help again. With surprising gentleness, they pick up their babies in their mouths and flip them into their throat pouches, before carrying them down to the water.

Although adapted to life in water, dwarf crocodiles, like most crocodilians, make shelters on land. These are underground dens dug into the banks of rivers and lakes. They are connected to the outside world by entrances and exit tunnels, both of which can be several metres (tens of feet) long.

Dwarf crocodiles are also known as broad-fronted crocodiles, because of their broad, blunt snouts. People once thought they were cannibals as they carry their young in their mouths.

NON-VENOMOUS SNAKES

Most snakes do not have a venomous bite and are completely harmless to humans. The largest African snakes – the pythons – are non-venomous. They kill by squeezing their prey until their victims suffocate. Colubrids, typified by the grass snake of Europe, are the largest group of snakes. Most colubrids are non-venomous, although a few use their saliva to stun their prey.

Grass snake

Natrix natrix

Grass snakes have dark green bodies with black flecking and whitish-yellow collars around their necks. They inhabit Britain as far as the Scottish border counties.

The grass snake is the most common snake in Britain. It owes its success to its versatility, being able to hunt both on land and in the water. It prefers to prey on frogs, toads and fish, when it can. To acquire enough heat to be able to function properly, the grass snake has to spend much of its time basking in sunlight. However, this does leave it rather exposed to attack from birds of prey. Foxes, badgers and hedgehogs will also make a meal out of it if they get the chance, but this isn't easy. When threatened, a grass snake has a range of defensive tactics including loud hissing, inflating its body with air, biting, producing a foul-smelling secretion from its anus and playing dead.

Not only is keeping warm a problem for adult grass snakes, it is a problem for the eggs, too. If they are too cold they will take too long to develop, or not hatch at all. Female grass snakes combat this problem by travelling large distances to find suitable places to lay them. Heaps of rotting vegetation, such as compost heaps, are favoured.

Distribution: Europe from Scandinavia south to the Mediterranean, North Africa and central Asia east to Lake Baikal, Russia.
Habitat: Prefer damp grasslands, ditches and river banks.
Food: Amphibians, fish, small mammals and small birds.
Size: 0.7–2m (2.25–6.5ft).
Maturity: Not known.
Breeding: 8–40 eggs laid in June, July or August depending on the latitude, about 8 weeks after mating.
Life span: 20 years.
Status: Common.

Western whip snake

Coluber viridiflavus

The western whip snake ranges from the Spanish side of the Pyrenees to Brittany. It is also found in the foothills of the Alps and throughout Italy. The snake is also a resident of Corsica and Sardinia. Northern Croatia is the eastern limit of its range, where it gives way to its close relative, the Balkan whip snake.

The snake is found in thickly vegetated areas and woodlands. It shelters under rocks and in crevices and is often seen among the ruins of buildings. It is a diurnal hunter and is most common in the south of its range. The western whip snake hunts a variety of small animals, most commonly lizards and rodents. The snake hunts by sight and moves in for the kill very quickly. Smaller prey is grabbed in the mouth, while larger prey is constricted.

Distribution: South-western Europe, Corsica and Sardinia.
Habitat: Rocky areas, woodlands and shrubs.
Food: Lizards, small mammals, nesting birds and smaller snakes.
Size: 1.5m (5ft).
Maturity: 3–5 years.
Breeding: Up to 15 eggs laid each year.
Life span: 20 years.
Status: Common.

Adult western whip snakes have charcoal-grey backs with pale yellow bellies, though a few individuals have striking yellow markings.

African house snake

Lamprophis fuliginosus

African house snakes exhibit a large number of colour forms in different parts of Africa. In southern Tanzania, for example, the snake is known as the brown house snake, while in the north the snake is chocolate brown with white stripes and in Kenya it is called the sooty house snake.

This species of snake is one of the most successful of all the snakes in Africa. It lives virtually everywhere south and west of the Sahara Desert. However, many naturalists now consider the species to be a complex (a mixture of subspecies and completely separate species). The precise relationship between the continent's house snakes is uncertain, but the snakes appear in so many colour forms that it is likely that in the future they will be recognized as several distinct species.

African house snakes hunt for rodents and go wherever they can find prey. In the wild that takes them to most mild habitats, such as grasslands and woodlands. However, the snakes avoid deserts and dense jungle.

Rodents are common residents of human settlements too, and African house snakes have followed them. They are harmless to humans, and, since they ensure that rats and mice are kept to a minimum, most people are happy to see these snakes in their homes.

Distribution: Sub-Saharan Africa.
Habitat: Woodland and savannah.
Food: Rodents.
Size: 60–120cm (23.5–47.25in).
Maturity: 6 months.
Breeding: About 15 eggs laid in summer.
Life span: 8 years.
Status: Common.

Aesculapian snake

Elaphe longissima

The Aesculapian snake is reputed to be the species depicted on the rod of Aesculapius, widely recognized as a universal symbol of healing and often depicted on the side of ambulances. The snake itself is rather nondescript: it is long and slender with a small head and a uniformly grey body. The individual seen below has a juvenile colour pattern. Adults are more uniformly coloured.

This snake lives in central and eastern Europe. The western limit of its range is the Atlantic coast of France, although it is absent from the north of that country. To the east, the snake appears in Poland and Ukraine, and it is also found in northern Italy and southern Greece, home to the Greek god Aesculapius after which it is named. Another species, the Italian Aesculapian, lives in pockets of southern Italy. Some people suggest that these populations stem from Aesculapian snakes introduced to these areas by Romans for the snakes' reputed healing powers.

Aesculapian snakes live in shrubs and woodlands and tend to prefer dry and sunny areas. They are hunters and prey on small mammals, lizards and birds. Adults eat every three or four days. The rest of the time they lie hidden under stones and in tree hollows.

Males travel widely in search of mates and often fight other males for access to females. The females lay a dozen pear-shaped eggs in holes at the base of trunks. The eggs are then covered with dead leaves. As these decay they produce heat and keep the eggs warm.

Distribution: Northern Spain, southern France, Switzerland, northern Italy, Austria, Czech Republic, Poland and Ukraine. Also found in Turkey and east to northern Iran.
Habitat: Dry woodlands, especially in sunny clearings.
Food: Mice, voles and squirrels.
Size: 2m (6.5ft).
Maturity: About 3 years or when they reach 1m (3.25ft).
Breeding: Single clutch of elongated 12–18 eggs produced each year. Hatchlings are about 20cm (8in).
Life span: 20 years.
Status: Common.

Dice snake (*Natrix tessellata*): 80–130cm
(2.5–4.25ft)
A close relative of the grass snake, the dice
snake lives across southern and central Europe.
The western limits of its range are Italy in the
south and the Czech Republic in the north, and
the species is found as far east as Ukraine. The
species is also seen across southern Asia. Most
dice snakes have several large dark spots on
their pale skin. These spots, resembling the dots
on dice, are spaced regularly along the back.
Dice snakes are an aquatic species and live in
lowland rivers. They hunt underwater for fish
and amphibians. In several places dice snakes
occur in large numbers, with one snake found
in every two or three metres of river bank.

Montpellier snake (*Malpolon monspessulanus*):
2m (6.5ft)
Very fast and shy, Montpellier snakes will flee
at the first sign of a disturbance. They prefer
open and dry grassland with stones and slopes
exposed to sunlight, where they are active only
on warm and sunny days. They feed mainly on
lizards, which are hunted by sight.

False smooth snake (*Macroprotodon
cucullatus*): 60cm (23.5in)
The hooded snake lives in stony parts of Spain,
Portugal and North Africa. It preys on lizards,
which it attacks while they are sleeping,
paralyzing them with a mild venom harmless to
people. The hooded snake can move quickly and
if surprised it will throw its head back to show
its underside before fleeing for shelter.

Leopard snake

Elaphe situla

Lacking any significant amount of venom,
leopard snakes are constrictors – they
squeeze their prey to death. While the young
feed mainly on small lizards, adults prefer to
eat rodents. It is this fondness for rats and
mice that has made leopard snakes popular
pets in some parts of their range. Active by
day, leopard snakes are attracted to human
settlements by the abundance of rats and
mice to be found there. In some parts of
Greece, far from being feared, people used
to actively introduce these snakes into their
homes as a way of controlling pests.
They are even considered to
be good-luck charms by
superstitious people.

   The leopard snake's
good reputation, and
its ability to live
alongside humans,
has played highly
in its favour, and it
is still a common
sight throughout much
of its range in south-eastern Europe.

Distribution: South-eastern
Europe.
Habitat: Dry, rocky slopes.
Food: Small mammals and
birds.
Size: 1m (3.25ft).
Maturity: Not known.
Breeding: Clutches of 2–5
eggs laid in July or August.
Life span: 15 years.
   Status: Common.

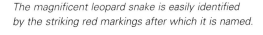

*The magnificent leopard snake is easily identified
by the striking red markings after which it is named.*

Smooth snake

Coronella austriaca

Distribution: Southern
England, France and northern
Spain and Portugal.
Habitat: Heathland and rocky
areas.
Food: Small mammals,
lizards and nestlings.
Size: 70cm (27.5in).
Maturity: 3–4 years.
Breeding: About 6 babies
born in autumn.
Life span: 18 years.
Status: Common.

Britain's rarest snakes, smooth snakes are restricted to just a handful of sandy heathlands in
southern England. Across the Channel, the snakes are found across France and in northern
and central parts of the Iberian Peninsula. These snakes are colubrids, sometimes described
as typical snakes, largely because they are the most numerous type. Like the great majority
of colubrids, they are not venomous at all: they kill their prey by constricting them with
their coils. Grass snakes and house snakes are also colubrids.

   Smooth snakes hunt during the day. They are secretive reptiles and will slither away into
cover if they detect something coming. They are also slow moving. They do not chase prey
but stalk it by following its scent and ambushing it as it emerges from a burrow.

   These snakes breed in spring. They
are the only European species to give
birth to their young rather than lay
eggs. The young take anywhere
between four and five months to
develop inside the mother.

*Smooth snakes are so called because, unlike grass snakes,
which have keel-shaped scales, they have flat, smooth scales.
Female smooth snakes are generally larger than the males.
The snakes are smaller in the northern parts of their range.*

Malagasy leaf-nosed snake

Langaha madagascariensis

Also known as twig mimic snakes, the habits of these peculiar looking snakes are not very well known. Lying motionless for hours in the canopy of the tropical forests of Madagascar, leaf-nosed snakes blend into their background incredibly well, becoming extremely difficult to spot. The snake is long and thin like many tree-living snakes, which helps it to spread its weight over a wide area. The slender brown body also creates the illusion that the snake is a twig, and this camouflage is perfected by the remarkable protrusions from the front of their faces. Males possess long, spiky projections, making them look even more like twigs, whereas the females have leaf-like structures instead.

Leaf-nosed snakes are only active for about one hour in every day, normally waiting until midday, the hottest part of the day, before rousing themselves to go hunting. By remaining inactive, the snakes save a lot of energy, which allows them to have long breaks between foraging trips. A decent meal can keep a leaf-nosed snake going for four days or more, before it feels the need to go hunting again. The snakes prey on small tree-living animals, such as frogs, lizards and nestlings.

The leaf-like snout of the female Malagasy leaf-nosed snake helps to camouflage it among leaves and twigs.

Distribution: Madagascar.
Habitat: Tropical rainforests and dry forests.
Food: Tree frogs, small birds and reptiles.
Size: 1m (3.25ft); 50–80g (0.1–0.2lb).
Maturity: Not known.
Breeding: Clutches of around 10 eggs laid in November or December.
Life span: 10 years.
Status: Common.

Common egg-eating snake

Dasypeltis scabra

Very few other snakes share the dietary habits of this fascinating species. Generally most active at night, egg-eating snakes hide out during the day in sheltered areas under rocks or logs. During the night they mainly prey on the eggs of weaverbirds. They are very adept at climbing trees to get to their nests. The snakes test the eggs with their tongues to check whether they have gone off or not. This is important because they cannot spit rotten eggs out once they have swallowed them.

Having found a fresh egg, a snake holds it tightly between its coils and slowly pushes its mouth over and around it. Once the egg is inside the snake's body, it passes farther down the throat until it meets a series of tooth-like structures attached to the vertebrae. These pierce the egg when the snake makes a series of sharp sideways movements of its head. The contents of the egg then drain out of the shell to be digested. Once empty, the egg shell is crushed up and regurgitated from the body. This ability to deal with shells is rare among snakes.

Egg-eating snakes can swallow eggs up to three times the size of their own heads.

Distribution: Southern and central parts of Africa, south of the Sahara Desert.
Habitat: Lowland evergreen forest.
Food: Birds' eggs.
Size: 50–90cm (19.75–35.5in).
Maturity: Not known.
Breeding: 6–25 eggs laid each year.
Life span: 14 years.
Status: Common.

Mole snake

Pseudaspis cana

Distribution: East and southern Africa.
Habitat: Grasslands.
Food: Moles and burrowing rodents.
Size: 1–1.80m (3.25–6ft).
Maturity: 4 years.
Breeding: 90 young born in summer.
Life span: 20 years.
Status: Common.

A grassland species, mole snakes specialize in hunting for burrowing mammals, such as moles (hence their name), although moles are actually only rarely taken. Most of the snake's prey are burrowing rodents, such as African mole rats.

These snakes have a painful bite but they are not a venomous species. They kill by constricting their prey with their thick, coiled body. Constricting does not crush an animal to death, although bones may be broken by it. Instead the snake steadily tightens its grip and as it does so the victim finds it harder and harder to draw breath. In the end the animal is suffocated to death.

After mating, female mole snakes do not lay eggs. Instead the eggs are retained inside the body of the female for several weeks. The young hatch out while still inside their mother, and are born soon afterwards. Mole snakes have been known to produce huge litters, with over 90 young born at once.

The mole snake is a large, thick-bodied snake. It has a slightly hook-shaped snout, which is typical of snakes that move through underground burrows. The juveniles are pale brown with cream and black markings. The adults are dark green.

Emerald snake (*Hapsidophrys smaragdina*): 60–110cm (23.5–43.25in)
The emerald tree snake is a forest snake. It lives in the Central African jungles, hunting in the trees for lizards and frogs. However, it is often found hunting in thick vegetation close to the ground, especially along banks of rivers. Like many arboreal snakes, the body is long and thin. The tail makes up 30 per cent of the body. (Although it is hard to differentiate, a snake's tail begins behind the genital opening.) The long body is an adaptation to a climbing lifestyle.

Splendid tree snake (*Rhamnophis aetiopissa*): 1–1.5m (3.25–5ft)
The splendid tree snake is a large tree snake living in the lowland rainforests of Central Africa. It has a green body with a brown stripe down the back and black and yellow bands and stripes on either side. It hunts for lizards and frogs by moving slowly up through the branches, using its length to spread its weight over a wide area so that it is supported by several thin branches. It kills with a powerful bite. It is not venomous and is harmless to people. When it is threatened, however, the splendid tree snake inflates its neck to make itself look fiercer than it really is.

Cape wolf snake

Lycophidion capense

The Cape wolf snake lives in the savannahs of Africa. It is distributed mainly through East and southern Africa, from Sudan in the north to Namibia and South Africa. It is a night-time hunter: it has vertical pupils that open very wide and allow its eyes to collect enough light to see by in the gloom of twilight and in the burrows of its prey.

It specializes in eating burrowing animals, especially skinks and sand lizards. While the snake rests in a burrow by day, these lizards forage for food on the surface. As dusk approaches, the snake emerges from hiding and tracks a lizard as it makes its way back to its burrow. The small wolf snake follows its victim into its hiding place. The snake then uses its long curved teeth to make a firm grip on its prey so it can be dragged from the safety of the burrow. The snake generally bites its victims on the back of the neck and, once it has them out in the open, constricts them until dead. Breeding takes place in the wet season. The female lays between three and eight eggs.

Distribution: East and southern Africa.
Habitat: Savannah.
Food: Skinks.
Size: 30–50cm (12–19.75in).
Maturity: 1 year.
Breeding: Up to 8 eggs laid in wet season.
Life span: Unknown.
Status: Common.

The Cape wolf snake catches its food underground, so it has a small, flattened head that is easy to fit into the burrows of its prey. The snake is named after its backwards-curved teeth, which are not for delivering venom but for hooking on to struggling prey as they are pulled from their burrows.

Schlegel's blindsnake

Rhinotyphlops schlegelii

Schlegel's blindsnake has very small eyes that are barely capable of vision. The snake's tiny head is covered by large protective scales called scutes. These are often referred to collectively as the "beak".

Schlegel's blindsnake is exceptionally large, being over twice as long as nearly all other blindsnakes. These snakes spend most of their lives underground, earning them their alternative name: worm snakes. The subterranean environment they occupy has meant that blindsnakes' eyes are mere vestiges of those of their above-ground relatives. However, like Schlegel's blindsnake, few are completely blind.

This species is also typical in that it only has teeth in the upper jaw of its small, blunt head. These are all the teeth it needs, because the blindsnake spends most of its time around ant and termite mounds, where it feasts on the soft bodies of the developing insects. The protective beak over the snake's head helps it to tunnel through soft soil without injury. The snake's long, thin body is also covered in smooth, shiny scales that aid in burrowing.

Although they are totally harmless, it is unwise to harass blindsnakes. They have well-developed glands near their anuses, packed full of the most noxious-smelling secretions, which they eject upon attack.

Distribution: Southern Africa from Kenya to South Africa.
Habitat: Soft, sandy or loamy soils.
Food: Pupae, eggs and larvae of ants, termites and other subterranean insects.
Size: 1m (3.25ft).
Maturity: Not known.
Breeding: Lays up to 60 eggs underground, which hatch after 4–6 weeks.
Life span: Not known.
Status: Common.

Zambezi blindsnake

Rhinotyphlops mucrosa

The Zambezi blindsnake lives in the soils of eastern Africa. It is most common close to the Zambezi River's watershed in Tanzania, Mozambique and Zambia. This snake is typical of other blindsnakes or worm snakes in that its body is cylindrical, and the head is covered in a scaly beak that helps the snake shovel through the soft soil in search of food. The scales also cover the snake's eyes. The snakes cannot see in the true sense of the word, but their eyes are able to detect whether the animal is in daylight or within the dark of a burrow.

These blindsnakes specialize in eating social insects such as ants and termites. They break into the insects' nest and gorge themselves on the eggs and larvae. Much of this food is stored as fat inside the snake's body. As a result, blindsnakes need to eat just two or three times a year. The rest of the time, the snakes lie dormant underground. The snakes only rarely come to the surface, since their food is all underground. They are most commonly seen after floods. Flash flooding caused by heavy rains waterlogs the soil, so the snakes must come above ground to breathe.

Distribution: Southern Tanzania and northern Mozamibibua.
Habitat: Soil.
Food: Ants and termites.
Size: 70cm (27.5in).
Maturity: 1–2 years.
Breeding: Large clutches of eggs laid each year.
Life span: Unknown.
Status: Common.

Blindsnakes find it difficult to find mates, so when they do they make the most of it and produce a large number of eggs. Some reports suggest that there can be as many as 60, but half this number is probably more typical. The eggs are laid in an underground chamber and hatch after about six weeks.

The Zambezi blindsnake is found in two colour forms. Just after the snake sheds its old skin, its new skin is a blue-grey with black, blotchy markings. Soon, however, the skin darkens to a rich red-brown that matches the colour of the soil more closely.

Royal python

Python regius

Royal pythons are Africa's smallest pythons. They are generally active at night, when they hunt using eyes that are well adapted to low light levels. They also have special heat-sensing pits around their mouths to detect prey in the dark. Since these pits pick up heat in the form of infrared radiation, they are well equipped to detect the body heat released by their prey.

Pythons are not venomous; they are constrictors. They grab hold of their prey and throw a number of coils around it, holding so tightly that the animal cannot breathe. Constrictors do not crush their prey; they suffocate them.

During the hot dry season, pythons lie inactive (aestivate) in underground burrows. They emerge when the rains arrive in order to mate. However, royal pythons only mate once every three or four years, so that they reproduce at a low rate. This means that their populations are particularly vulnerable to over-hunting. Royal pythons are endangered in the wild because they are collected for the pet trade, as well as being hunted for their flesh and skins.

Distribution: Central Africa.
Habitat: Grassland.
Food: Small mammals, birds, lizards and other species of snakes.
Size: 1.2m (4ft).
Maturity: 3–5 years.
Breeding: 4–10 unusually large eggs.
Life span: 25 years.
Status: Threatened.

Royal pythons are also known as ball pythons because when they are threatened they coil up into tight balls with their heads well protected inside.

Sand boa (*Eryx jaculus*): 80cm (31.5in)
The sand boa is a European relative of pythons and anacondas. It is a constrictor like these relatives, but is substantially smaller. As its name suggests, it is specialized to a life in dry, sandy habitats. It lives in the southern Balkans and east to the Caspian Sea and central Asia. The snake is also found throughout the Middle East and into North Africa. The snake spends the day in burrows. It might dig its own, but often takes over one dug by a rodent. At night the snake comes to the surface and hunts for prey, which include lizards, insects and small rodents. It generally chases its prey into their burrows and catches them there. However, it also lies buried just below the surface and grabs victims as they walk past.

Worm snake (*Typhlops vermicularis*): 40cm (15.75in)
As their name suggests, these snakes look more like large worms than snakes. They are blind and have teeth only on the top jaw. This species is found in the Balkans and east to the Caucasus. They live underground and prefer to make their homes in grassy areas. They eat ants and other underground insects.

Central African python

Python sebae

Central African pythons live across Africa south of the Sahara Desert. They are found in both forested and savannah habitats. Large adults can consume juvenile crocodiles, small antelopes and domestic goats. Most pythons do not survive long enough to grow to that sort of size, and their diet consists of rodents and ground-living birds. The snake hunts in the dark, when most small mammals are on the move. It locates prey using heat-sensitive pits on its snout, which pick up the body heat of prey in the darkness.

Females incubate their eggs to ensure they hatch. The snake wraps its body around several dozen orange-sized eggs. She then shivers her body to generate the heat needed to incubate the eggs.

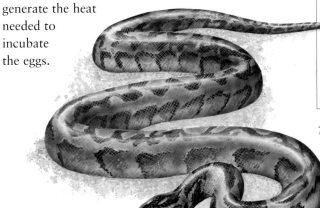

Distribution: Sub-Saharan Africa.
Habitat: Forest and savannah.
Food: Crocodiles, pigs, goats, birds and antelopes.
Size: 3.5–7.5m (11.5–24.5ft).
Maturity: 3–5 years.
Breeding: 100 eggs incubated by mother.
Life span: 30 years.
Status: Common.

The Central African python is the largest snake in Africa. One specimen from the Ivory Coast was nearly 10m (32.75ft) long. However, this was an unusual size, and today pythons over 6.5m (21.25ft) are very rare.

VENOMOUS SNAKES

About 10 per cent of all snakes use modified fangs to inject prey with venom. The main groups of venomous snakes are the vipers, elapids and colubrids. Most of the venomous snakes in Europe are vipers, including the adder, the only venomous species in Britain. One of the largest venomous snakes in the world is the Gaboon viper. However, many African elapids, such as the black mamba, are much more dangerous.

Boomslang

Dispholidus typus

Distribution: Southern Africa.
Habitat: Open woodland.
Food: Reptiles, mammals and birds.
Size: 1.3m–2m (4.25–6.5ft).
Maturity: Not known.
Breeding: 8–13 eggs laid in early summer.
Life span: 18 years.
Status: Common.

Weight for weight, the venom produced by the boomslang is more potent than that of either mambas or cobras. However, the boomslang's shy nature has led to it having less of a fearful reputation than its better-known relatives. Boomslangs also lack the large front fangs of mambas and cobras, having small teeth located at the backs of their mouths. To inject a large amount of poison, boomslangs have to deliver more prolonged bites than front-fanged snakes.

The word boomslang means "tree snake" in Afrikaans – the colonial language of South Africa. This name is very apt, since they are very agile snakes that can slide gracefully through the branches of trees, helped by their strong prehensile tails. Nevertheless, while hunting they will come down to the ground on a fairly regular basis in search of prey.

Most of a boomslang's life is spent coiled and immobile among branches. So effective is their camouflage that birds, which make up a substantial part of their diet, have been known to actually perch on them.

When immobile in trees, boomslangs are very hard to spot. Their green bodies blend perfectly with the foliage. These highly venomous snakes are members of the colubrid snake family, unlike mambas and cobras.

Banded water cobra

Naja annulata

The banded water cobra is thought to have at least two subspecies. The first has a yellow-brown body with thick black rings along its length. The less common subspecies, known as the storm water cobra, has just two or three rings near the neck. The rest of the body is more yellow with a blue tinge. The tail is jet black.

The banded water cobra lives in the waterways of Central Africa. Most are located in the rainforests that grow in the Congo Basin, but the snakes also live around the Great Lakes of East Africa. The banded water cobra spends long periods in water. It is an excellent swimmer and makes long dives to catch prey. It can dive to a depth of 30m (98.5ft) and stay underwater for 10 minutes. Being a cold-blooded reptile, its metabolic rate is low so it can survive perfectly well without a fresh supply of oxygen for this time. The snake hunts for fish underwater. Like all cobras, this species is venomous but as yet biologists are not sure how effective the venom is underwater.

When not hunting for fish, the cobra rests under rocks and in thickets beside the water. It is a frequent visitor to jetties and wrecks close to the shore. However, the cobra is a shy species and will avoid contact with people.

Distribution: Congo River Basin and Great Lakes of East Africa.
Habitat: Forest lakes, rivers and other bodies of water.
Food: Fish.
Size: 1.5–2.7m (5–9ft).
Maturity: Unknown.
Breeding: Unknown number of eggs laid each year.
Life span: Unknown.
Status: Common.

Spitting cobra

Naja pallida

Distribution: Eastern and Central Africa from southern Egypt to northern Tanzania.
Habitat: Savannah grasslands.
Food: Amphibians, small mammals, birds, eggs and other reptiles.
Size: 0.7–1.5m (2.25–5ft).
Maturity: Not known.
Breeding: Clutches of up to 15 eggs.
Life span: 20 years.
Status: Common.

As its name indicates, this snake has a particularly effective method of defence. When it feels threatened, the spitting cobra rises up in typical cobra fashion, extending its hood, which is quite narrow by cobra standards. Holding its head high off the ground, it then spits large quantities of venom over a distance of more than 2m (6.5ft), aiming for the attacker's eyes.

The venom is very potent, causing blindness if it does reach the eyes, and bites can be fatal to humans. These cobras, however, are very reluctant to bite, preferring a "spit-and-run" tactic, making off while their enemy's eyes are stinging. Of course, cobras do not hold back when they come across prey animals. These are rapidly killed by the powerful venom injected via the snake's fangs.

Adults are predominantly nocturnal, hiding inside termite hills, old logs or piles of leaves during the day. Young cobras are active during the day, and with good cause: adult cobras will eat them.

The colour of spitting cobras is very variable. Individuals may be red, yellow, pinkish or steely grey. Cobras (members of the Naja *genus) are a sizeable group associated more with Asia.*

Forest cobra (*Naja melanoleuca*):
1.5–3m (5–10ft)
The forest cobra holds the record, along with the anaconda, for being the longest-living snake. It is capable of reaching the impressive age of 30 years. It is found all over western and southern Africa, inhabiting many different habitats. Forest cobras have a reputation for being ill tempered and dangerous. Their venom is extremely toxic. They chase attackers off with mouths agape and ready to bite.

Rinkhal (*Hemachatus haemachatus*):
1–1.5m (3.25–5ft)
Rinkhals closely resemble cobras in that they have hoods, which they spread when feeling threatened. Found in southern Africa, they differ from true cobras by having differently shaped scales, and by giving birth to live young (whereas cobras lay eggs). In the wild, rinkhals mainly eat toads, but will make meals of rodents or any other small animals unfortunate enough to come too close.

Green mamba (*Dendraspis angusticeps*):
1.8–2.3m (6–7.5ft)
The green mamba is a smaller and less-dangerous cousin of the mighty black mamba. The green mamba lives high in the trees of coastal forests of Kenya and Tanzania. There it preys on small mammals and birds by moving silently through the branches and setting ambushes for its victims. Females slither down to the ground after mating to lay about 10 eggs in the leaf litter.

Black mamba

Dendroaspis polylepis

The black mamba is probably Africa's most feared snake, and justifiably so. It is an aggressive animal, armed with venom capable of killing humans in four hours.

Raising its head up off the ground to a height of 1.2m (4ft), black mouth agape, the mamba charges. It can reach a speed of 16kph (10mph), making it one of the fastest snakes in the world. Hunting by day using its excellent eyesight, it usually bites its prey a couple of times and then lets go. The stricken animal may make off but in a short time it is paralyzed by the snake's toxins, and then swallowed headfirst.

Distribution: Southern and Central Africa.
Habitat: Tropical forests and savannah.
Food: Mainly small mammals and birds.
Size: 3.5m (11.5ft).
Maturity: Not known.
Breeding: Clutches of 14 eggs laid after a long courtship period.
Life span: 26 years.
Status: Common.

Black mambas are actually grey with white bellies. Their name refers to the colour of the insides of their mouths.

Cat snake

Telescopus fallax

The cat snake lives in the Balkans and Greece. It is found as far north as Bulgaria and the north-east corner of Italy. The snake's range continues east through the Caucasus to western Asia. The snake is considered sacred on some Greek islands.

Although it is more or less harmless to humans, the cat snake does use a weak venom to subdue its prey. It hunts in twilight using its large eyes to see in the gloom. Its vertical pupils allow its eyes to capture as much light as possible.

The snake is small and cannot tackle prey much bigger than a mouse or medium-sized lizard. Its favoured prey are small lizards, which it tracks by scent and sight through rocky habitats. The snake generally follows its victims into their hiding places and kills them with a bite. However, a few victims are also stalked. The prey is paralyzed by the venom, which is delivered along a groove in the snake's two fangs. It is weak and slow acting: the snake must hook a small lizard in its mouth for five minutes as it waits for its victim to die. The snake is relatively harmless to humans because its mouth is too small for its fangs to pump venom into the skin.

The cat snake earns its name from the pupils in its eyes, which resemble those of a cat. In strong light the pupils close into a vertical slit, not into a ring like human eyes. Pupils like this can be opened more widely than round ones, allowing more light in for night vision.

Distribution: South-east Europe from the Adriatic coast of the Balkans to south-east Bulgaria. It is also found on several Aegean islands including Crete and Rhodes.
Habitat: Stony habitats, such as hilly woodlands, ruins, walls and also sandy areas with bushes.
Food: Small lizards, slow worms and rodents.
Size: 1m (3.25ft).
Maturity: 3 years.
Breeding: 5–9 eggs laid each year.
Life span: Unknown.
Status: Common.

Green water snake

Philothamnus hoplogaster

Green water snakes belong to a group of snakes called racers. They have fangs for delivering venom, but these are positioned at the back of the mouth, instead of at the front as in more familiar biting snakes, such as cobras. The venom of green water snakes is very mild. It is thought to be harmless to humans, but may cause paralysis in frogs, the snake's main prey.

The green water snake lives in the swamps and still backwaters of southern and East Africa. It is an active swimmer and patrols the shallow waters for small frogs and any other water animals it comes across.

Like most snakes, the green water snake prefers to keep out of the way of people and as a consequence it is not well understood. When it is encountered, it seems to be a gentle species. It does not inflate its throat like other snakes in an attempt to frighten off attackers and it rarely bites. However, its size and colouring make it hard to distinguish from the green mamba – a deadly snake.

The green water snake is long and thin. Juveniles have dark crossbars, but most of these fade in adulthood. The adults are either a uniform pale green or more muted grey-blue. Many individuals also have a yellow patch on the throat.

Distribution: Southern Kenya to Tanzania, Mozambique and across southern Africa.
Habitat: Backwaters, marshes and other areas of shallow water.
Food: The main prey are frogs, but any small animal will be eaten if the opportunity arises.
Size: 60–93cm (23.5–36.5in).
Maturity: Unknown, probably about one year.
Breeding: Up to 8 elongated eggs laid at all times of year.
Life span: Unknown.
Status: Common although rarely seen.

Eastern twig snake

Thelotornis mossambicanus

Distribution: South-east Africa.
Habitat: Wooded areas of savannah.
Food: Lizards and birds.
Size: 90–140cm (35.5–55in).
Maturity: 2–3 years.
Breeding: Eggs laid in summer.
Life span: Unknown.
Status: Common.

The eastern twig snake lives in the savannahs of south-eastern Africa as far north as Tanzania. Savannahs are often characterized as grasslands, but they also contain a good number of small wooded areas. It is there that the twig snake makes its home.

The twig snake is named after the wood-like pattern on its body, which helps it to hide among the branches. It hunts for newly hatched birds and small lizards, locating its prey using its sense of smell and vision. Like many tree snakes, this species has horizontal keyhole-shaped pupils. These give the snakes a wide field of view but also allow them to retain forward binocular vision, in which both eyes look at the same object, which is essential for the twig snakes to be able to judge distances. Twig snakes kill with a very potent venom that causes their victims to die from internal bleeding.

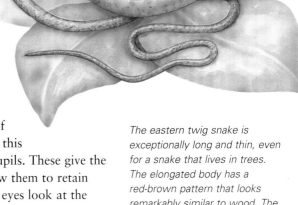

The eastern twig snake is exceptionally long and thin, even for a snake that lives in trees. The elongated body has a red-brown pattern that looks remarkably similar to wood. The snake never leaves the trees, since it would be too conspicuous among the green grass.

Giant centipede eater (*Aparallactus modestus*): 35–65cm (13.75–25.5in)
This large burrowing snake lives in the forests of the Congo Basin. It has a small head and short tail which makes it able to burrow through soil. Adults are a dark grey-green, while juveniles can be identified by the pale patch on their heads. The snake digs through the soft forest soil and leaf litter in search of soft-bodied invertebrates. Centipedes certainly make up a part of their diet, but earthworms, slugs and beetle grubs are probably a more common meal. Venom is delivered through fangs at the rear of the mouth. It is harmless to humans.

Eastern tiger snake (*Telescopus semiannulatus*): 60–100cm (23.5–39.5in)
This species of eastern African snake is so named after the thick orange and brown bands on its body. The snake hunts on the ground and in trees. Its main prey are birds and lizards, but it also takes roosting bats. The tiger snake is an aggressive species and will bite when provoked. The venom is pumped through fangs at the back of the mouth and a few bites are capable of delivering a harmful dose.

Dagger tooth snake (*Xyelodontophis uluguruensis*): 80–130cm (31.5–51in)
This species was first described only in 2002. It lives in the evergreen forests that grow on Uluguru Mountain near the coast of north-eastern Tanzania. When threatened, the snake stiffens its body and inflates its throat. It will readily bite attackers but the potency of its venom is still to be investigated.

Rufous beaked snake

Rhamphiosis rostratus

The rufous beaked snakes live in the sandy grasslands of East Africa, from Somalia and Sudan in the north to Mozambique in the south. They are common in the dry lowland areas on the coastal plains.

The snake has a small head but a powerful body. The head is used to shovel sandy soil out of the way as the snake digs a burrow. It shelters by night in this burrow and emerges to hunt at dawn. The snake kills with a venom that is delivered through fangs located at the back of its mouth. The venom paralyzes the muscles of victims and eventually causes them to stop breathing. However, the venom is weak and prey may be eaten when immobilized but still alive. The venom is harmless to humans.

Distribution: Eastern Africa.
Habitat: Sandy grasslands.
Food: Small mammals, lizards and small snakes.
Size: 1.2–1.4m (4–4.5ft).
Maturity: Unknown.
Breeding: A dozen eggs laid singly of the course of several days.
Life span: Unknown.
Status: Common.

The head of the rufous beaked snake is small and has a sloping snout. This is an adaptation to a burrowing lifestyle, making it well suited for pushing through soft soil. However, this species should not be confused with the blindsnakes, another group of burrowing snakes, also with a similar beak-like snout and sometimes called beaked snakes because of it.

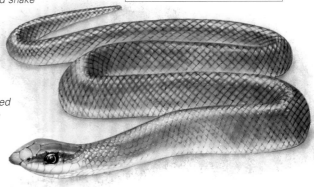

Egyptian cobra

Naja haje

The Egyptian cobra is one of the most deadly snakes in Africa. Its venom is more toxic than most other familiar cobras, such as the Indian cobra, famed for its use in snake charming, and even the king cobra, the world's largest venomous snake. The Egyptian cobra's venom first causes paralysis and soon after death, as the heart and other chest muscles give out. Humans bitten by an Egyptian cobra will die unless an antivenin drug is administered within an hour or two. The death is reputed to be painless. Legend has it that Queen Cleopatra, the Ptolomeic ruler of Egypt during Roman times, chose to use a bite from an Egyptian cobra to commit suicide after hearing of her lover Mark Antony's death.

Egyptian cobras live in any habitat where there is a good supply of food. They sometimes live among humans, attracted by the rodents that also live in human settlements. In the wild young snakes eat toads and birds' eggs, while older individuals eat small mammals. The largest Egyptian cobras eat other snakes. They seem to be particularly fond of puff adders. Eggs are laid in a termite mound to protect them from predators. The eggs are also kept warm by the heat produced by the insects' nest, and after 60 days of incubation the young hatch.

The Egyptian cobra is the largest cobra in Africa. It is also known as the brown cobra. Like other cobras, this species has a hooded neck; the hood is opened when the snake rears up into a threat posture. The belly below the hood has dark bands before changing to pale brown.

Distribution: Northern and eastern Africa and most of the Middle East as far north as Syria.
Habitat: Grasslands, woodlands and deserts.
Food: Mammals, eggs and other snakes.
Size: 1.3–2.5m (4.25–8.25ft).
Maturity: 3 years.
Breeding: Up to 20 eggs laid in termite mounds. The eggs hatch after 60 days, and the young are already venomous but have smaller hoods than the adults.
Life span: 25 years.
Status: Common.

Adder

Vipera berus

The majority of members of the viper family are venomous, and the adder – or common viper – is no exception. However, it poses little threat to humans. Adders rarely bite humans, and, even when they do, the consequences are usually no more than a painful swelling around the area of the bite. Adders spend most of their day basking in the sunshine, and go out to hunt in the late afternoon. As winter closes in, adders prepare to hibernate, usually burrowing underground to sleep through the cold weather. The duration of hibernation varies with latitude.

The active periods of adders can be divided into three distinct phases. The first phase occurs during spring, when they come out of hibernation and disperse. This is when the males, having shed their skins, go in search of females, and mating occurs.

The second phase begins at the onset of summer, when adders migrate along hedgerows and ditches to prime feeding grounds, such as wet meadows. They stay in these areas until summer starts to draw to a close, at which time they head back to drier areas – the third phase. Female adders give birth to their young – they do not lay eggs – which immediately prepare to hibernate, too.

Distribution: Throughout Europe and northern and western Asia.
Habitat: Open places such as heaths, meadows and woodland edges.
Food: Lizards, small mammals, nestlings and insects.
Size: 65cm (25.5in).
Maturity: Not known.
Breeding: 10 young born in late summer.
Life span: 15 years.
Status: Common.

The adder's predominantly grey-brown colour, with zigzag markings down the back, is very different from the coloration of the grass snake, yet people often confuse the two.

Asp viper

Vipera aspis

Distribution: Western and central Europe.
Habitat: Rocky hillsides and scrublands.
Food: Small mammals, frogs, lizards and birds.
Size: 60cm (23.5in).
Maturity: 3–4 years.
Breeding: About 7 young born every 2–3 years.
Life span: 18 years.
Status: Common.

The asp viper lives in rocky areas of western and central Europe. The viper prefers dry habitats but is also present in damp climates, such as those on the slopes of the Pyrenees and Alps. The northern side of the asp viper's range overlaps with that of the adder. In these areas, the asp viper is restricted to dry and warm locations.

The asp viper is mainly diurnal, although it will hunt at night when the temperature is too high in some parts of its range. Males may hunt over a large home range, while the females tend to stay close to a single den. The snake's diet is mainly composed of mammals, lizards and birds. The venom is relatively weak and victims often manage to run away after being bitten before dying close by. The vipers use their excellent sense of smell to track down their dying victims.

Females breed once every two or three years. They do not lay eggs but give birth to six or seven young three months after mating.

The asp viper has a broad triangular head that is typical of the vipers, although its body is somewhat more slender than other viper species. Its nose is also only slightly upturned. There are many colour forms across its range.

Desert horned viper (*Cerastes cerastes*): 30–60cm (12–23.5in)
The desert horned viper is a resident of the Sahara Desert. Its name also refers to the pointed projections above both its eyes. The powerfully built snake has heavily keeled scales (scales with a marked ridge on them). The keels help the snake to squirm beneath the soft desert sands, where it hides during the heat of the day. The desert horned viper hunts at night and often buries itself in order to ambush its prey. Its victims include rodents and lizards and the occasional bird. When the prey is in range, the snake launches itself out of the sand. When threatened itself, it coils its body and shakes itself to make the keeled scales clatter together and produce a menacing rustling sound.

Horned adder (*Bitis caudalis*): 30–50cm (12–19.75in)
The horned adder lives in the deserts and savannahs of south-western Africa. It has a very similar life to the desert horned viper. The southern species also has roughly keeled scales to help it grip loose ground as it side-winds (moves in sideways loops). The scales also help the snake to shuffle under soft sandy soil when resting or forming an ambush. The horned adder always hunts at night. It buries itself just below the surface but leaves the tip of its tail visible. Small mammals see the tail wriggling in the sand and come to investigate, only to be met with the adder's deadly fang. Like its more widespread northern relative, the common adder, this species does not lay eggs, but instead gives birth to live young.

Nose-horned viper

Vipera ammodytes

The nose-horned viper ranges from Austria and Italy in the west, through the Balkans, Greece and Turkey to the Caucasus and then beyond into western Asia. This species is one of the deadliest in Europe. Modern medical intervention has made deaths rare today, but bites to bodily extremities may cause severe swelling and tissue damage. The viper's venom is a neurotoxin (a substance that attacks the nervous system). The nose-horned viper has fangs that are 1cm (0.4in) long. When not in use they fit into a soft sheath at the top of the mouth, a feature common to all vipers and adders. The fangs are hollow and venom is pumped through them deep into a victim's body tissue, where it can act immediately.

Nose-horned vipers are diurnal hunters. They prey on mammals, but in certain parts, such as the Aegean Islands, lizards form their staple diet.

Distribution: Central and south-eastern Europe and western Asia.
Habitat: Dry habitats.
Food: Small mammals, birds and other snakes.
Size: 65cm (25.5in).
Maturity: 3–4 years.
Breeding: A dozen young born in summer.
Life span: 15 years.
Status: Common.

The nose-horned viper is named after its upturned snout. It is the only snake in eastern Europe to have such as distinctive "horn". Males tend to be larger than the females. The males are light grey, while the females are a darker grey-brown. Both sexes have the zigzag pattern characteristic of vipers.

Puff adder

Bitis arietans

The puff adder is a large snake, despite being relatively short. The body is very bulky and this is made all the more apparent when the snake inflates its body to scare off potential threats. The dark grey chevrons on the sandy background provide the snake with excellent camouflage as it slithers slowly through dry grasses in search of prey.

Along with the Egyptian cobra, the puff adder is responsible for more deaths than any other African snake. The snake is very aggressive and will bite with only the slightest provocation. The venom is a cytotoxin and begins to break down the body tissue in the region of the bite. That area swells and fills with liquid and becomes excruciatingly painful. A large adult puff adder will inject three times the amount needed to kill an adult human with each bite. The venom is slow acting, however. The destruction of tissue spreads slowly through the body and takes more than 24 hours to cause death, which is often caused by vital body fluids draining from the damaged tissue. If antivenin drugs are not administered quickly, even non-fatal injuries to the body can be permanent. Male puff adders tend to be smaller and more brightly coloured than the females. The females are large because they produce the largest litters of any live-bearing snake: it is not uncommon for 40 babies to emerge in one go. The maximum recorded is 154 for a single adder.

Distribution: Most of sub-Saharan Africa.
Habitat: Grasslands. Uncommon in forests.
Food: Small mammals.
Size: 1m (3.25ft).
Maturity: 3–4 years.
Breeding: Females release a scent to attract males. The males wrestle each other for access to mates. After mating, 20–40 young are born in a single litter in summer.
Life span: Unknown.
Status: Common.

Gaboon viper

Bitis gabonica

The Gaboon viper, sometimes known as the Gabon viper, is a forest species. Its pattern of purple and brown diamonds and zigzags provides excellent camouflage among the deep leaf litter of the African rainforest. It is found chiefly in the Congo Basin, but also lives in the forests that grow along the southern coast of West Africa.

This viper hunts at night. It is the heaviest snake in Africa and Europe and so never climbs into trees. Instead, it lies motionless in an ambush for small mammals, lizards and the occasional bird to come within reach. Victims receive a huge dose of venom through the viper's mighty fangs. The venom is weaker than many African vipers, but the size of the dose means that it is likely to be deadly if no medical treatment is received. To service such large fangs, the snake needs to have equally large venom glands. These are located inside the head behind the eyes. This arrangement produces the arrow-shaped heads of vipers and is the reason for the broad triangular-shaped head of the Gaboon viper.

Gaboon vipers mate during the rainy season – for this reason, captive breeders are able to stimulate their pets into action by spraying them with water. The young develop inside their mother for seven months. Up to 60 baby vipers are born in a single litter, although a third of that is normal. The newborn babies are 30cm (12in) long.

Distribution: Central and West Africa.
Habitat: Forest.
Food: Rodents, birds and frogs.
Size: 1.20m (4ft).
Maturity: 3–4 years.
Breeding: About 20 young born every 2–3 years.
Life span: Unknown.
Status: Common.

The Gaboon viper is the largest of all viper species. Some other species may grow longer but none achieves the size of the Gaboon viper. The snake has an extremely broad, arrow-shaped head, which contains large venom glands. The viper's fangs are the longest of any snake at 4cm (1.5in) long.

Yellow-bellied sea snake

Pelamis platurus

Distribution: Coast of East Africa and around Madagascar.
Habitat: Sea water.
Food: Fish.
Size: 60–110cm (23.5–43.25in).
Maturity: 2–3 years.
Breeding: Young born in water.
Life span: Unknown.
Status: Common.

The yellow-bellied sea snake is the only sea snake to reach Africa. It is found on the coast of East Africa and Madagascar. The same species lives throughout the northern Indian Ocean, around Southeast Asia and into the Pacific. The species is at home on the high seas. However, most snakes prefer inshore water, where small fish are plentiful.

The snakes breathe air at the surface but also extract oxygen from the water through their skin. As a result they can stay underwater for more than three hours. They spend the night resting in deep water, rising to the surface to breathe two or three times at night. During the day they hunt at the surface, using their venom to kill fish. The snake is a good swimmer but is still at the mercy of currents.

The yellow-bellied sea snake never needs to come on to land and is helpless out of water. Mating takes place at sea, as does the birth of the young.

The yellow-bellied sea snake has a body adapted for swimming. The tail is flattened into a paddle that is waved from side to side to push the snake through the water. The upper body is black and the lower section is a pale yellow. The snake swims at the surface of the ocean, so these colours make it hard to spot from above or below.

Lataste's viper (*Vipera latasti*): 60cm (23.5in)
Lataste's viper lives in most of Spain and Portugal bar the far north and is also found in the Maghreb, between Morocco and Algeria. The viper closely resembles the asp viper, which is found to the east. However, Lataste's viper has a snout that is more upturned into a slight horn. This species of viper lives in rocky areas. It preys on small mammals but also hunts small lizards, slow worms and other snakes. Its venom is harmless to humans. Females of this species breed every two years and produce a litter of about six young. The young eat large invertebrates, such as centipedes and scorpions. They become sexually mature once they reach half their full size.

Ottoman viper (*Vipera xanthina*): 1.2m (4ft)
This is the largest venomous snake in Europe. Most of its range covers western Asia, but the viper is found on a few Greek islands and in the north-eastern tip of the Greek mainland. The size alone is enough to differentiate it from other vipers, but this species is also identifiable by the red-brown colouring. The Ottoman viper has cytotoxic venom (a poison that destroys body tissues). Bites are often fatal without medical attention.

Green night adder

Causus resimus

Green night adders live in most of the savannahs of Central Africa. These habitats grow around the edges of forests and typically have a few trees and tall stands of grasses and similar plants. There is an isolated population of these snakes on the coast of Kenya, but most live in damper locations, such as around Africa's Great Lakes.

The green night adder is a largely ground-living species. It hunts for the frogs and toads that frequent the damp grasslands during the dry season. The green night adder is sometimes found in tall overhanging sedges, from where it can pick off prey from the ground. The night adders have short fangs and produce only a weak venom. However, like some other night adders, this species has long venom glands that are located in the body and not just the head, as in most venomous snakes. As a result, they can deliver a large amount of venom in a single bite. A bite from a green night adder can cause painful swelling despite the weakness of the venom.

Green night adders lay eggs rather than giving birth. The females lay about 12 eggs one by one throughout the wet season.

Distribution: Central Africa.
Habitat: Savannahs.
Food: Frogs and toads.
Size: 40–75cm (15.75–29.5in).
Maturity: 2–3 years.
Breeding: 12 eggs laid in wet season.
Life span: Unknown.
Status: Common.

The green night adder has a remarkably vibrant body, with bright green scales on top of an electric-blue skin. When the snake inflates itself to ward off predators, the scales are pushed apart and the blue skin is exposed to startle any attackers away.

CATS

The cat family Felidae consists of two groups: big cats and small cats. The former includes lions, cheetahs and leopards, and the latter includes lynxes, caracals and servals. Typically, cats hunt alone by night, using their acute senses of hearing, sight and scent to locate and stalk their prey. Once within pouncing distance, they unsheath their curved claws and deliver neck bites with dagger-shaped teeth.

Lion

Panthera leo

The social behaviour of lions is unique among wild cats. A typical pride contains about ten related females with their cubs and one or two males. Females do most of the hunting. They may work together to isolate and kill large prey such as zebra or buffalo. Males in a pride help themselves to the females' kills and rarely hunt for themselves. They spend much of the night patrolling, marking territory and driving away rival males. A pride male's reign rarely lasts longer than three years before he is usurped. Once adolescent males are evicted from the prides where they were born and reared, they may stay together in hunting groups, or hunt alone before eventually joining other groups.

Male lions have thick manes of hair, while the females do not. The manes are symbols of the dominance level in males.

Distribution: Africa, south of the Sahara, and Gir Forest, India.
Habitat: Open country.
Food: Grazing animals.
Size: 2–2.7m (6.5–9ft); 125–180kg (275.5–397lb).
Maturity: 3–4 years.
Breeding: 1 litter of 2–5 cubs in alternate years.
Life span: 16 years.
Status: Vulnerable.

Cheetah

Acinonyx jubatus

Distribution: Most of Africa, Middle East to Turkestan.
Habitat: Savannah and open, dry grassland.
Food: Gazelles or antelopes.
Size: 1.6–2.1m (5.25–7ft); 30–45kg (66–99lb).
Maturity: Females 3 years; males 3–4 years.
Breeding: 2–6 kittens every 2–3 years.
Life span: 15–20 years.
Status: Endangered.

Cheetahs differ from typical cats in several ways. Instead of stealth, they use speed to run down their prey, assisted by blunt claws that grip the ground. The dew-claws, however, which are used to grasp the prey, are curved and sharp. A cheetah is built like a racing dog, with a small head and long legs and body, but the teeth and jaws are too small and weak to deliver an effective death bite, so the cheetah is forced to suffocate its prey. After the sustained effort of catching and killing a prey animal, a cheetah may need to rest for half an hour before starting to eat.

The cheetah is well known as the fastest animal on land. Sadly, despite captive breeding programmes, it is now an endangered species. A breeding female requires a hunting range of up to 800sq km (300sq miles) and, apart from some national parks and isolated populations, suitable territories are mainly restricted to Namibia and parts of South Africa.

The cheetah's long, flexible spine helps to lengthen the stride of the animal at full sprint. It is the fastest terrestrial animal, capable of sprinting at 110kph (70mph).

Eurasian lynx

Lynx lynx

Eurasian lynx have three distinct coat patterns: stripes, spots or plain. These markings can be either faint or clearly visible.

This golden, delicately marked cat hunts small game by night in cool mountain forests and woodland. A shortened tail helps to conserve body heat, but it hinders communication between cats to a certain degree. As with other short-tailed cats that live in cold climates, the lynx has developed conspicuous ear-tufts to send visual signals instead.

Lack of a tail also impairs a cat's balance when running and climbing; the lynx hunts mainly by the techniques of stealth or ambush. Its feet are densely furred, even on the pads, giving a good grip as well as warmth on frozen ground. Most lynxes live in dense forests, but they may also wander into more open country. They build rough beds under rocks and fallen trees, or inside shrubs, resting during the day and hunting at night. While out and about, the lynx climbs trees and fords rivers – swimming if necessary – as it travels far and wide in search of food. It relies on its senses of vision and smell to locate prey, which it then stalks through the trees.

Distribution: Eastern Europe, Pyrenees and northern Eurasia, with distinct races in some regions.
Habitat: Montane forest and woodland.
Food: Rabbits, hares, birds and small deer.
Size: 0.8–1.3m (2.5–4.25ft); 18–21kg (39.75–46.25lb).
Maturity: 12–15 months.
Breeding: 2–4 cubs, weaned at 12 weeks, independent at 12 months.
Life span: 10–20 years.
Status: Endangered in south-eastern Europe.

Spanish lynx (*Lynx pardinus*): 65–100cm (25.5–39.5in); 5–13kg (11–28.5lb)
The Spanish, or Iberian, lynx resembles the more common Eurasian lynx in appearance, with tufts on the ears and jaw and a short, bobbed tail. However, on average, members of this species are smaller. As the name suggests, these cats are found on the Iberian Peninsula. The species is highly endangered, with as few as 1,000 individuals now restricted to a few isolated populations in dry woodland areas of Spain and Portugal.

Jungle cat (*Felis chaus*): 50–75cm (19.75–29.5in); 4–16kg (9–35.25lb)
The jungle cat is a fierce and robust little predator. It has a sandy grey to reddish coat with tabby stripes along its legs, a dark tail tip and black tufts on its large ears. It has good hearing and is very agile, often leaping almost 2m (6.5ft) into the air to catch birds. This cat ranges from North Africa to South-east Asia. It was sacred to the ancient Egyptians, who trained them to catch birds in an early example of domestic cats.

Caracal

Caracal caracal

The name caracal is Turkish for "black ears". Caracals are also known as desert lynxes because they have short tails and ear-tufts like their northern cousins, an adaptation for cold weather. This has led scientists to conclude that the caracal's ancestors once lived in colder regions.

This adaptation to the cold comes in handy during the night, when caracals generally hunt. It is not unusual for desert temperatures to plunge below 0°C (32°F). Caracals prey on anything they can find and kill, including insects, snakes, lizards, gazelles and even brooding ostriches.

Caracals set up home in the abandoned burrows of porcupines or any other suitable crevices. Like other types of lynx, the caracal hunts at night, stealing up close to its prey before leaping the last few metres in huge bounds. The caracal is the fastest cat of its size. Prey is stalked and then captured after a quick dash or leap. The caracal is easy to tame and has been used as a hunting cat in Iran and India. However, it is also persecuted in this region as a pest.

Distribution: Southern Africa to Senegal and India, excluding the Congo and Arabian Desert.
Habitat: Dry scrubland, but avoids sand areas.
Food: Rodents, hyraxes, hares and small antelopes.
Size: 66–76cm (26–30in); 18kg (40lb).
Maturity: 6 months to 2 years.
Breeding: Litter of 3 young born every year.
Life span: 15 years.
Status: Lower risk (threatened in Asia).

Caracals have narrow, pointed ears with long tufts of hair at their tips. These are used to signal to other cats.

Leopard

Panthera pardus

The leopard is widespread across most of Africa and southern Asia, ranging from open grassland to tropical rainforest and mountain highlands. It is an opportunistic feeder, choosing mainly large hoofed mammals, such as deer and antelope, but will take birds, rabbits and even dung beetles if prey is scarce.

Leopards are well adapted for climbing trees and have been seen hiding the corpses of prey in the branches to eat later. They hunt mostly at night but may switch to the daytime to avoid competition with nocturnal lions and hyenas. Leopards vary greatly in colour depending on their habitat. On the savannah they are usually a sandy ochre, while the high mountain leopards are very dark gold. They tend to have short legs on long bodies, and their fur is covered in black spots or rosettes. The rosettes help to keep the cats hidden in the dappled light of forests Completely black leopards (black panthers) are usually found only in forests, but they do not represent a different subspecies, merely an infrequent mutation.

Solitary and nocturnal, the leopard is rarely seen, even though it often lives in close proximity to humans. A melanistic (black, or nearly black) form is found (mainly in Asia), known as the black panther.

Distribution: Atlas Mountains of Morocco, sub-Saharan Africa and southern Asia, from Pakistan to Vietnam and Malaysia. Small groups living in Arabia, the Caucuses and Iran.
Habitat: Forest, mountains and grassland.
Food: Antelope, deer and rabbits.
Size: 1–1.9m (3.25–6.25ft); 20–90kg (44–198.5lb).
Maturity: 33 months.
Breeding: 2–4 cubs.
Life span: 10–15 years in the wild; 25 in captivity.
Life span: Endangered.

Black-footed cat

Felis nigripes

The black-footed cat is widespread across the semi-deserts and dry grasslands, or veld, of Botswana, Zimbabwe and Namibia. They are solitary and generally most active at night to avoid the extreme heat of the day.

The hairs on its feet not only provide insulation against the hot ground but also act as sensors that can pick up the movements of small prey animals, such as rodents or insects that are moving on or under the ground nearby. The black-footed cat kills by stalking and pouncing. It delivers a deadly bite with its long canine teeth. During the day the cat rests in a burrow commandeered from a neighbouring animal, such as an aardvark or springhare.

Male black-footed cats control a territory that includes the home ranges of several females. This suggests that each male fathers more than one litter each year. However, the mating season is very short, and males may miss the opportunity to mate. Transient males without territories who travel through an area may be able to mate as successfully as the resident males.

Black-footed cats are among the smallest of all cat species. The soles of the feet are black and are covered in hairs, which act as protective insulation from the burning-hot ground.

Distribution: South Africa, Namibia, Botswana, Zimbabwe and Zambia.
Habitat: Dry steppes and grasslands.
Food: Rodents, spiders, birds and insects. The cats also scavenge on carcasses.
Size: 33–50cm (13–19.75in); 1.6–2.1kg (3.5–4.5lb).
Maturity: 21 months.
Breeding: Litter of 2–3 kittens born in November and December. Kittens are raised by mother only.
Life span: Unknown; similar species live for 12 years.
Status: Common.

European wildcat (*Felis sylvestris sylvestris*): 35–75cm (13.75–29.5in); up to 5kg (11lb)
In parts of its forest range, extending from Scotland to eastern Europe, this subspecies interbreeds with domestic cats, making its pedigree uncertain. The pure wildcat resembles a robust dark grey tabby cat, with short legs and a bushy, blunt-tipped tail. Unlike feral domestic cats, it is entirely solitary apart from a brief association between mates in the breeding season.

African wildcat (*Felis sylvestris lybica*): 30–75cm (12–29.5in); up to 5kg (11lb)
Genetic fingerprinting tells us that the African subspecies of wildcat is the closest ancestor of modern pet house cats. The sandy-coloured African wildcat was probably domesticated by the ancient Egyptians.

Sand cat

Felis margarita

Sand cats are found in three distinct populations. All live in very dry locations. The first is spread across the Sahara Desert from Algeria to Morocco and Niger. The second lives in deserts of the Arabian Peninsula, while the third is found in dry parts of Turkmenistan, Pakistan, Iran and Afghanistan.

As their name suggests, sand cats are one of the few carnivores to survive in dry, sandy areas that can support only the thinnest covering of vegetation. In such places the daytime temperature can exceed 50°C (122°F) but then plummet to below freezing at night.

The sand cat survives in these extremes by hunting at night. Thick fur protects it from the worst of cold night-time conditions. It relies on its sensitive hearing to locate prey in the dark. The species has a larger inner ear compared to other cats. They eat almost anything they can find. By day the cat digs a burrow in the sand to stay cool.

Distribution: Sahara Desert, Arabia and Central Asia.
Habitat: Deserts.
Food: Rodents, snakes, lizards and insects.
Size: 45–57cm (17.75–22.5in); 1.4–3.4kg (3–7.5lb).
Maturity: 1 year.
Breeding: 4–5 kittens born in June and July.
Life span: 13 years.
Status: Vulnerable.

Sand cats are similar in size to domestic cats but have tapered outer ears that are larger than those found on pet cats. This cat hunts using its hearing, so large ears are useful.

Serval

Leptailurus serval

Distribution: East and southern African.
Habitat: Grassland.
Food: Hares, ground-living rodents, frogs and small birds. In spring, the servals also prey on newborn antelopes.
Size: 67–100cm (26.5–39.5in); 13.5–18kg (30–40lb).
Maturity: 1–2 years.
Breeding: Females are pregnant for about 2 months. Litters of 3 cubs born at anytime of year. Male young leave home first.
Life span: Unknown.
Status: Endangered.

Servals are expert grassland hunters. They specialize in hunting in long grass, where they cannot see, only hear, their prey. They use their huge ears to pinpoint the rustling produced by their intended victims and then pounce with great accuracy. They may not even see their prey until they have trapped it under their paws. Prey are killed by a bite to the neck, which breaks the spine and severs the windpipe.

Servals live alone, staying out of each other's way. The cats are seldom found far from water, where stands of tall grass are more common. They are most active at dawn and dusk, when the changing temperatures and light levels disorientate their prey. At other times, the cats hide out in a den among the tall grass. As well as pouncing on prey (they can leap 3m/ 10ft into the air), servals also catch prey in water. They are known to kill flamingos, for example. Their slender bodies also allow them to reach a long way into burrows to get at prey such as mole rats.

Servals have the longest ears and legs compared to their body size of any cat. They locate prey by the sounds their victims make and then pounce on them in a single giant bound.

HYENAS

Hyenas are heavily built, long-legged and long-necked carnivores with large, padded feet and short, hairy tails. Their front legs are longer than their back legs and their shaggy coats are either striped or spotted. There are four species, all of which can be found in Africa. The striped hyena, the widest-ranging species, also lives in Turkey, the Middle East and parts of India.

Spotted hyena

Crocuta crocuta

Spotted hyenas are dog-like, with sloping backs and long thick necks. They are the only mammal to disgorge indigestible hair, along with grass, hooves, horn and bone.

Spotted hyenas live in female-dominated groups known as clans. The mothers rear all of the cubs together in a communal breeding den that is only big enough for the cubs to enter. The entrance to the den is guarded by one or two adults, helping to reduce the number of young killed by other carnivores or hyenas.

Spotted hyenas have a complicated greeting ceremony, involving a variety of interactions using scents and physical gestures. These are only used by certain individuals in a clan and are uncommon between females and low-ranking males. They help to reduce stress in the group. Females are very aggressive and, to help them dominate their clans, they have developed false genitals to look like males. They will fight other females to win over and mate with favoured males. Hyenas are very vocal and their wails – howling screams and "laughter" – can inform other clan members of a food source from up to 5km (3 miles) away.

Distribution: Most of Africa outside rainforest.
Habitat: Woodlands, savannahs, subdeserts, forest edges and mountains.
Food: Hunt antelope, buffalo and zebra. Scavenge from the kills of other large carnivores.
Size: 1.2–1.8m (4–6ft); 60–80kg (132.25–176.5lb).
Maturity: Cubs weaned after 18 months.
Breeding: Litter of 1–2 cubs born at any time of the year.
Life span: 12 years, and up to 25 years in captivity.
Status: Declining in all areas.

Aardwolf

Proteles cristatus

The aardwolf is a specialist feeder and mainly consumes harvester termites. These give off a very toxic spray, and few other predators are able to overcome the chemicals emitted. Aardwolfs find the termites by listening for their movements.

Unlike the spotted hyenas, which have large crushing teeth, aardwolfs only have small peg-like teeth, ideal for crunching small insects. The aardwolf is mainly nocturnal and lives alone, in pairs or in small family groups. Females often live together in the same den to help increase the chances of survival for their pups. Burrows are either taken over from other species or dug by the aardwolfs themselves.

When feeding, adults may travel up to 10km (6 miles) in one night and in this time they may consume 250,000 termites. When threatened, they raise their long manes and erect their tails but, unusually, they keep their mouths closed – the aardwolf has such tiny teeth that it would appear almost harmless if it opened its mouth.

The aardwolf is slimmer and more agile than the other three species of hyena. When attacked, the aardwolf raises the mane along its back and secretes a foul-smelling odour from its anal glands.

Distribution: Southern Africa and north-east Africa.
Habitat: Heavily grazed and trampled grasslands, and sandy plains and plateaux.
Food: Termites plus other invertebrates including grasshoppers and maggots.
Size: 0.8–1m (2.5–3.25ft); 6–11kg (13.25–24lb).
Maturity: Weaned after 16 weeks.
Breeding: Litter of 1–4 pups born at any time of the year.
Life span: Not known.
Status: Uncommon.

Brown hyena
Parahyaena brunnea

Distribution: Southern Africa – most common in Namibia and dry parts of Botswana.
Habitat: Semi-desert.
Food: Carrion, bone marrow, and small animals.
Size: 1.2–1.6m (4–5.25ft); 37–47kg (81.5–103.5lb).
Maturity: 30 months.
Breeding: 2–3 young born in August to November.
Life span: 24 years.
Status: Endangered.

Brown hyenas have long hairs on their necks and backs. Male and female brown hyenas are more or less the same size.

Brown hyenas are scavengers. They are nocturnal and travel huge distances across the semi-deserts and dry grasslands of southern Africa following the scent of a rotting dead body many miles away. Like other hyenas, this species has short but wide jaws that are capable of producing a bite powerful enough to crack bones. Their large cheek teeth are blunt, making them good for crushing food.

Brown hyenas feed on the carcasses of large antelopes such as wildebeest. Unlike other scavengers, such as jackals or vultures, hyenas can access the meaty bone marrow inside bones. This food is rich in nutrients and allows these large animals to survive in arid habitats. They are especially common in the Kalahari Desert. On the sand-strewn Skeleton Coast of Namibia, the brown hyena is known as the beach wolf because it patrols the coast looking for the stranded bodies of whales, seals and other sea mammals.

Brown hyenas do hunt for small animals when possible and will also eat mushrooms. They live in small clans comprising a breeding pair and their close relatives and offspring. The clan den together but rarely scavenge as a group. Only the highest ranking females and male produce young each year.

Striped hyena
Hyaena hyaena

Distribution: North and East Africa. Also lives in smaller numbers across western and southern Asia.
Habitat: Dry scrublands and grasslands.
Food: Carrion.
Size: 1.2–1.4m (4–4.5ft); 26–41kg (57.25–90.5lb).
Maturity: 2–3 years.
Breeding: Litters of up to 6 cubs born at all times of the year.
Life span: 25 years.
Status: Lower risk.

The striped hyena is the only hyena species to live outside Africa. However, it is most common on the grasslands of East Africa, which it shares, to apparently no ill effects, with its larger and fiercer relative, the spotted hyena. Beyond this region, the population of striped hyena falls dramatically, but it is still found as far east as India and as far north as the Caucasus.

Unlike its sometime neighbour the spotted hyena, which is a skilled hunter, the striped hyena finds almost all its food by scavenging. Like other hyenas, it has powerful jaws for crushing bones. It specializes in scavenging large and medium-sized animals, such as zebras and impalas. They are largely solitary animals, trotting through the night to find food. They follow their noses to carcasses and will also readily pick through the rubbish produced by humans. In parts of Africa, rubbish is left outside villages so that striped hyenas can dispose of it.

Striped hyenas have probably kept the same striped pattern as their civet-like ancestors while other species have lost this primitive pattern. Striped hyenas have a mane that is erected when the animal feels threatened.

CIVETS AND GENETS

Civets and genets are small carnivores. Most of them are in the viverrid family, although a few, such as the African palm civet and the species from Madagascar, are more distantly related. Most viverrids live in trees. They have long, slender bodies and many have spotted fur. Biologists think that civets and genets closely resemble the ancestors of today's cats and hyenas.

Common genet

Genetta genetta

A row of black erectile hairs is usually present along the middle of the back of the common genet. The tail has black and white rings. A genet's claws can be withdrawn inside the paws, just like a cat's.

Common genets, also called small-spotted genets, are related to civets. They are common in Africa, and a few are found in western Europe, although biologists think that these are descended from genets introduced to the area many years ago.

Genets live alone or in pairs, resting by day in sheltered spots or abandoned burrows. They feed at night, hunting for small animals in a range of habitats, from dense forest to open grassland. They climb trees to prey on roosting birds or silently stalk victims on the ground.

Genets mainly communicate by sound and smell, but also use their tails to signal. In warmer parts, genets breed during the wet season, with a few females managing to produce two litters each year.

Distribution: South-western Europe, including France and Spain, and Africa, excluding tropical rainforests and deserts.
Habitat: Forests and grasslands.
Food: Rodents, birds, small reptiles and insects.
Size: Length 42–58cm (16.5–23in); 1–3kg (2.25–6.5lb).
Maturity: 4 years.
Breeding: 2 litters of 1–4 kittens every year.
Life span: 13 years.
Status: Common.

Fossa

Cryptoprocta ferox

The fossa is the largest carnivore in Madagascar. Looking very similar to a cat, it hunts by leaping through the trees to prey on lemurs and other small animals, such as birds and frogs. The fossa lives alone, patrolling its forest territory at dawn and dusk and sheltering in caves or inside disused termite mounds by day.

Fossas sometimes attack domestic animals, such as pigs and poultry, and are often killed as pests by people, who also unnecessarily fear that the fossas may attack them. This persecution, combined with the destruction of their forest habitat, means that fossas have become very rare, like much of Madagascar's native wildlife.

Fossas only spend time with other members of their species during the breeding season, which is between September and October. The females give birth three months later, in the height of summer.

Distribution: Madagascar.
Habitat: Forests.
Food: Rodents, birds, frogs, reptiles and young lemurs.
Size: 61–80cm (24–32in); 7–12kg (15.5–26.5lb).
Maturity: 4 years.
Breeding: Twins born once per year.
Life span: 17 years
Status: Endangered.

Fossas walk in a flat-footed manner on their soles, like bears, rather than on their toes, like cat and dogs.

Falanouc

Eupleres goudotii

Distribution: North-western and eastern Madagascar.
Habitat: Lowland forests.
Food: Earthworms.
Size: 45–65cm (17.75–25.5in); 2–4kg (4.5–8.75lb).
Maturity: 1 year.
Breeding: Litter of 1–2 young born in dens between November and January.
Life span: Unknown.
Status: Endangered.

Along with many of Madagascar's mammals, falanoucs are in danger of extinction. The boggy lowland forests they occupy are being drained and cut down to make way for farms and other human developments. In addition, the small Indian civet has been introduced to the island, and this species appears to be contributing to the falanouc's downfall.

Falanoucs are nocturnal foragers. By day they sleep inside hollow logs or in rocky crevices. They live alone but might form into groups in areas that have plenty of food. Falanoucs forage by rooting through leaf litter for worms and other buried invertebrates. They have long claws for digging into the soil to find food. The falanouc's cheek teeth are pointed and are used for stabbing prey. The teeth resemble those of moles and shrews more than they do other small carnivores, which have teeth built for slicing.

This animal is a little larger than a domestic cat. It has a pointed snout for probing through leaf litter and a thick, cylindrical tail.

Malagasy civet (*Fossa fossana*): 42cm (16.5in); 1.75kg (3.75lb)
The Malagasy civet is found throughout Madagascar, where it occupies most of the island's types of tropical forest. The local name for this fox-like species is fanaloka. They have a thick coat of short, brown fur, which has four lines of dark spots along the back. This species of civet preys on small rodents and unusual insectivores called tenrecs – another of the island's many unique species. They also feed on small birds, crabs, frogs and reptiles. During periods of drought, when food is less easy to come by, the civets survive by metabolizing fats stored in their tails during times of plenty. Malagasy civets mate between August and September and a single young is born three months later.

Large-spotted genet (*Genetta tigrina*): 50–60cm (19.75–23.5in)
This species is found mainly in the Cape region of South Africa – another name for it is Cape genet – although its range does extend as far north as southern Sudan. As its name suggests, this species has large grey-brown spots on its back, which are surrounded by paler fur. An alternative common name is blotched genet. This species of genet is found in habitats that contain plenty of good hiding places. They live among tall grasses and dense woodland, and in drier parts of their range are found in the thick vegetation along river banks. Large-spotted genets prey on a variety of small mammals, birds, reptiles and invertebrates. They also supplement their meat diet with fruits.

Aquatic genet

Osbornictis piscivora

The aquatic genet is a very rare cat-like animal that is found in the dense tropical forests of the Congo. Very little is known about the habits of this secretive animal. It is thought that they live alone and spend a lot of time in or near water, feeding on fish. There are also reports that they eat frogs and the roots and tubers of aquatic plants.

Most of what is known is surmised from studying the anatomy of the species. Unlike other genets, aquatic genets do not have hairs on their palms. This difference helps the genets feel for prey in muddy water holes and also grip on to more slippery victims. They also have small olfactory bulbs in their brains, which suggests that they do not have a very good sense of smell – not particularly important for locating prey in water. The aquatic genet's premolars are larger than the molars farther back in the mouth. This is likely to be another adaptation that helps the animal grip on to slippery, struggling prey.

Distribution: Central Africa.
Habitat: Rainforests.
Food: Fish.
Size: 45cm (17.75in); 1.5kg (3.25lb).
Maturity: 1 year.
Breeding: 1 young born each year.
Life span: Unknown; other species reach 20 years old.
Status: Unknown.

Unlike other genets, this species does not have spots on its back. It has white spots between the eyes.

Angolan genet

Genetta angolensis

Angolan genets have dark red fur with large black or brown spots forming a symmetrical pattern on either side of the spine. The longer hairs along the spine stand up into a crest when the genet is threatened. Like in other genets, this species has large eyes for seeing in the dark. Each eye is set facing forwards, so the animals can judge distances accurately.

Angolan genets live across southern African between the latitudes of 5 and 15 degrees south. Their range includes the countries of Angola, Democratic Republic of Congo, Zambia, Malawi and Mozambique. They are most commonly found in forests but will venture out on to savannahs that receive enough rain for tall grasses to grow.

Angolan genets occupy a small territory in which they prey on a range of small animals, including rodents, birds, lizards and reptiles. They hunt mainly in the treetops, using their long agile bodies to weave through the dense branches. They are nocturnal creatures and avoid contact with other genets. They mark the borders of their territories with smelly anal secretions, which are also expelled in larger quantities when the genet is under attack. A male's territory encompasses those of several females, and he will mate with each female once or twice a year. Litters are born 10 weeks after mating.

Distribution: Southern Africa, from Zambia and Mozambique to the Congo.
Habitat: Rainforest and savannah.
Food: Small vertebrates and invertebrates.
Size: 40–50cm (15.75–19.75in); 1.5kg (3.25lb).
Maturity: Unknown.
Breeding: 2 litters of up to 4 young produced each year. The young are hairless and blind and born in a tree hollow.
Life span: Unknown, but other genets live for 20 years.
Status: Common.

African linsang

Poiana richardsonii

African linsangs are among the smallest viverrids in the world. They differ from Asiatic linsangs in that the Asian species have smaller spots and these never run into bands or stripes on the body, just the head and shoulders.

African linsangs live in the rainforests of equatorial Africa around the Congo Basin. They are nocturnal animals and forage for food among the branches. By day they sleep in nests made from small branches and leaves. They will use this den for a few days before moving to another part of their territory and constructing a new one. This behaviour ensures that they exploit as much of the food supply in their territory as possible.

Little is known about the social behaviour of African linsangs. For much of the year they live alone. They are seen foraging in twos sometimes and it is possible that these are breeding pairs. Some nests have been found containing several linsangs. These might be a family group with adolescent offspring who have stayed with their mother after weaning. It is likely that the young are born at all times of year, and that they are cared for in a den.

Distribution: West Africa, from Sierra Leone and Gabon to Cameroon and the Congo. Also found on Bioko Island, in Equatorial Guinea.
Habitat: Forests and woodlands.
Food: Insects, birds, fruits and nuts.
Size: 33–38cm (13–15in); 500–700g (17.5–24.75oz).
Maturity: 1 year.
Breeding: Litters of 2–3 produced once or twice a year.
Life span: 5 years in captivity, probably more in the wild.
Status: Unknown

African civet

Civettictis civetta

Distribution: Southern and Central Africa, from Senegal to Somalia in the north to the Transvaal of northern South Africa.
Habitat: Forest and grasslands.
Food: Fruits, carrion, rodents, insects, eggs, reptiles and birds.
Size: 68–89cm (26.75–35in); 7–20kg (15.5–44lb).
Maturity: 1 year.
Breeding: Each female produces 2–3 litters of up to 4 young each year.
Life span: 20 years.
Status: Common.

The African civet lives all over sub-Saharan Africa, being equally at home in open grassland and dense forest. They are rarely found far from rivers or another permanent source of water. Its coarse hair is black with yellowish spots and stripes. During the day, civets hide in thickets of grass. At night they cross large distances, even swimming across rivers, in search of carrion, small animals, eggs, insects and fruit. They are also sometimes found out and about during cloudy days.

African civets live alone and only settle in one place when nursing young. Breeding takes place at any time throughout the year. The mother can suckle up to six young at a time, but litters of more than four are rare. The young are raised in a den made inside a burrow that has been deserted by another animal. The mother transports her young by clasping the loose skin on the backs of their necks in her mouth.

Like many other viverrids, the African civet has a mane down its back that can be erected to make the animal appear larger than it really is to attackers. The dark, mask-like pattern across the eyes makes this civet resemble a raccoon, but the two carnivores are not closely related. Unlike genets, in civets the claws are not retractile – they are always sticking out from the paws.

African palm civet

Nandinia binotata

Distribution: Central Africa from Equatorial Guinea, including Bioko, to Sudan, Angola and Mozambique.
Habitat: Tropical forests and woodlands.
Food: Rodents, carrion, fruits, insects and eggs.
Size: 50cm (19.75in); 1.7–2.1kg (3.75–4.5lb).
Maturity: 1 year.
Breeding: 2 litters of up to 4 young produced in May and October.
Life span: Unknown; other similar species live for about 15 years.
Status: Common.

African palm civets spend most of the time in the branches of trees. They also forage on the ground and have been known to venture out of the forest into more open habitats in search of food. African palm civets are omnivores – they eat all types of food. When catching live prey, such as rodents or birds, with their forepaws, the civets use their long tails, which are generally the same length as their body, as a balance. The flexible hind feet can also be twisted considerably to get a good grip.

Civets are most active in the hours just after sunset and before dawn. They have scent glands between their toes, which exude a brown sticky substance. Along with other secretions this is used to mark territory. However, the foot glands might also be used to leave a trail of scent that the civet can follow back to its resting place in the dark.

The mottled coat of an African palm civet helps it to blend in to the background in the dappled light of the forest. Although common animals, they are seldom seen.

DOGS

There are several members of the wild dog family, Canidae, including the African hunting dog, Ethiopian wolf, foxes and jackals. Long legs and muzzles enable these mammals to chase and capture prey. Most have a bushy tail and feet with four toes at the back and five at the front. Small canids are solitary hunters, medium-sized canids hunt alone or in small family groups and large canids hunt in large cooperative groups.

African hunting dog

Lycaon pictus

Hunting dogs are highly social and live in large packs of around 100 animals. A pack is formed by a group of brothers from one pack meeting with a group of sisters from another. A dominant pair emerges and breeds. Females will fight each other for the top breeding position.

These dogs are truly nomadic carnivores. They are on the move all the time to mark their territories and to avoid conflict with lions. Movement is reduced when there are small pups in the den. Unlike most canids which howl to show their presence, wild dogs use scents that last for months. When packs contain about 20 adults, the older offspring leave to form subgroups and hunt independently.

Individual dogs are capable of killing large prey such as impala antelope, although most hunting is done in packs. Pups typically leave at two to three years of age but sometimes stay to help rear more young. Packs stay together for no more than six years, usually two, when the founder members die. The remaining dogs separate into single-sex groups to find new opposite-sex groups and start all over again.

The African hunting dog has black, white, brown and yellow-brown blotches. It has large, round ears, a broad, black muzzle and a tufted tail, usually with a white tip. It is also the only carnivore except hyenas to have five toes on all four feet.

Distribution: Non-forested, non-desert areas of Africa.
Habitat: Desert plains, open and wooded savannah, and bushed country.
Food: Antelope, eland, buffalo and wildebeest.
Size: 1–1.5m (3.25–5ft); 17–36kg (37.5–79.5lb).
Maturity: Pups follow pack after 3 months and join in hunting at 12–14 months.
Breeding: Average of 7–10 pups born in the dry winter months from March to July in the south.
Life span: Not known.
Status: Endangered.

Ethiopian wolf

Canis simensis

Ethiopian wolves' main prey are giant mole rats (*Tachyoryctes macrocephalus*), which make up nearly half of their diet when available. During the day, the wolves lie on the mounds made by the giant mole rats. These make good ambush sites to catch their prey. Ethiopian wolves live in packs with two or more adult females, five closely related males and the current offspring of the dominant pair. The females do not always mate with the males in their pack; indeed, three-quarters of matings may be with males from neighbouring packs.

These wolves are extremely vocal, using all types of howls, yelps and screams to mark their territories, which may be 2.4–12sq km (1–4.5sq miles) in size. They forage alone, but the animals will meet in the morning, midday and evening to rest, play, sleep, feed their pups and mark boundaries. This is when they are most vocal.

Ethiopian wolves have reddish-ginger coats, with white throat patches, inner ears, underparts and lower legs, and dark tails. They have long legs, long muzzles and squared-off noses and upper lips.

Distribution: Restricted to the Ethiopian Highlands of Africa.
Habitat: Alpine moorlands.
Food: Naked mole rats and other rodents, hares and antelope calves.
Size: 1.3m (4.25ft); 11–19kg (24–42lb).
Maturity: Not known.
Breeding: 2–6 pups born from August to December.
Life span: Not known.
Status: Critically endangered.

Golden jackal

Canis aureus

Distribution: Southern Europe, Middle East, northern Africa and southern Asia.
Habitat: Open savannah and grassland.
Food: Opportunistic feeders.
Size: 0.6–1.1m (2–3.5ft); 7–15kg (15.5–33lb).
Maturity: Females 11 months; males 2 years.
Breeding: 6–9 pups born after 63 days of gestation.
Life span: 6–8 years.
Status: Common.

The golden jackal is widespread, living across southern Europe, the Middle East and south Asia. It is the only jackal that ranges into North Africa, where it was held sacred to the Egyptian god Anubis in ancient times. It usually sports a golden-brown or yellow coat of short, coarse fur and a black-tipped tail.

Golden jackals mate for life and typically raise pups together. They live in clearly defined scent-marked territories, often in small family groups. Some offspring remain as helpers, taking care of newborn pups and leaving their mothers free to gather food for their families.

The jackals are found mainly in open grassland terrain. They are opportunistic feeders, eating whatever carrion and small mammals they can find, as well as a lot of plant matter. However, golden jackals hunt more than other species, and often compete with hyenas and lions, which will try to steal their prey. The jackals eat very quickly, without chewing their food, and will often bury their kills to hide them from other scavengers.

Golden jackals can often be seen rummaging around landfill sites near human settlements, looking for tasty refuse.

Side-striped jackal (*Canis adustus*): 96–120cm (3.1–4ft); 9.7kg (21.5lb)
This species of jackal lives in Central Africa. They live alongside other jackals on the grasslands and share a similar body form and lifestyle. However, side-striped jackals are also found in moister habitats, such as mountain woodlands. They are easily distinguishable due to a white stripe along their flanks between a rusty saddle-shaped section of fur on the back and dark sides.

Sand or **pale fox** (*Vulpes pallida*): 61–74cm (24–29.25in); 2–3.6kg (4.5–8lb)
Found across the Sahel belt in northern Africa, the sand fox lives in family parties comprising an adult pair and their offspring. They dig their own burrows and come out at night or early evening to feed on fruit and berries, which provide them with their daily supplement of water. The sand fox feeds on small mammals and insects.

Royal or **hoary fox** (*Vulpes cana*): 40–60cm (15.75–23.5in); 2–3kg (4.5–6.5lb)
A shy, cat-like fox with dense, sandy-coloured fur, the royal fox lives in rock crevices and shelters from Pakistan to northern Egypt. It has excellent hearing to find insects. It will also feed on berries. The tail is long with thick fur, which is thought to help the animal evade predators that may try to catch it. If a predator grasps the tail, the royal fox has a chance to run away even if it means the predator being left with a mouthful of fur or even a piece of the tail itself.

Raccoon dog

Nyctereutes procyonoides

The raccoon dog originated in eastern Asia. In 1927 it was introduced to eastern Europe for fur-farming and is now seen as far west as the French–German border and northern Finland. Unusually for a member of the dog family, the raccoon dog is an agile climber. Adults form pair bonds and have distinct home ranges. However, these are relatively flexible and they will often roam into other raccoon dog territories.

Males and females both help to care for offspring, taking it in turns to guard young while the others hunt for food.

Distribution: Siberia and north China; introduced into eastern and central Europe.
Habitat: Damp lowland forest.
Food: Carrion, fruits, fish, frogs and birds. Scavenges food scraps from near human settlements.
Size: 50–60cm (19.75–23.5in); 4–10kg (8.75–22lb).
Maturity: 9–11 months.
Breeding: 4–9 young born in April–June.
Life span: 11 years.
Status: Widespread.

The raccoon dog looks like a grey and black raccoon, with its characteristic black face mask and bridled greyish body fur.

Black-backed jackal

Canis mesomelas

Distribution: Southern Africa and East Africa.
Habitat: Dry savannahs.
Food: Omnivorous diet.
Size: 0.7–1.3m (2.25–4.25ft); 6–12kg (13.25–26.5lb).
Maturity: Not known.
Breeding: Usually 3–4 pups born July–October in southern Africa.
Life span: Not known.
Status: Not endangered.

The black-backed jackal is reddish-brown with a white-streaked black band along its back. The thick, hairy tail is also black, particularly at the tip. In parts of South Africa, black-backed jackals used to cause problems by feeding on large numbers of pineapples.

Black-backed jackals live in closely bonded pairs, sometimes with one or two older offspring staying to help rear the pups. The older offspring increase the survival rate of young pups by providing extra food and guarding the den from predators, such as hyenas. When the parents arrive back from hunting, the pups start begging and this encourages the adults to regurgitate food which they have caught and swallowed earlier.

The jackals communicate with screaming yells followed by three or four short yaps. They make these calls more often during the winter when they start mating. In South Africa, where black-backed jackals are the only species of jackal present, howling is common.

Black-backed jackals have very varied diets, feeding on anything from young antelope, rodents and hares through to birds, reptiles, carrion, invertebrates, wild berries and fruit.

Red fox

Vulpes vulpes

The red fox is a very successful and adaptable species. It is mainly active at night but will forage during the day, particularly when there are hungry cubs to feed. It also enjoys curling up and sunbathing in exposed but private spots, often by railway lines or roadsides.

A pair of foxes shares a home range, often with young from the previous breeding season. Mating takes place from December to February. After a few months, females – also known as vixens – give birth to between 3 and 12 cubs. The availability of food determines whether vixens breed and how many cubs they produce. During the mating season, females and occasionally males give out spine-tingling shrieks.

Red foxes mark their territories with a distinctive scent, which lingers and tells when a fox has been in the area. The scent is left with urine or faeces and is produced by special glands at the base of the tail. There are further scent glands between the pads of foxes' feet and around their lips.

Distribution: Europe, Asia and North Africa. Introduced to Australia.
Habitat: Able to colonize almost any habitat available.
Food: Small vertebrates, invertebrates, kitchen scraps, fruit and carrion.
Size: 85–95cm (33.5–37.5in); 4–8kg (9–17.5lb).
Maturity: 10 months.
Breeding: 3–12 pups born in early spring.
Life span: 9 years.
Status: Common.

The red fox is a large fox with a rusty, red-brown coat and a darker bushy tail with a white tip.

Fennec fox

Vulpes zerda

The fennec fox is the world's smallest fox and lives in the hot deserts of North Africa. The animal gets most of its water from solid food. Its body also ensures that the least amount of water is wasted. Fennec foxes are only active at night, when the temperature is much lower.

The fox's very large ears are used to detect the sounds made by prey, such as grasshoppers and other insects, in or on the sand. The large ears also radiate excess body heat. Cream-coloured fur helps keep fennec foxes well camouflaged against the sand when resting during the day. They are able to dig very quickly to catch any fast-moving prey living in the sand.

Fennec foxes are usually seen in pairs. In the breeding season, females are very protective of their pups and will be very aggressive if anything threatens them.

The fennec fox is a small cream-coloured fox with short legs, huge ears, a small pointed muzzle and a black-tipped tail.

Distribution: Sahara Desert through to the Nubian Desert. Also found in North Arabia.
Habitat: Sandy deserts.
Food: Various animal and plant foods, particularly insects.
Size: 42–72cm (16.5–28.5in); 1–1.5kg (2.25–3.25lb).
Maturity: Suckled for 2 months and mature by 6 months of age.
Breeding: Mating between January and February. Give birth to 1–5 pups.
Life span: Not known.
Status: Common.

Bat-eared fox

Otocyon megalotis

Bat-eared foxes have very large ears that listen for the movements of harvester termites. Their very thick fur coats protect the foxes from the painful bites of soldier termites that they encounter. They have 46–50 teeth, whereas most mammals have far fewer than this. Their teeth are used to slice up insects that have hard shells and pincers. With the ability to move their lower jaws up and down five times a second, insects are hurriedly chewed and eaten. The bat-eared fox also has very strong claws on its front feet, enabling it to dig very fast.

A pair normally lives together with up to six offspring. They mate for life and have a home range that may be 0.25–3sq km (0.1–1sq miles) in size. Sometimes a second female will join the pair and share the breeding den. Individuals feed by walking long distances over their territories, continually listening for small invertebrates. When they hear something underground, they dig vigorously, catching the prey before it has a chance to get away.

Distribution: Southern Africa and East Africa.
Habitat: Open country, including short scrub, grassland, steppes, lightly wooded areas and farmland.
Food: Harvester termites, beetles and other insects.
Size: 75–90cm (30–36in); 3–5kg (6.5–11lb).
Maturity: Not known.
Breeding: 1–6 pups born from September to November.
Life span: Not known.
Status: Common.

Bat-eared foxes are smaller than most canids. They have huge ears and dark, bushy tails.

Cape fox

Vulpes chama

Cape foxes are small, silver-grey foxes with reddish tinges to the head and forelegs. The hind legs have black patches on them. The bushy tail is about half the length of the body.

The Cape fox is found only in the arid areas of southern Africa. Its range covers Namibia, Botswana and western and central South Africa. This small, slim fox lives in dry grasslands and scrub areas. It avoids forest.

The Cape fox has large pointed ears for detecting faint sounds. Like other dogs, it also has an acute sense of smell. The fox uses these senses to hunt at night. It runs long distances in search of a wide range of food. Most victims are small, such as rodents, lizards and insects, although Cape foxes have been known to attack larger animals, such as young antelopes and livestock.

The foxes always hunt alone, even those within a breeding partnership. Breeding pairs stay together for the breeding season and may pair up again in the following years. They produce pups in late summer and autumn. Several breeding pairs will share a territory and may even den together. The dens are the modified burrows of other mammals, such as aardvarks.

Distribution: Southern Africa.
Habitat: Grasslands and semi-desert.
Food: Rodents, rabbits and insects.
Size: 86–97cm (33.75–38.25in); 2.4–4kg (5.25–8.75lb).
Maturity: 9 months.
Breeding: Females are pregnant for 7 weeks and between 3–5 pups are born from September to November.
Life span: Unknown.
Status: Common.

Arctic fox

Alopex lagopus

Arctic foxes have the warmest coat of any mammal – some species have more hair but it is not as warm as the fox's. They exhibit two colour forms. Those that live in exposed tundra regions are more or less white all year around, becoming paler in winter. In warmer places where the snow melts in summer, the white foxes become grey. By contrast, the foxes that live in coastal areas, which are generally less exposed, are a pale brown in summer and tinged pale blue in winter.

The Arctic fox lives in the far north of Scandinavia and is also found in Greenland, Siberia and the high Arctic of North America. The fox's habitat is barren tundra along the coast of the Arctic Ocean. They also stray into pine forests found in the far north and on high mountain slopes. In winter they move out on to the frozen sea.

The temperatures in these habitats often plunge to far below freezing. Arctic foxes keep out the cold by having a extra thick coat that even grows over the soles of the feet.

There is not very much food among the snow and ice, and Arctic foxes feed on anything they can find. In summer, they feed on small mammals, such as lemmings, but in winter they have to diversify their diet to survive, eating insects, berries, carrion and even the faeces of other animals. When the land is iced over, they rely on sea birds and fish for their meat.

Arctic foxes have difficulty constructing dens because the ground is frozen. As a result, many generations of Arctic foxes den in the same place, often at the foot of cliffs or mounds, sometimes for hundreds of years.

Distribution: Scandinavia, Greenland, Canada, Alaska, northern Russia and Siberia.
Habitat: Arctic tundra, pine forests and sea ice.
Food: Lemmings, fish and carrion of large mammals and birds, plus insects and berries in summer.
Size: 50–60cm (19.75–23.5in); 4kg (8.75lb).
Maturity: 10 months, although many young stay with parents for second year.
Breeding: Mating takes place in spring; litter of 5–8 cubs born two months later.
Life span: Unknown, although between 5 and 10 years is normal for other fox species.
Status: Common.

Grey wolf

Canis lupus

Distribution: Patches of northern and eastern Europe, western and northern Asia, Canada and some locations in the United States.
Habitat: Tundra, pine forest, desert and grassland.
Food: Moose, elk, musk ox and reindeer. Wolves are also known to prey on domestic animals, such as sheep and cattle.
Size: 1–1.6m (3.25–5.25ft); 30–80kg (66–176lb).
Maturity: 22 months.
Breeding: Once per year; only the alpha pair breed.
Life span: 16 years.
Status: Vulnerable.

All domestic dogs are descended from grey wolves, which began living alongside humans many thousands of years ago. The wolves were once common in the ancient forests of the Northern Hemisphere. Human hunters have wiped them out in most parts of the world.

Grey wolves are the largest dogs in the wild, and they live in packs of about ten individuals. A wolf pack has a strict hierarchy, with a male and female "alpha pair" in charge. The alpha dogs bond for life and are the only members of the pack to breed. The rest of the pack is largely made up of the alpha pair's close relatives and their offspring.

In summer, pack members hunt alone for small animals such as hares. In winter the pack hunts together for much larger animals, such as deer or wild cattle. Grey wolves are strong runners and can travel 200km (125 miles) in one night. They detect prey by smell and chase them down. The pack harries a victim until it becomes exhausted. The wolves then take turns to take a bite at its face and flanks until the victim collapses.

Grey wolves howl to communicate with pack members over long distances. Each individual can be identified by its howl.

Rueppell's fox

Vulpes rueppellii

Distribution: North Africa, from Morocco to Egypt, Arabia. Also found in western and south Asia.
Habitat: Sand and stone deserts.
Food: Insects, small mammals and roots.
Size: 34–56cm (13.5–22in); 1.1–2.3kg (2.5–5lb).
Maturity: 1 year; many yearlings will stay with their parents for a second year.
Breeding: Females are pregnant for 50 days and cubs born in March.
Life span: 12 years.
Status: Unknown.

Rueppell's fox is a desert animal. It has large ears, which help it to lose excess body heat (their large surface area allows the blood inside to be cooled by the air). The large ears often result in Rueppell's fox being confused with the fennec fox, but this species is generally significantly larger. The fox also has hairs on the soles of its feet to protect the paws from burning on the hot sand.

This species of fox is a nocturnal hunter, being most active before dawn and at dusk. It will eat whatever it can find in the desert. Most of the diet is made up of insects and other arthropods, such as scorpions.

Rueppell's foxes live in small groups, which are probably primarily composed of family members. Like other fox species, Rueppell's fox cubs often stay with their parents for a year or more. This behaviour allows them to learn how to raise their own young – and be better parents when their time comes. It also helps their parents to raise the next litter more successfully. The helper can guard the young while the mother rests or feeds herself. As a result more of the litter survives.

Rueppell's fox exists in two colour morphs (types). Most have sandy-coloured fur, which helps them blend into their desert habitat. In rocky places, however, the foxes have grey flashes, helping it blend in with the broken landscape. All members of the species have a white tip to their bushy tails.

SMALL CARNIVORES

Some of the small carnivores, the mustelids, are very fast and efficient hunters. They can tackle prey much larger than themselves. Mustelids tend to be solitary animals, defending their territories from all newcomers. Their long, lithe bodies, short legs and sharp claws mean that they are often skilful climbers, capable of reaching the most inaccessible of places and leaving their prey few places to hide.

Stoat

Mustela erminea

Although rarely seen, stoats are common in the countryside, where they mainly feed on rodents. However, the large males will often prey on rabbits, even though rabbits are considerably larger. Stoats are famed for mesmerizing their prey by dancing around them, before nipping in for the kill. This is not just an old wives' tale. Stoats have been observed leaping around near rabbits in a seemingly deranged fashion. This curious "dance" seems to have the effect of confusing the rabbits, which just watch the stoat draw slowly closer and closer, until it is too late to escape.

As winter approaches, populations of stoats that live in cooler, northern areas change the colour of their coats. In summer, they are a chestnut colour but, by the time the first snows have fallen, the stoats have changed to pure white. White stoats are known as ermines, and their fur was once prized for its pure colour and soft feel.

In mild climates, stoats have chestnut fur all year round. In colder areas, they moult into white fur in winter. Stoats are distinguished from their smaller cousins, the weasels, by having black tips to their tails.

Distribution: Widespread in northern and central Europe extending into Asia and across northern North America. Introduced to New Zealand.
Habitat: Anywhere with enough cover.
Food: Mammals up to the size of rabbits.
Size: 16–31cm (6.25–12.25in); 140–445g (0.25–1lb).
Maturity: 1 year.
Breeding: 1 litter per year of 5–12 young.
Life span: 10 years.
Status: Common.

Zorilla

Ictonyx striatus

Zorillas have an uncanny resemblance to skunks, although they are more closely related to ferrets and polecats. Their alternative name is the striped polecat. Not only do they share black and white markings with their North American relatives, but they also eject a foul-smelling liquid from glands near their anuses if alarmed. When faced with enemies, zorillas puff up their fur in an attempt to look bigger, and then squirt their noxious liquid towards their assailants. If the liquid gets in a predator's eyes, it causes intense irritation, as well as smelling very unpleasant. This strategy is extremely effective, with few predators prepared to risk the stinking spray.

Zorillas are nocturnal animals, resting during the day in burrows or rock crevices. At night they hunt small animals, as well as eating the eggs of ground-nesting birds, which are a particular favourite. Zorillas are predominantly ground-living, but they are also proficient swimmers and climbers.

Distribution: Sudan to South Africa.
Habitat: A wide variety, including temperate forest, tropical forest, savannah and grasslands.
Food: Rodents, large insects, eggs, snakes, birds, frogs and reptiles.
Size: 33–38cm (13–15in); 1kg (2.25lb).
Maturity: 1 year.
Breeding: 1 litter of 1–3 young born each year.
Life span: 13 years.
Status: Common.

With their bold black and white markings, zorillas are easily mistaken for skunks.

Sable

Martes zibellina

Distribution: Northern Russia and Siberia.
Habitat: Mountainous forests.
Food: Rodents, birds, fish, nuts and berries.
Size: 35–56cm (13.75–22in); 0.7–1.8kg (1.5–4lb).
Maturity: 16 months.
Breeding: Litter of 3–4 young born in summer.
Life span: 15 years.
Status: Lower risk.

This carnivore lives in mountainous wooded areas, usually near streams, and an individual may have several dens beneath rocks or large roots. The sable hunts by day or night, roaming across a territory that may be as large as 3,000ha (7,400 acres). Mostly it hunts rodents, but it will also eat small birds, fish, honey and berries.

Sables form individual territories, which are fiercely defended against intruders, but in the mating season the males are more forgiving to passing females. The young are born small and blind during the spring. They open their eyes after around 30 days and are independent by 16 months.

The sable has a luxurious silky coat, usually dark brown or black, and has been hunted for many years. During the 18th century, thousands of animals were trapped for their pelts, and the sable is now raised on farms for the fur industry.

An elegant relative of the pine marten, the sable was almost hunted to extinction for its sumptuous pelage (fur). The fur is thicker with longer hairs in winter than in summer. Males are slightly larger and heavier than the females.

European pine marten (*Martes martes*): 45–58cm (17–23in); 0.5–1.8kg (1–4lb)
This species of mustelid is found across Europe and Asia. It is found as far south as the Mediterranean islands and as far east as the Pacific coast of Siberia. The pine marten was once common in the British Isles, but it is now found only in Ireland and the far north of Great Britain. Despite their name, pine martens live in all types of forest – pine, broad-leaved, or a mixture of both trees. The martens are most at home in ancient forests where the tops of the trees join together. That forms a protective canopy under which the pine martens can hide from their chief prey – eagles. Recently planted forests – or those that are regularly disrupted by people – do not have such a canopy, and martens do not thrive there. In Scotland pine martens often leave forests and hunt on moorlands. Pine martens are nocturnal. They rest in tree hollows, discarded squirrel and bird nests and rocky crevices during the day. The martens eat mainly small rodents, such as voles.

Beech marten

Martes foina

Not found in Britain but common in continental Europe, the beech marten was originally an animal of woodland and hilly habitats. However, it has greatly increased its range by exploiting the habitats humans have created. In some regions of France, Germany and Switzerland, beech martens have become very common in towns, frequently occupying the loft spaces of people's homes.

They can actually be quite a nuisance, chewing electrical wiring and making off with roof insulation to use as bedding. Beech martens have also been reported to have developed a liking for cars. The learned behaviour of sleeping under car bonnets, where it's nice and warm, has spread across central Europe. Every day, up to 40 cars in Switzerland are damaged by beech martens chewing through the wires under their bonnets. This compulsive chewing behaviour is a consequence of the marten's dietary flexibility. Youngsters will test anything and everything to see if it is edible or not.

Distribution: Throughout Europe.
Habitat: Deciduous woodland, open rocky hillsides and urban habitats.
Food: Rodents, fruit and eggs.
Size: 42–48cm (16.5–19in); 1.3–2.3kg (2.75–5lb).
Maturity: 1–2 years.
Breeding: 1 litter of 1–8 kittens per year.
Life span: 18 years.
Status: Common.

Beech martens have a silky dark brown coat with a white throat patch. People tolerate them in towns partly because they help to control rodents. Their main enemies are birds of prey and foxes.

Least weasel

Mustela nivalis

Weasels are common throughout much of the Northern Hemisphere, from Japan and China, across Russia and Europe, including Great Britain but not Ireland, and right across the northern half of North America. They also occur in North Africa.

These animals survive in a wide variety of habitats, though they avoid thick forests, sandy deserts and any overly exposed spaces. For example, they are absent from Arabia and much of the Middle East.

Least weasels have very long bodies, with a long neck and flat head. This allows them to move through broken ground and inside burrows easily. The size of the weasel's body appears to depend on where it is: the largest specimens live in North Africa, and the smallest ones live in North America, where they are called least weasels.

Weasels live alone when not breeding. Males occupy territories that are also home to two or more females. Young are born in summer. They forage at all times of the day or night. They watch and listen for signs of prey before launching an attack, and kill by biting their captured animal in the neck.

Distribution: North Africa, northern Europe, northern Asia and North America.
Habitat: Forest, moorland, steppe, farmland and semi-desert.
Food: Small rodents, such as mice and voles, eggs, nestlings and lizards.
Size: 16–20cm (6.25–8in); 30–55g (1–2oz).
Maturity: 8 months.
Breeding: 2 litters of up to 7 offspring born during spring and late summer. Females are pregnant for a month.
Life span: 7 years, although many die in first year.
Status: Common.

Least weasels have large eyes and ears compared to their body size. In summer the brown fur is about 1cm (0.4in) long, while in winter it more than doubles in length. In the far north, the brown coat also turns white in winter. The animal's flat head helps it to wriggle into burrows and other cramped spaces to catch prey.

Wolverine

Gulo gulo

Wolverines are giant relatives of the weasels and, along with the giant otter, they are the largest mustelids in the world. The name wolverine primarily refers to the North American population. In northern Europe and Siberia, the animals are also known as gluttons due to their liberal feeding habits and voracious appetites.

Wolverines are generally nocturnal but will forage by day if they need to. Their diet varies throughout the year. In summer, they feed on small animals, such as mice and other rodents and ground-living birds, such as pheasants. They also readily feast on summer fruits.

In winter, when most other carnivores are hibernating or sheltering from the cold, wolverines may tackle bigger prey, even something as large as a moose, which is 20 times the size of the predator. The wolverine's wide feet act as snowshoes, allowing them to walk over deep snow, in which hapless deer or wild sheep are easily bogged down, becoming defenceless and unable to make their escape.

Wolverines mate in early summer and young are born in underground dens the following spring. They are weaned at ten weeks and leave their mothers in the autumn.

Distribution: Scandinavia, Siberia, Canada and northern United States.
Habitat: Tundra and conifer forest.
Food: Carrion, eggs, rodents, berries, deer and sheep.
Size: 65–105cm (25.5–41.25in); 10–32kg (22–70.5lb).
Maturity: 2–3 years.
Breeding: Litter of 2–4 born in early spring every 2 years.
Life span: 10 years.
Status: Vulnerable.

Wolverines have large heads and heavily built bodies with dense coats of hairs of different lengths to prevent winter snow and ice from getting too close to the skin, causing heat loss.

European mink

Mustela lutreola

Distribution: Europe.
Habitat: Beside rivers and lakes.
Food: Water rodents, birds, frogs, fishes and insects.
Size: 37cm (14.5in); 590g (1.25lb).
Maturity: 1 year.
Breeding: 4–5 young born in April and May.
Life span: 8 years.
Status: Vulnerable.

European mink once ranged from northern Spain all the way through mainland Europe to the Ob River Valley, east of the Ural Mountains of Russia. They are now almost extinct across this range and only a few populations survive in the south of France and in Spain. European mink have never lived in the British Isles. The mink species found in Britain is the American mink, which was introduced as a source of fur. The American species has become widespread across Europe and its presence has been one of the factors in the downfall of the indigenous European mink. Other problems have been hunting and habitat destruction.

European mink live along the banks of rivers and lakes, where they hide in dense waterside vegetation. They may dig their own burrows or modify those of water rats and other aquatic mammals. The minks are most active at dawn and dusk. They spot their prey in the water, then pounce.

Mink have a thick coat of underfur that helps to repel water when the animal is swimming. The undercoat is especially thick in winter to enable the animal to stay warm when wet.

Kolinsky (*Mustela sibrica*): 25–39cm (9.75–15.25in); 650–800g (1.5–1.75lb)
This species, also known as the Siberian weasel, ranges from the European region of Russia to Korea and Japan. It has a dark brown coat that becomes paler during winter, especially in the north of its range. It has a dark "mask" across the eyes.

European polecat (*Mustela putorius*): 35–51cm (13.75–20in); 0.7–1.4kg (1.5–3lb)
European polecats are the wild form of ferrets. This form is rare in the British Isles but is found across all forested areas of continental Europe. A large population of feral polecats has also formed in New Zealand. Male polecats are up to twice the size of females. Polecats prey on burrowing animals such as rabbits and rodents. Ferrets were originally bred to flush out or kill rabbits that had gone to ground. Domestic ferrets are inquisitive and affectionate and can be house trained. As a result they make good pets. They sleep for about 18 hours a day, so require less attention than other domestic animals.

American mink (*Mustela vison*): 33–43cm (13–17in); 0.7–2.3kg (1.5–5lb)
American mink are small carnivores that live close to water, where they feed on small aquatic animals. They originally came from North America, but were brought to Europe and Asia to be farmed for their fine fur. They have since escaped or been released into the wild and are now a common pest. They are also competition for the similar, and now very rare, European mink species.

African striped weasel

Poecilogale albinucha

The African striped weasel is a skilled burrower. It can dig a tunnel with great speed and spends most of its time underground. When it does emerge to hunt, it does so at night. This behaviour protects it from large birds of prey.

The weasel locates prey by smell and kills or disables it with a bite to the back of the head. Struggling prey are subdued with powerful kicks. The weasel returns to its burrow to feed, taking the meal down to a rounded chamber underground. Food is often stored in this chamber, including injured victims, which are left to die. African striped weasels prey mainly on rodents, and may eat three or four each night.

Most African striped weasels live alone, although small family groups sometimes share a burrow. Courtship between male and female involves the pair growling at each other, while they take it in turns to drag each other around by the scruff of the neck – a practice that mimics the way prey is carried.

Distribution: Sub-Saharan Africa.
Habitat: Grasslands, marshes, forest edges.
Food: Birds, snakes, small rodents and insects.
Size: 25–36cm (9.75–14.25in); 230–380g (8–13.5oz).
Maturity: 20 months.
Breeding: Up to 3 pups born from September to April.
Life span: Unknown.
Status: Common.

Even for a mustelid, this species of weasel has very short legs in comparison to its body. The weasel's stripes mean that this species is often confused with the zorilla, an African polecat.

Honey badger

Mellivora capensis

Honey badgers are secretive hunters and are rarely seen, despite having a wide range that spans most of Africa and southern Asia. The badgers are also known as ratels.

The moniker honey badger might give the impression of sweetness but it belies this hunter's fearsome nature. The name is derived from the animal's love of honey. The badger has evolved a symbiotic relationship with the honey guide bird to locate sources of this food. The honey guide leads the badger to a tree containing a bees' nest. The badger then climbs the tree, knocks the nest down and rips it apart to expose the honeycomb inside. The badger licks at the honey while the honey guide feeds on the beeswax and bee larvae.

Honey badgers generally forage at night. They usually move around alone but sometimes small family groups hunt together. The badgers do not have a den like other species of badger. Instead they roam large distances in search of food, resting in temporary shelters before moving on again. Without a safe place to retreat to, honey badgers will readily fight any threat; in fact they are known for being especially fierce in fights. They will attack an unsuspecting human if cornered and have been known to even bite cars.

Distribution: Africa, Middle East, central Asia, India, Nepal and Myanmar.
Habitat: Grasslands, rocky areas, semi-deserts, forests and woodlands.
Food: Honey, fruits, insects snakes, lizards, rodents, birds, eggs and carrion.
Size: 80cm (31.5in); 9–12kg (19.75–26.5lb).
Maturity: 14 months.
Breeding: Females are pregnant for six months. 1–4 cubs, usually 2, are born in April or May.
Life span: Unknown; other badgers live 20 years.
Status: Common.

Although the honey badger does not have stripes on its face like other species of badger, it does have a silver-grey "cape" on its back, which extends from just behind the eyes to the tip of the tail. A few honey badgers do not have a cape at all. The young are rusty brown in colour. Males are only slightly larger than the females.

Badger

Meles meles

Large members of the mustelid family, badgers have a much more diverse diet than most of the small carnivores. Adept at making a meal out of most situations, badgers will eat anything they find, including berries, fungi and carrion. Worms are a particular favourite, and on warm, damp nights badgers can regularly be observed patrolling through pastureland.

One of the badger's greatest assets is its mouth. The way a badger's skull is structured means that it is physically impossible for the animal to dislocate its jaw, allowing badgers to have one of the most powerful bites in the natural world. This trait makes the badger a fearsome foe for any animal that happens to cross its path.

Unlike most other mustelids, badgers are very social animals. They live in large family groups centred on communal dens, or setts.

The badger's black and white face makes it instantly recognizable.

Distribution: Throughout Europe (but not north of Arctic Circle) and Asia.
Habitat: Favours a mixture of woodland and pastureland, also moving into urban habitats.
Food: Omnivorous diet.
Size: 65–80cm (25.5–31.5in); 8–12kg (17.5–26.5lb).
Maturity: 1–2 years.
Breeding: 1 litter of 1–5 young per year.
Life span: 15 years.
Status: Common.

European otter

Lutra lutra

Distribution: Europe, Asia and North Africa.
Habitat: Rivers and lakes.
Food: Fish, shellfish, frogs, eggs and insects.
Size: 57–70cm (22.5–27.5in); 13kg (28.5lb).
Maturity: 2 years.
Breeding: Pups born mainly in summer.
Life span: Unknown.
Status: Vulnerable.

This species is perhaps more aptly named the Eurasian otter because it is found as far east as Manchuria. It is also found as far north as the tundra line of Siberia and Scandinavia and as far south as the coastal plain of North Africa.

European otters spend most of their waking hours in water, though they build their nests on land. The nests are often made up of a network of tunnels dug into the river bank or running through roots and thick shrubs. Each otter defends a short stretch of river bank, marking its territory with secretions from a scent gland under the base of the tail.

Within the territory an otter has a designated area for entering the water, basking in the sun and playing. Otters are very playful. They are often seen rolling in grass and sliding down muddy slopes into the water.

Otters can dive for up to two minutes at a time. Once in the water they use sensitive whiskers to detect the currents produced by the movements of their prey. Air bubbles trapped in the fur keep the skin dry.

The European otter has a brown coat, which is paler in Asian populations. The feet are generously webbed to aid with swimming. Each foot is also equipped with large claws.

Spotted-necked otter (*Lutra maculicollis*): 85–105cm (2.8–3.4ft); 4kg (8.75lb)
Spotted-necked otters live in the Great Lakes region of East Africa. They do not swim in cloudy water and are often found foraging beside clear mountain streams. As its name suggests, this species has white spots on its neck and throat against a background of brown fur. They have strongly webbed feet and large claws, which suggests they catch most of their food while swimming in open water. Fish makes up most of their diet, but they also eat frogs, freshwater crabs and insect larvae.

African clawless otter (*Aonyx capensis*): 1m (3.25ft); 5kg (11lb)
This species is slightly larger than its close African relative, the Congo clawless otter. It lives in eastern and southern Africa. Like its relative, the African clawless otter has feet with less webbing than most otters and only rounded claws on the hind feet. Members of this species feed on creatures that live on the bottom of rivers and streams, such as crabs and frogs. They locate this prey by touch, using their dexterous, clawless hands.

Congo clawless otter

Aonyx congicus

Congo clawless otters live in the waterways of the mighty Congo Basin, the largest river system in Africa. The otters avoid the main watercourses and are more often found in streams, swamps and ponds in the deep tropical rainforest.

These bodies of water have little or no current and are consequently heavily clouded with sediment. Lacking claws, these nocturnal otters are much better able to feel for slippery prey in this muddy water and overturn stones in search of food than their clawed cousins.

Clawless otters also have shorter whiskers than other species. This suggests that they are not as reliant on whiskers for detecting prey underwater as other otters. This species of otter catches fish and frogs and collects prey, such as shellfish, from the muddy bottom of the river.

The otter's teeth are also more suited to a wide range of food than other otters, which all have teeth adapted for gripping slithering fish. This feature, along with the short whiskers, suggests that Congo clawless otters spend a lot more time foraging on land than other species. Little is known about the breeding habits of this allusive species, but they are probably broadly similar to other species.

Distribution: Congo River Basin.
Habitat: Swamps and ponds in tropical rainforests.
Food: Fish, frogs and shellfish.
Size: 78–98cm (30.75–38.5in); 15–25kg (33–55lb).
Maturity: 1 year.
Breeding: Litters of 2–3 young.
Life span: 15 years.
Status: Unknown.

Unusually for otters, this species has no claws or webbing on its forefeet. There is a small amount of webbing on the hind feet and a simple peg-like claw on the three middle toes. Clawless feet help the otters to feel objects under muddy water as they search for prey.

MONGOOSES

Mongooses form a family of carnivores called the Herpestidae. They look similar to most small carnivores, including the mustelids and viverrids, in that they have short legs, long slender bodies and pointed whiskered snouts. This body form is ideal for searching for and tackling prey in tight places. Unlike most small carnivores, which hunt alone, mongooses tend to live in large units, or bands.

Banded mongoose

Mungos mungo

Distribution: Africa south of the Sahara.
Habitat: Grassland and dry woodland.
Food: Insects and millipedes.
Size: 30–45cm (12–18in); 1.5–2.5kg (3.3–5.5lb).
Maturity: 9–10 months.
Breeding: Litters of 3 or 4, up to 4 times per year.
Life span: Up to 12 years.
Status: Common.

The banded mongoose is one of the most common mongooses in Africa. It lives in open grassland and areas of dry woodland, and is also found in rocky, broken country. It lives in bands of up to 40 individuals, sharing dens inside old termite mounds or abandoned aardvark holes. The dens have central sleeping chambers, which are reached from several holes.

Dens are used for only a few days at a time, with bands regularly moving on to new foraging sites. Banded mongooses feed during the daytime, returning to their dens before sunset. Their diet consists of invertebrates, such as beetles and millipedes.

Banded mongooses have excellent senses of smell, hearing and vision. Their bands are highly social, with members rarely straying far from each other and communicating by making several distinct sounds. All females in a band breed at the same time. The young are raised together, and are suckled by all the adult females in the band.

Banded mongooses have brownish-grey fur with dark brown stripes, or bands, across their backs and tails. Each foot possesses five long claws.

Meerkat

Suricata suricatta

Meerkats are relatives of mongooses, which live in large bands in the arid, semi-desert areas of southern Africa. They are efficient diggers and live in large underground burrows.

Meerkats live in highly organized societies. While feeding, at least one band member keeps a look-out for danger, communicating to the others with an array of sounds. For example, howling warns that a bird of prey is approaching, while double-barking informs the band that a terrestrial predator has been spotted.

A meerkat band has between 10 and 15 individuals, with two or three pairs of males and females which do all the breeding. The young kits stay close to their dens and are looked after by at least one adult while the rest of their band forages for food.

Meerkats live in dry, open country in southern Africa, especially in the semi-desert regions of Namibia, southern Angola, Botswana and western South Africa.

Distribution: South-western and southern Africa from Angola to South Africa.
Habitat: Semi-desert and scrubland.
Food: Insects, scorpions, small vertebrates and eggs.
Size: 25–35cm (9.75–13.75in); 600–975g (1.25–2.5lb).
Maturity: 1 year.
Breeding: Litters of 2–5 kits born once per year in November.
Life span: 10 years.
Status: Common.

Gambian mongoose

Mungos gambianus

Distribution: Southern coastal region of West Africa.
Habitat: Grassland and woodland.
Food: Insects.
Size: 30–45cm (12–17.75in); 1–2kg (2.25–4.5lb).
Maturity: 10 months.
Breeding: Up to 4 litters produced each year.
Life span: 10 years.
Status: Unknown.

Gambian mongooses are found from Gambia and Senegal to Nigeria. They avoid thickly forested areas and are found instead in grassland and open woodlands.

This species lives in groups of 10–20 individuals. Each group has an equal split of males and females. Some groups swell to up to 40 members, but these tend to split into smaller groups that can exploit sources of food more effectively.

The Gambian mongoose dens as a group in disused burrows, hollow logs and rock crevices. The group moves between dens regularly to avoid depleting food supplies in one area. The Gambian mongoose is diurnal. It hunts as a group, moving in a fixed formation as the animals search for insects. Members of the group communicate with each other by growls and screams. Twittering sounds help the group stay together while feeding, and louder barks warn of approaching danger.

Gambian mongooses have a uniform grey-brown fur. The only obvious markings are a dark streak on the neck. Males and females are about the same size.

Long-nosed cusimanse
(*Crossarchus obscurus*): 30–45cm (12–17.75in); 1.5kg (3.25lb)
Cusimanses are small mongooses that live in patches of swampy forest in West Africa. Their bodies are covered in long brown-grey-yellow hairs. Cusimanses travel in large groups and appear to be most active during the day but are also seen on the move by night. The group takes shelter when convenient in temporary dens. They feed on fruit, seeds, insects and small reptiles, foraging by pushing their long snouts through leaf litter, scratching at soil and overturning stones. Long-nosed cusimanses also crack snail shells and eggs by hurling them between their back legs on to hard stones.

Pousargues's mongoose (*Dologale dybowskii*): 25–30cm (9.75–12in); 300–400g (10.5–14oz)
This small species of mongoose lives in the woodlands and grasslands of Central Africa from southern Sudan to the Central African Republic. It is common around the shores of Lake Albert between the Democratic Republic of Congo and Uganda. This mongoose has a bushy tail and a grey face, long claws and simple teeth. This suggests that its diet contains a lot of invertebrates, which the mongoose digs out from underground.

Black-footed mongoose

Bdeogale nigripes

The black-footed mongoose lives in the rainforests of southern Nigeria and those around the mouth of the River Congo in the Democratic Republic of Congo and northern Angola. They are most often found near to rivers. They do most of their foraging on land and rarely climb trees but will move in and out of water as they move around.

Black-footed mongooses are nocturnal. They are most often seen alone, but pairs are also spotted. These may be breeding pairs who are living together for a short period during the mating season or a mother and her juvenile offspring. Breeding takes places in the dry season.

Black-footed mongooses survive by eating mainly insects, most commonly ants, termites and beetles. They also feed on carrion, small mammals and snakes and will take frogs and salamanders from shallow water. While most other species of mongoose have sharp teeth built for killing large prey, the teeth of this species are more adapted for crushing small prey.

Distribution: Central Africa.
Habitat: Rainforests.
Food: Insects.
Size: 37–60cm (14.5–23.5in); 0.9–3kg (2–6.5lb).
Maturity: 1 year.
Breeding: Litter born between November and January.
Life span: 15 years.
Status: Common.

This species of mongoose lives near to water and has slightly webbed feet to help it swim strongly. Its coat is also adapted to life in and out of water, with long, thick guard hairs over a softer undercoat.

Slender mongoose

Galerella sanguinea

The slender mongoose is one of the smaller members of the mongoose family. It is also one of the most widespread of all the African mongooses, with a range that stretches across most of the continent south of the Sahara Desert.

While it avoids the dense tropical rainforests of the Congo Basin, this species is found in a wide array of other habitats, from lush grasslands and savannahs to rock fields and semi-desert. Slender mongooses are also agile climbers and often look for food in the branches of large shrubs and among the trees of open woodlands.

A single male slender mongoose occupies a territory that overlaps those of several females. Females defend their territories from each other, but the male is tolerated by a female when she is ready to mate. Most mating takes place between October and March. At all other times of the year the males forages alone. Mothers and their young sometimes form small groups, but these are short-lived as the offspring leave to find their own territories.

There are more than 40 recognized subspecies of slender mongoose. These show a range of different colour forms, from yellow and red to brown. Many individuals are spotted.

Distribution: Sub-Saharan Africa.
Habitat: Grasslands, scrub and semi-deserts.
Food: Insects, lizards and fruit.
Size: 27–40cm (10.5–15.5in); 350–900g (12.25–31.75oz).
Maturity: 1 or 2 years.
Breeding: Single male fathers several litters.
Life span: 10 years.
Status: Common.

Egyptian mongoose

Herpestes ichneumon

Egyptian mongooses are widespread across Africa but are not found in the rainforests that grow in the Congo Basin and along the coast of the Gulf of Guinea. In addition, the species is not very common in southern Africa. However, they have been introduced to Madagascar – to the detriment of native species – and Italy.

They live around trees that grow beside waterways. This habitat is one of the few to have increased in abundance due to human activity. Today, Egyptian mongooses are equally at home beside a canal or irrigation channel as they are next to a natural river.

These mammals live alone, in pairs or in small groups of up to seven individuals, depending on the availability of food in their area. The species is diurnal and forages for food on the ground, in trees and in the water.

Each mongoose has a sac above the anus that produces a strong-smelling substance. When mongooses travel together at night, the following animal walks with its nose pressed to the anal sac so it can keep in contact with the leader in the dark. The leader is generally a mother being followed by its offspring or a female being courted by a male. Mongooses also mark their territories with these anal secretions.

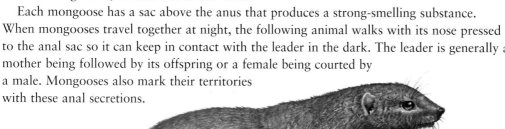

Egyptian mongooses have claws and teeth adapted for their lifestyle. The long claws are used for digging dens, while the teeth are able to slice through meat and grab fish easily.

Distribution: Southern Europe, Middle East, North and Central Africa.
Habitat: Trees near rivers, lakes, canals and ditches.
Food: Fish, insects, snakes and frogs.
Size: 54cm (21.5in); 2.85kg (6.25lb).
Maturity: 2 years.
Breeding: Female's genitals swell and redden when on heat. Gestation is 11 weeks and 2–4 kits are born in summer.
Life span: 12 years in the wild but almost twice that in captivity.
Status: Common.

White-tailed mongoose

Ichneumia albicauda

Distribution: Sub-Saharan Africa.
Habitat: Woodland and grassland.
Food: Insects.
Size: 58cm (22.75in); 4kg (8.75lb).
Maturity: 2 years.
Breeding: Litters born in rainy season.
Life span: 12 years.
Status: Common.

Like many other African species of mongoose, the white-tailed mongoose is found across the continent south of the Sahara but is absent from the jungles of Central Africa and the deserts of southern Africa.

White-tailed mongooses are nocturnal. By day they rest inside thickets of vegetation or in burrows abandoned by other animals. When night falls the mongooses forage alone. They are secretive animals and rarely leave the cover of ground vegetation. White-tailed mongooses eat mainly ground-living insects, such as locusts, beetles and mole crickets. They will also eat small vertebrates if given the opportunity. They sometimes steal domestic poultry. This species is also an egg eater: it breaks an egg by throwing it between its hind legs on to a rock. Kits are born in the wet season. They become independent at nine months.

This large mongoose has a grizzled coat of pale brown underfur with long black guard hairs over it. Only the last half of the large bushy tail is white. The palms are naked and this hairless area extends to the wrists of the forepaws.

Dwarf mongoose (*Helogale parvula*): 24cm (9.5in); 320g (11.25oz)
The species shares the title of smallest mongoose with the brown mongoose of Madagascar. The dwarf mongoose lives across Central Africa from Ethiopia to Angola and in parts of eastern South Africa. It occupies savannahs, woodlands and mountain brush. Dwarf mongooses have brown-and-grey speckled coats. They live in a complex social system, where an older, reproductively active female is dominant. Her mate is the group's second-ranking animal. The next most dominant member is the youngest offspring. Other members of the group are ranked according to age, with females always outranking males. Dwarf mongooses eat eggs, small vertebrates and insects, which they find in leaf litter and under rocks.

Liberian mongoose (*Liberictis kuhni*): 45cm (17.75in); 2.3kg (5lb)
The Liberian mongoose is the most endangered mongoose species on the African mainland. Only the Madagascan mongooses are similarly endangered. The individuals that do survive live in northern Liberia and Côte d'Ivoire. They are naturally rare and have suffered from overhunting. They are diurnal insect eaters that live in small groups of about five.

Yellow mongoose

Cynictis penicillata

Yellow mongooses are most common in the dry region of southern Africa that spreads from the Transvaal to northern Angola. However, this mongoose does not populate the driest habitats in this region, being found instead in grass and scrublands. It never ventures into forest or very high up in mountains.

These animals are primarily diurnal but they do sometimes forage at night, especially in areas where they are disturbed by people during the day. The yellow mongoose emerges from its den after sunrise and warms itself in the sun for a short while before heading off for a day-long foraging trip. The animals live in social groups made up of a male and female breeding pair and their younger offspring. Older offspring tend to leave the group, but unrelated older individuals may join from other neighbouring groups.

Males roam through the territories of other groups, which means that the relationships between group members might be more complex than a simple family structure.

Distribution: Southern Africa.
Habitat: Dry grasslands.
Food: Insects.
Size: 31cm (12.25in); 800g (1.75lb).
Maturity: 1 year.
Breeding: Young born in August to November.
Life span: Unknown.
Status: Common.

There are currently 12 subspecies of yellow mongoose. They differ in the colour and length of their hair and size of tail. Southern yellow mongooses are larger than those in the north, which also have a greyer coat.

Ring-tailed mongoose

Galidia elegans

Like many Malagasy mammals, the ring-tailed mongoose is in danger of extinction. This threat is largely from the destruction of the African island's tropical forests but is compounded by the fact that this species of mongoose reproduces at a much slower rate than its more fecund relatives – producing only a single kit each year. Madagascan forests are not normal rainforests. They are prone to long periods of drought, which makes food hard to come by. The mongoose's small litter size therefore ensures that mothers will be able to find food for their young each year.

Ring-tailed mongooses are seen alone or in pairs. They are sometimes also found in small groups. Little is known about the social behaviour of this species, but evidence suggests that they form breeding pairs and that groups are family units made up of the parents and two or three offspring. The mongooses are good climbers and will forage for food in trees as well as on the ground. The bushy ringed tail helps individuals keep track of other mongooses while they move through the branches.

The ring-tailed mongoose should not be mistaken for another resident of Madagascar, the ring-tailed lemur. Like the lemur, ring-tailed mongooses probably use their bushy, striped tails to communicate with each other among thick vegetation.

Distribution: Madagascar, most common in the north, east and west-central regions of the island.
Habitat: Subtropical and tropical dry forests.
Food: Small mammals, insects, spiders, lizards, fish, eggs and fruits.
Size: 32–38cm (12.5–15in); 700–900g (24.5–31.75oz).
Maturity: 2 years.
Breeding: Gestation period is 3 months. A single kit born in July to February.
Life span: 8 years, although 13 years has been recorded in captivity.
Status: Vulnerable.

Broad-striped mongoose

Galidictis fasciat

As its name suggests, the broad-striped mongoose has dark stripes running from the neck to the lower part of the tail. This species is easily mistaken for the small Indian civet, which has been introduced to Madagascar. This introduction has been at great cost to the native species of carnivore, such as this mongoose, and their prey animals alike.

Broad-striped mongooses live in the forests of Madagascar, where they lead solitary nocturnal lives. Madagascar is divided by a range of mountains that runs north to south. Most sightings of the broad-striped mongooses are made at an altitude of about 800m (2,600ft) on the eastern side of the mountains.

Being a forest dweller, the broad-striped mongoose is a good climber and forages for food in the trees. Its diet is dominated by small vertebrates, such as rodents, lizards and amphibians. It also eats insects and other invertebrates. There are some reports that this species also preys on small lemurs, some of which are little more than the size of a rodent.

Little is known about the breeding habits of the broad-striped mongoose. When compared to its close relatives, it is likely to follow a similar breeding pattern to them, in which adults form temporary pairings to help raise the single offspring.

Distribution: Madagascar; most commonly spotted on the eastern slopes of the island's mountains.
Habitat: Mountain forest below 1,500m (4,900ft).
Food: Insects, small rodents and birds.
Size: 57cm (22.5in); 600g (21.25oz).
Maturity: 2 years.
Breeding: Single young born in July–February. Gestation is between 10 and 12 weeks.
Life span: 10 years.
Status: Vulnerable.

Giant-striped mongoose

Galidictis grandidieri

Distribution: South-western Madagascar.
Habitat: Spiny desert, an arid region of cactus-like plants covered in sharp spines.
Food: Insects, scorpions and small vertebrates, such as lizards.
Size: 40cm (15.75in); 500g (17.5oz).
Maturity: 2 years.
Breeding: Single offspring born at all times of the year. Gestation period is between 10 and 14 weeks
Life span: Unknown, but could be as much as 20 years.
Status: Endangered.

This type of mongoose lives in the "spiny desert" of southern Madagascar. The species is very rare, and all individuals are found in an area of 430sq km (165sq miles). The spiny desert is so called because most of the plants that grow there are covered in thorns. This makes it very difficult for large animals, including humans, to travel through the habitat. Consequently, giant-striped mongooses have only rarely been observed in the wild, and many details about their lives remain a mystery.

Giant-striped mongooses are nocturnal. They avoid the heat of the day by resting inside hollows in the limestone outcrops that are common in the region. They form monogamous pairs that stay together all year round. If one is injured, the partner will stay nearby.

These animals eat insects, especially the hissing cockroach, which is now quite familiar as a pet across the world. The mongoose also has long legs and powerful jaws. This suggests that it can also catch and eat larger prey than insects, such as scorpions.

Despite their name, giant-striped mongooses do not have stripes that are particularly large. They have eight in all, which run down the back from the ears to the base of the tail. Male and female giant-striped mongooses appear to be the same size as each other, although females have a scent pouch near the anus.

Narrow-striped mongoose

Mungotictis decemlineata

Distribution: South and western Madagascar, although not seen in the south for 20 years.
Habitat: Savannah.
Food: Insects, eggs and small vertebrates.
Size: 25–35cm (9.75–13.75in); 600–700g (21.25–24.5oz).
Maturity: 2 years.
Breeding: Single young born in summer. Mating takes place in early spring
Life span: Unknown; other species reach 20.
Status: Endangered.

Narrow-tailed mongooses live in the sandy savannahs of southern and western Madagascar. They are active during the day, foraging on the ground and in the small trees that grow sparsely across the region. Like the similar Malagasy mongooses, this species is primarily an insectivore, though they are also known to eat eggs and can tackle small mammals and lizards when given the opportunity. When narrow-tailed mongooses catch prey, they lie on their sides and hold the food with all four feet as they eat it.

These mongooses live in breeding pairs, which are often joined by juvenile offspring. In areas that can support a high population of mongooses, larger social groups form containing up to 20 non-related individuals, though these are becoming very rare as the surviving wild population of narrow-striped mongooses becomes increasingly fragmented. Most foraging is done alone or in pairs. In winter, any larger group breaks up into its constituent pairs.

Mating takes place between December and April, with a peak in March. Kits are born in the summer and weaned within two months.

Narrow-striped mongooses have between eight and ten thin bands running along the back. The tail is bushy and ringed.

RODENTS

The Rodentia, with over 2,000 species distributed all around the globe, is by far the largest order of mammals. All rodents have two upper and two lower chisel-like incisor teeth. These incisors grow continuously throughout their lives, so, unlike many other animals, they can gnaw everything without their teeth getting worn away.

Edible dormouse

Glis glis

When awake, all species of dormouse belie their dozy reputation, being incredibly lithe and agile climbers – the edible dormouse being no exception. These dormice spend virtually their entire lives in the treetops, searching for food, and are very reluctant to leave the safety of the branches. If they cannot leap between trees, they will not cross the open areas on the ground. Roads and tracks cut through woodland can therefore inhibit the movement of dormice.

Dormice are champion sleepers, being one of the few types of mammal to enter a true state of hibernation. Come autumn, dormice descend into the bases of hollow trees, wrap themselves into balls and fall into a state of very deep sleep. They allow their body temperature to drop very low, barely more than the temperature of the air around them. Heart rate and breathing also slow right down. By doing this, they are able to conserve enough energy to last them through the winter. When spring arrives, the dormice's metabolism speeds up again, bringing them out of six or seven months of uninterrupted sleep.

Distribution: Throughout central and eastern Europe, extending west through northern Spain. Introduced into England.
Habitat: The canopy of mature deciduous woodland.
Food: Nuts, fruit, fungi, bark, insects and occasionally eggs and nestlings.
Size: 13–19cm (5–7.5in), 70–300g (0.15–0.66lb).
Maturity: 2 years.
Breeding: 1 litter of 2–9 offspring born in summer.
Life span: 7 years.
Status: Common.

Also known as fat dormice, edible dormice were kept by the Romans in jars, called gliraria, to fatten them for the table.

Water vole

Arvicola terrestris

Distribution: Widespread across Europe and Asia.
Habitat: Banks of slow-flowing rivers and streams.
Food: Grasses, rushes and sedges.
Size: 14–22cm (5.5–8.5in); 150–300g (0.33–0.66lb).
Maturity: 2 months.
Breeding: 3 or 4 litters of 5 young born throughout spring and summer.
Life span: Up to 3 years.
Status: Common.

Water voles are also known – confusingly – as water rats. Ratty, of *The Wind in the Willows* fame, was really a water vole, and, like him, these rodents are found living alongside slow-moving rivers, ditches, dykes and lakes. In areas of central Europe, however, water voles do not live by water, preferring dry habitats instead. In some places they are considered to be a serious agricultural pest.

Water voles excavate extensive burrow systems in the banks of the rivers, with plenty of entrance and exit holes so that they can escape from the various predators they encounter – both in and out of the water. Even so, the average life span of a water vole is a mere five months. Herons, barn owls, brown rats and pike are all known to prey on water voles, but the rodents' most important predators are stoats and mink. Indeed, the introduction of the American mink to Britain has been blamed for the species' recent and rapid decline.

Water voles are often mistaken for rats, but they differ from rats by having blunter snouts, more rounded bodies, smaller ears and shorter, hairy tails.

Siberian lemming

Lemmus sibericus

Contrary to popular belief, lemmings do not commit suicide. During favourable years, the lemmings' ability to reproduce very quickly leads to population explosions of amazing proportions. As the population size goes up, space becomes more and more difficult to find, and young are pushed away from the best habitat, down the mountains and into the valleys.

Lemmings are good swimmers when they have to be, but they don't know their limits. During dispersal, youngsters often try to cross large bodies of water, drowning in the process. It is this behaviour which gave rise to the misconception that they kill themselves.

During the summer, lemmings spend much of their time underground in burrows, but, when the ground starts to freeze in autumn, the lemmings cannot dig through the ground and are forced to forage on the surface. The lemmings do not hibernate during the harsh Siberian winter, but construct tunnel systems under the snow in search of food. The tunnels keep them out of sight of hungry predators, such as great grey owls, which are heavily reliant on lemmings as a source of food.

Unlike other species of lemming, the Siberian lemming does not change the colour of its coat in winter.

Distribution: Siberia and northern North America.
Habitat: Tundra grassland.
Food: Moss and grass.
Size: 13–18cm (5–7in); 23–34g (0.05–0.07lb).
Maturity: 5–6 weeks.
Breeding: These prolific breeders may produce 8 litters of up to 6 young each throughout the summer.
Life span: Less than 2 years.
Status: Common.

Alpine marmot (*Marmota marmota*):
45–60cm (17.75–23.5in); 3–4.5kg (6.5–10lb)
Alpine marmots live in the Alpine and sub-Alpine pastures of the Alps. Like many other marmots, Alpine marmots live in family groups, consisting of a breeding pair and their offspring from previous years. Older male offspring are known to help keep their younger siblings warm during the cold Alpine winters. Litter sizes tend to be small – about two pups. The pups stay with their parents until they are three years old.

Southern birch mouse (*Sicista subtilis*):
5–9cm (2–3.5in); 6–14g (0.015–0.03lb)
These tiny mice inhabit the forests, moors, meadows and steppes of eastern Europe and Asia. They excavate shallow burrows, in which they build oval-shaped nests of dry grass and cut plant stems. They travel over the ground in leaps and bounds. They are also great climbers. Strong outer toes grip twigs, and their prehensile tail curls around other branches for additional support.

Wood lemming (*Myopus schisticolor*):
10cm (4in); 33g (1.25oz)
The wood lemming lives in the taiga (forests of conifer trees) of Scandinavia and is also found across Siberia as fat east as northern Mongolia. It digs tunnels with its teeth in the thick moss. It eats the moss and make stores of it in autumn to see it through the winter. As with other lemmings, the population of wood lemmings fluctuates wildly. In good years a population explosion results in migrations of large numbers in search of feeding sites.

Eurasian beaver

Castor fiber

Eurasian beavers are the largest rodents in Europe and Asia. They live in or beside woodland waterways. Beavers live in family groups of four or five individuals, with each family defending a small area of river and woodland. The family lives inside a den called a lodge, which is a simple tunnel dug up into the bank from below the water line. In places where this construction is not possible, beavers build a castle of mud, stones and branches. To ensure that the entrance to the lodge is underwater, the beavers build a dam across the river to make a deep pool of calm water. On occasion, the lodge is built into the dam.

Beavers dig canals from the river into the woodland. Using their huge teeth, they cut down small trees and cut them into chunks, floating the timber down the canal into the dammed area. The wood is eaten along with water plants, or stored underwater for eating later.

Distribution: Northern Europe and Siberia.
Habitat: Lakes and rivers.
Food: Wood and river plants.
Size: 80–110cm (2.5–3.5ft); 17–32kg (37.5–70.5lb).
Maturity: 3 years.
Breeding: Litters of about 3 born early summer.
Life span: 14 years.
Status: Near threatened.

The Eurasian beaver is similar to the American beaver, but is slightly smaller. It is a powerful swimmer, thanks to a flipper-like tail and webbed feet.

Hamster

Cricetus cricetus

The common hamster is also named the black-bellied hamster because of the dark stripe that runs from the shoulders along the belly to the base of the tail. Most pet hamsters belong to another species as domestic breeds of the golden hamster – a smaller species living in the Middle East.

Within Europe, the common hamster is mainly a resident of cultivated fields, where it feeds on the grains of cereal crops, potatoes, beets and other root crops. This diet is mirrored in more wild habitats, such as the great Eurasian steppe. Common hamsters also eat any insect larvae they find in the soil, especially beetle grubs. Despite their relatively small size, these stocky rodents are known to eat small birds, frogs and smaller rodents, such as shrews.

Hamsters stash a lot of their food, making large stockpiles within burrow systems. Food intended for storage is carried back home in the animal's cheek pouches, which gives the hamster's face its characteristic look.

The stored food is consumed over the winter. The hamster sleeps for several days at a stretch during this period but then wakes to eat part of its food cache. In warmer periods, the hamster is active at dawn and dusk, emerging from its intricate network of burrows to forage.

The hamster's breeding season is between April and August. Each female produces two litters each summer. Newborns weigh 7g (0.25oz). They are weaned in three weeks.

Distribution: Europe and Siberia.
Habitat: Steppe and agricultural land.
Food: Seeds, fruits, roots and insect larvae.
Size: 20–27cm (8–10.5in); 200–500g (7–17.5oz).
Maturity: Females 43 days; males 56 days.
Breeding: 2 litters of up to 12 young born in summer. Gestation period is 20 days.
Life span: 2 years.
Status: Common.

Crested rat

Lophiomys imhausi

The crested, or maned, rat lives across eastern African from Somalia and Sudan in the north to Tanzania in the south. Fossil records show that the rodents also once lived as far north as Israel. They are woodland animals and are common in highland areas that rise up on either side of the region's Great Rift Valley.

Crested rats are nocturnal. By day they rest in rock crevices and hollow tree trunks. They are slow movers and, instead of dashing for cover, they have evolved an elaborate array of defensive behaviours to ward off attackers. At first the rats raise their mane to make them appear larger than they really are. The mane also highlights white stripes that point to anal glands under the tail. If the attacker is undeterred, the crested rat will squirt a foul-smelling liquid from those glands. At the same time, the rat snorts and hisses, snaps its teeth and thrashes its body.

If none of this puts the attacker off, the crested rat has one last line of defence. Its skull has a unique structure (it is strengthened with extra bones and has unusual projections over the eye sockets), and it is presumed that this is a defensive adaptation.

The crested rat has a bristled mane running from the top of the head and merging with the long bushy tail. The females are generally larger than the males.

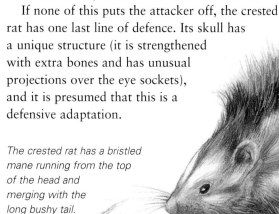

Distribution: Eastern Africa including Somalia, Sudan, Ethiopia, Uganda, Kenya and Tanzania.
Habitat: Forests and woodlands. Especially common in highland regions.
Food: Fruit and roots. The rats hold food in their forepaws.
Size: 22–36cm (8.5–14.5in); 750g (26.5oz).
Maturity: 1 year.
Breeding: 2–3 young in each litter. Probably a single litter produced each year. Newborns are fully haired.
Life span: Unknown.
Status: Common.

Gambian pouch rat

Cricetomys gambianus

Distribution: Sub-Saharan Africa.
Habitat: Sheltered areas.
Food: Fruits, seeds, leaves and insects.
Size: 91cm (35.75in); 4kg (8.75lb).
Maturity: 6 months.
Breeding: Up to 5 offspring born in summer.
Life span: 5 years.
Status: Common.

Gambian pouch rats live south of the Sahara Desert, reaching as far south as Zululand in South Africa. They have very little body fat under the skin and so are very susceptible to the cold. They are primarily found in the humid tropical region of Africa where temperatures stay more or less constant all year around. Nevertheless, they are also intolerant of extreme heat, so the rats stay in cool dens tunnelled under the ground during the day.

Although these rats are indeed giant, they are not commonly seen because they do not venture out into the open very much. Instead they search for food under the cover of darkness and populate only those areas that provide plenty of cover. They hoard food in their dens, carrying it back home in cheek pouches.

Gambian pouch rats do not have many natural predators. Adults are rarely preyed upon by anything except humans, who in many parts of Africa traditionally consider the rat to be a delicacy.

The Gambian pouch rat is the largest rat in the world. Including the tail, it can grow to nearly 1m (3.25ft) long.

Mouse-like hamster (*Calomyscus bailwardi*): 10cm (4in); 30g (1oz)
The mouse-like hamster lives in western Asia and south-eastern Europe. Its preferred habitat is highland meadows and it is rarely found below 400m (1,300ft). As its name suggests, the species resembles a mouse in size and body form, but its teeth show that it belongs to a different family. The mouse-like hamster becomes mature at four months and produces one litter of five offspring in summer. Outside of the breeding season, the hamsters are solitary animals. They feed on grains and grasses. In summer they forage for food at night, but in winter, when night temperatures can be very low, they begin to forage in the day.

Delany's swamp mouse (*Delanymus brooksi*): 6.5cm (2.5in)
Delany's swamp mouse lives in the eastern half of Central Africa in the marshy forests that grow on mountains. They do not live below 1,700m (5,500ft). They eat seeds and build small nests out of grass that sit in the branches of a shrub. They forage at night. They can climb through the shrubs using flexible feet with opposable toes for gripping and a prehensile tail used as a fifth limb.

Pouched mouse

Saccostomus campestris

The pouched mouse lives in the savannahs and steppes of southern Africa, from Angola and Malawi through to South Africa. It forages on the ground looking for seeds and nuts. It dens under the ground, either by digging its own burrow or by taking over one abandoned by another grassland animal.

Pouched mice are so called because they have cheek pouches, which are used to store food for carrying back to the burrow, where the food is either eaten or stored underground for later consumption. In time of plenty the mice might store nearly three-quarters of everything they find. The stored food is used by nursing mothers, who cannot leave the den until the young are more independent. The stores are also used during droughts when seeds and other plant food are hard to come by. When the food supply is used up and no more food is to be found, the mice enter a torpor, or dormant state similar to hibernation.

Female pouched mice tend to avoid other members of the species, but there is a window of a few hours when females allow males to come near enough to mate. The females then turn violent against the mates. Litters are born 50 days later.

Distribution: Southern Africa.
Habitat: Grasslands.
Food: Seeds.
Size: 19cm (7.5in); 85g (3oz).
Maturity: Unknown.
Breeding: Litters of 5 young born in January–September.
Life span: 3 years.
Status: Common.

Pouched mice have bodies built for digging. The legs are short, and the rounded head and small ears make it easier for the mice to move along tunnels.

Chestnut climbing mouse

Dendromus mystacalis

Chestnut climbing mice live across Africa, south of the Sahara Desert. They are found in grassland areas and shrubs from Somalia to the coast of Nigeria and south to Angola in the west and the northern tip of South Africa in the east. They do not live in desert areas, such as the Kalahari of Namibia and Botswana, and are not found in the dense forests of the Congo Basin.

These mice are closely associated with a short herby weed plant named namirembe. They are also common pests in banana groves and gardens. The mice climb through shrubs and tall grasses in search of food. They spend almost all of their time off the ground, but will cross areas of bare earth if needed.

Chestnut climbing mice build nests from shredded leaves or grasses. The nests are spherical and are suspended from bushes or trees. They have a single entrance and are lined with finely shredded dry leaves.

In equatorial regions most litters of the chestnut climbing mouse are produced between November and January. However, to the north and south, the seasons follow a different pattern and young are produced at other times.

This species is not always chestnut in colour: the fur can be anything from dark brown to yellow and a few have a pale stripe down the back. The females are slightly smaller than the males.

Distribution: Africa south of the Sahara, from Ethiopia to Nigeria and south to Angola and eastern South Africa. Absent from Namibia.
Habitat: Grasslands, farms and scrub. Absent from the tropical rainforests of the Congo.
Food: Seeds, grass and insects.
Size: 7cm (2.75in); 17g (0.5oz).
Maturity: 1 year.
Breeding: Litter of 3–4 young born in November–January.
Life span: 3 years.
Status: Common.

White-tailed mouse

Mystromys albicaudatus

White-tailed mice live in eastern South Africa and Swaziland. Their preferred habitat is dry grassland and semi-desert areas where there are plenty of large cracks in the arid soil. The mice make their burrows in these cracks and hide in them during the day to keep out of the baking heat. At night they emerge to feed.

These mice live in monogamous breeding pairs and produce litters throughout the year. However, they spend much of their time alone, searching for food. Although they forage for seeds and leaves, they will also eat insects when given the opportunity. In laboratory studies they consistently opt for animal food over plant material, but in the wild their diet is likely to consist largely of plant food.

The mice become most active during the short rainy season, when plants are growing at their fastest rate and producing seeds in large numbers. Plants in this habitat have only a short time in which to reproduce and release their seeds, and the white-tailed mouse is used by many as a distributor. The mice digest the seeds' outer coats, and the seeds then pass out in the faeces, ready to germinate.

The white-tailed mouse has a pale grey upper coat but is white on the belly, and this colour extends on to the whole of the tail. The males are about 25 per cent larger than the females.

Distribution: Eastern South Africa and Swaziland.
Habitat: Grassland and semi-desert with dry soils suitable for burrowing.
Food: Seeds, leaves and insects. Known to eat dead offspring.
Size: 18cm (7in); 87g (3oz).
Maturity: 150 days, probably older in the wild.
Breeding: Litter of 2–5 young produced every 10 weeks. Breeding pairs are probably monogamous.
Life span: 4 years in the wild, double that in captivity.
Status: Endangered.

Malagasy giant rat

Hypogeomys antimena

Distribution: Western Madagascar.
Habitat: Sandy coastal forests.
Food: Fallen fruit.
Size: 30cm (12in); 1.2kg (2.75lb).
Maturity: 1–2 years.
Breeding: 1–2 young born in rainy season.
Life span: Unknown.
Status: Endangered.

Malagasy giant rats live in the deciduous forests that grow along the western coast of Madagascar. These forests are being put under extreme pressure by human activities and have been greatly fragmented. Consequently, the population of giant rats has suffered also and the species is endangered.

Malagasy giant rats dig deep burrows in the sandy forest soil. They have several entrances and reach down 5m (16.5ft) at their deepest point. A burrow is home to a family unit of rats made up of an adult male and female and their offspring from the two previous breeding seasons. Maturing females leave the burrow to set up home nearby, while males migrate further distances to avoid mating with closely related females. Malagasy giant rats mate for life. This strategy ensures that both parents will be present to defend their young against predators. The rats are in considerable danger of being eaten by fossas and boas.

Both male and female Malagasy giant rats are about the same size. They have long hind feet and sturdy claws, which are used for digging tunnels.

Grey climbing mouse (*Dendromus melanotis*): 13cm (5in); 12.5g (0. 5oz)
The grey climbing mouse is a relative of the chestnut climbing mouse. It is found further south than its relative in the drier regions of southern Africa. The grey climbing mouse lives in grasslands and brush from coastal areas to mountainsides. This species has a dark stripe along its back. The tail is long and prehensile and is used when the mouse is climbing through long grass or flimsy branches. The mice move around at night, foraging for insects and seeds. They build their own nests using grasses and leaves but have also been found living in the abandoned nests of weaverbirds and sunbirds.

Bastard big-footed mouse (*Macrotarsomys bastardi*): 10cm (4in); 20g (0.75oz)
The bastard big-footed mouse is the smallest Malagasy mouse. It lives in the dry forests of southern and western Madagascar. The species is named after its hind feet, which are more than a third as long as the whole body. The mice live in pairs. They move around by hopping on their large hind feet. By day they lurk in a burrow with the entrance sealed from the inside. At night they forage for plant foods.

Golden spiny mouse

Acomys russatus

Golden spiny mice live in the north-eastern area of the Egyptian desert. Its range spreads into Asia, through the Sinai and across Arabia to Oman and Yemen – a region characterized by its aridity. The spiny golden mouse is most common in areas that receive at least some running water each year. They take up residence in the cracked mud of the banks of dried-up seasonal rivers or in crevices in rock fields. The mice live in greatest numbers in the areas where agriculture is possible. Their population has been boosted in recent years because irrigation has been used to green parts of the desert.

Golden spiny mice eat whatever they can find. They do not need to drink because they can extract moisture from their food. The mice are diurnal, which is unusual for a desert rodent. In many parts of their range, the golden spiny mouse lives alongside a close relative, the Cairo spiny mouse. This second species is nocturnal, and it would appear that this forces the golden spiny mice to forage by day. In places where the Cairo spiny mice do not live, the golden spiny mice become nocturnal.

Distribution: Egypt and the Middle East.
Habitat: Rocky grassland and deserts.
Food: Snails, insects and seeds.
Size: 13cm (5in); 45g (1.5oz).
Maturity: 3 months.
Breeding: Most litters born in wet season.
Life span: 3 years.
Status: Common.

This rodent is covered in bristles. These are thickest on the back, where they more resemble spines, but lack a sharp tip. The bristles are tipped with black, making the coat a grizzled brown.

Setzer's hairy-footed gerbil

Gerbillurus setzeri

This species of hairy-footed gerbil lives in the Namib Desert in Namibia and southern Angola. They dig burrows in the soil of dried river beds, where the top layer is loose gravel washed along by the seasonal flow of water, while deeper layers are damp compacted sand.

The burrows have several entrances and there are numerous branches and chambers off the main tunnel. If the river beds get too crowded, younger gerbils are forced to make less stable homes in sand dunes.

The hairy-footed gerbil avoids the heat of the day by staying underground. If the heat is so intense that even the burrow gets too hot, the rodent spreads saliva over its head and neck to cool itself down. If a predator enters the burrow, a gerbil will thump the ground rapidly with its hind feet to warn others of danger.

The gerbils emerge after sunset to forage for insects and seeds. They move around by jumping. When not feeding, the rodents take sand baths to remove any parasites from their fur.

Distribution: Namib Desert in Namibia from the Kuiseb River as far north as the southern fringe of Angola.
Habitat: Areas of desert with gravel soils.
Food: Insects, leaves, dried flowers, dried fruits, and seeds.
Size: 23cm (9in); 35g (1.25oz).
Maturity: Unknown.
Breeding: Litters produced all year round.
Life span: Unknown.
Status: Common.

This species is one of the largest gerbils. The soles of the feet are covered with hairs to protect the feet against the intense heat of the ground – a feature common among desert creatures.

Fat-tailed gerbil

Pachyuromys duprasi

Fat-tailed gerbils have shorter tails than other gerbils. The tails, which are club-shaped and lack hairs, act as a storage organ for fat and water, like the hump of a camel.

Fat-tailed gerbils live in the small desert areas that are scattered across the coastal region of North Africa, west of the Nile to Tunisia and Algeria. They are nocturnal creatures and spend the day in burrows dug up to 1m (3.25ft) into the ground. The gerbils will dig their own burrow if necessary, but often opt to modify a burrow left abandoned by another desert resident. Like other tunnelling creatures, the fat-tailed gerbils play an important ecological role by aerating the upper layers of soil, which makes it easier for plants to put down roots.

A normal burrow contains several individuals. At dusk the fat-tailed gerbils leave their burrows to feed. They generally choose to forage alone. Their diet consists of large amounts of plant material, but they also eat any insects and other invertebrates they find.

During courtship, both sexes are reported to rear up on their hind legs and produce shrieks. This behaviour is often mistaken for fighting.

Fat-tailed gerbils have never been observed giving birth in the wild. Females are pregnant for between two and three weeks. A typical litter comprises between three and nine young. They are hairless and blind when born and raised by the mother in an underground nest. The father plays no part in caring for the young. The young are weaned at the age of three weeks.

Distribution: North Africa from Egypt to Libya, Tunisia and Algeria.
Habitat: Sandy desert.
Food: Insects, such as beetles and crickets, and other invertebrates, such as worms and scorpions.
Size: 11cm (4.25in); 37g (1.25oz).
Maturity: 3–6 months.
Breeding: Litters of up to 9 young born 3 times a year. Captive specimens give birth between April and November.
Life span: 5 years, up to 7 years in captivity.
Status: Common.

Libyan jird

Meriones libycus

Distribution: North Africa and the Middle East.
Habitat: Desert depressions.
Food: Seeds and grass.
Size: 15cm (6in); 85g (3oz).
Maturity: Unknown.
Breeding: Litters produced several times per year. Gestation is 20 days.
Life span: Unknown.
Status: Common.

Libyan jirds live across the Middle East, ranging from Iran to Libya in North Africa. They are most common in lowland areas and deep depressions and valleys in the deserts of Egypt and Libya. They make their homes in oasis areas where some vegetation grows.

The jirds are social animals, living in large groups that share communal burrows. Members of the group communicate with each other frequently by stamping their feet and using a series of sounds.

Jirds are largely diurnal and move quickly when out in the open to avoid being targeted by a predator. They are active all year round in warmer parts of the range but may hibernate for a short time in colder regions to the east.

Libyan jirds are very passive and are not easily disturbed when living near to humans. Due to this tolerance, they have become a popular pet. However, many pet owners have found that a peaceful colony of jirds can suddenly turn very violent, with members biting each other, often with fatal results.

Jirds are relatives of gerbils. This species shares many of the features of a gerbil, except it has a slightly narrower head.

Sundevall's jird (*Meriones crassus*): 25cm (9.75in); 70g (2.5oz)
This jird lives in north-west Africa, the Middle East and central Asia. It is a desert creature, living in burrows under sparse vegetation. Like those of other gerbils and jirds, the burrows are a complex network of tunnels connecting several chambers. This jird eats leaves and twigs in winter and seeds in summer, as well as insects and small worms and scorpions. Foraging takes place at night. Food is carried back to the burrow, where most of it is eaten and some is stored for later.

Angoni vlei rat (*Otomys angoniensis*): Length unknown; 120g (4.25oz)
The Angoni vlei rat lives in South Africa. It is a medium to large rat and has red-brown fur that is paler at the throat. The rat survives in a range of habitats from dry grasslands and semi-deserts to wet mountain habitats. It is most common in moister areas, where it forages for grasses, roots and bark. The Angoni vlei rat is generally diurnal and spends most of the time alone. Only while breeding will the rat form pairs for a short while. Mature at four months, the Angoni vlei rat can produce up to 15 young in a year in three litters.

Fat sand rat

Psammomys obesus

Fat sand rats live across the Sahara Desert of North Africa, from Mauritania to northern Sudan and Egypt, as well as in parts of the Arabian Peninsula. They are ground-dwelling animals, most commonly found in sandy areas but also occupying rocky deserts, scree and salt marshes. They dig burrows close to food sources.

These animals are active during the day unless it gets too hot at this time, at which point they switch to foraging at night. During colder periods they spend a long time basking in the sun to warm up before feeding. Males have a territory that overlaps those of several other males. Each adult has a complex burrow with several chambers for storing food or waste.

Fat sand rats eat succulent plants that store water in their leaves. This water is often very salty, which would cause problems for most mammals that consumed it, but fat sand rats have very efficient kidneys that can remove all the excess salt.

A male fat sand rat occupies a territory that covers the home range of several females. He mates with all the females, who produce up to seven young between December and April. Most females produce three or four litters per year.

Distribution: North Africa and Arabia.
Habitat: Deserts.
Food: Succulent plants.
Size: 19cm (7.5in); 200g (7oz).
Maturity: 4 months.
Breeding: Up to 4 litters produced in December–April.
Life span: 2–3 years.
Status: Common.

Fat sand rats resemble gerbils in some ways, such as having a tufted tail. This rodent also has black skin under its fur to protect the body from the desert sunlight.

Wood mouse

Apodemus sylvaticus

The wood mouse, also often referred to as the long-tailed field mouse, is the most common wild mouse in Europe. It lives right across the continent except in the far north of Scandinavia. It is found on the British Isles including the smaller, surrounding islands. The wood mouse also ranges across northern Asia except the cold northern regions and is found south of the Himalayas and as far east as the Altai Mountains of northern China. The mice also live in north-western Africa.

With such a wide distribution, it is not surprising that wood mice are able to survive well in several habitats – anywhere with places for the mice to shelter, such as meadows, woodlands, gardens and cultivated fields. They do occupy houses and other buildings on occasion, especially during cold periods, but generally they dig themselves deep burrows and line them with dried leaves. Newborns are raised in the den for the first three weeks.

Long-tailed field mice are excellent swimmers, climbers and jumpers and can forage successfully almost anywhere. They have typical self-sharpening rodent teeth so are able to tackle most foods. They are most active in the twilight of dawn and dusk.

The wood mouse has large eyes so it can see well at night time and a long nose that is sensitive enough to smell seeds buried underground. The mouse has a long tail but it is not prehensile.

Distribution: British Isles, mainland Europe, North Africa and northern and eastern Asia.
Habitat: Meadows and woodlands. Sometimes live in homes or other buildings, especially during winter.
Food: Roots, fruits, seeds and insects.
Size: 15cm (6in).
Maturity: 2 months.
Breeding: 4–7 young born in litters produced up to 4 times a year. Gestation period is about 3 years.
Life span: 1 year.
Status: Common.

African grass rat

Arvicanthis niloticus

African grass rats live in the fertile areas of Egypt and Sudan around the Nile River Valley. They also follow the Blue Nile into Ethiopia and range in the other direction as far west as Mali. The mice's range also continues south to Central Africa, although it does not continue further south than that.

The African grass rat lives in colonial burrows that are dug under well-covered ground, be it by brush, rocks or even a termite mound. These conditions exist in a range of habitats across the rat's range. The burrows run at just 20cm (8in) below the surface and have several entrances, where the residents are often seen associating. They all help to maintain the runways that lead from the burrow's entrances to foraging grounds. These runways are most obvious during the dry season, when grass is trimmed. It is thought that runways serve as high-speed escape routes that lead rats to the burrow when predators appear.

There are equal numbers of males and females in a colony of grass rats. Breeding takes place after the dry season in March. Females are pregnant for three weeks. The newborn females stay in the colony, while the males leave after the age of about three months.

Male African grass rats are slightly larger than the females. The hind feet are long and used for digging, while the forefeet are smaller with a small opposable thumb that makes them relatively dexterous.

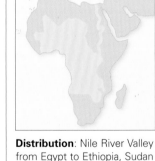

Distribution: Nile River Valley from Egypt to Ethiopia, Sudan and to the Great Lakes region of East Africa. The population extends west to Mali and south to Central Africa.
Habitat: Grassland, semi-desert and woodland.
Food: Grasses, stems, seeds and bark.
Size: 13cm (5in); 120g (4.25oz).
Maturity: 4 months.
Breeding: About 5 young born in a litter produced after the dry season.
Life span: 1 year.
Status: Common.

Black rat (*Rattus rattus*): 16–22cm (6.25–8.5in); 70–300g (2.5–10.5oz)

Thought to be originally from India, the black rat, also known as the house rat or ship rat, is now one of the most common rodents in the world. It is found wherever humans have settled, including across Europe and Africa. It even survives in Arctic settlements. A few have travelled to Antarctica with human explorers and scientists, but no sustainable population exists on that cold continent. The secret of the black rat's success is its adaptability. Its medium-sized body makes it a good climber, jumper, swimmer and runner; its long teeth allow it to tackle almost any food it comes across, and its high intelligence means that it can investigate areas quickly and remember where suitable food sources can be found. The black rat will forever be remembered for spreading the Black Death – a disease passed to humans by the rat's fleas.

Brown rat (*Rattus norvegicus*): 40cm (15.7in); 140–500g (5–17.5oz)

Like the black rat, the brown rat has spread from its native forest habitat in China to become one of the most common rodents in the world. Travelling with human migrants, this species, also known as the Norway rat, is now common on all continents except Antarctica. Considerably larger than the black rat, brown rats still share the characteristics that make its relative such a success. A female brown rat can produce 60 offspring in one year if the conditions are right, which shows just how quickly these rodents can take over a new habitat.

Eurasian harvest mouse

Micromys minutus

The Eurasian harvest mouse is a little rodent that lives across temperate parts of Europe from northern Spain to Russia. Its range extends into Asia, running through Siberia as far east as Korea. The mouse occupies areas of tall grass and consequently is a common resident of fields of cereal crops, including rice paddies.

Eurasian harvest mice each occupy a territory. These overlap, but the mice will avoid coming into contact with each other. When cold weather forces the mice to seek shelter, they congregate in the same place and become more tolerant of each other. Each mouse builds a nest out of grasses, where they sleep for about three hours at a time. Each sleep period is followed by a similar time spent foraging.

Distribution: Europe and northern Asia. Northern limit of range is the Arctic Circle.
Habitat: Tall grasses.
Food: Seeds, fruits and grains.
Size: 7cm (2.75in); 11g (0.5oz).
Maturity: 35 days.
Breeding: Litter of 3–8 young born every 20 days.
Life span: 6 months.
Status: Common.

The Eurasian harvest mouse has large ears that allow it to hear the slightest sound. The tail is prehensile and provides extra support while the mouse is climbing.

House mouse

Mus musculus

Distribution: Every continent of the world, including Antarctica.
Habitat: Generally near human habitation.
Food: Waste food, insects plant matter.
Size: 15–19cm (6–7.5in); 17–25g (0.04–0.05lb).
Maturity: 5–7 weeks.
Breeding: Usually around 5–10 litters of 3–12 offspring during the year.
Life span: 12–18 months.
Status: Abundant.

The key to the house mouse's phenomenal success as a species is its ability to follow humans around the globe, and the way it is able to make use of whatever food sources people provide. By stowing away on ships and, latterly, aeroplanes, house mice have been able to colonize every continent of the world.

Mice were first domesticated, and in some instances worshipped, by the Romans and ancient Greeks. However, these days house mice are considered to be a major pest. They cause billions of dollars' worth of damage to food stores worldwide every year. They also damage buildings, woodwork, furniture and clothing, and are known to carry various dangerous diseases, including typhus and salmonella.

However, house mice are virtually unrivalled by other mammals in their capacity to adapt to new surroundings. Their generalist habits, rapid breeding rate and talent for slipping into places unnoticed have enabled the house mouse to become possibly the most numerous mammal in the world today.

A common sight all over the world, the house mouse is capable of making the most of any opportunity.

Gundi

Ctenodactylus gundi

The North African gundi lives in parts of Morocco, Algeria, Tunisia and Libya. They are found in arid areas that have plenty of rocky outcrops and also survive on the slopes of the region's mountains.

Gundis resemble guinea pigs, but are more closely related to mice and squirrels. They live in large colonies. The size and area occupied by each colony is dependent on the amount of food available. A gundi colony is divided up into territories controlled by a family unit. A family may be made up of an adult male and female and their offspring, though other families are matriarchies, with several adult females and their young.

The families den under rocks, which are a useful heating system: warming up slowly during the day, so that the den stays cool, then cooling more slowly at night than the surrounding land so that the den stays warm. In cold weather gundi huddle together for warmth. To warm up in the morning, they bask on sunny rocks before feeding.

A female gundi is pregnant for about 40 days during the dry season. She produces a litter of two young. Unusually for rodents, the newborns are fully furred with their eyes open.

Gundis are small diurnal rodents that have very short legs, flat ears, big eyes and long whiskers. Their long but thin fur makes their bodies appear to be almost spherical in windy conditions.

Distribution: North Africa from south-eastern Morocco, northern Algeria, Tunisia and the Libyan Desert.
Habitat: Deserts with many rocky outcrops.
Food: Leaves, seeds and stems.
Size: 16–20cm (6.25–8in); 175–195g (6.25–6.75oz).
Maturity: Unknown.
Breeding: 2 young born fully furred. Gestation is 40 days, young are weaned in 4 weeks.
Life span: 3–4 years.
Status: Common.

Lesser-Egyptian jerboa

Jaculus jaculus

The lesser-Egyptian jerboa is distributed from Morocco to central Asia. It lives in desert areas and rocky meadows. Like other jerboas, this little rodent is nocturnal in habit to avoid the intense heat of the day. The jerboas are solitary foragers and live alone in a burrow dug into compacted sand or under rocks. The burrows follow a clockwise spiral and go down to a depth of about 1.2m (4ft). Each burrow has two or three entrances and the nest area is located at the deepest point.

Lesser-Egyptian jerboas stay in the burrow during the hottest and driest periods of the year. Without eating, they enter a dormant state similar to hibernation but called aestivation because it is a response to heat rather than cold.

Being able to jump 1m (3.25ft) in a single bound, the jerboas can forage over a huge area for such a small creature. Some have been found 10km (6 miles) from their burrow.

Males mate with several females but a female jerboa probably mates only once. Breeding takes place twice a year at six monthly intervals.

The lesser-Egyptian jerboa is the smallest of the desert-living jerboas. It is built like a kangaroo, with long hind feet that are used for hopping. The hind legs may be three-quarters of the length of the body. The long tail helps the rodent balance while jumping.

Distribution: North Africa, the Middle East and central Asia.
Habitat: Deserts and semi-deserts with areas of sand and stone.
Food: Roots, grass, seeds and insects. They do not drink liquid water and get all they need from their food.
Size: 10cm (4in); 55g (2oz).
Maturity: 8–12 months.
Breeding: 2 litters of 3 young produced in late summer and early winter. The gestation period is 25 days.
Life span: 2 years.
Status: Common.

Mzab gundi (*Massoutiera mzabi*): 24cm (9.5in); 195g (6.75oz)

This species, also known as Sahara gundis, lives in the heart of the Sahara Desert of Algeria, northern Chad, Mali and southern Libya. They are sand-coloured and have plenty of long fur to protect them against the extreme cold of the desert night. They are diurnal creatures, spending the night in crevices between rocks, and have long whiskers to help them orientate themselves in the darkness. Mzab gundis forage for plant food that is on or growing out of the ground.

Four-toed jerboa (*Allactaga tetradactyla*): 26cm (10.25in); 52g (1.75oz)

This large jerboa lives in the deserts of Libya and Egypt and across the Middle East to central Asia. They live in coastal salt marshes and semi-desert areas. By day they lurk in burrows before foraging for seeds and other plant foods at night. The jerboas hibernate in cooler parts of their range, especially in central Asia. They dig deeper and more complex burrows for the winter.

Cameroon scaly-tail (*Zenkerella insignis*): 22cm (8.75in); 220g (7.75oz)

This species of squirrel is related to the gliding scaly-tailed squirrels: it has the scales on the tail but lacks the gliding membrane, and consequently cannot glide from tree to tree. The scaly-tail lives in Cameroon and Gabon. It rarely leaves the high canopy of the rainforest, where it feeds on mainly bark. It is a diurnal animal, unlike its gliding relatives, which are all nocturnal foragers.

Forest dormouse

Dryomys nitedula

Forest dormice live across Eurasia from northern Europe to Japan, where they are most often seen in thick forests made up of a mixture of deciduous trees and evergreen conifers. The species also survives in the rocky groves of North Africa.

These animals rarely leave the trees. They can climb well and are good jumpers, regularly making leaps of up to 2m (6.5ft). They are nocturnal and retreat to a nest of leaves built in the trees. The dormice do not just sleep in the nest; instead they become torpid, and enter a more dormant state than sleep, which saves the animal's energy. This state is similar to hibernation, although it lasts only a few hours.

The forest dormouse does not hibernate in the normal sense of the word, but it does have long winter sleeps curled up into tight balls resting on its hind feet. In warmer regions, these sleeps are short or absent, while in other milder places the dormouse will wake regularly for foraging trips.

Distribution: Eurasia from northern Europe to Japan.
Habitat: Deciduous forests.
Food: Flowers, fruits and nuts.
Size: 13cm (5in); 34g (1.25oz).
Maturity: 1 year.
Breeding: Up to 3 litters each year.
Life span: 5 years.
Status: Lower risk.

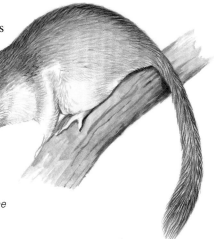

The forest dormouse has a long, muscular body that is more similar to a squirrel's than a mouse's. This helps it to climb more easily through trees. The tail is bushy but flatter than a squirrel's.

Lord Derby's scaly-tailed squirrel

Anomalurus derbianus

Distribution: West and Central Africa.
Habitat: Rainforests.
Food: Bark, fruit, leaves, flowers and nuts.
Size: 40cm (15.75in); 1.1kg (2.5lb).
Maturity: Unknown.
Breeding: Up to 3 young born each year.
Life span: Unknown.
Status: Common.

The scaly-tailed squirrels are named after rows of scales on the underside of the tail near the base. This species lives in the rainforest of Central Africa.

The squirrels glide (not fly) with their arms, legs and tails extended, stretching out the membranes. They can travel up to 250m (820ft) in this way. The scales on their tails are used as anchors, hooking on to the rough trunks of trees to prevent them from skidding when they land. These squirrels are almost helpless on the ground. They spend their time climbing into the treetops to feed on a range of plants. They then glide down to another suitable feeding tree and repeat the process. Gliding is also a useful escape technique. However, it also draws attention to the squirrel, so the rodent will scurry out of sight as soon as it lands.

Lord Derby's scaly-tailed squirrel is one of several so-called flying squirrels in Africa. It has a gliding membrane – a fold of skin that connects the front and back limbs on each side – which is hairy on top but largely naked underneath.

Blesmoles

Georychus capensis

Blesmoles have bodies built for tunnelling: they have short legs and rounded bodies. The large front teeth are used for gnawing through the soil as well as for feeding. Males and females are generally about the same size, although members of both sexes may grow to a giant size with twice the average weight.

Blesmoles are also called Cape mole rats. They live in areas of the Cape Province in south-western South Africa. They tunnel through hard, compacted soil in search of tubers and similar root storage organs and can be a destructive pest of root crops.

These animals live alone and build their own burrows. They loosen soil with their front teeth and then push it past the body with their feet. They tunnel for food and will also eat any insects that they come across as they dig with their teeth. The mole rats will avoid coming into contact with other moles if they break into an extant burrow. The tunnels will cover up to 10 per cent of the surface area, so it is common for burrows to connect.

The males drum their feet against the floor of the tunnel to advertise their presence. This has the dual effect of keeping rivals away and also attracting females in the breeding season.

After a pregnancy of seven weeks, females produce between three to five naked young. The newborns are weaned after just 17 days.

Distribution: South Africa.
Habitat: Grasslands areas with hard soils.
Food: Underground tubers (plant storage organs).
Size: 20cm (8in); 180g (6.25oz).
Maturity: 10 months for both sexes.
Breeding: 3–5 young born in August to December. The gestation period is 44 days.
Life span: 3 years, although probably less in the wild.
Status: Common.

African mole rat

Cryptomys hottentotus

African mole rats live on or rather under the plains of the Cape Province of South Africa. The rats spend their whole lives underground, tunnelling beneath grasslands where they eat tubers, bulbs and roots.

These animals live in complex societies, with a dozen or so rats sharing a network of tunnels. Most of the social group are adults, though only one pair of these adults is able to breed. The other adults are non-breeding workers who maintain tunnels, dig for food and fight off predators. In this way the society is similar to those of ants and termites, where all members of the group work to raise the offspring of a single female – a system known as eusociality. The breeding couple suppress the reproductive systems of the rest of the group using a chemical released in their urine.

Each group's members are all related, with the workers being sons and daughters of the breeders. Older mole rats, perhaps the breeders' brothers, sisters and cousins, do not do as much work as the younger ones. They are larger and spend time at the edge of the burrow where they lie ready to defend it. If attacked, the defender may be abandoned as the workers block up the tunnel behind him.

The body of an African mole rat forms a sturdy cylinder. The limbs are short so that they can move back and forth relatively easily inside narrow tunnels. The rats are blind but their bodies are covered in long, touch-sensitive hairs that work in the same way as whiskers.

Distribution: South-western region of Cape Province in South Africa.
Habitat: Soil beneath areas of grasslands.
Food: Roots, tubers, bulbs and other underground plant storage organs, herbs and grasses.
Size: 16cm (6.25in); 90g (3.25oz).
Maturity: Unknown, some individuals will not breed.
Breeding: 2 litters of up to 5 pups each year. Gestation is 44 days.
Life span: Unknown in the wild but captive mole rats live for about 10 years.
Status: Common.

Naked mole rat

Heterocephalus glaber

Naked mole rats live in societies which are more like social insects' colonies than those of other mammals. They live an entirely underground existence, and colonies can occupy 4km (2.5 miles) of tunnels, which are dug out by the rodents' claws and incisors. Some of these tunnels run just beneath the surface of the ground; others descend up to 2m (6.5ft) deep.

Like colonies of bees and ants, naked mole rat colonies are governed by queens, which give birth to the young. The queens are the largest individuals in the colonies, which usually comprise around 70 animals, but can number 300. The other individuals – the workers and drones – are separated into castes depending on their size. The members of each different caste have their own particular jobs, for example foraging, tunnel maintenance, caring for the young or nest defence.

Naked mole rats are the only mammals that have lost the ability to produce their own body heat. Instead, they bask in shallow tunnels warmed by the sun, or huddle together to keep warm.

As their name suggests, naked mole rats are almost hairless, with the pinkish skin showing through. They use their strong incisors and large claws for digging tunnels. These rodents are virtually blind.

Distribution: Kenya, Ethiopia and Somalia.
Habitat: Underground in arid savannah and grassland.
Food: Underground parts of plants, particularly the succulent tubers.
Size: 6–10cm (2.25–4in); 25–70g (0.05–0.15lb).
Maturity: 1 year.
Breeding: Usually about 12 young per litter, with 8 litters per year.
Life span: Over 20 years.
Status: Common.

East African mole rats (Tachyoryctinae subfamily): 16–31cm (6.25–12.25in); 160–930g (5.5–32.75oz)
There are 13 species of East African mole rat. They are found in Somalia and Ethiopia and across the Great Lakes region to the eastern part of the Democratic Republic of Congo. They live in woodlands, grassland and cultivated areas. They are mole-like in shape and spend most of their time in tunnels. Their tunnel networks are complex and they are constantly being expanded as the rats dig for food. The rats dig deep bolt-holes to hide in when predators, such as the Ethiopian wolf, attack. Other chambers are used for storing waste food and faeces. In cold weather this material produces heat as it rots and warms the burrow.

Blind mole rats (Spalacinae subfamily): 13–35cm (5–13.75in); 100–570g (3.5–20oz)
Another group of tunnelling mole rats, the blind mole rats live under the grasslands and woodlands of south-eastern Europe, the Middle East and north-eastern Africa. Their eyes are covered in skin because they are of no use underground, where the animals eat roots, though the rats do emerge on the surface from time to time to forage for leaves. They rely on their sense of hearing to detect other rats and approaching predators. They communicate with grunts and hisses and butt the ceilings of the tunnels with their heads to attract mates. This head banging produces low-frequency vibrations on the soil, which the rat's ears are highly attuned to detecting.

Springhare

Pedetes capensis

Hopping is a very efficient way to travel, and it allows springhares to bound rapidly around the African savannah at night. Usually they do not move too far from their burrows, but during times of drought they have been known to travel up to 40km (25 miles) in search of water.

Springhares have incredibly keen senses. As well as having fantastic sight, scent and hearing, they use their huge back feet to pick up vibrations from the earth.

Springhares need all their senses to be able to avoid the long list of predators that would happily make meals of them. They are small enough to be manageable for wild cats, jackals, ratels and large owls, but big enough to interest larger predators, such as lions and leopards, should they get close enough to be able to catch them.

Rather like a small kangaroo, the bizarre springhare is in a family all of its own.

Distribution: Southern and eastern Africa.
Habitat: Grasslands with sandy soil.
Food: Vegetation, mainly bulbs and grasses.
Size: 35–45cm (13.75–17.75in); 4kg (8.75lb).
Maturity: 1 year.
Breeding: Around 3 or 4 young per litter, with litters born about every 100 days.
Life span: 10 years.
Status: Common and widespread.

Red squirrel

Sciurus vulgaris

Red squirrels can be quite variable in colour, with some individuals being jet black, while others are strawberry blonde. The bushy tail helps them to balance in the treetops. These arboreal rodents are very acrobatic.

The red squirrel has undergone a well-documented decline in Britain due to its not being able to compete with the larger and more robust grey squirrel, which was introduced from North America. The two species actually hardly ever come to blows, and it is thought that the main problem may be that the grey squirrels harbour a viral infection that decimates red squirrels whilst leaving the greys unaffected.

These animals tend to be most active during early mornings and late afternoons. They rest in the middle of the day. As winter sets in, the squirrels rapidly put on weight, and settle down for a long period of inactivity. Squirrels do not truly hibernate. They never let their body temperatures drop, and they regularly wake up to stretch their legs, drink and feed from food caches made in the autumn.

Red squirrels are mainly solitary animals, and apart from when there is a large concentration of food readily available, the only time they get together in any numbers is when the females become ready to breed. Male squirrels fight over them at this time.

Distribution: Europe and Asia.
Habitat: Primarily coniferous forests.
Food: Seeds and nuts when available, and also fungi, eggs, flowers and tree sap.
Size: 25–35cm (10–13.75in); up to 350g (0.75lb).
Maturity: 9–10 months.
Breeding: 2 litters of 5–7 young per year.
Life span: 4–6 years.
Status: Rare in the UK, common elsewhere.

Grey squirrel

Sciurus carolinensis

Grey squirrels are native to the open woodlands of eastern North America. They have also been introduced into several parts of northern Europe, where they have begun to out-compete the smaller red squirrels for food and breeding sites.

These animals feed primarily on the nuts and buds of many woodland trees. In summer, when they are most active just after dawn and before dusk, grey squirrels also eat insects. In winter, when most animals of their size are hibernating, grey squirrels spend their days eating stores of food that they had buried throughout the previous summer. Grey squirrels may make dens in hollow trees, but are more likely to make nests, or dreys, from twigs and leaves in the boughs of trees.

There are two breeding seasons each year: one beginning in midwinter, the other in midsummer. Males begin to chase a female through the trees a few days before they are receptive to mating. One female may be chased by several males at once. When females are ready, their vulvas become pink and engorged. Litters of three are born six weeks later.

Grey squirrels have, as their name suggests, greyish fur, although many individuals have reddish patches. Their tails, which have many white hairs, are bushier than those of most other squirrels.

Distribution: South-eastern Canada and eastern United States. The species has been introduced to Britain and northern Europe and is now the most common species in deciduous forests.
Habitat: Woodlands, parks and gardens.
Food: Nuts, seeds, flowers and buds.
Size: 38–52cm (15–20.5in); 300–700g (10.5–24.5oz).
Maturity: 10 months.
Breeding: 2 litters each year with 2–4 young per litter after a gestation of 3 months. Mating takes place in late summer and winter. Breeding is later in a cold winter.
Life span: 12 years.
Status: Common.

Siberian flying squirrel

Pteromys volans

Distribution: Scandinavia, Russia and northern Asia.
Habitat: Forests.
Food: Fruit, seeds and leaves.
Size: 12–23cm (4.75–9in).
Maturity: 1 year.
Breeding: 2 litters born in spring and summer.
Life span: Unknown.
Status: Lower risk.

These animals live across northern Asia. Their range extends from Scandinavia in the west to the Pacific coast of China in the east. The squirrels live in forests of aspen, birch and coniferous trees. This type of forest grows in cold lowland areas and is often referred to as taiga.

Siberian flying squirrels nest in tree hollows. They stay in the nests during the day and leave them by night to look for food, such as young leaves, berries and seeds. In lean winter months, the rodents survive on less nutritious foods, such as nuts and pinecones.

The squirrels rarely touch the ground. They have short legs that are not well suited to walking on all fours, so instead the squirrels climb up tree trunks and then glide on their outstretched membranes across gaps in the forest. Without a rear membrane between the hind legs, the Siberian flying squirrel must adopt a different posture to other flying squirrels when in flight. The forelimbs point out sideways, as is normal, but the hind legs are held backwards. This gives the gliding squirrel an unusual triangular shape.

Unlike many species of flying squirrel, the Siberian variety does not have a gliding membrane connecting its hind limbs to the base of the tail. Instead, all the gliding is done using membranes between the forelimbs and hind legs.

African pygmy squirrel

(*Myosciurus pumilio*): 7.5cm (3in)
The African pygmy squirrel is the smallest squirrel in the world: it is about as large as a person's thumb and the tail is about two-thirds of the length of the body. It lives high up in the forests of West and Central Africa and is also found on the island of Bioko. Pygmy squirrels are omnivores: in addition to plant food they also eat ants and termites.

Gambian sun squirrel

(*Heliosciurus gambianus*): 15–21cm (6–8.25in); 250–340g (8.75–12oz)
Gambian sun squirrels live in the woodlands of Central Africa. This habitat is found between the dry savannah south of the Sahara and the rainforests of the Congo Basin. Despite their name, Gambia is the western limit of their range, and the squirrels are found right across Africa to Kenya. Gambian sun squirrels live in the branches of trees. They also make foraging trips into lusher rainforests. There are at least seven subspecies of Gambian sun squirrel, each with its own distinctive colouring.

Striped ground squirrel

Xerus erythropus

The striped ground squirrel is also known as Geoffrey's ground squirrel. It is a common species that lives along the fringes of North Africa's Sahara Desert. It is especially common in the grasslands of the Sahel along the desert's southern fringe.

This animal is a sturdy rodent. It is named after the pale stripes that run from both shoulders along the side of the body to the rump. The squirrel has long claws, which are used for digging burrows.

Striped ground squirrels live in colonies of about ten squirrels. Most of the group are females, the rest are their young. Adult males are allowed to join the group only when the females are ready to mate. Litters are produced at all times of year, but all the females in a group come into season at the same time.

Members of a group communicate with sounds such as chirps and squeaks. They also let each other know how they are feeling using their long and bushy tails. Relaxed squirrels drag the tail along the ground; frightened squirrels hold the tail straight out behind them; while a squirrel that is alert will curl its tail over its back.

Distribution: North Africa.
Habitat: Dry savannah.
Food: Nuts, leaves, fruit, leaves and small animals.
Size: 20–46cm (8–18in); 300–945g (10.5–33.25oz).
Maturity: 1 year.
Breeding: Colony's females produce litters of 3 young all at the same time.
Life span: 2 years.
Status: Common.

The colour of the striped ground squirrel's fur often matches that of the surrounding soil. The squirrels may have a mixture of red, yellow and grey hairs. The flattened tail is always darker than the rest of the body.

Cape porcupine

Hystrix africaeaustralis

The Cape porcupine shares its habitat with a whole array of dangerous predators, but its sharp quills can repel even lions and hyenas. A mane of long, white bristles runs down the neck to the back. The rodent has special hollow quills attached to its tail, which can be rattled together as a warning to any unsuspecting animal that gets too close for comfort. Covering the lower back are 40cm (16in) long quills, equipped with tiny barbs. These quills are only loosely held in the skin and will embed themselves easily into any animal attempting to attack.

Porcupines have keen hearing and an excellent sense of smell, which they use to locate nutritious bulbs underground. The Cape porcupines, like other rodents, also chew bones from carcasses to obtain calcium, phosphorus and other essential minerals. Chewing bones also helps to keep their incisor teeth sharp. Porcupines will often share burrows, forming clans comprising adult pairs and up to four offspring of varying ages. Members of the clan share common runs, trails and latrines, and also common feeding sites and refuges.

Distribution: Widespread in Africa south of the Sahara Desert.
Habitat: Grassland.
Food: Roots, bark, herbs and fruit.
Size: 0.7–1m (2.25–3.25ft); up to 17kg (37.5lb).
Maturity: 9 months.
Breeding: Mated females produce up to 2 offspring at a time.
Life span: Up to 20 years.
Status: Endangered in some parts of its range, but common elsewhere.

The Cape porcupine has the longest quills of any species of porcupine in the world.

North African crested porcupine

Hystrix cristata

Like other porcupines, the North African species has thickened hairs on its back that form sharp quills. These quills, which form a crest along the back and neck, are meant as a deterrent to attackers. Thicker quills also stick out from the sides and back.

The North African crested porcupine is most common along the coast of North Africa and through eastern Africa to the fringes of the Congo's equatorial rainforests. The species is also found in Sicily and Italy, but is very rare in that country.

This animal is able to adapt to a range of habitats, from dense forest to deserts and mountain meadows. It finds shelter in abandoned burrows and caves, but will also dig its own den if required. Adults pair up for life and live in small family groups.

Crested porcupines are nocturnal, although they will stay in when the moon is bright to avoid predators. At other times, they rely on their armoury of quills to protect them. Unlike other Old World porcupines, this species has a rattle of quills on its tail, which is used to warn off predators. The porcupine also raises a crest of quills to make itself look larger. If the predator continues to attack, the porcupine charges at them backwards, stabbing the attacker with a quill.

Distribution: Central and North Africa and southern Italy.
Habitat: Forests, rocky areas and fields.
Food: Roots, bulbs, fruit, bark and grasses. Porcupines also gnaw on bones.
Size: 60–93cm (23.5–36.5in); 10–30kg (22–66lb).
Maturity: 2 years.
Breeding: 1 litter per year.
Life span: Up to 20 years but probably less.
Status: Common.

Greater cane rat

Thryonomys swinderianus

Distribution: Africa south of the Sahara Desert from Gambia and Sudan to Namibia and eastern South Africa. Absent from Cape Province.
Habitat: River and marsh banks. Also common in plantations and irrigated fields.
Food: Grasses and sugar cane.
Size: 48cm (19in); 4.5kg (10lb).
Maturity: 1 year.
Breeding: 2 litters of 4 young produced in rainy season.
Life span: 4 years.
Status: Common.

The greater cane rat is found across Africa south of the Sahara Desert. The southern extent of its range is the dry grasslands of Namibia and South Africa. Cane rats are grass eaters. In this context, "cane" is a general term for the tall reed-like grasses that grow on river banks and in shallow water. The rats fell these tall stems using their large incisors.

Like all rodents, the rat's incisors grow continuously. They are worn down by the tough plant food so they never get too long. (The teeth are also self-sharpening: with each bite, the lower teeth cut a chisel-edge on the upper teeth.) The cane rat's teeth make a characteristic chattering sound as they bite through the grasses. As well as grass, greater cane rats eat bark and fallen fruits. They are also well equipped to tackle crops such as sugar cane and corn.

These animals live in small groups made up of a single male, several females and any offspring under one year old. The rodents feed at night and make simple nests among the grass to rest in during the day. The rats escape from danger by jumping into the water. They also warn other rats by stamping their hind feet and grunting.

Although they are called rats, cane rats are more closely related to porcupines and guinea pigs. They are sometimes called grasscutters. The greater cane rat has brown fur with several flattened bristles growing on the back.

Dassie rat

Petromus typicus

Distribution: Angola, Namibia and western South Africa.
Habitat: Rocky hillsides and deserts.
Food: Flowers, seeds and leaves.
Size: 14–21cm (5.5–8.25in); 170–300g (6–10.5oz).
Maturity: 9 months.
Breeding: Single litter of up to 3 young born in February or March – the start of the rainy season – after a gestation period of 3 months.
Life span: Unknown.
Status: Lower risk.

This species of rat is the only member of the Petromuridae family of rodents. This name literally means "rock mouse", but dassie rats are not closely related to mice. Nor is the species a badger, despite the fact that the name dassie means "badger" in Afrikaans. In fact, the dassie rat isn't even a rat, but rather a distant relative of guinea pigs, chinchillas and other rodents that are now found mainly in South America. The rodent's closest African relatives are the cane rats.

Dassie rats live in the rocky semi-deserts of southern Angola, Namibia and western South Africa. They spend the night in small crevices among rocks. They are most active during the early morning and late afternoon, when they forage for plant food. The rats are unique among rodents because they regurgitate their food for a second chew. As with cattle chewing their cud, this helps to break down the tough plant food.

The animals lie flat on rocks and bask in the sun. At the slightest hint of danger, they dart for cover, squeezing into the nearest rock crevice. Females give birth to a small litter and have teats on their sides so that they can suckle their young even when squashed into a narrow space.

The dassie rat's fur is grey and brown to blend in with the rocks of its habitat. It has short legs, which it often stretches out when jumping. As with a flying squirrel, this helps the rat to travel a little farther with each leap. The soft and silky coat has no insulating underfur, unlike most mammals.

RABBITS

There are 54 species of rabbit and hare, all of which belong to the same family, the Leporidae. They are found in many parts of the world, and some species have been introduced to areas well outside their original range. Strictly speaking, "hare" is the name given to members of the genus Lepus, *while all other species in the family are referred to as rabbits.*

Brown hare

Lepus europaeus

Unlike rabbits, hares do not live in burrows. They spend most of the time alone, although a few may be seen together at good feeding sites. Hares are mostly active by night. During the day they crouch in small hollows in the grass called forms, sometimes leaving their backs just visible over the vegetation. In Europe, the main breeding season is in spring, and at this time hares can often be seen during the day, with males fighting one another and pursuing females.

A number of predators target hares, and in Europe these include foxes and eagles. If a predator detects a hare, the hare flees, running at speeds of up to 60kph (37mph) and making sharp, evasive turns. Injured or captured hares are known to make high-pitched screams.

In order to reduce the risk of losing all of their young leverets to predators, females hide them in different locations in specially dug forms, and visit them one by one to nurse them. Although brown hares are common, changing farming practices have caused a decline in hare numbers in some countries, such as Britain.

Brown hares are easily distinguishable from European rabbits by their larger size and longer ears and limbs.

Distribution: Southern Scandinavia, northern Spain and Britain to Siberia and north-western Iran.
Habitat: Grasslands and agricultural land.
Food: Grass, herbs, crop plants and occasionally twigs and bark.
Size: 60–70cm (23.5–27.5in); 3–5kg (6.5–11lb).
Maturity: 1 year.
Breeding: Litter of 1–8 young; 2 or more litters per year.
Life span: 7 years.
Status: Common.

Cape hare

Lepus capensis

Cape hares have red-brown fur and white hair on the inside leg. They are also known as brown hares by African people, although they should not be confused with the Eurasian brown hare.

The Cape hare is found across areas of Africa that are not covered by forests. The species is also found in the Middle East and as far east as central Asia. The Cape hare survives in a range of habitats from damp, highland meadows and marshes to arid rock fields.

There is even a population of Cape hares that lives in the Sahara Desert, cut off from the rest.

Cape hares not only look similar to Eurasian brown hares but also behave in a very similar way. The males box each other when competing for mates. They do this standing on their long hind limbs.

The hind limbs are used to propel the hare along at speeds of 77kph (48mph). The hares can also use them to make leaps of 2.5m (8.25ft).

Unlike rabbits, hares do not dig burrows; instead, they live in shallow dips called forms. (In the cold steppes of Mongolia, Cape hares actually make their homes underground – unique for hares. They take over the burrows of ground squirrels.)

Distribution: Africa and western and central Asia.
Habitat: Meadows, fields and marshes.
Food: Leaves, seeds, berries and mushrooms.
Size: 55cm (21.75in); 4.5kg (10lb).
Maturity: 8 months.
Breeding: Litters of 3–4 young born every 3 months.
Life span: 5 years.
Status: Common.

Distribution: Originally the Iberian Peninsula and southern France. Introduced to most of Europe, north-west Africa, Australia and many other countries.
Habitat: Farmland, grassland and dry shrubland.
Food: Grass, herbaceous plants, bark and twigs.
Size: 35–45cm (13.75–17.5in); 1.25–2.25kg (2.75–5lb).
Maturity: 1 year.
Breeding: 1–9 young per litter; up to 7 litters per year.
Life span: 9 years.
Status: Common.

European rabbit

Oryctolagus cuniculus

The rabbit has had a long association with humans, who have prized it for its soft fur and tasty meat. This species was probably introduced to the Mediterranean from its original home in the Iberian Peninsula more than 3,000 years ago. Rabbits often live in large colonies, inhabiting complex labyrinths of burrows, or warrens, that may have hundreds of entrances. Although rabbits live in close proximity to one another, there is a strong dominance hierarchy within a warren. Each male defends a territory, especially during the breeding season.

Rabbits are famed for their rate of reproduction, and a single female has the potential to produce 30 young per year. Rabbits have been introduced to some areas, such as Australia, where there are no predators capable of controlling their numbers. In these places they have created huge problems, crowding out local species and destroying crops. Ironically, rabbit populations in the species' original range in Spain are too small to support their rare predators such as the Iberian lynx and the imperial eagle.

There are as many as 66 domestic breeds of rabbit, and they vary considerably in size, shape and coloration. In Australia, rabbits occurred in such high numbers that they left little food for local marsupials, and even threatened the sheep industry. Diseases have been successfully introduced to control them.

Riverine rabbit (*Bunolagus monticularis*): 43cm (17in); 1.65kg (3.75lb)
The riverine rabbit inhabits a small part of South Africa. It lives among the scrub that grows along the seasonal rivers of the Karoo Desert in Cape Province. For much of the year the river bed is dry at the surface. If there is any water, it flows through the deep sandy bed. When the rains come, the river is flooded with a rush of water. This flood provides the habitat's plants with most of the water they get all year. The riverine rabbit survives by feeding on the succulent salty plants that grow along the banks. The vegetation is similar to what might grow in a salt marsh close to the sea. The riverine rabbit is one of the rarest mammals in the world. It is endangered by virtue of having such a specialized lifestyle. The species' low numbers are not helped by the fact that females produce only one baby every year, which is highly unusual for a rabbit. This is probably because the harsh environment makes it tough to feed more young.

Bunyoro rabbit (*Poelagus marjorita*): 47cm (18.5in); 2.5kg (5.5lb)
Bunyoro rabbits live in several small populations across Africa. Most are found in the Great Lakes region of eastern Africa. The largest population is in southern Uganda, but other populations are found as far north as southern Sudan and west as northern Angola. Despite its name, this species is actually a hare, although its short legs mean that it is often mistaken for a smaller rabbit. Bunyoro rabbits eat grasses and roots and are nocturnal.

Steppe pika

Ochotona pusilla

This species of pika is the only one to live in Europe. Its distribution extends from the Volga River in southern Russia to the Irtysh River in Siberia. The steppe pika eats grass and lives out on the vast Eurasian grassland known as the steppe.

The pika digs a burrow for shelter. While most pika species are diurnal, the steppe pika is found out of its burrow at all times of day or night. Also unusually for pikas, this species does not hibernate. Instead, it remains active in winter, when the steppe may be covered in snow for months on end, which means that the pika has to dig down to the grass below. Their dark bodies stand out against the snow, so pikas restrict their movements to darker days when they are less easy to spot. It is generally too cold at this time of year to feed at night.

Male pikas occupy a home range that overlaps those of many females. It is likely that groups of pikas seen together are families with an adult male and one or more adult females and their offspring.

Distribution: South-eastern Europe and Kazakhstan.
Habitat: Steppe.
Food: Grass.
Size: 15cm (6in); 400g (14oz).
Maturity: 1 year.
Breeding: 3–5 litters born each year.
Life span: 5 years.
Status: Vulnerable.

The steppe pika does not have a visible tail. The head and body are covered in long, thin hairs to keep it warm and the soles of the feet are also covered in thick fur.

BATS

With nearly 1,000 species, bats form one of the largest groups among the mammals, living in almost all temperate and tropical parts of the world. They are the only mammals to have truly mastered flight, and more than half of the species use echolocation for navigating and capturing prey at night. Different bats are specialized for eating insects, fruit, flowers, blood, fish and small animals.

Greater mastiff bat

Mops condylurus

This species is also known as the Angolan free-tailed bat, reflecting the disagreement in its classification. Some scientists place the greater mastiff bat in the same group as the free-tailed bats, while others place it in a separate group.

The greater mastiff bat roosts in caves, mines, hollow trees and can even be found under thatched roofs and in attics. The bats form groups of several hundred individuals. At sundown they fly out of their roosts to hunt insects. A colony of 500 individuals can consume a tonne of insects per year, and ecologists are considering using these bats to control insect pests in Africa, such as mosquitoes that carry malaria. Scientists have designed artificial roosts or bat "hotels" to encourage the bats to feed in areas where insect pests breed. While designing these roosts, researchers discovered that the bats are capable of tolerating up to 45°C (113°F) at midday.

This bat is characterized by having wrinkly lips and a band of skin joining the ears, over the top of its head.

Distribution: Africa south of the Sahara Desert, including Madagascar.
Habitat: Forest, savannah and dry brushland.
Food: Insects.
Size: 5–6cm (2–2.25in); 7–64g (0.015–0.15lb).
Maturity: 3 months.
Breeding: 2 breeding seasons per year, with a single young produced per season.
Life span: Not known but most bats live for 5 years.
Status: Common.

Hammer-headed fruit bat

Hypsignathus monstrosus

This is the largest bat in Africa, and is remarkable in having the greatest difference between males and females (sexual dimorphism) of any bat species. Males are nearly twice as heavy as females and, unlike females, they have an unusually large square-shaped head, giving the species its name. The male head-shape is one of several adaptations for calling, which include a greatly enlarged voice box, allowing males to produce a continuous and very loud croaking and quacking, probably to attract females.

Twice a year, male hammer-headed fruit bats congregate into groups of up to 130 individuals, in order to compete for mates. The males attract attention by croaking as loudly as possible and flapping their wings. The females are very selective, and most opt to mate with just a few of the noisiest males. When the bats are not breeding, they roost quietly during the day in small groups high up in the treetops. At night, hammer-headed bats fly up to 10km (6 miles) from their roost sites to find trees with ripened fruit to eat.

The male's head is large and square, and the muzzle is hammer-shaped. The males also have large lips and warty snouts. Females have thinner, fox-like muzzles.

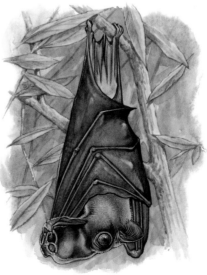

Distribution: Central and western Africa.
Habitat: Forests, swamps, mangroves and river margins.
Food: Fruit, and also reported to have killed and eaten tethered chickens.
Size: Up to 90cm (35.5in); up to 0.5kg (1.1lb).
Maturity: Females 6 months; males 18 months.
Breeding: Give birth to single young, or sometimes twins, once or twice per year.
Life span: Not known.
Status: Common.

Little flying cow (*Nanonycteris veldkampi*): 5–7.5cm (2–3in); 19–33g (0.04–0.07lb)
This small flower-feeding bat can be found in parts of western and Central Africa. It gets its curious name from the apparently calf-like appearance of its head. This species migrates from forests to savannahs during the rainy season.

Butterfly bat (*Glauconycteris variegata*): 3.5–6.5cm (1.5–2.5in); 6–14g (0.01–0.03lb)
This African bat gets its name from its beautifully patterned wings and butterfly-like flight, and can be found roosting in small groups under palm fronds or banana leaves. Butterfly bats feed on small insects, sometimes foraging in broad daylight.

Lesser noctule (*Nyctalus leisleri*): 83–113mm (3.25–4.5in); 11–20g (0.4–0.7oz)
This species lives as far west as Ireland and is found across North Africa and the Middle East. It lives in mature woodlands where there are plenty of hollow trees. As its name suggests, this bat is the small relation of the common noctule. It hunts at dawn and dusk and migrates to warmer regions in winter.

Noctule bat

Nyctalus noctula

The noctule bat is one of the largest and most common European bats. In winter, noctules roost in hollow trees or old woodpecker holes, and occasionally in buildings. In some parts of Europe, groups of 1,000 individuals may roost together.

Noctules hunt insects in flight, and are capable of flying at speeds of 50kph (30mph) or more. Usually they forage at dusk, catching insects over woodland or close to water, and sometimes they are seen hunting insects that gather around street lamps in towns.

Although noctules are capable of surviving in cold conditions without food for up to four months, they also migrate to warmer areas where there is more food. Noctules have been known to migrate as far as 2,347km (1,455 miles). In late summer, solitary male noctules set up breeding roosts in tree holes, attracting up to 20 females with mating calls and pheromones. In early summer, pregnant females form groups of related individuals, then they help one another nurse their young.

Distribution: Europe to Japan.
Habitat: Forests.
Food: Insects, especially beetles, and also midges and moths.
Size: Wingspan 40cm (15.75in); 15–40g (0.03–0.09lb).
Maturity: Females 3 months; males 1 year.
Breeding: Single litter of 1, 2 or occasionally 3 young born per year.
Life span: 12 years.
Status: Declining in some parts of its range.

The colour of the noctule bat ranges from a golden brown to a dark brown on the back, usually with paler brown coloration on the belly.

Pipistrelle bat

Pipistrellus pipistrellus

These small bats are common throughout most of Europe, but have declined in some countries due to the loss of natural roosting sites in trees. The reduction is also due to toxic chemicals that have been used to treat wood in the buildings where many pipistrelles roost during winter time. In some parts of Europe, pipistrelles hibernate in winter, either individually or in groups, hidden in crevices in buildings and trees. However, very cold weather may force wintering pipistrelles to move to warmer areas.

Mating usually takes place in autumn, when the bats congregate at traditional breeding roosts. Females give birth to their young in summer, when they come together in large maternity colonies to suckle and care for them.

Pipistrelles leave their roosts early in the evening to feed, chasing after insects in a characteristic fast and jerky pursuit flight, using echolocation. A single pipistrelle can eat as many as 3,000 insects in one night. Usually the high-pitched squeaks that pipistrelles make for echolocation are inaudible to humans, but some people can hear the lower-frequency parts of their calls.

There are two subspecies of pipistrelle bat, distinguished by the pitch of their calls. One is known as the tenor, while the other is the soprano. The largest colonies may number many thousands.

Distribution: Europe, North Africa, south-western and central Asia, and possibly Korea and Japan.
Habitat: Forests, farmland, wetlands and urban habitats, nesting in lofts.
Food: Insects.
Size: Wingspan 19–25cm (7.5–9.75in); 3–8g (0.006–0.017lb).
Maturity: Females 6 months; males 1 year.
Breeding: 1 young or occasionally twins produced per year.
Life span: 16 years.
Status: Common.

Heart-nosed bat

Cardioderma cor

Heart-nosed bats live in the lowland areas of eastern Africa, where they are found in moist grasslands and woodlands from eastern Sudan to northern Tanzania and southern Zambia. By day the bats roost in large numbers in dry caves or in hollows in the immense baobab trees that grow on the open grasslands.

The heart-nosed bat's habitat experiences two rainy seasons. One runs from March to June, the other covers October to December. Most pups are born during these periods, although young are found in small numbers at all times of year.

Like all small bats, this species is nocturnal. They emerge from their roosts just before sunset. The bats hang from a branch and wait for prey to show itself. During the wet seasons, when insects are more common, the heart-nosed bats hunt on the wing, swooping through the air to snatch large flying insects, such as moths or locusts. They also snatch small vertebrates, such as frogs, from leaves and branches. In the dry seasons, the bats grab beetles from the ground. Insects are less common at these times of year, so the bats also target scorpions and centipedes.

Distribution: Eastern Africa from eastern Sudan to northern Tanzania and southern Zambia.
Habitat: Dry lowland grasslands often near the coast. The bats are especially common close to caves and baobab trees.
Food: Insects.
Size: 7.5cm (3in); 28g (1oz).
Maturity: 1 year.
Breeding: Single pups born in rainy seasons.
Life span: Unknown.
Status: Lower risk.

The heart-nosed bat is named after the shape of its nose leaf – a flap of skin that focuses the bat's echolocation calls. The bat has the largest eyes of any small bat in Africa.

Sucker-footed bat

Myzopoda aurita

Sucker-footed bats have small pads on each ankle and wrist. These pads work as suckers, enabling the bats to cling to flat surfaces such as large leaves. Some American bats have similar suckers but biologists believe that this species evolved separately from them.

The sucker-footed bat is the only one of its kind in the Old World (Eurasia and Africa). Once relatives of this species lived across East Africa, but today only one species survives. This lives on the Masoala Peninsula of eastern Madagascar, which is the location of the island's largest palm forests. There are similar bat species living in South America, but it is uncertain if they are closely related to the Malagasy bat.

As with many Malagasy species, the sucker-footed bat is facing extinction due to the loss of its habitat. About 90 per cent of the island's unique palm forests have been destroyed during the last century.

Being so rare, little is known about the life of the sucker-footed bat. It is nocturnal and is thought to feed on small flying insects, such as small moths. The bat needs to be an extremely agile flyer to catch such prey, which are themselves very acrobatic. Sucker-footed bats also have an unusual echolocation call that is made up of several elements that are thought to help it detect even the tiniest flying creatures. These two factors also make the bat very hard to catch because it can detect even the finest nets and can easily flit around them.

During the day the bats rest on palm leaves. They use their suckers to cling on in an upright position rather than upside down like many roosting bats.

Distribution: Masoala Peninsula in eastern Madagascar.
Habitat: Forests of palm trees.
Food: Small flying insects, such as moths.
Size: 11cm (4.25in); 9g (0.25oz).
Maturity: 1 year.
Breeding: Unknown.
Life span: Unknown.
Status: Vulnerable.

Yellow-winged bat

Lavia frons

Distribution: Central Africa from Gambia to Angola and Ethiopia.
Habitat: Savannahs and woodlands.
Food: Insects.
Size: 7cm (2.75in); 32g (1oz).
Maturity: 1 year.
Breeding: Pup born in April.
Life span: Unknown.
Status: Common.

The yellow-winged bats live in woodlands and savannahs with some tree cover. They are found across Central Africa. They live in monogamous pairs that may stay together for years. The pairs roost in trees and are especially common in umbrella thorn trees. They eat insects, such as ants and grasshoppers, that also live in the tree. Yellow-winged bats do not fly in search of food. Instead they wait for their prey to come to them.

A pair of bats roost about 1m (3.25ft) apart, keeping their distance from other pairs, which are always at least 20m (65.5ft) away. The pair forage independently by flitting from branch to branch and clambering around close to their roosting site. Just before dawn, the pair rendezvous back at the roost. The bats are often out in the open in view of predators, and frequently twist their heads almost completely around as they scan for danger.

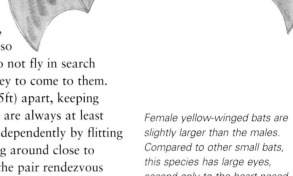

Female yellow-winged bats are slightly larger than the males. Compared to other small bats, this species has large eyes, second only to the heart-nosed bats in their size. The bat uses sight to find prey more than most small bats.

Woermann's bat (*Megaloglossus woermanni*): 6–8cm (2.25–3.25in); 14g (0.5oz)
Woermann's bat lives in the rainforest of the western part of Central Africa. It is found from northern Angola and Guinea to the eastern part of the Democratic Republic of Congo. The bat lives on pollen and nectar from banana and sausage tree flowers. It hangs from branches above the flowers and laps up its food using a tongue that is almost half as long as the body, from which it gets its other name of long-tongued fruit bat. This species of bat is an important pollinator for the plants it visits. As it feeds, the bat picks up pollen grains on its body. Some of these are transferred to the next flower that it visits. The pollen fuses with the female part of the flower, which then goes on to develop seeds and fruits. Flowers pollinated by day tend to be colourful, but those visited by bats at night are white. Woermann's bats roost under banana fronds, in trees and in houses.

Soprano pipistrelle (*Pipistrellus pygmaeus*): 3.5–5cm (1.5–2in); 6g (0.25oz)
It is more or less impossible to tell this species of bat from the common pipistrelle just by looking. Indeed, until recently biologists believed that they all belonged to one species. However, some bats produce more high-pitched calls than others, and these calls include the ones used to attract mates. It was discovered that the bats fall into two groups: high-pitched, or soprano, pipistrelles, which breed only with each other, and lower-pitched, or tenor, pipistrelles, which breed among themselves. Soprano pipistrelles are most common along river banks.

Egyptian slit-faced bat

Nycteris thebaica

Egyptian slit-faced bats live across Africa. They are also found on parts of the Arabian Peninsula, and small populations live in southern Europe, the largest of which is on the Greek island of Corfu. Slit-faced bats are most common on savannahs, but outside Africa they live in dry habitats, such as scrub and olive groves. The bats live in small groups. They roost in any sheltered spots, such as caves, hollow trees and among thick foliage. This species is also often found inside built structures.

Slit-faced bats eat mainly moths, but also catch other insects, such as grasshoppers and beetles. They also eat arachnids, such as spiders and scorpions. The bats catch flying prey on the wing, scooping the prey into their mouths with a membrane of skin around the tail. The bats also hang from trees and listen for the sounds of prey on the ground.

Distribution: Africa, Arabia and southern Europe.
Habitat: Savannahs and other dry habitats.
Food: Insects.
Size: 8–16cm (3.25–6.25in); 6.5–16g (0.25–0.5oz).
Maturity: 1 year.
Breeding: Single pups born at all times of year.
Life span: Unknown.
Status: Common.

The Egyptian slit-faced bat is named because its large nose leaf is split in two. The bat's fur varies from brown to grey, with bats living in drier places tending to have paler fur than those living in damper habitats.

Straw-coloured fruit bat

Eidolon helvum

The straw-coloured fruit bat is the most common and widespread fruit-eating bat in Africa. It is found across the continent south of the Sahara Desert – and there is also a population in Arabia. The bats live wherever there is fruit available and so can survive everywhere from humid rainforests to the most parched savannahs.

The bats roost in large groups in tall trees or in caves during the day. At night they fly off in small groups in search of food. The bats have long but narrow wings, which help them to fly long distances more efficiently. However, the wings do limit the bat's manoeuvrability. Straw-coloured fruit bats do not eat the flesh of fruits. Instead, they suck out the juice, spitting out any pulp. The bats feed while hanging beside the fruit. Favourite fruits include dates, mangoes, pawpaws, avocados, figs and custard apples.

The colony mates during the dry season, which is generally in early summer. This mating creates embryos, but these do not develop straight away. Their growth is timed so that the pups are born after the rains, when there is plenty of food available.

Only the neck and back of the straw-coloured fruit bat are actually straw-coloured: the rest of the body is a dull brown-grey. The male bats are slightly larger than the females.

Distribution: Africa south of the Sahara Desert and Arabia.
Habitat: Forests, woodlands, and savannahs. These bats do not live in deserts.
Food: The juice of fruits such as mangoes, figs, dates and custard apples.
Size: 18cm (7in); 290g (10.25oz).
Maturity: 1 year.
Breeding: Single pup born after rainy season.
Life span: 15 years.
Status: Common.

Gambian epauletted fruit bat

Epomophorus gambianus

Gambian epauletted fruit bats are found across the non-forested areas of Central Africa, distributed from Senegal and Mali to Ethiopia and also south to eastern South Africa. They roost in small groups in trees and are most common along the edges of woodlands. (The trees are more widely spaced in a woodland than in a forest.)

This species of bat eats figs, mangoes, guavas and bananas. They also suck nectar from some large flowers. Like most other fruit bats, it does not echolocate; instead, it finds food primarily using its sense of smell, following the scent of ripe fruits through the dark. The bat's large eyes allow it to see well in the darkness so it can avoid obstacles while in the air.

Gambian epauletted fruit bats live in mix-sexed groups. Males mate with several females during both the spring and autumn breeding seasons. Pups are nursed by other females in the roosting group, most of which are probably the pup's aunts. In most bat species, mothers must leave their pups in the roost when they go to feed, but the pups of this species come along for the ride, clinging to their mother's chest as she flies.

Male epauletted fruit bats have pouches of white fur on their shoulders, hence the name. The pale fur is normally hidden, but the males flash their white patches while courting females.

Distribution: Central and southern Africa from Senegal and southern Mali to Tanzania and South Africa.
Habitat: Woodland and savannah.
Food: Fruits, such as banana, guava, figs and mangoes. Also feeds on nectar.
Size: 12–25cm (4.75–19.75in); 40–120g (1.5–4.25oz).
Maturity: 1 year.
Breeding: 2 litters born each year.
Life span: 20 years.
Status: Common.

Peter's dwarf epauletted fruit bat

Micropteropus pusillus

Distribution: South of the Sahara Desert.
Habitat: Woodlands.
Food: Fruits and nectar.
Size: 6.5–10cm (2.5–4in); 24–34g (0.75–1.25oz).
Maturity: 6 months to 1 year.
Breeding: Single pups born twice a year.
Life span: Unknown.
Status: Lower risk.

This small species of epauletted fruit bat lives in woodland areas of western, Central and south-western Africa. From the south, the species is distributed from Angola to Ethiopia and Senegal. The bat does not live deep in the Congo rainforests.

Peter's dwarf epauletted fruit bats roost alone or in pairs, sleeping in the lower branches of trees. When roosting, the wings are wrapped around the body and the bat's eyes are closed, but the ears are constantly scanning the surroundings for signs of danger. Like most fruit bats, this species does not echolocate. Its ears are relatively small compared to those of echolocating bats, and its eyes are large.

This species feeds in the early evening. It lands on large fruit but hovers in front of smaller food, taking a bite on the wing. A mouthful of food is sucked and chewed for about 30 seconds. The juice and soft pulp are swallowed while the tougher fibres are spat out.

Like other species of epauletted bat, the males of this species have shoulder pouches filled with white hairs. Females have shallow pouches but no white fur.

Schreibers's long-fingered bat (*Miniopterus schreibersi*): 5.5cm (2.25in); 9.5g (0.25oz)
This species of bat is one of the most widespread in the world. It lives across southern Europe, Africa and Asia. It is also located in the Philippines and parts of Australia. The bat has very long fingers, which support broad wings. The third finger is so long that it has to be folded back on itself when the wing is not being used. The long-fingered bats are very fast and agile flyers. They seldom fly far from their cave roosts. They are nocturnal and hunt for insects such as small beetles. They hunt at 10–20m (33–66ft) above the ground.

Whiskered bat (*Myotis mystacinus*): 6.5–9cm (2.5–3.5in); 4–8g (0.15–0.25oz)
This bat is most common in central Europe, but it is found across northern Asia and North Africa. The species is distinctly furry, with coarse brown hairs on the head and back. Whiskered bats roost in large groups. When the females are nursing young in summer, the males leave the roost and live alone. The bats hunt for small insects such as flies, often hunting over water.

Rodrigues flying fox

Pteropus rodricensis

The Rodrigues flying fox is an extremely large and rare species of bat that lives on the island of Rodrigues, about 1,500km (930 miles) east of Madagascar. Rodrigues is part of the state of Mauritius.

Most bats are nocturnal, but the Rodrigues flying foxes are crepuscular (most active during the twilight of dawn and dusk). They are not able to echolocate like smaller bats. They still use their ears to find prey, but they rely on their eyes to orientate themselves while flying. Their ears are much smaller than most bats, hence this species' resemblance to a fox. Like other fruit bats, their eyes are large to collect more light so the bats can see objects in low light levels.

Most large bats are fruit eaters. The Rodrigues flying fox does eat fruits, but it also hunts for large flying insects, such as moths. The bat catches these insects in mid-air, using its large wings as a net. The size of the Rodrigues flying fox has a detrimental effect on its flying ability and it cannot get aloft in strong winds.

These bats were on the brink of extinction in 1976. As an island species, they are especially at risk of disruption to their habitat. Today the bats are bred in captivity, and other measures have seen the island's wild population reach 3,000 in recent years.

Distribution: Rodrigues Island.
Habitat: Mangrove and rainforest.
Food: Insects.
Size: 35cm (13.75in); 285g (10oz).
Maturity: 1.5–2 years.
Breeding: Single pup born each year.
Life span: Unknown.
Status: Critically endangered.

The Rodrigues flying fox has a brightly coloured head. The fur is a mixture of red and yellow fur. This species of bat has a wingspan of 90cm (3ft). It is named a flying fox because of the shape of its snout, which lacks the acoustic adornments of other species.

Giant leaf-nosed bat

Hipposideros commerson

The giant leaf-nosed bat is found across the equatorial region of Africa and on the island of Madagascar. It is divided into at least five subspecies, including the Malagasy population. Another subspecies occupies the islands of São Tomé and Principe in the Gulf of Guinea to the west of the African mainland. The most common subspecies lives across eastern and southern Africa, from Somalia to Namibia and South Africa.

Giant leaf-nosed bats live in forested areas that have plenty of open spaces for them to fly along. Such flyways are uncommon in the middle of tropical rainforest, so the species is most common along the edge of jungle and woodlands. When not on the move along the flyways, the bats perch to the side. The bat is nocturnal, and the largest roosts are inside caves. Smaller groups of bats will see out the day inside hollow trees. Pups are born in the wet season and the nursery roosts are generally based in caves.

Giant leaf-nosed bats have sharp fangs and powerful jaws, which are used to crush the hard bodies of large beetles. The bat's prey lives on the ground, and it searches for food from a perch or scans the ground as it flies along at a height of 60cm (2ft).

Distribution: Sub-Saharan Africa, Madagascar and several surrounding islands.
Habitat: Forest edges and clearings.
Food: Beetles.
Size: 11–15cm (4.25–6in); 130g (4.5oz).
Maturity: 1 year.
Breeding: Single pups born once a year. Mating takes place between February and June and the pup is born about 4 months later.
Life span: Unknown.
Status: Common.

This is one of the largest insect-eating bats, with a wingspan of more than 50cm (19.75in). These bats have elaborate nose leaves used in echolocation. Males have a large crest of bone running down the head.

Lesser mouse-tailed bat

Rhinopoma hardwickei

The lesser mouse-tailed bat is a widespread desert species. It lives in dry habitats across North Africa, the Middle East and southern Asia. Its distribution stretches as far east as Myanmar (Burma). The bat is well adapted to life in the dusty desert. For example, the wind often whips dust and grit into the air, which could easily cause a problem for a flying bat by blocking its airways. However, lesser mouse-tailed bats are able to continue flying in windy conditions because their nostrils are equipped with a valve inside that closes to keep the dust out.

Most of where the lesser mouse-tailed bats live is treeless, so the bats have only a few places to sleep. They prefer cliffs, caves and walls and other artificial structures. Consequently they crowd into any suitable sites and roost in huge numbers. A large cave will contain many thousands of bats. As is normal with small bats, when the female bats are nursing young, they live in separate roosts to the males.

Mouse-tailed bats are insect eaters. In dry periods, insects are hard to come by, so the bats must stay in their roosts to conserve energy. During this time, the bats become torpid, entering a dormant state, or torpor, similar to hibernation. They survive these periods of inactivity by consuming fat supplies that are stored in the tail.

Distribution: North and East Africa, Middle East, and southern Asia.
Habitat: Deserts and other dry treeless areas.
Food: Insects snatched from the air and gleaned from the ground.
Size: 7cm (2.75in); 10g (0.25oz).
Maturity: 1 year.
Breeding: Single young born in summer, although pups arrive earlier in southern parts of the bat's range.
Life span: Unknown.
Status: Common.

This bat and its close relatives are the only species to have such a long tail, which can be longer than the body in some cases. It plays no part in flight, being a food-storage organ.

Greater horseshoe bat

Rhinolophus ferrumequinum

Distribution: Europe, north-west Africa and central and south Asia.
Habitat: Woodland and shrublands.
Food: Large insects.
Size: 6.5cm (2.5in); 25g (0.75oz).
Maturity: 3 years.
Breeding: Single pup born in summer.
Life span: 30 years.
Status: Lower risk.

The greater horseshoe bat is the largest horseshoe bat in Europe. It is also found in north-western Africa and across most of Asia as far east as Japan. Horseshoe bats belong to the *Rhinolophus* genus, which means "nose crest".

The greater horseshoe bat is an insect eater. It hunts at night and specializes in catching large insects such as moths and beetles. They fly close to the ground, scanning for prey with pulses of sound, the echoes of which enable them to locate insects. They catch prey mainly in the air. Horseshoe bats prefer to hunt on warm nights, because most insects cannot fly in cold weather. In the northern parts of its range, where winters are colder, members of this species will not leave their roosts for weeks on end.

Greater horseshoe bats roost in caves and smaller holes under rocks. They mate in the autumn, but the females' eggs are not fertilized by the sperm until the following year. Pups are born during the late summer.

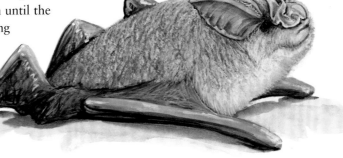

The greater horseshoe bat is named after the shape of its nose. The upper nose leaf is pointed but the larger flap below the nose forms a horseshoe shape.

Egyptian rousette (*Rousettus egyptiacus*): 15cm (6in); 126g (4.5oz)
This species is also called the Egyptian fruit bat. It is found across most of Africa south of the Sahara Desert and extends up the Nile Valley into the Middle East. From there the bats range into Turkey, Cyprus and east to Pakistan. Unlike all other fruit bats, rousettes use basic echolocation to orientate themselves while flying in the day, although they are more reliant on their eyesight for avoiding obstacles. The bat has a very sensitive nose that can smell even the tiniest morsels of fruit. Egyptian rousettes roost in large groups. They congregate in caves and many of the ancient ruins across their range. As well as fruits, they eat flowers, buds and leaves.

Livingstone's fruit bat (*Pteropus livingstonii*): Wingspan: 1.4m (4.5ft); 700g (1.5lb)
The Livingstone's fruit bat, or black flying fox, lives on the Comoro Islands, which are located at the northern end of the deep channel that separates the African mainland from Madagascar. The bat is found on only two of these islands, where dense jungles grow on the sides of steep mountains. It uses its huge wingspan to catch thermals so that it can soar high up the mountainside. The bat is a fruit and flower eater, with much of its diet consisting of figs. The bat locates food by sight and smell and is seen foraging during both day and night. Livingstone's fruit bat is one of the most endangered of all bat, and indeed mammal, species: there are thought to be just 400 left in the wild.

Mediterranean horseshoe bat

Rhinolophus euryale

Like all the horseshoe bats, the Mediterranean horseshoe bat has a semicircular nose leaf below the nostrils. Horseshoe bats emit their echolocation calls through their noses, and the nose leaf is shaped to focus the sound into a beam that can detect a certain size of prey.

Mediterranean horseshoe bats prey on small moths. Many moths are able to hear the high-pitched calls of the bat species and so fly away to safety, but they cannot detect the sounds produced by these bats and so are unable to hear the hunters coming.

The females are slightly larger than the males. Both sexes roost together in caves and other hidden places. The bats prefer places that stay the same temperature all year around. Their wide wings are not long enough to wrap around their bodies as they sleep, so if it gets too cold in the roost the bats become dormant to save energy.

Distribution: Southern Europe.
Habitat: Mountain forests.
Food: Flying insects.
Size: 8cm (3.25in); 17g (0.5oz).
Maturity: 2 years.
Breeding: Single pup born each year.
Life span: 27 years.
Status: Vulnerable.

Mediterranean horseshoe bats have broad wings, which are typical of bats that live in forests. They make the bats agile flyers that are able to twist and turn in the air.

Lesser woolly bat

Kerivoula lanosa

Lesser woolly bats live close to the rivers, lakes and wetlands of south-eastern Africa. Their range extends from the south of the Democratic Republic of Congo through Zambia and Zimbabwe to Mozambique and Botswana. Recently the same species has been found in another population that lives in West Africa.

   The bats are associated with water habitats, which are few and far between and often seasonal. As a result, despite having a very wide distribution, the lesser woolly bat is relatively rare, especially in the western part of the range.

   Its rarity makes this species difficult to study in the wild and its breeding and other behaviours are not well understood. It is assumed that it lives in a similar way to other small bats. Like other insect eaters, this species hunts at night. They are not fast flyers and tend to flutter in tight circles as they hunt. Many bats hunt over water, where insects are generally more common.

   The lesser woolly bat has a long tail membrane supported by a heel bone. The tail membrane extends beyond the toes. The tail might be used for scooping prey off the surface of water or out of the air.

Distribution: Sub-Saharan Africa from the Ivory Coast to the Congo, Zimbabwe and Botswana.
Habitat: Rivers, lakes and wetlands. Some specimens have been found in forested regions.
Food: Small insects caught on the wing or snatched from leaves and the ground.
Size: 8cm (3.25in); 7g (0.25oz).
Maturity: 1 year.
Breeding: Single pup born after 40 day gestation.
Life span: Unknown.
Status: Common.

Like all woolly bats, this species has a thick coat of curly hair. The fur is grizzled, meaning it is darker at the base than at the tips, which gives the fur an overall silvery look. All species have high foreheads, making their heads rounded.

Western barbastelle

Barbastella barbastellus

The western barbastelle lives in hill forests, apart from those in cold regions. For example, in Great Britain it survives only in the milder southern regions. The species is more common in southern Europe and the Mediterranean islands. In summer the bats roost in hollow trees and other relatively open spots, where they often squeeze behind patches of loose bark. In winter the barbastelles retreat to more secluded roosts, such as caves, where they hibernate without becoming completely dormant: they will leave the roost every week or two to hunt.

   These bats prey on moths and other soft-bodied insects. They do not seem to eat beetles, which have hardened wingcases and tend to have tougher bodies than most insects. The bats snatch prey in mid-air or grab insects as they perch on leaves and branches. Barbastelles hunt along the edges of forests, where there are more flyways for them and their prey.

   Across its entire range, this species is under threat. The main reason for this is the loss of its habitat, in particular a lack of hollow trees in which the bats can roost.

Distribution: Great Britain, western and central Europe, Morocco, and the Canary Islands.
Habitat: Highland forests in summer but retreat to subterranean caves and mines in winter.
Food: Moths and other soft-bodied insects.
Size: 6cm (2.25in); 8g (0.25oz).
Maturity: 1 year.
Breeding: Single pups born in summer. Pups reach full size in about 3 months.
Life span: Unknown.
Status: Vulnerable.

Western barbastelles have dark hairs with yellow tips. The neck and chin have long hairs that give the impression of a beard. The feature that distinguishes this species from other bats is the ears, which join across the forehead.

Brown big-eared bat

Plecotus auritus

Distribution: Western Europe, excluding the British Isles, and east to South-east Asia.
Habitat: Forest edges.
Food: Moths.
Size: 5cm (2in); 8g (0.25oz).
Maturity: 1 year.
Breeding: Mating takes place in autumn.
Life span: 15 years.
Status: Common.

The brown big-eared bat is most common in wooded hills. It has a vast range that extends from Spain to Japan and India. The bat is most often found flying along the edges of the forests or in clearings. The species' main food is moths, but the bats also eat beetles, flies, earwigs and spiders. The long-eared bats catch prey in three ways: they snatch prey on the wing, swoop down to the ground to grab it or hover beside a tree or bush and listen for insects moving on the leaves and branches. This is where the bat's ears come into their own. Being so huge, the ears can collect a lot of sound waves. The bat filters out the sounds of prey and swoops in for the kill. All of this takes place in darkness, although the bat has relatively large eyes, which might be used in the final approach to the prey.

The bats roost in hollow trees. Pups born at the end of summer might be abandoned if the weather turns too cold for the mother to produce milk.

This bat has enormous ears that are almost as long as the rest of its body. They point forward during flight to keep the bat streamlined. When the bat is resting, the ears are folded sideways.

Grey big-eared bat (*Plecotus austriacus*): 6cm (2.25in); 10g (0.25oz)
This close relative of the brown big-eared bat also lives across Europe, Asia and northern Africa. It prefers warmer climes to its brown-haired cousin's habitat. It roosts in caves, under rocks and even hanging from large tropical flowers. It catches prey using its tail membrane to scoop victims toward the mouth.

Daubenton's bat (*Myotis daubentonii*): 5cm (2in); 10g (0.25oz)
Daubenton's bat ranges from Britain to Japan. It is a relative of the mouse-eared bats. Most members of this species live in woodlands and are always close to a supply of water. In summer the bats roost under bridges and in trees. They withdraw into caves and more sheltered spots in which to hibernate over the winter. This species hunts for insects that fly over water. In a single night a bat can eat more than half its body weight in insects. Thanks to conservation measures, which protect bat roosting sites, this species is increasing in numbers across Europe.

Long-tailed bat (*Rhinopoma microphyllum*): 5–9cm (2–3.5in); 6–14g (0.01–0.03lb)
This species, also known as the greater mouse-tailed bat, has a tail nearly as long as its body, and lives in dry, treeless regions in northern and western Africa, parts of the Middle East and southern India. Long-tailed bats can often be found roosting in houses, and in Egypt they are believed to have roosted in the great pyramids for thousands of years.

Greater mouse-eared bat

Myotis myotis

The greater mouse-eared bat was declared extinct in Britain in 1990. This is in contrast to its relative, the Daubenton's bat, which is one of the few European species that are increasing in number.

The greater mouse-eared bat is one of the largest bats in Europe. It is found across the continent and also in much of southern and eastern Asia and parts of North Africa. The species lives in open woodland areas, roosting in caves and trees. However, considering its range, this bat is also a common resident of churches and other quiet, high-vaulted buildings. A good roost is one where the temperature stays more or less stable for the whole winter.

The greater mouse-eared bat forages for food over an area about 8km (5 miles) from its roost. It feeds on a number of insects, including many flying creatures, but most of its diet consists of beetles plucked from the ground. The ideal hunting ground for this species is thin woodland with grass covering the ground.

Distribution: Europe, Asia and North Africa.
Habitat: Woodlands.
Food: Beetles.
Size: 9cm (3.5in); 30g (1oz).
Maturity: 1 year.
Breeding: Pups born in early summer.
Life span: 13 years.
Status: Lower risk.

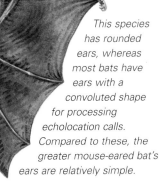

This species has rounded ears, whereas most bats have ears with a convoluted shape for processing echolocation calls. Compared to these, the greater mouse-eared bat's ears are relatively simple.

AARDVARK AND PANGOLINS

These two types of mammal specialize in eating ants and termites, but recent scientific work has shown that, although aardvarks and pangolins share some superficial resemblance and behaviour, they do not have common ancestry. Rather, specialist ant-eating mammals evolved independently several times. This is not surprising, given the abundance of ants and termites found in almost all habitats around the world.

Aardvark

Orycteropus afer

Distribution: Sub-Saharan Africa.
Habitat: Woodland, savannah, grassland and shrubland.
Food: Ants, termites, other insects, small mammals and vegetable material.
Size: 1–1.5m (3.25–5ft); 40–70kg (88–154lb).
Maturity: 2 years.
Breeding: 1 or occasionally 2 young per year.
Life span: 20 years.
Status: Common.

These animals are often found foraging out in the open at night, systematically covering the ground in search of ants or termites. Aardvarks travel long distances in looking for food, often travelling 10km (6 miles) in a single night. Not surprisingly, given their long tubular ears and snout, they have acute hearing and a good sense of smell with which to detect their prey. They use their powerful front claws to dig open ant and termite nests, and their long sticky tongues to collect the insects. These animals have very thick skin, and seem to be immune to insect bites.

The aardvark's skin is so tough that it also saves it from bites by predators. Aardvarks are very well adapted for digging. When alarmed, they will either run away or start digging a burrow. A single aardvark can dig a hole faster than several people using shovels. Temporary aardvark burrows are less than 3m (10ft) deep, with end chambers large enough for the animals to turn in. More permanent burrows can be 13m (42.75ft) long with several chambers and entrances.

The word aardvark means "earth-pig" in Afrikaans, reflecting both the burrowing habits and pig-like features of this unusual animal. It has long ears, an elongated snout, a shaggy body and powerful tail. It folds its ears back while making its burrows.

Cape pangolin

Manis temmincki

There are four species of pangolin, also known as scaly anteaters, living in Africa. Two of them are tree-living animals with long prehensile tails, which they use when climbing. The other two species, which include the endangered Cape pangolin, live in burrows and forage on the ground.

Pangolins feed solely on ants and termites. They have several adaptations, such as having no teeth, which help them in this regard. Like other ant-eating mammals, they have sticky tongues up to 25cm (10in) long for collecting their prey, and strong claws to tear open termite nests. Unlike any other mammals, however, pangolins have scales rather than hairs, giving them a reptilian appearance. When a pangolin is threatened, it rolls up into a tight ball, protecting its soft underparts and presenting a formidable, scaly barrier to predators. The Cape pangolin has declined in numbers because, like its Asian cousins, it is in demand for its scales, which are used in local medicines.

Distribution: Chad and Sudan to Namibia and South Africa.
Habitat: Savannah and shrubland.
Food: Ants, termites and occasionally other insects.
Size: 40–50cm (15.75–19.75in); 15–18kg (33–39.75lb).
Maturity: 2 years.
Breeding: 1 or occasionally 2 young.
Life span: Not known.
Status: Threatened.

Pangolins usually walk on their knuckles to save wear and tear on their claws, which they use for opening ant and termite nests. Sometimes they walk on their back legs, using the trailing tail to keep balance.

Giant pangolin

Manis gigantea

Distribution: Central Africa from Senegal to Uganda and Angola.
Habitat: Rainforests and grasslands.
Food: Ants and termites. Up to 200,000 ants are eaten in one night.
Size: 1.25–1.4m (4–4.5ft); 33kg (72.75lb).
Maturity: 2 years.
Breeding: Litters born in September and October.
Life span: 10 years.
Status: Common.

The giant pangolin is the largest of all seven pangolin species (only four of which live in Africa) and lives in the forests of Central Africa. It forages on the ground in the dead of night. A giant pangolin seldom emerges from its burrow before midnight. It digs its own burrow using the long and sturdy claws on its forepaws. The burrows can be immense affairs, reaching 40m (130ft) in length.

When walking through the forest, the giant pangolin puts most of its weight on to its thick back legs. It uses its tail as a counterbalance so that it can free up its forepaws for digging for food. When it does walk on all fours, the forefeet have to be twisted to the side to protect their crucial claws.

Like all pangolins, this species is highly adapted to eating termites and ants. The mighty claws are used for ripping into nests and mounds; then the pangolin uses its long, sticky tongue to lick up the exposed insects.

As with all pangolins, the only hairs on a giant pangolin are its eyelashes. Instead of hairs, it is covered in thick scales. The claws on the forelegs are long. They are used for ripping open ants' nests.

Tree pangolin (*Manis tricuspis*): 35–45cm (13.75–17.75in); 2kg (4.5lb)
This is the smallest of all pangolin species. It lives in the rainforests that skirt the grasslands of East Africa. Like other tree-living pangolins, this species has a long tail that is used to provide support and balance. The tree pangolin also forages on the ground, specializing in cocktail ants and termites. The pangolin sniffs out its prey's nests and licks the insects up with its long tongue. When pulled back into the mouth, the tongue is held in a sheath that extends halfway along the body's length. The pangolin has no teeth and so cannot chew its meal. This function is transferred to the gut lining, which is lined with thin scales that grind the food into a paste as the stomach churns. The pangolin swallows grit and pebbles as it eats, which also help with the grinding process.

Long-tailed pangolin

Manis tetradactyla

The long-tailed pangolin is found in forests across Central Africa in a range that begins in southern Uganda and extends west to Senegal and south to Angola. It is arboreal (built for living in trees), and most of its time is spent in the high canopy of the rainforest; indeed, some individuals may never come down to the ground.

Like its relatives, this species survives on ants. Pangolins have a very long tongue that it is half as long as the body and coated with sticky saliva. The pangolin spends the day licking up ants that are moving along the forest branches. It sleeps in a hollow by night.

The tongue is not the only long body part. This species of pangolin also has a very long, flexible tail. The tip is naked of scales and is highly sensitive to touch. It acts as a feeler and fifth limb and can be wrapped around branches to provide that extra bit of support. When surprised, these pangolins will curl up into a ball and squirt a foul-smelling liquid from anal glands. If the location allows it, the pangolins are known to leap from the branches into the safety of water.

Distribution: Central Africa.
Habitat: Rainforest.
Food: Ants and termites.
Size: 40cm (15.75in); 3kg (6.5lb).
Maturity: 2 years.
Breeding: Single young born at all times of year.
Life span: 10 years.
Status: Common.

The most striking feature about this little tree-living pangolin is its hugely long tail, which is roughly twice as long as the body.

INSECTIVORES

The insectivores are a wide-ranging group of small mammals, all with sensitive and highly mobile noses, small eyes and relatively small brains. They are generally solitary, nocturnal animals, the majority of which eat insects, earthworms and other invertebrates. Their teeth are well designed for eating insects, with long incisors for seizing their prey and sharp molars for dealing with their tough bodies.

Hedgehog

Erinaceus europaeus

Few members of the insectivore family have been able to grow much larger than moles because the food they eat – insects – are so small that they would need to eat a very large quantity. Hedgehogs, however, are more eclectic in their tastes, with a diet that includes earthworms, birds' eggs, frogs, lizards and even snakes. Eating these larger foods has allowed hedgehogs to grow much bigger than is the norm for the group.

Nonetheless, being larger can have its disadvantages, not least being more conspicuous to predators. This is where the hedgehog's most famous asset comes in handy. All over its back the hedgehog has rows of thickened hairs, which narrow at their tips into sharp, prickly points. Using muscles located around the base of the coat, which act like drawstrings, the hedgehog can roll into a ball, becoming an impregnable mass of prickles, which is very effective at deterring the advances of predators.

The hedgehog's Latin name Erinaceus *is derived from the word* ericius, *meaning a spiked barrier. Hedgehogs are mostly solitary, but when they do come together they follow a pecking order.*

Distribution: Western Europe and Northern Russia.
Habitat: Woodland, grassland and gardens.
Food: Invertebrates.
Size: 22–28cm (8.75–11in); 0.4–1.2kg (1–2.75lb).
Maturity: 2–3 years.
Breeding: 2–6 young born in summer.
Life span: 3–4 years.
Status: Common, but declining in the UK.

Southern African hedgehog

Atelerix frontalis

Like Eurasian hedgehogs, this species is covered in short spines. It stands out from others because it has a thick white band across the forehead.

The southern African hedgehog lives in two populations. The first is found in south-western Africa, stretching from Angola to northern Namibia, and the second, larger, group lives in Zimbabwe, Botswana and the Cape Province of South Africa. This species' catholic tastes for food mean that it can survive in most places as long as there is plenty of cover.

The southern African hedgehog lives alone. It forages at night and rests by day. This species eats mainly ground-living insects, such as beetles and grasshoppers, but it often scratches around for earthworms and centipedes. The hedgehogs are also known to supplement their diet with mushrooms, lizards and carrion. Mating takes places throughout the year. The male must court the female by walking around her several times. Litters can contain up to ten young. An older female may have several litters in one year.

Distribution: Angola, Namibia, Zimbabwe, Botswana and South Africa.
Habitat: Grasslands, rocky areas and gardens.
Food: Insects, worms and centipedes.
Size: 15–20cm (6–8in); 150–555g (5.25–19.5oz).
Maturity: 1 year.
Breeding: Litters of between 4 and 10 young born several times a year.
Life span: 3 years.
Status: Common.

Russian desman

Desmana moschata

Distribution: South-western Russia and eastern Europe.
Habitat: Slow rivers and oxbow lakes.
Food: Aquatic invertebrates, including insects, amphibians, crustaceans and molluscs, and also fish and plant roots.
Size: 18–22cm (7–8.75in); 100–220g (0.2–0.5lb).
Maturity: 1 year.
Breeding: Litters of 1–5 young.
Life span: 2–3 years.
Status: Vulnerable.

Looking somewhat like a cross between a shrew and a mole, there are only two species of desman alive in the world today. The Pyrenean desman lives in northern Spain and Portugal, and its relative the Russian desman inhabits areas in Russia and eastern Europe.

Desmans have webbed feet and broad tails fringed with stiff hairs. These adaptations help them swim, and it is underwater that desmans do most of their hunting, feeling around with their long whiskers for prey items such as dragonfly larvae and tadpoles.

These animals do not just swim; they also burrow, looking for worms. They tunnel into river banks, making networks of burrows which can extend for many metres. The entrances to the systems of tunnels are always located below the waterline, so that the desmans can come and go as they please, without having to worry about any predators that may be watching from above. There are many predators that will feed on desmans, including hawks, kestrels, foxes and weasels. Several desmans share the tunnel network, although they tend to have their own dens within the burrow.

Like their close relatives the shrews, desmans must feed almost constantly to keep up their energy reserves.

Pygmy white-toothed shrew (*Suncus etruscus*): 3.5–5.2cm (1.5–2in); 1.5–2.5g (0.003–0.005lb)
One of the world's smallest mammals, pygmy white-toothed shrews are found across southern Europe. These shrews have scent glands on their sides, which secrete a pungent odour. The glands are especially well developed in the males during the breeding season, when they are trying to intimidate their rivals and impress females.

Alpine shrew (*Sorex alpinus*): 6–7.5cm (2.5–3in); 5.5–11.5g (0.01–0.025lb)
Inhabiting alpine grasslands up to an altitude of 3,400m (11,333ft) above sea level, alpine shrews are often found in rocky habitats. They are especially common on stony banks and beds of fast-flowing mountain streams, seeking out invertebrate prey. Unlike most shrew species, alpine shrews are adept climbers.

Blind mole (*Talpa caeca*): 9.5–14cm (3.75–5.5in); 65–120g (0.14–0.25lb)
Unlike the common European mole, the blind mole of southern Europe is physically unable to open its eyes. It has membranous coverings over them, which it cannot pull back. However, the membranes do allow some light through, and it is said that blind moles are not totally insensitive to the visual world, being able to react to changes in light and dark.

European mole

Talpa europaea

The European mole lives across most of Europe, including large parts of Britain, but does not live in southern Europe, which is too dry. However, the species is found across northern Asia as far as China.

Like all moles, this species is a tunneller. It digs using the large claws on its forefeet. Its rounded body and short fur make it easy for the mole to push through loosened soil. The mole needs relatively deep soil to dig in. It pushes the excavated soil out on to the surface, making a molehill.

It is most common in woodlands, where deep soil is held together by tree roots. However, the moles are also found under fields and in gardens. Their tunnels can undermine the structure of the soil, and the molehills ruin lawns.

Distribution: Europe and Asia.
Habitat: Woodland, fields and meadows.
Food: Earthworms.
Size: 9–16.5cm (3.5–6.5in); 70–130g (2.5–4.5oz).
Maturity: 1 year.
Breeding: Single litter of about 3 young born in summer.
Life span: 3 years.
Status: Common.

The European mole is adapted for life underground. It has short but sturdy forelegs equipped with wide claws, which are used for digging tunnels and pulling the animal along. The hind legs are much smaller.

Golden mole

Eremitalpa granti

There are no species of true mole in Africa. Their niche is filled by another group of insectivores called the golden moles. Found mainly in dry sandy areas, golden moles lead entirely subterranean lives, feeding mainly on insects, such as termites. Golden moles also consume small reptiles, such as geckoes and legless lizards, which the moles encounter buried in the sand. Their underground existence means that the moles have little need for vision, and consequently they have lost the power of sight.

Since it is impossible to construct burrows in the dry sands of their desert habitats, golden moles constantly have to plough their way through the sand. Their small but powerful forelimbs are well designed to help them "swim" through sand. They are active at night. By day the golden moles enter a deep sleep, or torpor, which helps them conserve energy. The young are born between October and November. They are suckled for two to three months in a grass-lined nest.

Golden moles may not be able to see, but they do have incredibly acute hearing, being able to pick up the noises made by their insect prey as they move on the surface. Golden moles can pinpoint the precise location of their prey and emerge from below to snatch their meals.

Distribution: Cape Province, Namaqualand in South Africa and the Namib Desert.
Habitat: Coastal sand dunes.
Food: Insects and lizards.
Size: 76–87mm (3–3.5in); 120–150g (0.25–0.33lb).
Maturity: Not known.
Breeding: 1 litter of 1–2 young born every year.
Life span: Not known.
Status: Vulnerable.

A layer of skin grows over the golden mole's useless eyes, giving them a somewhat bizarre appearance.

Tailless tenrec

Tenrec ecaudatus

Like other tenrecs, this is an island species. It lives on Madagascar and the Comoro Islands, which lie between Madagascar and the African mainland. The insectivore has also been introduced to several other Indian Ocean islands, including the Seychelles and Mauritius.

The tailless tenrec is a forest animal, but it is highly adaptable and will eat whatever it can find. The species has therefore not suffered from the deforestation that has occurred in Madagascar and elsewhere. Instead it has adapted to life alongside humans and is found everywhere apart from arid habitats.

The insectivores are solitary creatures. They forage at dusk and before dawn among rubbish tips for waste food. In the wild the tenrec survives mainly on insects and other invertebrates but also eats fruits and leaves and hunts for lizards, frogs and small mammals.

Tailless tenrecs give birth in the rainy season after a pregnancy of 9 weeks. Up to 32 young are born in a single litter, but half this number is more usual. The young begin to feed themselves at the age of three weeks.

Distribution: Madagascar and Comoro Islands. Introduced to Mauritius, Reunion and Seychelles, all islands in the Indian Ocean.
Habitat: Areas with running water where shrubs and bush grow. Most common in the humid forests of eastern Madagascar.
Food: Insects, fruits, small vertebrates and rubbish.
Size: 39cm (15.25in); 2.4kg (5.25lb).
Maturity: 1–2 years.
Breeding: 10–20 young born in rainy season. Young are independent at 6 weeks.
Life span: 6 years.
Status: Common.

The tailless tenrec is one of the largest insectivores. When young, the tenrecs have a row of white spines along the back. Adult tenrecs shed the spines and grow a mane in its place.

Aquatic tenrec

Limnogale mergulus

Distribution: Madagascar.
Habitat: Mountain streams.
Food: Insects, frogs and crayfish.
Size: 24cm (9.5in); 100g (3.5oz).
Maturity: Unknown.
Breeding: Litters of 3 young born in March and April.
Life span: Unknown.
Status: Endangered.

The aquatic tenrec lives in the fast-running streams that flow through the highland region of eastern Madagascar. There are only eight locations where the tenrecs have a sustainable population. Like other aquatic mammals, this species is especially sensitive to water pollution and habitat destruction.

It hunts underwater by night. Its main prey is the larvae of insects such as dragonflies, but it also catches small frogs and crayfish. The tenrecs swim against the rapid current using their large, webbed hind feet. (The species is often also referred to as the web-footed tenrec.) The thick tail is used as a rudder.

Aquatic tenrecs use short whiskers on the their snout to locate prey. The whiskers pick up the tiny eddies created in the water by the movements of small prey. The eyes and ears are small and of less use. By day they rest in bank-side burrows.

This small tenrec does not have the spiny coat of other species. Instead its sleek fur resembles that of an otter. Unlike other tenrecs, this species has a rounded snout and webbed hind feet.

Large-eared tenrec (*Geogale aurita*): 10cm (4in); 6g (0.25oz)
Large-eared tenrecs are small shrew-like tenrecs that live in the south of Madagascar. They inhabit dry forests and scrub. This sort of habitat is generally hot. This species of tenrec is unusual because its body temperature rises and falls with that of its surroundings, whereas most mammals maintain a constant body temperature, either cooling or warming themselves. These insectivores use their large ears to pick up the sounds of prey. They hunt at night and have poor vision. Large-eared tenrecs consume mainly termites, but also eat other types of insects.

Lesser hedgehog tenrec (*Echinops telfairi*): 17.5cm (7in); 200g (7oz)
Tenrecs are generally considered as relatives of the insectivores, such as moles, shrews and hedgehogs. However, recent research suggests that they might be more closely related to aardvarks and elephants. This fact makes the lesser hedgehog tenrec all the more interesting. This small mammal from Madagascar looks very similar to the hedgehogs found throughout Africa, Asia and Europe. It has a coat of spines and short legs for shuffling around undergrowth. Unlike true hedgehogs, however, this species is often seen to climb into trees. The lesser hedgehog tenrec occupies dry habitats in southern and western Madagascar, such as scrubland and dry monsoon forests, that rely on a single deluge of rain for their survival. The tenrecs are night-time foragers. They eat insects, small mammals and plant food.

Giant otter shrew

Potamogale velox

The giant otter shrew is a relative of the Malagasy tenrecs, but it lives on the African mainland. It occupies wetlands and streams that run through the rainforests of Central Africa. In the rainy season, otter shrews cross dry land to hunt in many of the temporary pools that form.

The giant otter shrew swims with its tail, which is flattened to form a vertical flipper. The tail is swung from side to side to power the otter shrew through the water. The legs play no role in swimming. The paws are not webbed and the hind legs are tucked against the body and have a flap of skin along the inside edge that flattens against the body to maintain its streamlined shape.

Otter shrews hunt at night and rely on their sense of touch to find prey. Without webbing, their fingers and toes remain relatively dexterous, but it is their thick whiskers that are their main sense organ. The otter shrews grab prey in their mouths or pin down larger victims with their forepaws.

Distribution: Central Africa.
Habitat: Forest streams and swamps.
Food: Crabs, frogs and fish.
Size: 58cm (22.75in); 625g (22oz).
Maturity: Unknown.
Breeding: Mating takes place in rainy season. Litters usually made up of twins.
Life span: Unknown.
Status: Endangered.

The otter shrew has a long, rounded body covered in a sleek brown coat, which consists of long, oily guard hairs over fine underfur. A layer of air trapped between the two layers keeps the animal's skin dry and warm. The nostrils are sealed during swimming.

Eurasian water shrew

Neomys fodiens

The Eurasian water shrew is found across Europe and Asia. The western limit of its range is Britain. It does not live in Ireland. To the east, the species' range extends all the way to the Pacific coast of Siberia.

Most water shrews live close to fresh water, defending a small area of bank in which their burrow is located. Some members of this species live farther away from flowing water, in damp areas such as hedgerows.

The shrews live alone. They hunt at all times of the day and night, mostly in water. The tail has a keel of hairs on the underside, which helps with swimming. The shrew's fur traps a blanket of air as the animal submerges, which prevents the little mammal from losing body heat too quickly.

These animals eat about half their own body weight each day. They catch prey in their mouths and stun it with mildly venomous saliva. Only a handful of other mammals deploy venom.

Water shrews breed during the summer. Each female is capable of producing several litters in that time. A typical litter contains about five or six young, although twice this number is possible. The young are weaned after 40 days. Females born early enough can breed in their first year.

Distribution: Most of Europe, including Great Britain, and Asia from Turkey to Korea.
Habitat: Freshwater streams and ponds.
Food: Snails, insects and fish.
Size: 10cm (4in); 18g (0.75oz).
Maturity: 6 months.
Breeding: Several litters of between 3 and 12 young produced in summer after a 20-day gestation.
Life span: 18 months.
Status: Lower risk.

The Eurasian water shrew is the largest shrew species in Britain. The species is one of the red-toothed shrews. Red-coloured iron compounds coat the tips of its teeth, which makes them more hard-wearing.

Eurasian shrew

Sorex araneus

The Eurasian shrew, known simply as the common shrew in Britain, lives in damp habitats across Europe. Its range stops at the Pyrenees and the shrew does not live in Spain or Portugal or in much of southern France, where it is too dry for them. The range extends to the east as far as Lake Baikal in western Siberia.

The common shrew lives in meadows, woodlands and in broken habitats covered in rocks. It survives on mountainsides as high up as the snow line.

Common shrews live alone and forage for food at dusk and before dawn. They feed on small invertebrates and must consume 90 per cent of their body weight each day. (Being such tiny mammals, they lose body heat very quickly and therefore must eat huge amounts to stay alive.) Hibernating is not an option because the shrews could not build up enough body fat to survive the winter without feeding.

Common shrews produce large litters of about six young. After a couple of weeks, the young emerge from their burrow for the first time and can be seen following their mother in a "caravan". The shrews form a train, with each one holding the tail of the shrew in front. The young continue to hold on even when the mother is lifted off the ground.

Distribution: Europe from Great Britain and the Pyrenees to Lake Baikal in western Siberia.
Habitat: Woodlands, grasslands, rock fields and sand dunes.
Food: Woodlice, insects, spiders and worms. Also eat plant foods.
Size: 6cm (2.25in); 9.5g (0.25oz).
Maturity: Between 9 and 10 months.
Breeding: 2 litters produced in summer after a gestation of 20 days. The young are weaned after 30 days.
Life span: 2 years.
Status: Lower risk.

The Eurasian shrew has a tri-coloured fur coat: the back is reddish brown, the underside is pale grey and the flanks and face are brown. Young shrews have paler fur.

ELEPHANT SHREWS

Elephant shrews, or sengis, are small African mammals. Despite their name, they are not shrews or members of the insectivores. Elephant shrews are known for having flexible snouts – evocative of a trunk – and long legs. They also have a unique form of tail line with thick bristles. No one is sure what the bristles are for, but they may be important for scent marking during fights and courtship.

Rock elephant shrew

Elephantulus myurus

Distribution: South-eastern Africa.
Habitat: Savannah grassland.
Food: Insects.
Size: 10–14cm (4–5.5in); 40–55g (0.09–0.12lb).
Maturity: 2 months.
Breeding: 1 young per litter.
Life span: 1–3 years.
Status: Common.

It's not easy being a small diurnal mammal in the African bush. There is a whole host of other animals that are intent on making them their next meal, from hawks and eagles to small cats, mongooses and a multitude of snakes. Rock elephant shrews are well aware of the danger that surrounds them, and they are always on the run from it. They carefully maintain tracks throughout their home ranges, linking feeding areas to bolt holes. These tracks are kept meticulously tidy, and for good reason. The elephant shrews sprint along them at breakneck speed, relying on being simply too fast for their predators to catch them.

Home ranges may be up to 1sq km (0.4sq miles) in size. This is a large area for an animal only 10cm (4in) long to maintain, but, where food is scarce, it needs to search a large area to remain well fed. In places where food is much easier to come by, the home ranges tend to be considerably smaller. Young rock elephant shrews are born very well developed, and after just two days they are able to sprint nimbly around with their mothers.

Elephant shrews get their name from their elongated, mobile snouts. They are also known as jumping shrews or sengis.

Four-toed elephant shrew

Petrodromus tetradactylus

Distribution: Central and East Africa.
Habitat: Forests and rocky areas.
Food: Ants and termites.
Size: 21cm (8.25in); 200g (7oz).
Maturity: 2 months.
Breeding: Litters of 1–2 young born all year round.
Life span: 4 years.
Status: Common.

This is one of 15 elephant shrew species, all of which live in Africa. This one is found across Central and East Africa, where it lives in forest, on rocky ground and in other areas with plenty of thick cover.

Four-toed elephant shrews forage on the ground. They maintain paths, or runways, through the undergrowth, which they scamper along on their long legs, holding their tail up as they run. The shrews use their long snouts to root around among vegetation and into tiny holes to find their prey, which is generally ants or termites.

Elephant shrews do not have nests; instead they sleep outside in thickets. They form monogamous breeding pairs, which work together to maintain a territory. The pair may breed at all times of year.

A single young is the norm, but twins are also seen. Female elephant shrews are pregnant for a long time, up to 65 days, for such a small animal. The young are highly precocious: they can run almost as fast as the adults soon after birth.

This species of elephant shrew gets its name from having just four toes on its hind foot. All elephant shrews also have a long flexible snout, which resembles an elephant's trunk.

APES

There are three species of great ape in Africa: the chimpanzee, gorilla and bonobo. Within the group of gorillas there are three races, though it is not certain whether they are separate subspecies. The great apes are human beings' closest animal relatives; in fact, humans share 98 per cent of their genetic code with them. Our common ancestor – Kenyapithecus – lived in Africa 15 million years ago.

Chimpanzee

Pan troglodytes

Chimpanzees are tool-users, and they are also skilled at communication, which they do with vocalizations and facial expressions.

These intelligent, social animals are very closely related to human beings, and give us some indication of the kind of animal from which we evolved. Chimps have a number of characteristics that were once thought to be exclusively human. For example, they construct tools – tasks that few other species, except humans and orang-utans, are capable of. One tool used by chimps is a probe, made of a twig stripped of leaves. It is poked into termite nests to extract these insects, which are then eaten.

Chimps live in groups comprising 15–80 animals, which have complex social structures. The dominant males are not necessarily the strongest individuals, but the ones best able to recruit the most allies. Chimps are territorial, and neighbouring groups are aggressive towards one another. Indeed, chimps share an unpleasant characteristic with humans: they go to war, and sometimes individuals of one group will hunt and kill members of rival groups.

Distribution: Gambia to Uganda.
Habitat: Tropical forest and woody savannah.
Food: Fruit, leaves, flowers, bark, insects and animals.
Size: 1–1.7m (3.25–5.5ft); 26–70kg (57.25–154.25lb).
Maturity: Females 13 years; males 15 years.
Breeding: Single young born every 3–6 years.
Life span: Around 60 years.
Status: Endangered.

Western-lowland gorilla

Gorilla gorilla gorilla

The armspan of a gorilla is greater than its height – up to a huge 2.75m (9ft). This illustration shows a male silverback.

Currently, three different races of gorilla are recognized: the western-lowland gorilla, the eastern-lowland gorilla and the mountain gorilla. The western-lowland gorillas are separated from the nearest population of eastern-lowland gorillas by at least 1,000km (620 miles).

Western-lowland gorillas live in relatively small groups of only about six animals. Each group is led by dominant males, or silverbacks – so called because of the grey-white fur only found on the backs of older males.

Although gorillas are large and extremely powerful, they are gentler than chimpanzees. Gorilla groups tend to avoid one another although, on occasion, groups will meet amicably for a short time. Sometimes meetings are not peaceful, and a dominant silverback may respond to intruders by standing up, hooting and beating his chest with cupped hands, followed by a display of strength by breaking branches. This display may lead to an all-out fight between the large males.

Distribution: South-eastern Nigeria, west-central and southern Cameroon, south-western Central African Republic, Guinea, Gabon and the Congo.
Habitat: Lowland tropical forests.
Food: Leaves and shoots.
Size: 1.25–1.75m (4–5.5ft); females 70–140kg (154.25–308.75lb); males 135–275kg (297.5–606.25lb).
Maturity: Females 7 years; males 15 years.
Breeding: Single young, or occasionally twins.
Life span: 50 years.
Status: Endangered.

Mountain gorilla

Gorilla gorilla beringei

Distribution: The Virunga volcanoes lying between Congo, Rwanda and Uganda.
Habitat: Montane forest and bamboo forest.
Food: Leaves and shoots.
Size: 1.5–1.8m (5–6ft); females 110–140kg (240–300lb); males 200–275kg (440–605lb).
Maturity: Females 7 years; males 15 years.
Breeding: Single young, or occasionally twins, born after 9 months' gestation. Females usually give birth to only 2–3 surviving young in a lifetime.
Life span: 50 years.
Status: Critically endangered.

Although there is doubt as to whether mountain gorillas constitute a separate subspecies, genetic analysis has shown that they are more closely related to the eastern-lowland gorillas than to the western-lowland gorillas. Mountain gorillas tend to be larger, and have much longer and silkier fur, especially on their arms, than their lowland cousins. They also occupy a very different habitat, and are found almost exclusively in cold mountain rainforests of bamboo, at altitudes over 2,000m (6,560ft).

Scientists George Schaller and Dian Fossey, who spent many years living in close contact with mountain gorillas, studied these enigmatic animals in detail. They found that they live in relatively large groups of up to 30 individuals, and that they communicate with a wide range of calls.

Gorillas travel up to 1km (0.6 miles) in search of food each day, and build crude nests out of leafy branches, usually on the ground, where they sleep at night. Mountain gorillas are only found in the region of the Virunga volcanoes (two of which are active) and Bwindi Forest in Uganda. They number little more than 600 animals in the wild. Mountain gorillas have suffered heavily from poaching and accidental trapping.

The long, silky fur of the mountain gorilla helps to protect it from the freezing conditions sometimes found in its mountain habitat.

Bonobo

Pan paniscus

Distribution: Central Congo.
Habitat: Lowland forests.
Food: Mostly fruit, occasionally leaves and seeds, rarely invertebrates and small vertebrates.
Size: 70–83cm (27.3–32.75in); 27–61kg (60–135lb).
Maturity: 9 years.
Breeding: Single young, or occasionally twins, born every 3–6 years after a gestation of 227–232 days.
Life span: Probably similar to that of the closely related chimpanzee.
Status: Endangered.

Although commonly known as the pygmy chimpanzee, this species is often the same size as its close relative – *Pan troglodytes* – and is also very similar in appearance, though less powerfully built. Unlike chimpanzees, bonobos have never been observed to use tools in the wild, though in captivity they have been seen to use leaves to clean themselves, and sticks to pole-vault over water.

Bonobos are very social animals, and live in groups of 40–120 individuals. These groups move about by day searching for fruiting trees. When a food source is located, individuals make loud calls, probably to alert other members of their group and warn off members of other groups. Like chimps, bonobos construct temporary nests made from leafy branches, to sleep in at night.

Bonobo societies are much less aggressive than groups of chimps. Serious fighting is rare, and they never make deliberate lethal raids on neighbouring groups. Unlike chimp societies, females have equal ranking with males in bonobo groups, and form the cores of bonobo societies. A curious characteristic of bonobo behaviour is the use of sexual contact to settle arguments or to calm down aggressive situations.

In bonobo groups it is frequently the females that adopt the leadership roles, unlike in chimpanzee societies.

MONKEYS

There are nearly a hundred species of monkey found in the Old World (Africa and Eurasia), all of which belong to the family Cercopithecidae. Most species are well adapted for life in trees and can move with great agility, jumping from branch to branch. Many monkeys live in tropical regions, where leaf and fruit production is year-round, providing these active animals with continuous food.

Hamadryas baboon

Papio hamadryas

There are five species of baboon living in Africa, although some are known to be able to interbreed, leading some scientists to suggest that they are just different varieties or subspecies. If suitable resting sites are rare, hamadryas baboons can be found congregating in large groups, called troops, consisting of 100 or more individuals.

When baboons start looking for food in the morning, they split up into bands, each consisting of several groups of four or five females and young, led by a dominant male. When a female is ready to mate, the dominant male prevents other males from approaching, striking out when an intruder gets close. Sometimes young male baboons form temporary partnerships to defeat dominant males and get access to females. One of the pair distracts a dominant male by starting a fight with him, while the other mates. At a later time, the individuals in the partnership swap roles, and the one who had to fight last time will have the opportunity to mate.

Distribution: North-eastern Africa and western Arabian peninsula.
Habitat: Open woodland, savannah and rocky hill country.
Food: A wide range of plants and small animals.
Size: 61–76cm (24–30in); 14–41kg (30.75–90.5lb).
Maturity: Females 5 years; males 7 years.
Breeding: Single young.
Life span: 30 years.
Status: Threatened.

Male hamadryas baboons have bright red faces and wild silvery hair. Females are smaller, sometimes only half the size of males, and have paler faces with brown hair.

Anubis baboon

Papio anubis

Anubis baboons are the most widespread of all baboon species. A few small populations live along the southern edge of the Sahara Desert, but most live farther south in Central and West Africa's tropical forests and grasslands. While most monkeys are arboreal, baboons spend most of their time on the ground. They walk on all fours.

Anubis baboons are highly social monkeys, living in well-ordered troops of about 40 animals. Each troop is run by a loose alliance of dominant males. All adult males have a rank. Individual's ranks are frequently challenged and altered by the males of a troop as dominant males age and new males arrive from outside.

The higher-ranking males have access to most of the females. Females also have a hierarchy, which dictates which ones mate with the highest-ranking males. Young male baboons are chased from the troop as they mature. Females stay in the same troop for their whole lives, alongside their sisters and aunts.

Distribution: Africa south of the Sahara Desert.
Habitat: Grasslands and rainforests.
Food: Fruits, leaves, roots, insects, eggs and small vertebrates.
Size: 48–76cm (19–30in); 14–25kg (30.75–55lb).
Maturity: 8–10 years.
Breeding: Single young born at all times of year.
Life span: 30 years.
Status: Lower risk.

As with all species of baboon, male anubis baboons are considerably larger than the females. The males also have large canine teeth, which they often display to rivals with a threatening yawn.

Mandrill

Mandrillus sphinx

This is the largest monkey in the world, with males weighing up to 54kg (120lb). The adult males are particularly colourful, with bright blue and purple nose ridges, scarlet noses and lilac buttock pads. There is a strong hierarchy among male mandrills, and it has been shown that the males with the most prominent facial coloration and the biggest rumps have the most success in attracting females and fathering young.

Mandrills move about in groups of up to ten adult females – with or without infants – around ten juveniles, and single dominant males.

Foraging mandrills cover around 8km (5 miles) per day. Usually the male stays close to the back of the group, but when there is danger he moves to the front to defend the group. Although mandrills are famous for their formidable appearance and ferocity, captive individuals are usually quite gentle.

A male mandrill's face is very brightly coloured, especially when he becomes excited. Females have duller, blue faces and are less heavily built than males.

Distribution: Southern Cameroon, Equatorial Guinea, Gabon and Congo.
Habitat: Dense lowland rainforest.
Food: Mostly fruit, nuts and other vegetable material, and also invertebrates and occasionally small mammals.
Size: 61–76cm (24–30in); 30–54kg (66–120lb).
Maturity: Females 3.5 years; males probably much older.
Breeding: Single young born each year.
Life span: 45 years.
Status: Threatened.

Drill (*Mandrillus leucopaeus*): 61–76cm (24–30in); 12–25kg (26.5–55lb)
The drill is a very rare type of forest monkey. It lives in a small area of northern Cameroon and on the island of Bioko, which forms part of Equatorial Guinea. Drills live in lowland rainforests. They prefer pristine forests that have not been changed in any way by human activity, and consequently there are few places left for them to thrive. Drills resemble their close relatives the mandrills in stature, though drills are less brightly coloured. Instead they have a more uniform pale brown coat. The only hint of colour is a male's bright red bottom lip and the bright genital region of the females. This changes from pink to bright blue when the female is on heat. Male drills are twice the size of females and they tend to stay on the ground. Females and the young monkeys are small enough to climb through the lower branches in search of fruits and other plant food.

Chacma baboon (*Papio ursinus*): 50–115cm (19.75–45.25in); 15–31kg (33–68.25lb)
Chacma baboons are the largest and heaviest of the five true baboon species. They live in southern Africa, specializing in dry woodland and savannah habitats. As with all baboons, they are highly social and live in troops of 20–80 individuals. Living in dry habitats, the troop must move long distances in search of food, which it does in a defensive formation with dominant males surrounding the females and young. If a threat appears, the males dash forward to attack, while the other troop members flee in the opposite direction.

Gelada

Theropithecus gelada

The gelada baboon is the only species of grazing monkey. It is not closely related to other types of baboon. It is so named because it shares the characteristic of living on the ground with true baboons.

Geladas live in a very specific habitat: the grasslands found high up in the highlands of Ethiopia and Eritrea. The monkeys live in large groups, which are often based near rocky gorges where members can find sleeping sites on the cliffs that are relatively safe from predators. Each troop is broken down into harems, which contain a single dominant male and several females. The members of a harem frequently groom each other to maintain a strong social bond.

Geladas have the most dexterous hands of any African monkey. They are used to pluck just the juiciest grass stems and dig up roots. Geladas have been known to raid cereal crops, which are a manmade grassland. Despite being protected, geladas are often killed by farmers.

Distribution: Ethiopian highlands.
Habitat: Highland meadows.
Food: Grass.
Size: 50–72cm (19.75–28.25in); 14–20kg (30.75–44lb).
Maturity: 5 years.
Breeding: Single young born each year.
Life span: 30 years.
Status: Vulnerable.

Geladas have long side whiskers, a mane of hairs on the neck and three bare red patches of skin on the chest and throat. Males have facial hair and a cloak-like mantle of hair.

Vervet

Cercopithecus aethiops

Male vervets possess bright blue scrotums, which are used in signals of dominance over other males in a group.

Like many monkey species, vervets are very social, forming communicative groups of up to 50 individuals. These monkeys have a broad repertoire of calls, and are able to express alarm, excitement, rage and even sadness. Vervets forage in trees and occasionally on the ground. If predators are spotted, particular alarm calls are given, depending on the type of predator approaching. When vervets hear their snake alarm call, they all stand upright, scanning the surrounding grass for pythons. If they hear their leopard alarm call, they run into the trees, keeping their eyes on the leopard, and if they hear their eagle alarm call, they hide deep in the tree canopy.

Female vervets tend to remain in the groups into which they they were born, whereas males are forced to leave when they become sexually mature, moving into new groups.

Vervets have adapted well to living alongside people. They are common in even the suburbs of big cities. Many people welcome their presence, but others treat them as pests because they can damage property and crops.

Distribution: Eastern and southern Africa.
Habitat: Riverine woodland, wooded savanna, open forests and agricultural land.
Food: Fruit and vegetable material, insects, crustaceans, birds' eggs and vertebrates.
Size: 35–66cm (13.75–26in); 2.5–9kg (5.5–19.75lb).
Maturity: Females 3 years; males 5 years.
Breeding: Usually a single young born each year.
Life span: 30 years.
Status: Common.

Patas monkey

Erythrocebus patas

Patas monkeys are ground-living monkeys. They are found in woodland and savannah areas across the central region of Africa. They do not live south of the Congo rainforest, but are found from Senegal in the west to the huge savannahs of East Africa. This species is one of the few monkeys to be expanding their range. Although deforestation is thinning the African rainforest, patas monkeys stay out of dense jungle and are now found in forest clearings and along the edges of roads cut into the forest.

These monkeys are omnivores. They will eat a range of plant and animals foods and can survive just as well on waste thrown away by people.

Patas monkeys live in groups of 10–40 individuals. One type of group contains the adult females, which are generally closely related to each other, and their offspring of both sexes. The adult males live alone or in small male-only groups. Adult males visit the females in the summer to mate. Rather than actively courting mates, a male will wait for females to choose him. Successful males will build up a harem of mates, which he defends from other males while the females are on heat. In some groups, however, monkeys have a promiscuous mating system in which both males and females breed with several mates. Young are born after a pregnancy of 170 days.

Male patas monkeys are larger than the females, though both sexes have distinctive white beards and moustaches. The monkeys combine a lean body with long legs, which is a good build for running on all fours across the ground. Patas monkeys, however, are also agile climbers and dash into trees or on to other high points if they feel threatened.

Distribution: Western and eastern Africa. Most common in east.
Habitat: Savannah and woodland.
Food: Fruits, roots, leaves and insects.
Size: 70cm (27.5in); 13kg (28.75lb).
Maturity: 3–4 years.
Breeding: Most births occur in December and January after a gestation of 24 weeks.
Life span: 20 years.
Status: Common.

Talapoin

Miopithecus talapoin

Distribution: Western central Africa.
Habitat: Forests.
Food: Insects, leaves, fruits, eggs and small vertebrates.
Size: 32cm (12.5in); 1.4kg (3lb).
Maturity: 5 years.
Breeding: Births occur from November to March.
Life span: 25 years.
Status: Lower risk.

Talapoins live a range of forest types in the western side of central Africa, including mangroves and rainforests. They are also often spotted in and around human settlements close to the forest. The monkey's distribution runs from Cameroon to northern Angola.

They are highly social monkeys. They live in large groups, or troops, of 70–100 monkeys. Each troop contains adults of both sexes, although there are generally a few more females than males. Dominant males lead the troops, deciding where to forage and when to move on. The males also keep guard over the troop at night. The young and females rest at the centre of the troop, while the males are posed as sentinels at the edges.

Females are ready to breed from May to September. Their perineum swells up as a signal that they are fertile. Females are pregnant for about five months. The young are precocious: they can look after themselves soon after birth, and at just two weeks a young talapoin is able to climb independently of its mother. It is fully independent at three months.

This species is the smallest monkey in Africa. Both sexes have cheek pouches for storing food, but the females have paler fur than the males.

Diana monkey (*Cercopithecus diana*): 55cm (21.75in); 7kg (15.5lb) The Diana monkey is a resident of the forests of West Africa. They are found only in untouched rainforest, where they eat leaves, fruits and insects. As a consequence of their reliance on this habitat, Diana monkeys are vulnerable to extinction. They are mainly black but also have a white throat ruff and a pointed beard. A white stripe also runs down the thighs. The back of the legs is orange. These patches are visible as flashes of colour as the monkey moves through the dense forest. Diana monkeys are polygynous (the males mate with several females in one season).

Mona monkey (*Cercopithecus mona*): 53cm (20.75in); 4kg (8.75lb) Mona monkeys live in the rainforests of Central Africa. They range from Uganda in the east to Gambia in the west and Angola in the south. This species has also been introduced to the Caribbean island of Grenada. Mona monkeys are very colourful: they have red-brown fur on the back, the rump and front are white, while the face is blue with a pink snout. Mona monkeys live in small groups ruled by a single male. These small harem groups often band together into troops of about 50 monkeys.

Barbary ape

Macaca sylvanus

Barbary apes are a type of monkey called a macaque. Most macaque species live in Asia, where they have adapted well to life alongside humans. The Barbary ape is a North African species, which lives in the dry cedar forests of Morocco, Algeria and Tunisia. The species is most common in the forests that grow on the slopes of the Atlas Mountains, where snow is common in winter. This macaque is the only monkey species to survive in Europe. It was introduced to Gibraltar by the Romans, and a small community still lives there.

The animals forage for food on the ground, in trees and on top of buildings. They feed on a range of plant and animal foods. The European population is highly dependent on humans for its survival.

The social behaviour of the European monkeys is less stable than in the African populations. Natural populations live in mixed sex groups: females in a group are sisters and cousins while the males are drawn from a mixture of neighbouring troops. The males in a troop are organized into a hierarchy, and the top-ranked males mate with most of the females.

Distribution: North Africa and Gibraltar.
Habitat: Dry forest.
Food: Roots, flowers, fruits and insects.
Size: 63cm (24.75in); 12.5kg (27.5lb).
Maturity: 4 years.
Breeding: Single young born once a year.
Life span: 30 years.
Status: Vulnerable.

Barbary apes are not apes at all but monkeys. Their common name comes from the fact that they lack a tail, which is one of the characteristic features of true apes, such as gibbons, gorillas and humans.

Red-capped mangabey

Cercocebus torquatus

Red-capped monkeys are large and very vocal. Their calls can be heard from over 1km (0.6 miles) away. Groups of red-capped mangabeys consist of about 30 individuals, and unlike many species of monkey, their groups may include several adult males, who live peacefully alongside one another and the females. All mangabeys have pale upper eyelids, which they flutter to attract attention and signal sexual intentions and status.

Although mangabeys spend a lot of time in the treetops searching for fruit, they will also forage on the ground, searching the leaf litter for mushrooms and small animal prey.

Mangabeys are territorial when food is relatively scarce in the dry season, and their loud calls help neighbouring groups maintain their distance from one another. At other times of the year, when food is in plentiful supply, mangabey troops come together without conflict.

Mangabeys are threatened by the loss of their forests to logging. However, the red-capped mangabey seems to be quite adaptable to new habitats, hopefully making this species less susceptible to problems in the future. Nevertheless, the monkey is also being hunted to meet the growing demand for bushmeat.

The fur on the top of this species' head is a dark maroon-red. The white hair on the sides of the head extends around the neck like a collar, giving rise to the other common name of this species: the collared mangabey.

Distribution: Senegal to Congo.
Habitat: Mostly tropical rainforest, but also mangroves, degraded forest, swamps and agricultural land.
Food: Mostly fruit, but other vegetable matter and insects and small animals are also taken.
Size: 38–89cm (15–35in); 7–14kg (15.5–30.75lb).
Maturity: Females 4 years; males 5–7 years.
Breeding: Single young, or occasionally twins, born at an average 16-month interval.
Life span: Probably around 30 years.
Status: Endangered.

Blue monkey

Cercopithecus mitis

Most blue monkeys live in the rainforests of the Congo Basin, although they are also found in other habitats farther afield in southern and eastern Africa. Blue monkeys occupy humid places that have plenty of tall trees and a lot of running water available.

Male blue monkeys are generally larger than the females and also have more white facial hair. A single male rules a blue monkey troop, which can contain up to 40 members. The males in an area compete for ranks and only the highest-ranking alpha male mates with the troop's mature females, which come into season at any time throughout the year. The females pout over their shoulder at the male during mating. Alpha males are frequently deposed by younger males moving up the ranks.

Blue monkey troops are very aggressive toward each other. The alpha male leads an attack by the grown males, but the females also join in. Interestingly, blue monkey troops will team up with a group of another species, such as its close relative the black-cheeked white-nosed monkey, to defend an area from other troops and predators. The two species forage for food in different parts of the forest, so they do not compete for resources. Both benefit from working together to keep hold of the territory.

Only a few blue monkeys are actually blue. Most have dark coloured fur with just a faint bluish tinge to the hairs around the face. Blue monkeys are also called diademed monkeys because of the tiara-shaped triangle of white fur on their heads. There are six subspecies of blue monkey.

Distribution: Central, eastern and southern Africa. Most common in Congo.
Habitat: Forest.
Food: Fruits and leaves.
Size: 65cm (25.5in); 6kg (13.25lb).
Maturity: 3 years.
Breeding: Each female produces a single young each year. Birth occurs at all times of the year. A single male fathers all the young in a troop.
Life span: 20 years.
Status: Vulnerable.

Black-cheeked white-nosed monkey

Cercopithecus ascanius

Distribution: Central and southern Africa.
Habitat: Forests.
Food: Fruits, insects and gums.
Size: 38–46cm (15–18in); 3–4kg (6.5–8.75lb).
Maturity: 4–6 years.
Breeding: Mating peaks in November to February.
Life span: 30 years.
Status: Common.

The black-cheeked white-nosed monkey lives in forests across central and southern Africa. They are most common in Uganda, but populations are further south and west. This species is primarily a rainforest monkey but it can survive in more open habitats as long as there is enough food. The monkeys are fruit eaters but they also consume resins, gums and insects.

Black-cheeked white-nosed monkeys live in groups run by a single male. The group forages and sleeps together. The group travels an average of 1.4km (1 mile) every day. Like many similar monkeys, members of this species often store food inside their cheek pouches. This allows them to carry food to a place where they can eat it safe from attack by predators or from being stolen by other monkeys. Black-cheeked white-nosed monkeys often live alongside leaf-eating monkeys and so do not compete with them for food.

The black-cheeked white-nosed monkey's name explains this species' most obvious features. Another of its common names is the redtail monkey, which refers to the chestnut-brown colouring on the underside of the tail.

Grey-cheeked mangabey (*Lophocebus albigena*): 72cm (28.25in); 11kg (24.25lb)
Grey-cheeked mangabeys are also known as black mangabeys. Most of their body is covered in dark fur, though the facial hairs and shaggy mantle are considerably paler. Males are about 20 per cent larger than the females. Both sexes have very long tails that are slightly prehensile. (This characteristic is unusual for an Old World monkey. It is the American monkeys that are most known for this feature.) Grey-cheeked mangabeys inhabit the lowland rainforests of Central Africa. They live in small groups and each group has just one male. Most of their diet is fruits and nuts.

Owl-faced monkey (*Cercopithecus hamlyni*): 40–65cm (15.5–25.5in); 4–10kg (8.75–22lb)
Owl-faced monkeys live in eastern Congo and southern Uganda. This species occupies bamboo forests that grow on the slopes of the Ruwenzori Mountains. The males are twice the weight of the females, but both sexes have similar olive-grey colouring. There is a pale yellow stripe running across the eyebrows and another crossing that one and running down to the upper lip. This T-shaped marking is the species' most obvious feature. The rump and genitals of both sexes are naked, with blue skin. Mature males sport a bright red penis, which stands out against the monkey's muted colouring. Owl-faced monkeys have extremely long fingers, which are used to grip smooth bamboo stems. (Bamboo grows in cold and wet locations, so the stems are also often slippery.) Owl-faced monkeys eat mainly bamboo shoots.

Allen's swamp monkey

Allenopithecus nigroviridis

Allen's swamp monkeys are found only in swamp forest: areas of low-lying tropical forest that are frequently flooded. In the case of Allen's swamp monkey, the swamps are fed by the Congo River. When the river breaks its banks and spills across the forest floor, the monkeys climb into trees for safety. During their time in the trees, the monkeys eat fruits and leaves.

Once the flood has subsided, however, the monkeys descend to the muddy forest floor once again. Their webbed feet help them to walk over the mud as they search for worms, beetles and other invertebrates.

The webbing is also useful during floods. If a monkey is threatened while up a tree, the monkey's first line of defence is to dive into the water, where it can swim away to safety. Allen's swamp monkeys are preyed on by large hawks, snakes and bonobos, which also live in the swampy forests. This species is polyganous, and females develop a sexual swelling when on heat.

Distribution: Congo Basin.
Habitat: Swamp forest.
Food: Fruits, water plants and insects.
Size: 60cm (23.5in); 3.5kg (7.75lb).
Maturity: 3–5 years.
Breeding: Single young born to females at all times of year.
Life span: 20 years.
Status: Lower risk.

Allen's swamp monkey has slightly webbed fingers and toes to help it move through shallow swamps. The males are slightly larger than the females.

Western red colobus

Procolobus badius

The western red colobus is one of the leaf monkeys. Like other colobus monkeys and their relatives the langurs, this species survives by eating leaves or, more specifically in the western red colobus's case, the petiole, or leaf stalk.

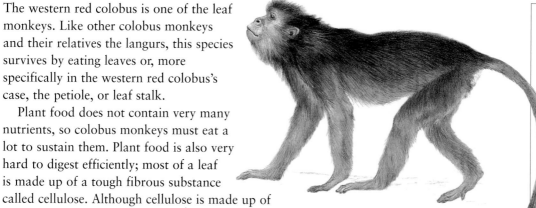

Plant food does not contain very many nutrients, so colobus monkeys must eat a lot to sustain them. Plant food is also very hard to digest efficiently; most of a leaf is made up of a tough fibrous substance called cellulose. Although cellulose is made up of chains of sugars molecules, it cannot be digested by a normal monkey. For this reason, the colobus species has a stomach split into four chambers (similar to that of a cow). The different stomach chambers contain bacteria that can break down cellulose fibres into an acidic sugary soup, which the monkeys can then digest themselves. This type of digestion takes a very long time, and so western red colobus monkeys often spend long periods sitting with full stomachs. (The process also produces a lot of gas, so the monkeys often look bloated.)

Having to sit still all the time, western red colobus are easy to hunt. Human hunters have nearly wiped them out in some places, but they are also the favourite prey of another ape – the chimpanzee.

The western red colobus has a very short, almost useless, thumb and four very long fingers, which it hooks over branches so that it can swing through the trees.

Distribution: West Africa.
Habitat: Rainforest, woodlands and savannah.
Food: Leaves.
Size: 45–67cm (17.75–26.5in); 5–11kg (11–24.25lb).
Maturity: Unknown.
Breeding: Single young born to each female every 2 years. Females mate with several males when on heat. The exact gestation period is uncertain but is probably about 100 days.
Life span: 20 years.
Status: Critically endangered.

Olive colobus

Procolobus verus

The olive colobus is found in the coastal rainforests of West Africa, from Sierra Leone to Togo. There is also a small population in eastern Nigeria. The monkey is most commonly seen in the dense undergrowth that grows beneath the high canopy. It moves higher up to sleep in the middle branches when night falls but never climbs to the top of the forest. It is often found close to running water.

Olive colobuses have larger feet than any of the related colobus species and also have very small thumbs. These adaptations allow the monkeys to grip branches as they climb, although reduce their ability to pluck food items.

Olive colobuses live in small groups of adult females, their young and a single adult male. Other males live in separate groups. Groups of olive colobuses are often seen with Diana monkeys. When a Diana monkey gives an alarm call to warn others of an approaching predator, the olive colobus monkeys freeze, their grey-green fur making them hard to spot among the leaves.

Olive colobus monkeys search out the youngest and juiciest leaves. When this food is not available, they will eat the stalks of older leaves, flowers and seeds.

These monkeys have no breeding season. A female reproduces every two years or so. When the female is on heat, her perineum swells. The pregnancy lasts between five and six months.

The olive colobus is the smallest of the African colobus monkeys. It has a drab coat of olive green. Males are the same size as females but have larger canine teeth. The teeth are used in fights.

Distribution: Coastal region of West Africa from Sierra Leone to Togo, with a small, isolated population living in eastern Nigeria.
Habitat: Understory and middle branches of rainforest generally near to water.
Food: Young leaves, seeds and shoots.
Size: 9–43cm (3.5–17in); 2.2–4.5kg (4.75–10lb).
Maturity: 3–4 years.
Breeding: Single baby born every 2 years.
Life span: 30 years in captivity, probably less in the wild.
Status: Lower risk.

Tana River red colobus (*Procolobus rufomitratus*):
45–67cm (17.75–26.5in); 5.8kg (12.75lb)
This critically endangered species of colobus
monkey lives in the forests around the Tana
River, which flows from the Kenyan Highlands
to the Indian Ocean. Flooding from the river
supports a tropical forest in a wider region
dominated by savannahs. Nevertheless, the
Tana River forest is considerably drier than the
habitats of other colobus monkeys. This forces
the species to be less reliant on leaves than
other colobus; in fact, less than half the
monkey's diet is made up of leaves. The rest
comprises fruits, seeds, buds and flowers. Living
in the isolation of the Tana River Valley, this red
colobus is not threatened by predators in the
same way as more common colobuses. As a
result, members of this species are less likely
to work together to fend off threats.

Angolan colobus (*Colobus angolensis*):
58.5cm (23in); 9kg (19.75lb)
Angolan colobus monkeys are close relatives of
the guereza and king colobus. Like these species,
the Angolan colobus has black and white fur.
It also has white epaulettes and white cheeks,
throat and brow. In addition to inhabiting Angola,
this species ranges as far north as Cameroon
along the western side of Central Africa. It
survives in a range of habitats from bamboo
rainforests to swamps and savannahs. Like other
colobus species, this monkey is primarily a
forest animal. It eats mainly leaves but survives
drought by consuming bark, clay and insects.
The monkeys often climb down beside streams
to eat the herb and water plants that grow there.

Guereza

Colobus guereza

Guerezas are found in a range of habitats,
including the rainforests of the Congo, the
forested hills of Nigeria's Donga Valley and
the wooded grasslands of East Africa. When
in dense jungle, guerezas spend their whole
lives in the trees, but, in
areas where trees are
more widely dispersed,
they often come down to
the ground to feed and
move between trees.

Guerezas eat mainly leaves.
Less than 20 per cent of their
diet is made up of other
items, mainly fruits.
When possible, the
monkeys eat fresh
shoots, but will move
on to tougher, older leaves when necessary.

Guerezas live in small groups made up of
one adult male, four or five adult females
and their offspring. The adult females are
close relatives. The young females stay with
their troop as they mature, while the males
are driven away by the resident male. When
the dominant male is replaced by another,
the new leader will kill the youngest infants.
This brings their mothers into season again
so the new male can breed with them.

Distribution: Central and
eastern Africa.
Habitat: Forest and
woodland.
Food: Leaves.
Size: 45–72cm
(17.75–28.25in);
5–14kg (11–30.75lb).
Maturity: 4–6 years.
Breeding: Breed
once every 2 years.
Life span: 20 years.
Status: Common.

*The male guerezas are
slightly larger than the
females. The thumb on
each hand is missing
completely, and
the remaining four
fingers are used
for swinging from
branch to branch.*

King colobus

Colobus polykomos

Distribution: West Africa.
Habitat: Monsoon forests.
Food: Leaves, fruits and
flowers.
Size: 45–72cm
(17.75–28.25in); 5–14kg
(11–30.75lb).
Maturity: 2 years.
Breeding: Single baby born
every 2 years.
Life span: 20 years.
Status: Endangered.

The king colobus lives in tropical forests that have long
periods of dry weather. Such forests are supplied by seasonal
rains or monsoons. West Africa has two monsoons each
year. Unfortunately, much of the land where monsoon forest
grows is also ideal for farming, which is why much of the
king cololubus's forest habitat has been cleared to make way
for fields. As a result, the species is currently endangered.

King colobus monkeys eat leaves during and following
the monsoons, but as drought takes hold of the forest the
monkeys turn to fruits and other plant foods to survive.
King colobus groups contain about twice as many females
as males. The males in the group are organized into a strict
hierarchy and rarely interact with each other. Fights are
rare, occurring only if a subordinate male believes
he can defeat a higher-ranking group member.
The ranking system is tested most frequently
during the breeding season, which coincides with the
rains. Males compete by calling; the dominant male
has the loudest call.

All members of the Colobus
*genus have black and white fur,
but the king colobus is distinctive
because most of its body is jet
black. Only the whiskers, chest
and tail are white.*

LEMURS

This is a group of primates that lives exclusively on Madagascar and some of its surrounding islands. The ancestors of lemurs arrived on Madagascar about 40 million years ago, before most modern primates – monkeys and apes – had evolved. The 30 species of lemurs that survive today have evolved from one common ancestor to live in all the varied habitats on the islands.

Ruffed lemur

Varecia variegata

Distribution: Eastern Madagascar.
Habitat: Tropical forest.
Food: Fruit.
Size: 51–56cm (20–22in); 3.2–4.5kg (7–10lb).
Maturity: 2–3.5 years.
Breeding: 1–6 young, most commonly twins.
Life span: 33 years.
Status: Endangered.

This is the largest of all the lemurs. Lemurs are prosimians that are found exclusively on Madagascar and some surrounding islands. Ruffed lemurs live in trees, and, although they are good climbers, they are not as agile as some other species of lemur.

Ruffed lemurs are most active at dusk, and at this time it is possible to hear their mournful territorial calls. Sometimes just a pair of ruffed lemurs occupies a territory, but more often groups of about 15 individuals will live together, sharing the same home range.

As well as calls, ruffed lemurs use scent-marking to signal their territorial boundaries. The males mark branches and other objects with a secretion from glands found on their necks. Scent-marking males are seen rubbing their chests, necks and chins on to trees or on the ground. Sadly, like many lemurs, these beautiful animals are in danger of extinction due to the overexploitation of their habitat and also overhunting of the animals themselves for their meat and fur, and for commercial exportation.

There are two subspecies of ruffed lemur. One has mostly black fur with white markings; the other has mostly red fur with white markings.

Ring-tailed lemur

Lemur catta

Ring-tailed lemurs are forest animals, but they spend quite long periods of time on the ground, searching for fallen fruit and other plant material. Although fairly common throughout their range in southern Madagascar, these animals are declining in number.

Their habitat is a dry forest, and the animals must endure long periods of drought. During these times they may eat insects, but they are reliant on dry fruits, such as those of the kily tree, a type of tamarind. Ring-tailed lemurs live in mixed-sex groups, but in most cases only one of the males is sexually active. During the breeding season, which runs from April to June, both sexes fight. The females are battling for resources, while the males are competing for access to mates. During a fight, the lemurs may never touch. Instead they do battle with smell. Each combatant in a stink battle coats its bushy tail with secretions from a gland on the wrists and near the genitals and wafts the strong smell toward its opponent.

From the age of three, a female produces one or two young every year. The newborn clings to its mother's belly, before moving to ride on the back by the age of two weeks. Weaning occurs at 5 months.

Distribution: Southern Madagascar.
Habitat: Forests and bushes.
Food: Plant foods.
Size: 38–45cm (15–17.75in); 2.3–3.5kg (5–7.75lb).
Maturity: 3 years.
Breeding: 1–2 young born in August to October. Young are independent by 6 months.
Life span: 30 years.
Status: Vulnerable.

Perhaps the most recognizable of all the lemur species of Madagascar, these animals are named after their striking tail markings.

Brown lemur

Eulemur fulvus

Distribution: Madagascar and the Comoro Islands.
Habitat: Forests.
Food: Leaves, fruits and bark.
Size: 40–50cm (15.75–19.75in); 2–4kg (4.5–8.75lb).
Maturity: 2 years.
Breeding: Single young born each year.
Life span: 25 years.
Status: Vulnerable.

Brown lemurs live in the forests in Madagascar and on the Comoro Islands. There are five subspecies, all with a very distinctive colouring. Both sexes of common brown lemurs have dark brown fur and pale beards. Female red-fronted lemurs have red-brown fur, while the males are grey with a crown of red fur. White-fronted lemurs have dark backs and a paler underside; males have pale heads, too. Male collared lemurs are grey-brown, with a darker stripe down the back; the females have redder fur. Both sexes have a red beard. Sanford's lemurs are smaller than the other subspecies. Both males and females are dark brown. Their most distinctive feature is a pale T-shape across the face.

Subspecies are often found mixed together, but each one is most associated with a habitat. The common brown and collared lemurs live in fragments of high forest in north-western Madagascar. The red-fronted lemur lives in monsoon forest along the coasts. White-fronted lemurs are found in rainforests, while the most rare subspecies, Sanford's lemur, lives along forest edges in northern Madagascar.

There are five subspecies of brown lemur. The common brown lemur is the only subspecies that is actually covered in just brown fur. Others have more distinctive markings that vary between the sexes.

Fork-marked lemur (*Phaner furcifer*): 22–28cm (8.5–11in); 300–500g (10.5–17.5oz)
This is one of the few species of lemur that is not classified as vulnerable to or endangered with extinction. It lives in most types of forest on Madagascar. The fork-marked lemur is named after the dark stripe on its forehead that splits in two and continues down either side of the face. Fork-marked lemurs are gum eaters. They have long upper teeth that point forwards to make a dental "comb". This comb is used to collect the sweet liquids that ooze from holes in tree trunks. Fork-marked lemurs live in pairs.

Crowned lemur (*Eulemur coronatus*): 34cm (13.5in); 2kg (4.5lb)
Crowned lemurs are named after the patch of orange hair on their heads. Males have brown bodies, while the females are more grey. Crowned lemurs live in northern Madagascar, where they are most common in that region's dry coastal forests. The lemurs are diurnal. They live in small groups and forage for fallen fruits. A typical group of these lemurs contains two adult pairs and a couple of young.

Bamboo lemur (*Hapalemur griseus*): 26–45cm (10.25–17.75in); 2.5kg (5.5lb)
This unusual lemur survives almost entirely on bamboo leaves. These are a difficult food because they contain high levels of the poison cyanide and are often covered in grains of hard silica that wear down the teeth. Bamboo lemurs live in small family groups. They forage in the trees and on the ground in the rainforests of eastern Madagascar.

Mongoose lemur

Eulemur mongoz

Most mongoose lemurs live in the dry forests of Madagascar. These forests are filled with deciduous trees that shed their leaves during periods of drought rather than when the weather turns cold. The lemurs also survive on two of the Comoro Islands, where they live in more humid rainforests.

During the dry season, mongoose lemurs are nocturnal. At this time of year the lemurs eat seeds and dry fruits that have fallen from the trees and are lying in wait for the rains. The mongoose lemur is an important disperser of these seeds. As the seeds pass through the lemur's gut, a hard outer coating is digested away, which prepares them for germination when the rains arrive.

In the colder, rainy season, mongoose lemurs are diurnal. At this time they also change their diet to leaves, flowers and pollen.

Mongoose lemurs are monogamous. A pair produces a single litter each year.

Distribution: Madagascar and Comoro Islands.
Habitat: Dry forest.
Food: Flowers, fruits and leaves.
Size: 35cm (13.75in); 2–3kg (4.5–6.5lb).
Maturity: 2 years.
Breeding: 1–2 young born in July–September.
Life span: 30 years.
Status: Vulnerable.

Male mongoose lemurs are pale grey with red patches on their flanks and face. The females are darker and have white patches instead of red. Newborns have a white beard.

Fat-tailed dwarf lemur

Cheirogaleus medius

Fat-tailed dwarf lemurs live in the west and south of Madagascar. They are found in the lower branches of both humid rainforests and drier monsoon forests. In areas that experience a dry season, which is most of Madagascar, these lemurs sit out the dry spells in a dormant state. They build nests in tree hollows and survive on the fat stored in their tails.

At other times of the year, fat-tailed dwarf lemurs are nocturnal foragers. They live alone and survive mainly on fruits, though they also eat petals, pollen and nectar. They also occasionally eat beetles and other insects.

During the wet season (October–March), the lemurs build up a supply of fat in their long tails. The tail triples in size at points by the beginning of the dry season. While lying dormant through the dry season, the lemur loses about 40 per cent of its body weight.

This species breeds in the wet season. They form monogamous pairs. The female is receptive for about 20 days and is pregnant for 62 days. Most litters are made up of twins, although three or four young are not uncommon.

These lemurs are about the size of a large rat. They have large eyes to help them see in the dark. Like cats, the lemurs have a reflective surface behind the eyes that makes them glow in the dark.

Distribution: Mainly in western Madagascar and parts of the south and east.
Habitat: Tropical rainforests and drier monsoon forests.
Food: Fruits, flowers, pollen and nectar.
Size: 20cm (8in); 142–217g (5–7.75oz).
Maturity: 1 year.
Breeding: Mating takes place in wet season and twins are born in January. Pairs produce litters each year,
Life span: 15 years.
Status: Endangered.

Hairy-eared dwarf lemur

Allocebus trichotis

Both sexes of hairy-eared dwarf lemurs have tufts of long hair on the ears. It is unknown what function this feature might have. The species is nocturnal, so using hairy ears as a visual signal is unlikely.

The hairy-eared dwarf lemur is one of the rarest primates in the world. Even before the habitats of Madagascar were devastated by human activities in the 20th century, biologists have suggested that this species was rare. Although the species was first described in 1875, it has been observed in the wild only twice for more than a century. In 1989 a small population was discovered living in the Mananara River in the north-east of the island but they still remain largely elusive.

Without being able to watch the lemur behaving naturally, biologists have had to surmise how it survives by looking at dead specimens. The hairy-eared dwarf lemur has long upper teeth that form a toothcomb. This suggests that at least part of the lemur's diet is made up of tree gums (sugary liquids that leak from holes in trunks). The species also has a long tongue compared to other similar lemurs. This tongue is useful for licking gums and also for extracting small food items, such as beetles and pollen.

Hairy-eared dwarf lemurs are monogamous. They live in family groups of one male, one female and their one or two offspring. Breeding occurs during the wet season in November and births occur two months later. Both the male and female help to raise the young.

Distribution: North-eastern Madagascar.
Habitat: Lowland forest in the Manarana River Valley.
Food: Long tongue used to lick up sticky plant gums, nectar. Insects make up about half the lemur's food.
Size: 13.5cm (5.25in); 85g (3oz).
Maturity: 1 year.
Breeding: Mating takes place at the beginning of the wet season in November and December and one or two young born in January and February.
Life span: 15 years.
Status: Endangered.

Aye aye

Daubentonia madagascariensis

This remarkable species is another prosimian found only in Madagascar. Aye ayes live alone. They are exclusively nocturnal and search for food high up in the trees, moving up to 4km (2.5 miles) a night within a small home range of around 5ha (12 acres). During the day, aye ayes sleep in spherical nests, made from branches and interwoven leaves. The nests are hidden in dense foliage in the forks of trees, and there may be several nests within a single home range.

Aye ayes have a most unusual way of finding food. Using a specially adapted finger, which is very long and thin like a probe, they tap the surface of decaying wood in search of tunnels made by insect larvae or ants and termites. Using a combination of a good sense of touch and a sort of echolocation with their sensitive ears – able to pinpoint a hollow sound from tapping – aye ayes locate the tunnels occupied by their prey. They then use their strong incisor teeth to make small holes in the wood, into which they insert their probe-like finger to extract their insect prey with a hooked claw. Unfortunately, these fascinating creatures are suffering from the loss of Malagasy forest. Local people also persecute them because they are seen as bad omens.

The aye aye uses its specialized third finger not only for locating and catching insects in decaying wood, but also for determining the milk content of coconuts and extracting coconut pulp.

Distribution: Northern, eastern and west-central Madagascar.
Habitat: Tropical forests, but seems adaptable to secondary forest, mangroves and even coconut groves.
Food: Fruit, seeds, nectar, other vegetable matter and insect larvae.
Size: 36–44cm (14–17in); 2–3kg (4.5–6.5lb).
Maturity: 3 years.
Breeding: Single young born every 2–3 years.
Life span: 20 years.
Status: Endangered.

Grey mouse lemur (*Microcebus murinus*): 10cm (4in); 60g (2oz)
Grey mouse lemurs are one of the smallest primates in the world. (The smallest is Peter's mouse lemur [*Microcebus myoxinus*] which is only 6.25cm/2.5in long.) The grey mouse lemur lives in the trees of Madagascar's dry forests, where it is a solitary forager. It spends all its life in the trees but is seldom far above the ground. Its diet is mainly insects. The mouse lemur is nocturnal, spending the day asleep in communal nests. Males sleep in pairs, while females gather together in groups of 15 or so.

Weasel sportive lemur (*Lepilemur mustelinus*): 24–30cm (9.5–11.75in); 500–900g (1.1–2lb)
This species of sportive lemur lives in deciduous forests in the eastern and western lowlands of Madagascar. As a sportive lemur its hind legs are longer and more powerful than the forelimbs, making the animal an excellent jumper. Weasel sportive lemurs are nocturnal. They eat mainly leaves, but will eat fruits, barks and flowers during dry periods. This species will also eat its own faeces to extract as many nutrients from its food as possible.

Northern sportive lemur (*Lepilemur septentrionalis*): 453cm (121in); 800g (1.75lb)
This species is confined to the northern fringes of Madagascar, where it lives in the high branches of dry monsoon forests. It eats leaves and fruits. Males and females only consort with each other during the breeding season from April to August.

White-footed sportive lemur

Lepilemur leucopus

The white-footed sportive lemur is found in two very different habitats in the south of Madagascar. In this dry region there exists both a unique type of spiny forest filled with succulent plants similar to cacti and also gallery forests (forests that grow beside a river), which are denser and more humid. Despite the great differences between these two forests, both habitats are occupied by this sportive lemur. It is found in the lower branches during the night, where it moves from trunk to trunk with bold leaps, and by day the lemur nests in a thicket or tree hollow.

White-footed sportive lemurs are leaf eaters. When leaves are scarce, they move on to fruits and flowers. Some reports suggest that this species extracts more of the nutrients from its food by eating the pellets of half-digested food that pass out of the anus, in the same way as rabbits.

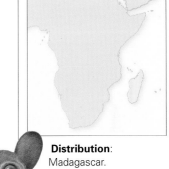

Distribution: Madagascar.
Habitat: Spiny forest.
Food: Leaves.
Size: 25cm (9.75in); 500g (1.1lb).
Maturity: 18 months.
Breeding: Single young born in October to December.
Life span: 15 years.
Status: Lower risk.

Like all sportive lemurs, this species has long limbs and especially powerful hind legs, which allow it to make enormous leaps. The hands have large pads for gripping on to vertical tree trunks.

INDRI AND SIFAKAS

As well as the various groups of smaller lemurs, Madagascar is home to three species of larger primates called sifakas, and the largest Malagasy primate, the indri. Like all primates living on Madagascar, the indri and sifakas are vulnerable to extinction. These large primate species are the closest surviving relatives of the giant lemurs that lived on Madagascar a thousand years ago.

Indri

Indri indri

The indri is the largest of all the living prosimians, and, like the lemurs, it is found only in Madagascar. Indris are arboreal and move about by jumping between tree trunks and stems. Sometimes indris come down to the ground, where they stand upright, moving in series of ungainly leaps.

They are mostly active by day and spend a lot of time feeding on leaves and fruit. Indris live in small family groups of up to five members, and occupy large home ranges. The central part of a home range is defended from others by the adult male, which uses scent markings and calls to signal the limits of the territory.

Sometimes several members of a group will make loud tuneful songs that can be heard up to 2km (1.25 miles) away. These songs are thought to signal occupancy of a territory to other groups, but also to unite groups and broadcast willingness to mate.

Indris have thick silky fur, which may be useful for living in cold mountain forests, as high as 1800m (6000ft) above sea level. There is considerable variation in fur colour, which ranges from black through browns and greys to white.

Distribution: North-eastern Madagascar.
Habitat: Tropical rainforest.
Food: Leaves, flowers and fruit.
Size: 61–90cm (24–35.5in); 6–10kg (13.25–22lb).
Maturity: 7–9 years.
Breeding: Single young born every 2–3 years.
Life span: Not known.
Status: Endangered.

Avahi

Avahi laniger

The avahi is also known as the woolly lemur because of its thick and curly fur. The fur is groomed with a toothcomb formed from the lower incisors.

Avahis live on both sides of Madagascar, and some scientists class the two populations as separate species. In the north-west, they live in the dry monsoon forest that grows on mountain slopes. On the eastern side, they live in lowland rainforests. Avahis cling to vertical trunks and move around by leaping between trees. When on the ground they hop along on their hind feet.

These animals often live in close proximity to indris, their close relative. Both species specialize in eating young leaves, but they avoid competition by foraging at different times: indris are diurnal while avahis feed at night. Avahis eat only the softest parts of a leaf, throwing away the midrib. During droughts, avahis survive by eating flowers and fruits. The avahi's food is low in quality so the primate does not have a lot of energy. As a result it spends long periods resting, waiting for its food to digest.

Distribution: Eastern and north-western Madagascar.
Habitat: Forest.
Food: Leaves.
Size: 37cm (14.5in); 950g (2lb).
Maturity: 2 years.
Breeding: Young born in July–September.
Life span: 20 years.
Status: Lower risk.

Verreaux's sifaka

Propithecus verreauxi

Distribution: South-west Madagascar.
Habitat: Tropical deciduous and dry evergreen and spiny forests.
Food: Leaves, fruits and flowers.
Size: 45–55cm (17.75–21.75in); 4–6kg (8.75–13.25lb).
Maturity: 3 years.
Breeding: A single young born in May to July after 5–6 months of gestation.
Life span: 23 years in captivity although probably less in the wild.
Status: Vulnerable.

Verreaux's sifaka lives in the forests of south-western Madagascar. It occupies two types of habitat – deciduous and evergreen forest. The trees of deciduous forests drop their leaves, not because of the cold, but because of drought. The evergreen forest is also dry, much of it is spiny forests found only in Madagascar.

This species lives in small groups of up to about 12 individuals. Groups contain more or less equal numbers of adult males and females. The group defends a small territory. They use their scent to mark the territory's boundary. Males have scent glands on their throats, while females use ones on their genitals. The sifakas mate in December, at the height of the dry season. A single young is born five months later and it is weaned after seven months.

Sifakas move through the trees by leaping. The distance they can jump is increased slightly by small flaps of skin under the animal's short forearms. These membranes allow the sifaka to glide slightly. On the ground, the sifakas move by hopping sideways on both hind feet. The forearms are held out to the side for balance.

Verreaux's sifakas eat all types of plant material apart from the roots. In the rainy season they prefer to eat easily digested soft fruits and flowers, but in the dry season they rely on wood, bark and leaves.

Verreaux's sifaka has a body built for leaping. The hind legs are very long for launching the animal into the air. This species can make jumps of 10m (33ft).

Diademed sifaka

Propithecus diadema

Distribution: Eastern Madagascar.
Habitat: Mountain and lowland rainforests.
Food: Fruits, flowers, shoots and leaves. Scientists suggest that the animal's athletic nature is due to the large amounts of caffeine and other alkaloids in its food.
Size: 45–55cm (17.75–21.75in); 6kg (13.25lb).
Maturity: 2–3 for females; 4–5 years for males.
Breeding: 1–2 young born in April and May.
Life span: 20 years.
Status: Endangered.

Diademed sifakas live in the high-altitude forests that grow above 800m (2,620ft) on the slopes of eastern Madagascar. This species is almost completely arboreal. They cling to trunks and make enormous leaps between trees, unlike other sifaka species, which often hop along the ground. These animals are diurnal. They live in small groups, which forage together for young leaves, fruits and other plant foods. The members of the group communicate to each other with a series of calls. They warn of a predator approaching on foot with a "tzisk" noise. Attacking birds illicit a honking call.

A group of sifakas contains several adult males and females. The males are organized into a mating hierarchy and only the highest-ranking male mates with the females in the group. During the summer breeding season (in December in Madagascar), the top-ranked male is frequently challenged by other males, which prevents it from mating with and guarding the females. While the alpha male is seeing off a threat, lower-ranked males often take the opportunity to mate with the females. One or two young are born four or five months later.

Diademed sifakas are named after the white tiara-like patch on the head. However, only one subspecies has this colouring: other members of the species are completely black or completely white.

BUSHBABIES

Monkeys and apes are not the only primates to live in Africa. Primitive primates, such as bushbabies, also live in the continent's forests. These are known as the prosimians, a name that means "before monkey". Biologists think that the ancestors of all the world's monkeys, apes and the lemurs of Madagascar resembled these small tree-living animals.

Potto

Perodicticus potto

These animals forage high up in the treetops at night, climbing slowly through the branches, using their wide, sensitive eyes to locate fruit in the moonlight, and a good sense of smell to find ants and other insects. Pottos also sleep high up in trees during the day.

Females occupy large ranges, big enough to provide food for themselves and their young. Males occupy larger ranges, which cover as many female ranges as possible. Pottos are fairly solitary creatures, but males and females in overlapping ranges make contact throughout the year, communicating with vocal calls and scent marks.

In the first few days of life, baby pottos cling to their mothers' bellies, but later the mothers leave their young hidden near their nests when out foraging. The young are collected at the end of the night. After a few months, the young pottos begin to follow their mothers around as they search for food. The mothers may carry their young on their backs. Young male pottos leave their maternal territories when they are only six months old, but young females stay with their mothers for much longer.

When threatened, pottos lower their heads between their forelegs, so that they are protected by their shoulderblades.

Distribution: Guinea to western Kenya and central Congo.
Habitat: Tropical forest.
Food: Fruit, insects and small vertebrates.
Size: 30–90cm (11.75–35.5in); 0.85–1.6kg (1.75–3.5lb).
Maturity: 18 months.
Breeding: Single young, or occasionally twins.
Life span: 25 years.
Status: Common.

Golden potto

Arctocebus calabarensis

This little prosimian has long, thick, woolly fur with a golden sheen. The animal grooms its fur with a long claw on the second toe of each foot.

The golden potto, alternatively known as the more exotic-sounding Calabar angwantibo, lives among the forests of western equatorial Africa. Its distribution runs from south-eastern Nigeria to southern Congo. The potto prefers areas of forest with dense undergrowth, where it feeds within 5m (16.5ft) of the ground. However, the most pristine rainforests have very little undergrowth because only small amounts of light penetrate the thick canopy of branches. For this reason, golden pottos tend to congregate around gaps in the forest where a tree has fallen, allowing enough light to flood into the gaps for shrubs to grow. Pottos are solitary animals. They forage for food at night, climbing slowly through the branches. They are cautious climbers: at all times three limbs are in contact with a solid surface. Pottos eat mainly insects. They can catch flying moths and will rub the poisonous hairs off caterpillars before eating them.

Distribution: Western Central Africa.
Habitat: Forest gaps.
Food: Insects.
Size: 23–30cm (9–11.75in); 260–460g (9.25–16.25oz).
Maturity: 18 months.
Breeding: Young born at end of rainy season.
Life span: 13 years.
Status: Lower risk.

Bushbaby

Galago senegalensis

Distribution: All parts of sub-Saharan Africa.
Habitat: Woodlands and savannahs.
Food: Mainly insects but also eggs, nestlings and fruits.
Size: 8–21cm (3.25–8.25in); 95–300g (3.25–10.5oz).
Maturity: 1 year.
Breeding: A single young, occasionally twins, are produced during both annual rainy seasons. The gestation period is 3–4 months.
Life span: 4 years.
Status: Common.

The bushbaby, or lesser galago, has the widest distribution of any species of African prosimian. It is found in the trees of open woodland and among the thickets of savannah habitats from Senegal to Tanzania. Bushbabies also live on Zanzibar.

Bushbabies are strictly tree-living animals. They have elongated feet that allow them to hop and leap a little like a kangaroo, but make them far from agile on the ground. The primates live in large crowds, although there is little social interaction. They sleep during the day, several bushbabies often sharing a nest in a thicket of vegetation or tree hollow. When awake in the day the bushbabies are sluggish and cautious, but when night falls the primates transform into agile climbers. They urinate on the hairless palms of their hands and soles of the feet to helps them grip better. The urine also leaves a trail of scent through the branches, which may help the bushbaby to find its way back to the nest in the darkness.

A bushbaby's favourite prey is grasshoppers. They also consume chicks, eggs and fruits. In periods of famine, the animals survive on sap and gum. Bushbabies are polyganous, and males fight for access to mates.

The bushbaby has wide eyes for seeing in the dark. It also has thickened pads on the tips of its fingers, which give the bushbaby more grip when climbing.

Greater galago

Otolemur crassicaudatus

Distribution: Eastern and southern Africa from Sudan to Angola and South Africa.
Habitat: Woodlands and forests.
Food: Gums, fruits and insects.
Size: 28–37cm (11–14.5in); 1–2kg (2.25–4.5lb).
Maturity: 2 years, but males will not breed until later.
Breeding: Litters of 2–3 young born once a year, in November in the south but earlier in equatorial regions.
Life span: 15 years in the wild but up to 18 years in captivity.
Status: Lower risk.

Greater galagos are found in forests from southern Sudan to eastern South Africa and Angola. Like other galago species, the greater galago has thick woolly hair. The animal grooms itself with its tongue, teeth and claws. Also, like its relatives, this species has pads on its fingers and toes to aid with gripping. (These are the same features that have evolved into the loose, wrinkles and folds on the palm of a human's hands.) However, unlike those of the bushbaby, the hind feet of the greater galago are not elongated. Consequently, the greater galago makes smaller leaps and generally moves by climbing from branch to branch.

Greater galagos survive on gums, fruits and insects. The composition of its diet depends on its location: in southern Africa nearly two-thirds of the animal's diet is made up of gum and saps, while in Kenya insects make up half its diet. Termites appear to be the most common insect eaten by greater galagos.

This species is polyganous. Males defend a large home range, which contains the territories of several females. Mating takes place between April and July, depending on geographical location.

This species is the largest species of galago. Males are larger than the females. The greater galago is also known as the thick-tailed galago on account of its bushy tail.

ELEPHANT AND HYRAX

There is only one living species of elephant in Africa, and it is the largest land animal in the world.
Although there is some disagreement among scientists, the closest relatives of the elephants are thought
to be sea cows, such as manatees and dugongs, and hyraxes. Neither of these groups bear much physical
resemblance to elephants, but similarities in their DNA codes reveal a shared ancestry.

African elephant

Loxodonta africana

One of the most distinctive features of an elephant is its trunk. It is a very adaptable tool, and can be used for picking up anything from peanuts to trees. It is used for feeding, drinking, fighting and communication.

There are two races of African elephants: the savannah elephant, which is the world's largest living land animal, and the smaller forest elephant that lives in the rainforests of Central and western Africa. The savannah elephants are social animals and, like Indian elephants, they form groups consisting of related female elephants and their young.

The leaders of elephant groups are always the eldest and largest females. Male elephants leave their groups at puberty, driven away by older females, to go and join groups of other young males. Males compete to mate, and usually these contests are settled by pushing and aggressive displays, but sometimes fighting leads to fatal injuries.

Forest elephants do not form large groups, but are able to maintain contact with other elephants in the dense jungle by producing deep, rumbling calls.

Distribution: Sub-Saharan Africa.
Habitat: Forest, savannah, marshland and semi-desert.
Food: Grass, leaves, shrubs, bark, twigs, roots and fruit.
Size: 6–7.5m (20ft–25ft); up to 7.5 tonnes (16,500lb).
Maturity: 10–20 years.
Breeding: Single calf born every few years.
Life span: 50–70 years.
Status: Endangered.

Rock hyrax

Procavia capensis

Close relatives of the elephant, these small rodent-like animals live in groups in rocky areas, where there are plenty of nooks and crannies in which to hide. Hyraxes are surprisingly agile, and can run up even the steepest, smooth rock surfaces with ease, gripping the rocks with the rubber-like soles of their feet. Hyraxes have many enemies, which include leopards, eagles and pythons, so they have to be quick and watchful. In fact, the dominant male of a family group, which typically consists of several females and young, and sometimes a subordinate male as well, usually stands guard while the rest of the group feeds or basks in the sun. If the sentry animal spots danger, he will warn the rest of the group with an alarm call.

Rock hyraxes don't like cold or wet weather, and will stay in their burrows if it is raining. When it is cold, groups of up to 25 animals will huddle together in a shelter to keep warm. On warm days, they come out to feed or bask in the sun. Hyraxes only come out at night if the weather is warm and there is plenty of moonlight, otherwise they stay in their burrows until daytime.

Rock hyraxes will eat almost any type of vegetation, even plant species poisonous to other mammals.

Distribution: Most of Africa, excluding the north-western regions.
Habitat: Rocky scrubland.
Food: Grass, leaves and shrubs.
Size: 30–58cm (12–23in); 4kg (8.75lb).
Maturity: 16–17 months.
Breeding: Litter of 1–6 young.
Life span: 11 years.
Status: Common.

HOOFED ANIMALS

Hoofed animals, or ungulates, walk on the tips of their toes. Their hooves are made from the same material as fingernails and claws – keratin. Walking in this way makes their legs very long, and most ungulates are fast runners because of this. Another shared characteristic of hoofed animals is that they are herbivores with highly developed digestive systems, allowing them to feed on tough plant material.

Ass

Equus asinus

Distribution: North Africa and Arabia.
Habitat: Hilly desert.
Food: Grasses.
Size: 2m (6.5ft); 250kg (550lb).
Maturity: 2 years.
Breeding: Single foal born in rainy season.
Life span: 30 years.
Status: Common.

The ass is the wild relative of the donkey. Donkeys were probably one of the first beasts of burden. Over the last few thousands years they have spread to all continents, though the natural range of wild asses is from Oman to Morocco.

Wild asses are now very rare, especially in Arabia. They live in small herds made up of a single male and several females. Sometimes larger groups come together, which contain several of these harem-type groups. The group grazes in the morning and evening. This allows it to seek shade and avoid the heat in the middle of the day. Asses are cautious animals and will shy away from the unfamiliar. This is the root of a donkey's stubbornness.

Asses can breed with horses and other members of the *Equus* genus. For instance, mules are a cross between a male donkey (jack) and a mare, a hinny is a cross between a stallion and a female donkey (jenny) and a zebra–donkey cross is called a zonkey.

The ass looks like a small and sturdy horse. Wild asses tend to be longer but more slender than domestic breeds of donkey.

Common zebra

Equus burchelli

Distribution: Ethiopia to southern Africa.
Habitat: Grassland and open woodland.
Food: Grass, herbs and leaves.
Size: 2.2–2.5m (7.25–8.25ft); 290–340g (640–750lb).
Maturity: 3 years.
Breeding: Single foal born every 1–2 years.
Life span: Up to 40 years.
Status: Lower risk.

There are three different species of zebra, all found in Africa and each with its own distinctive pattern of black and white stripes. The stripes make these hoofed mammals blend in to the natural patterns of light and shade in their habitat, making it more difficult for a predator to keep track of its quarry during a chase.

Zebras usually live in small family groups headed by dominant stallions, which lead groups of one to six mares with their young. When young male zebras reach maturity, they leave their family groups and form groups of bachelor males, while females stay behind. Males fight amongst each other for access to females, circling and trying to kick or bite one another. Within a group, zebras can be affectionate, and may spend a lot of time grooming one another.

The common or Burchell's zebra has the broadest stripes of the three zebra species, and its stripes usually join at the belly.

Black rhinoceros

Diceros bicornis

The black rhinoceros is the smaller and more abundant of the two species of rhino found in Africa, but it is still critically endangered. These animals form clans that sometimes come together at wallowing sites, where they have mud baths. The baths help to keep the skin healthy and free of parasites. Rhinos within a clan are usually tolerant of each other, though occasionally serious fights may occur between bulls that are courting the same female.

Black rhinoceroses can be quite dangerous. They have very bad eyesight and may charge at anything large enough to be a threat, including vehicles, tents and campfires. However, they usually run away when they detect the scent of humans. Indeed, rhinos have good reason to fear humans. Hunting has destroyed the populations of both of the African species. People have hunted the rhino for sport, for its tough hide, but mostly for its horn. A rhino's horn is made from the same material as hair, and can be carved into ornamental objects or ground into medicinal or aphrodisiac powders. Many countries have banned trade in rhino products, but illegal trading still occurs.

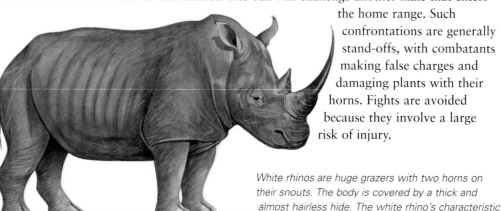

The black rhino can be distinguished from Africa's second rhino species, the white rhino, by its pointed, prehensile upper lip, as compared to the white rhino's squared, non-prehensile upper lip. Despite the names, there is no colour difference between them.

Distribution: Eastern and southern Africa from southern Chad and Sudan to northern South Africa.
Habitat: Scrubland and woody savannah.
Food: Twigs, buds and leaves. Also strips bark from woody stems.
Size: 3–3.75m (9.75–12.25ft); 800–1,400kg (1,760–3,080lb).
Maturity: Females 4–6 years; males 7–9 years.
Breeding: Single calf born every 2–5 years.
Life span: 30 years in the wild, but can exceed 45 years in captivity.
Status: Critically endangered.

White rhinoceros

Ceratotherium simum

The white rhino is among the rarest mammal species in the world. A little more than 150 years ago it was found across Africa from Sudan and Chad to northern South Africa. Today, however, only 400 individuals survive, and all of them live in reserves in eastern and southern Africa.

The reason for the white rhino's demise is hunting. In recent times the rhinos were being hunted for their horn, which could be sold for a high price in China, where it is believed to be an aphrodisiac. The huge black-market price for rhino horn makes poaching an ever-present problem.

White rhinos live in small groups. Each group never strays from a home range of about 8sq km (3sq miles). The groups are made up of females, while the dominant bulls live on their own but remain close to the females. The bull will challenge another male that enters the home range. Such confrontations are generally stand-offs, with combatants making false charges and damaging plants with their horns. Fights are avoided because they involve a large risk of injury.

Distribution: Eastern and southern Africa from Sudan to South Africa.
Habitat: Areas of open woodland and tropical grassland.
Food: Grass and other low-growing plants.
Size: 3.3–4.2m (10.75–13.75ft); 1.4–3.6 tonnes (3,080–7,920lb).
Maturity: 6 years in females; 10 years in males.
Breeding: Single calf born every 2 years.
Life span: 30 years in the wild but more than 40 when raised in captivity.
Status: Critically endangered.

White rhinos are huge grazers with two horns on their snouts. The body is covered by a thick and almost hairless hide. The white rhino's characteristic square lip is used for plucking grasses.

Giraffe

Giraffa camelopardalis

Giraffes are the world's tallest living land mammals, with some exceeding 5m (16.5ft) from top to toe. The giraffe's long neck has the same number of vertebrae as other mammals, but each one is greatly elongated. The giraffe's great height is an adaptation for feeding on young leaves in the upper branches of trees, which other browsing mammals cannot reach.

Giraffes have excellent sight, and because of their height they have the greatest range of vision of any terrestrial animal. If a giraffe spots danger, it will run away at speeds of up to 56kph (34mph). Occasionally, a giraffe will face its attacker, striking out with its front hooves or swinging its head like a club.

In order to reach fresh grass or drinking water, giraffes must splay their front legs apart, so that they can get their heads down to ground level. Giraffes settle on to their withdrawn legs to rest, and lie down when sleeping, resting their heads back on their hindquarters.

In times gone by, giraffes could be found in parts of North Africa, but due to a combination of over-hunting and the effects of climate change on vegetation they are now only thinly distributed south of the Sahara Desert.

Distribution: Sub-Saharan Africa.
Habitat: Open woodland and savannah.
Food: Leaves, grass and grains.
Size: 5.9m (19.25ft); 550–1,930kg (1,200–4,200lb).
Maturity: Females 3.5 years; males 4.5 years.
Breeding: Usually 1 young born every 2 years.
Life span: Up to 26 years recorded in the wild, and 36 years recorded in captivity.
Status: Conservation-dependent.

Giraffes have prehensile lips and long tongues to help them gather leaves. They also have short horn-like ossicones on their heads – a feature they share with okapis.

Horse (*Equus caballus*): 1.8m (6ft) tall; 2 tonnes (4,400lb) Today this species exists only as domestic breeds. These animals live on all continents of the world except Antarctica. In many places feral herds have appeared, such as in the Carmargue wetlands of southern France. The natural range of wild horses is thought to be the Eurasian steppes from Poland to Mongolia. Despite all being descended from domestic breeds, feral horses live in the same harem system as their wild ancestors, with a single male leading a small group of females. There are several breeds of horses, from the miniature Falabella and Shetland ponies to the mighty draft horses bred for hauling carts. Lighter horses were bred for speed. For example, the thoroughbreds used in racing are bred from fast-running Turkish and Arabic military breeds.

Okapi

Okapia johnstoni

The okapi is a close relative of the giraffe. Although okapis are nowhere near as tall as giraffes, they do have relatively long necks and legs. Females are usually larger than males. Okapis have a deep red-brown coloration with distinctive horizontal black and white stripes along their rumps and legs. Despite their large size and unique appearance, they were not known to science until 1900.

Okapis spend most of their time alone, and they are very wary, running into dense cover if they detect danger. Sometimes okapis form small family groups and communicate with vocalizations and mutual grooming.

It is thought that there are between 10,000 and 20,000 okapis in the wild, but their dense forest habitat makes it very difficult for scientists to estimate their true population status.

Male okapis have small, hair-covered, horn-like ossicones. They also have very long tongues, capable of reaching their eyes.

Distribution: Congo Region.
Habitat: Dense tropical forest.
Food: Leaves, twigs and fruit.
Size: 1.9–2.1m (6.25–7ft); 200–300kg (440–660lb).
Maturity: Females reach sexual maturity at 1.5 years; males probably do not have the opportunity to mate until older.
Breeding: Single offspring born after a gestation of 421–427 days.
Life span: 30 years.
Status: Threatened.

Common hippopotamus

Hippopotamus amphibius

These enormous animals spend much of their time in water, where they stay out of the hot sun and take the weight off their legs. Hippopotamuses lie in the water with only their nostrils, eyes and ears above the surface, and they can also submerge for up to 30 minutes, while walking on the bottom of the river or lake.

Hippopotamuses eat only plant food, which does not contain a large amount of nutrients. The water supports some of the weight of the hippos' massive bodies, so resting in water helps the animals conserve their energy and reduces the amount of food they need to eat. After dusk the hippos leave their watery refuge in search of grass, sometimes travelling more than 3km (2 miles) from water.

Large males set up territories along river banks, which they defend against other males. Although neighbouring territory-holders are usually peaceful, confrontations sometimes occur. When this happens, the males challenge each other with displays, including lunging, splashing, scattering dung with their short tails and displaying their tusks with great yawns of their mouths. If neither male backs off, fighting occurs, and sometimes they attack each other with their tusks – which can lead to fatal injuries, or deep gouges at the very least. Older males sport many scars from their past battles.

Males are aggressive towards intruders, including young hippos. Females are aggressive when they have young, and many consider hippos to be among the most dangerous of all African mammals.

Distribution: Most of Sub-Saharan Africa, although most common in tropical grassland areas of East Africa
Habitat: Deep water near reeds or grassland.
Food: Grass and other low-growing plants.
Size: 2–5m (6.5–16.5ft); 1–4.5 tonnes (2,200–9,900lb).
Maturity: Between 6 and 14 years.
Breeding: Successful males breed with several females. Mating takes place in water. Females are pregnant for 240 days. Usually a single young born during rainy season, with 2 or 3 years between births.
Life span: Up to 40 years.
Status: Common in general, although rarer in western and Central Africa.

The hippo's tusks – actually its canine teeth – can weigh up to 3kg (6.5lb) each, and are used in fighting. There have been some reports of hippos overturning small boats and biting the occupants to death.

Dromedary camel

Camelus dromedarius

Distribution: North Africa to western India.
Habitat: Deserts and scrubland.
Food: Vegetation and carrion.
Size: 2.2–3.5m (7.25–11.5ft); 300–690kg (660–1500lb).
Maturity: 3 years.
Breeding: Single young or twins every 2 years.
Life span: 50 years.
Status: Common.

These tough animals have been domesticated in and around the Arabian peninsula for more than 4,000 years, and are prized for their endurance in hot, dry conditions. The dromedary, or one-humped, camel can carry loads of more than 200kg (440lb) for several days.

Camels can survive for long periods without drinking water. However, when water is available they can drink up to 57 litres (12 gallons) at a time to restore normal levels of body fluids. Camels have almost no sweat glands, so they lose water much more slowly than other mammals. Contrary to popular belief, the camel's hump contains fat, not water, and serves as an energy reserve – although the blubber does hold some water. During the breeding season, dominant males defend groups of up to 30 adult females from other males. Younger males form groups of bachelor males.

As well as their characteristic hump, camels have other adaptations to the harsh conditions of the desert, including broad feet for walking on loose sand, long eyelashes, hairy ears, and nostrils that can be closed to keep out sand and dust.

Warthog

Phacochoerus africanus

This species gets its name from the warty protuberances located on the sides of the head and in front of the eyes, found only in the males. These powerful animals have large heads in proportion to the rest of their bodies, and both males and females have sharp tusks.

Unlike most species of wild pig, warthogs are active during the day, except in areas where they are likely to be attacked by humans. There they change to a nocturnal lifestyle in order to avoid human contact. When sleeping or rearing young, warthogs take refuge in holes – often those made by aardvarks.

If attacked by predators such as hyenas or lions, warthogs flee to the nearest available hole, backing into it so that they can face their attackers with their vicious tusks. Warthogs sometimes come together in groups called sounders, usually numbering 4–16 individuals. Although they are fairly abundant throughout their range, people hunt warthogs for their meat and to stop them eating crops. This poses a threat to warthog populations.

In male warthogs, the upper tusks can exceed 60cm (24in) in length. However, it is the smaller and sharper lower tusks that are the warthog's main weapon. Curiously, warthogs kneel down to feed on grass and roots.

Distribution: Throughout Africa from Mauritania to Ethiopia, and southward to Namibia and eastern South Africa.
Habitat: Savannah and open woodland.
Food: Grass, roots, berries, and sometimes carrion.
Size: 0.9–1.5m (3–5ft); 50–150kg (110–330lb).
Maturity: 18–20 months.
Breeding: 1–8 young.
Life span: Can exceed 18 years in captivity.
Status: Abundant, but the subspecies *P. a. aeliani* is classified as endangered.

Pygmy hippopotamus
(*Hexaprotodon liberiensis*): 1.5–1.7m (5–5.5ft); 160–270kg (350–600lb)
This animal is found in hot lowland jungles in parts of West Africa, and, although it looks like a miniature version of the hippopotamus, there are a number of notable differences. These include a more rounded head and eyes on the side, rather than the top of the head.

Giant forest hog (*Hylochoerus meinertzhageni*): 1.3–2.1m (4.25–7ft); 130–275kg (285–605lb)
These large wild pigs travel about their tropical forest habitats in groups, or sounders, of up to 20 individuals, led by old males. Males are aggressive, will charge intruding males, and have also been known to charge humans.

Bush pig (*Potamochoerus porcus*): 1–1.5m (3.25–5ft); 46–130kg (100–285lb)
These pigs have long pointed ears, long white whiskers, and white crests along their backs. They live in the jungles of West Africa, where they forage for a wide range of food types at night. Their numbers have increased, probably as a result of the reduction of leopard populations.

Wild boar

Sus scrofa

Although domestic pigs usually look quite different from wild boar, they are in fact the same species, and can readily interbreed. Wild boar live in groups called sounders, consisting of females and their young. The males live alone, but join sounders in the mating season, when they compete for access to females.

Male wild boar can be very aggressive. In Doñana National Park in Spain, they have been known to chase adult lynxes away from carrion. Wild boars sometimes construct shelters from cut grass, and female wild boars are the only hoofed animals that give birth and look after their young inside a crude nest.

These animals have an excellent sense of smell, and are able to sniff out nutritious tubers and roots underground, while they snuffle through the leaf litter. Foraging wild boars often leave telltale signs, frequently ploughing up large patches of soil. In some countries, where wild boar have been introduced, they have had a negative impact on local animals and plants, either by feeding on them directly, or by disturbing their habitats.

Only male wild boar have tusks, which are extended upper and lower canine teeth. Piglets have striped patterns, which they lose as they get older.

Distribution: Europe, North Africa and Asia.
Habitat: Forest and shrublands.
Food: Leaves, roots, fungi, small mammals and reptiles, eggs, carrion and manure.
Size: 0.9–1.8m (3–6ft); 40–350kg (88–770lb).
Maturity: 8–10 months.
Breeding: 1 litter of 1–12 young born annually.
Life span: 10 years.
Status: Common.

DEER

Deer are a group of hoofed mammals that are found across the Northern Hemisphere. They belong to the Cervidae family of mammals. In form and habit, deer resemble the horned antelopes of Africa, which are actually more closely related to sheep and cattle. However, instead of horns, deer grow antlers. In most species only males have them, and unlike horns which remain for life, antlers are shed annually.

Fallow deer

Dama dama

Fallow deer are easily distinguishable from other species of European deer by their somewhat flattened antlers and spotted summer coats. In some places fallow deer live alone, while in others they come together to form small herds of up to 30 individuals.

The breeding behaviour of this species is variable, and may depend on the way food is distributed. In some places males come together and attempt to attract females with dance-like rituals and bellowing, a behaviour known as a rut. In other places, males attempt to monopolize a group of females by defending good feeding areas from other males. Fallow deer have been introduced to many new places, but their original populations are falling because of hunting and climate change.

Only the male fallow deer sport antlers, which can span 80cm (32in) from tip to tip. Adults shed and re-grow their antlers every year.

Distribution: Originally from the Mediterranean and parts of the Middle East, but introduced to Britain, America and New Zealand.
Habitat: Open woodland, grassland and shrubland.
Food: Grass, leaves and twigs.
Size: 1.3–1.7m (4.25–5.5ft); 40–100kg (88–220lb).
Maturity: Females at 16 months; males at 17 months.
Breeding: A single fawn born annually.
Life span: 20 years or more in captivity.
Status: Common, but rare in its original range.

Reindeer

Rangifer tarandus

The reindeer, also known as the caribou in North America, is the only deer species in which both males and females possess antlers. Herds are organized into hierarchies based on the size of the deers' bodies and antlers. Most herds make seasonal migrations, moving to where food is available. Northern populations often travel more than 5,000km (3,000 miles). During the migration, reindeer groups congregate into great herds of up to half a million individuals.

Reindeer have been domesticated for 3,000 years, and there are huge numbers in northern Siberia.

The antlers of males can exceed 1m (3.25ft). Reindeer hooves are broad and flat – an adaptation for walking on soft ground and deep snow.

Distribution: Greenland, Scandinavia, Siberia, Mongolia, north-eastern China, Alaska, Canada, and northern USA.
Habitat: Arctic tundra, boreal forests and mountainous habitats.
Food: Plant material (especially new growth in spring), leaves, twigs and lichens.
Size: 1.2–2.2m (4–7.25ft); 60–318kg (130–700lb).
Maturity: 1.5–3.5 years.
Breeding: 1 fawn produced annually.
Life span: 15 years.
Status: Common.

Elk

Alces alces

Distribution: Northern Europe, Siberia, Alaska, Canada and northern parts of the United States.
Habitat: Marsh and coniferous woodland.
Food: Leaves, twigs, moss and water plants.
Size: 2.4–3.1m (8–10.25ft); 200–825kg (440–1,820lb).
Maturity: 1 year.
Breeding: 1–3 young born in spring.
Life span: 27 years.
Status: Common.

The name elk often causes confusion. In North America elks are known as moose. To compound this confusion, the name elk is also used in the Americas to refer to red deer. Elks are the largest deer in the world. They live in the cold conifer forests that cover northern mountains and lowlands. They are most common in Canada and Alaska but also live across northern Europe and Siberia.

These animals plod through forests and marshes, browsing on leaves, mosses and lichens. They often feed in rivers, nibbling on aquatic vegetation and even dive underwater to uproot water plants. In summer, they are most active at dawn and dusk. In winter, they are active throughout the day. They paw the snow to reveal buried plants and twigs.

Elks may gather to feed, but they spend most of the year alone. In the autumn mating season, the males fight each other for the females.

Male elks are almost twice the size of females. The males sport huge antlers – nearly 2m (6.5ft) across – and have flaps of skin hanging below their chins, called dewlaps.

Roe deer (*Capreolus capreolus*): 0.9–1.5m (3–5ft); 15–50kg (33–110lb)
This graceful deer is found over large parts of Europe, including Britain, where it lives in forests and on farmland. The smallest type of European deer, the roe deer lives alone or in small groups. Roe deer have been able to adapt well to habitat changes brought about by human activities, and they have actually increased in number. They eat more than 1,000 plant species across their natural range. When grazing out in the open, the deer form large groups of up to 90 members in order to reduce the risks of attack. In forests, where they are more protected from predators, the deer live in smaller groups of less than 15.

Water chevrotain (*Hyemoschus aquaticus*): 45–85cm (17.75–33.5in); 7–15kg (15.5–33lb)
The water chevrotain is a small African hoofed animal that lives south of the Sahara, from the coast of Sierra Leone to western Uganda. Chevrotains look like small deer but they actually form a separate group of hoofed animals, most of which live in Asia. Neither sex grows antlers, although males grow tusks. These are long upper canines that stick out of the mouth and extend to below the lower lips. The tusks are a feature shared with the muntjac deer of southern Asia, and may be primitive features now lost by most deer species. Water chevrotains are forest browsers. They are never more than 250m (820ft) away from a river. By day they stay hidden in undergrowth, but under the cover of darkness chevrotains come out into the open and feed in forest clearings and along river banks.

Red deer

Cervus elaphus

Red deer are one of the most widespread of all deer species. As with species that are spread across the world, the common names used can be confusing. In North America the species is known as elk, while populations of red deer living in the far north of Canada are also known as wapiti, though many biologists argue that wapiti are, in fact, a separate species from red deer. Red deer prefer woodlands, while wapiti are more common in open country. Nevertheless, the two groups of deer very closely resemble each other in most other ways.

Only male red deer have antlers, which reach up to 1.7m (5.5ft) across, and a dark shaggy mane. Adult males use their antlers during the rut, which takes place in autumn. The fighting establishes which males will control the harems of females. Antlers fall off in winter and re-grow in time for the next year's conquests.

Red deer only have red coats in summer. In winter, they grow longer and darker hairs.

Distribution: Northern Africa, Europe, Asia and North America.
Habitat: Woodlands.
Food: Grass, sedge, forbs, twigs and bark.
Size: 1.6–2.6m (5.25–8.5ft); 75–340kg (165–750lb).
Maturity: 2 years.
Breeding: 1 fawn born in autumn.
Life span: 20 years.
Status: Common.

ANTELOPES AND RELATIVES

Antelopes are a large group of hoofed animals that live mainly in Africa, with a few living in Asia. Antelopes belong to the same group of mammals as cattle, bison, sheep and goats. Gazelles also belong to this same group. Antelopes and their relatives have horns rather than antlers. These are made from bone and are permanent features on the heads.

Blue gnu

Connochaetes taurinus

The blue gnu, also known as the wildebeest, is one of the most abundant large mammals in Africa. There are thought to be 1.5 million individuals in the Serengeti alone, forming the greatest concentration of wild grazing animals on Earth. Some herds stay in the same place; others are nomadic, constantly searching for sources of food. Migrating gnus travelling in immense herds that number in the thousands are one of the wonders of the natural world.

The males leave their herds when they are over a year old, forming groups of young bachelors. At about three or four years old, males set up small territories, which they defend from other males, and attempt to mate with females entering their areas. Mating activity is seasonal, and is usually timed so that the majority of calves are born close to the beginning of the rainy season, when new grass is plentiful.

Although populations have increased in the Serengeti, numbers have declined in other areas, such as south-west Botswana. There, competition with livestock and destruction of crops has prompted farmers to kill gnus and set up long fences to prevent them from migrating to wetlands when there are seasonal droughts.

Gnus are named after the calls made by competing males – "genu". There are two species; this one is blue-grey, while the other is dark brown and black.

Distribution: Southern Kenya and southern Angola to northern South Africa.
Habitat: Savannah.
Food: Grass and succulent plants.
Size: 1.5m (5ft); 118–275kg (260–600lb).
Maturity: Females 2–3 years; males 3–4 years.
Breeding: Usually a single calf born each year.
Life span: Up to 21 years in captivity.
Status: Abundant, but continuing survival is dependent on conservation efforts.

Impala

Aepyceros melampus

Like many other antelopes, impalas have pointed, spiralling horns. Both sexes are similarly coloured, with a white belly, chin and tail, and black-tipped ears.

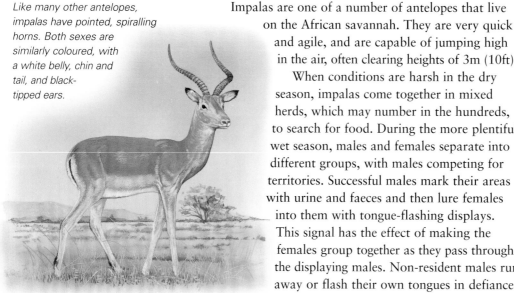

Impalas are one of a number of antelopes that live on the African savannah. They are very quick and agile, and are capable of jumping high in the air, often clearing heights of 3m (10ft).

When conditions are harsh in the dry season, impalas come together in mixed herds, which may number in the hundreds, to search for food. During the more plentiful wet season, males and females separate into different groups, with males competing for territories. Successful males mark their areas with urine and faeces and then lure females into them with tongue-flashing displays. This signal has the effect of making the females group together as they pass through the displaying males. Non-resident males run away or flash their own tongues in defiance.

Distribution: Kenya and southern Angola to northern South Africa.
Habitat: Savannah and open woodland.
Food: Grass, and leaves from bushes and trees.
Size: 1.1–1.5m (3.5–5ft); females 40–45kg (88–99lb); males 60–65kg (132–143lb).
Maturity: 1 year.
Breeding: Single fawn born at a time.
Life span: 13 years.
Status: Common.

Topi

Damaliscus lunatus

Distribution: Africa south of the Sahara Desert.
Habitat: Moist grasslands.
Food: Grass.
Size: 1.7m (5.5ft); 130–170kg (286.5–374.75lb).
Maturity: 2–3 years.
Breeding: Single calf born at end of dry season.
Life span: 20 years.
Status: Lower risk.

Topis are medium-sized antelopes that live in the savannahs of Africa. They prefer areas that are relatively damp – still too dry for a forest to grow but moist enough for bushes and small trees to grow in places. Topis are found south of the Sahara Desert, from Senegal to Sudan. Their distribution then extends through the plains of East Africa and across southern Africa.

Males defend a territory of grass, which will also be home to a few females and their young. At the centre of the territory is a mound or similar vantage point. The male uses this feature to display to the other topis in the area in order to reinforce his ownership of the territory and to attract more females to his herd. The females also stand on the mound in order to alert other topis of approaching danger.

The male has sole mating rights over the females. Gestation is about eight months, and young are born at the end of the dry season.

Both male and female topis have horns. Males are slightly larger than females and have darker coats. The coat is a pattern of dark blotches under a fine coat of red-brown hairs. The blotches range from black to dark purple.

Blue duiker (*Cephalophus monticola*):
72cm (28.25in); 10kg (22lb)
This small antelope lives across Central Africa. It is the smallest of the duikers, which are all much smaller than the grassland antelopes. The blue duiker is a forest animal. Being small helps it move through undergrowth. Both sexes have horns, although these are little more than short spikes. Blue duikers eat mainly fruits, shoots and buds, but also consume insects, snails and eggs. They live in breeding pairs that stay together for years. Blue duikers live for about 10 years.

Zebra duiker (*Cephalophus zebra*):
90cm (35.5in); 20kg (44lb)
This species of duiker, named after the black stripes running across its back, lives in the forests of West Africa. When not raising their young, zebra duikers live alone. They eat fruits and leaves. Most of the best food is located high in the branches and out of reach of the little antelopes. Zebra duikers survive on the leftovers of monkeys and other tree-living foragers who dislodge and drop food on to the ground.

Common duiker (*Sylvicapra grimmia*):
100cm (39.25in); 25kg (55lb)
The common duiker, also known as the grey or bush duiker, is the only species of duiker to live in both grasslands and forests. It is found south of the Sahara Desert. Common duikers live anywhere that there is cover for them to hide during the day. They eat a wide range of foods, which vary depending on their location. In forests they eat fruits, flowers and leaves, but in more open areas they dig up roots with their hooves.

Hartebeest

Alcelaphus buselaphus

Hartebeests look a little unusual because their horns grow from a single boney plate on top of the head. This antelope used to be widely distributed. Today, the species' habitat has been turned over to cattle pasture, and the hartebeests now live in several fragmented populations. These are centred on Botswana and Namibia in the south and the East African savannah.

Hartebeest live in large herds. They once gathered into herds of 10,000, but today a group of 300 is more normal. The herd is organized into four types of subgroups. Females and their young form the largest subgroups. The next subgroup contains two-year-old males. They may be sexually mature but are still growing and are rarely sexually active. The other subgroupings are solitary adult males – above the age of three. Younger adult males defend a territory within the herd. Males older than seven have generally been forced from their territories.

Distribution: East and south-western Africa.
Habitat: Grasslands and woodlands.
Food: Grass.
Size: 1.5–2.4m (5–8ft); 75–200kg (165.25–441lb).
Maturity: 12 months.
Breeding: Single calves born at all times of year.
Life span: 20 years.
Status: Lower risk.

Hartebeests are large antelopes. There are several subspecies that live in different parts of Africa; they are identified chiefly by the shape of their horns, which grow on both males and females.

Arabian oryx

Oryx leucoryx

The Arabian oryx is the only oryx found outside Africa. It is adapted to survive in very arid conditions. By the early 1970s the Arabian oryx was thought to be extinct in the wild, due to excessive hunting throughout the early 20th century. At this time, the only herds existed in zoos around the world. However, a captive-breeding programme was started in the 1960s, and oryx have been reintroduced into the wild in Oman, Jordan and Saudi Arabia. Wild populations now number around 500 individuals.

Since dry habitats contain relatively little nourishing plant material, oryx must range over vast areas to obtain enough food. Oryx are surprisingly good at detecting rainfall from a great distance, and will move towards areas where rain is falling so that they can eat fresh plant growth and drink water.

When water is not available, they eat succulent foods, such as melons or bulbs, to get the moisture they need. Oryx live in groups of around ten individuals, consisting of either a dominant male and females, or a group of young males. Although the oryx's exceptionally long and sharp horns are formidable weapons, most contests between males are settled by ritualized sparring.

Distribution: Originally in much of the Middle East, now only a few reserves in Oman, Jordan and Saudi Arabia.
Habitat: Dry habitats, including arid scrubland and deserts.
Food: Grass, shrubs, succulent fruit and bulbs.
Size: 1.5–2.3m (5–7.5ft); 100–210kg (220–463lb).
Maturity: 1–2 years.
Breeding: Single calf born.
Life span: 20 years.
Status: Endangered.

Oryx have striking black or brown markings on their heads and lower bodies, and very long, straight horns, up to 1.5m (5ft) in length.

Gemsbok

Oryx gazella

Gemsbok are large antelopes with long, slightly curved horns. Females have horns as well as the males, but they tend to be slightly shorter and more slender. Gemsbok living in the northern part of the range are darker than those living in the south.

Gemsbok are highland antelopes. They live in dry woodlands and more open grassland habitats. Many of the gemsbok's closest relatives are desert animals. High-altitude habitats are also often dry, and this species is also able to survive in areas where food is scarce for long periods. When food is plentiful, the gemsbok consume almost nothing but grass. As this food source reduces during the dry season, they become browsers and select leaves and other food items from bushes and trees. At the driest times, the antelopes use their hooves to dig out roots and other underground storage organs. They have been known to dig up melons and cucumbers, which are full of water and supply the gemsbok with the drink they need before the rains return.

Gemsbok are polygynous, which means that successful males will mate with several females. Small herds tend to contain just one dominant adult male, while in larger herds there are enough females for a few bulls to tolerate each other. There is no breeding season, and males mate with females soon after they give birth.

Distribution: Southern and East Africa. Most common in Zambia and Tanzania.
Habitat: Highland areas of savannah and grassland.
Food: Grasses, roots, leaves and fruits.
Size: 1.95m (76.75in); 210kg (463lb).
Maturity: 2 years.
Breeding: Single calf born every 9 months. Newborn calves hidden in thicket.
Life span: 18 years.
Status: Lower risk.

Addax

Addax nasomaculatus

Distribution: Sahara Desert.
Habitat: Desert.
Food: Grasses and shrubs.
Size: 1.5–1.7m (5–5.5ft);
60–125kg (132.25–275.5lb).
Maturity: 2–3 years.
Breeding: Single calf born
in spring.
Life span: 25 years.
Status: Endangered.

The addax antelope is found in the Sahara Desert and is well adapted to some of the driest and hottest conditions on Earth. The antelope rarely drinks liquid water, and can obtain most of the water it needs to survive from the plants it eats. It moves great distances in search of vegetation to eat and often spends long periods out in the open.

This species was once found across North Africa, although the scarcity of food in the desert meant that it was never present in large numbers. However, as one of the few large mammals to live in the deserts of North Africa, the addax has long been a target of hunters, who made use of its meat and hide. As a result of over-hunting in the last century, the addax now lives in a few tiny populations scattered across its original range. It is one of the most endangered of all antelope species. The species has some protection from extinction, however. Large numbers live in zoos.

During the summer, addaxes are almost white, but their coat darkens in winter. The paler coat helps to reflect the sun's heat during the hottest time of the year.

Scimitar-horned oryx (*Oryx dammah*):
1.7m (5.5ft); 204kg (449.75lb)
This desert antelope, also known as the white oryx, is thought to be extinct in the wild. It was once widespread across the Sahel – the African steppeland that borders the southern edge of the Sahara Desert. (Sahel means "shore" and refers to the "sea" of sand that is the desert.) Hunting was the downfall of this species in the same way as it was for its close relatives the addax and Arabian oryx. In the year 2000, after 35 years of monitoring, it was decided that no scimitar-horned oryxes survived in the wild. It is possible that some still remain in the remoter parts of northern Mali and Chad, but, even if they do, there would more than likely be too few to sustain a wild population in the future. The species survives in zoos. All is not lost, however: the Arabian oryx was saved from extinction by a captive breeding programme in the 1970s, one of the first conservation successes of this kind, so there is still hope for the scimitar-horned oryx.

Sable antelope (*Hippotragus niger*):
2.1m (7ft); 230kg (507lb)
The sable antelope, also called mbarapi, is known for the jet-black coat of the adult males. The females and immature antelopes have a red-brown coat. Both sexes have long, curved horns. Sables live in the savannahs of East and southern Africa. They are a favourite on safaris and are common in zoos. Like many grazing antelopes, sables live in small herds populated by several females and their juvenile offspring. The herd has just one adult male, who has sole mating rights over the females in the herd.

Roan antelope

Hippotragus equinus

The roan antelope is also known as the horse antelope. It belongs to a tribe of antelopes called the Hippotragini – the horse-like antelopes. This tribe includes the oryxes, sable and gemsbok, all of which share similarities with horses in the way they look. There is, of course, only a distant relationship with horses.

Roan antelopes live in thickets and areas of shrubs. It lives in two main populations. The first is found in the belt of grassland that grows south of the Sahara Desert and north of the Congo rainforest. Here the roan is found as far west as Gambia and ranges east to Somalia. The second group is centred on Botswana and the surrounding region.

Roan antelopes live in small herds, which rarely contain more than about 20 individuals. Each herd has a single bull and several females. The remaining members are their offspring.

Distribution: Africa, south of the Sahara Desert.
Habitat: Savannah.
Food: Grasses and leaves.
Size: 1.9–2.4m (6.25–7.75ft);
263kg (579.75lb).
Maturity: 2–3 years.
Breeding: Single calf born at all times of year.
Life span: 17 years.
Status: Lower risk.

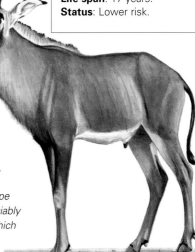

The roan antelope is one of the largest antelope species. Only the cattle-like elands are appreciably larger. Young roan have pale reddish coats, which darken as the antelope ages. Adults also have a mane of short black hairs.

Waterbuck

Kobus ellipsiprymnus

Only male waterbucks have horns. There are two races of waterbucks: the northern population has a flash of white on the rump against a background coat of reddish hairs while the southern group has a circle of white on the rump and a grey coat on the rest of the body.

As their name suggests, waterbucks are seldom found far from water. However, African grasslands are dry places where there is not enough rain for trees to grow, so as a result waterbucks are most often found in valley bottoms, where water drains from higher areas.

There are two populations of waterbuck. The Defassa waterbucks range from the Horn of Africa across the northern fringe of the Congo Basin to the savannahs of West Africa. The southern group, known as the Ellisprymnus waterbucks, lives in parts of south-eastern Africa, such as Zambia, Zimbabwe and South Africa.

Waterbucks live in small herds. The herds are primarily made up of females and their young. Solitary males may adopt a territory that overlaps with those of other herds. These males mate with any females that enter their territory. The females are attracted to the male because he protects them from harassment by younger males. Younger males are non-territorial and have a more opportunistic mating strategy.

Distribution: One population in the south-east and another in West and Central Africa.
Habitat: Grasslands close to rivers and waterholes.
Food: Grass and low-growing herbs.
Size: 1.7–2.3m (5.5–7.5ft); 160–300kg (352.75–661.5lb).
Maturity: 3–6 years.
Breeding: Northern population calves once a year, southern group calves every 10 months.
Life span: 20 years.
Status: Lower risk.

Kob

Kobus kob

Like their close relative the waterbucks, kobs are closely associated with water. They are found on river banks and beside watering holes on grasslands and along the edge of woodlands. Most feeding takes place in the early morning and evening.

Kobs employ what is known as a "lek" mating system – a system also used by some large deer, bats and birds. The males display in a lek – an array of small territories that are purely symbolic of the male's status because they are too small to hold enough resources to feed the male let alone a mate and young. Females move through the lek and choose which male to mate with. Most matings take place toward the centre of the lek, and territories there are highly contested. The dominant males fight for control of these central areas, and the best territories often change hands.

Only fully mature males can compete in the lek. Younger males stay with the females and young, where they may attempt to mate with females. This unwanted attention drives the females into the lek, where the younger males will not follow.

Outside the mating season, the males live in separate herds to the females and young. The males play no part in raising their young.

Male waterbucks have horns measuring about 44cm (1.5ft) long. Females do not have horns and they are also generally smaller than males.

Distribution: Western and Central Africa south of the Sahara Desert.
Habitat: Savannah and woodlands.
Food: Grasses and reeds.
Size: 1.6–1.8m (5.25–6ft); 105kg (231.5lb).
Maturity: Between 1 and 2 years; males are unlikely to mate for several years.
Breeding: Dominant males display together in small territories called a lek. Females choose mates and produce a single calf born at end of rainy season.
Life span: 20 years.
Status: Lower risk.

Lechwe

Kobus leche

Distribution: Southern Africa.
Habitat: Floodplains.
Food: Grasses.
Size: 1.3–1.8m (4.25–6ft); 60–130kg (132.25–286.5lb).
Maturity: 2 years; males unlikely to breed until the age of 5.
Breeding: Mating takes place before rainy season.
Life span: 20 years.
Status: Lower risk.

Like other members of the *Kobus* genus, lechwes live close to water. This species is most closely associated with floodplains, where the land is covered by shallow water for some of the year. Lechwes live in the floodplains of the Zambesi River, which runs through Zambia and Mozambique, and the Okavango, which rises in Angola and forms a huge wetland in Botswana.

Lechwes spend long periods wading through water, eating the lush grass that grows there. A grazing animal living in water must face a series of challenges not seen on dry land. For example, the normal fast-running gait of antelopes that allows them to escape from predators is not very efficient in water because the fur on their legs become waterlogged, slowing the antelopes down. The hairs on a lechwe's lower leg, by contrast, are waterproofed with oils to prevent this from happening. Lechwes also run in giant bounds rather than gallops. Overall this method is slower than running on land, but no other antelope can beat a lechwe through water.

Lechwes often feed while up to their chests in water. To help them walk through mud and across river beds, these antelopes have long hooves that spread the weight and prevent them from sinking into soft ground.

Nile lechwe (*Kobus megaceros*): 1.4–1.7m (4.5–5.5ft); 60–120kg (132.25–264.5lb)
Nile lechwes live in the marshlands of southern Sudan and western Ethiopia. Their wetland habitats are fed by water from the White and Blue Niles. Nile lechwes are smaller than their southern cousins. There is also a more obvious difference between the males and females: as well as lacking horns, the females have pale brown coats, while males are a blackish-brown.

Puku (*Kobus vardonii*): 1.5–1.7m (5–5.5ft); 62–74kg (136.75–163lb)
The puku closely resembles the lechwe and kob. Like these antelopes this species lives in rivers and wetlands. It is found in the savannahs south of the Congo rainforest. Pukus are not at high risk of becoming extinct, although they have had problems in the past in some of their range. For example, in the 1930s the entire puku population of Malawi was wiped out by hunting and wetland drainage. Today, pukus have been reintroduced to this area but are reliant on reservations and conservation measures for their survival.

Mountain reedbuck (*Redunca fulvorufula*): 1.1–1.4m (3.5–4.5ft); 30kg (66lb)
There are three populations of mountain reedbuck: a southern group lives in the Cape Province of South Africa; another is located in the highlands of East Africa, from Tanzania to Ethiopia; and the third lives in Cameroon. Each population consists of a separate subspecies. Mountain reedbucks are the smallest of all reedbucks, but, like their relatives, they live in alpine meadows or woodlands close to streams.

Southern reedbuck

Redunca arundinum

Southern reedbucks range from the southern fringe of the Congo Basin to northern South Africa. They are found close to water and spend most of their time hidden in thick cover. Reedbucks feed mainly at night. They are grazers and eat mainly grass and sedges.

They are solitary during dry periods, but when the rains come they gather into small family groups. Individuals communicate using whistles to greet and warn other herd members. The whistle is made by sharp exhalations through the reedbuck's nostrils.

The whistling sounds are also used during courtship. At this time the females also perform a dance that involves a series of pronks, or high, floating jumps. The jumps serve to spread the scent of glands located between her hind legs. The scent is released with a pop. After mating, the male defends the female from other males. Once the calf arrives, the male's role comes to an end, although he may return to the family once the calf is several months old.

Female southern reedbucks do not have horns and are slightly smaller than the males, though both sexes are slender.

Distribution: Southern Africa.
Habitat: Marshy areas and river banks.
Food: Grasses.
Size: 1.5m (5ft); 58kg (127.75lb).
Maturity: 2–3 years.
Breeding: Breeding peaks in summer.
Life span: 12 years.
Status: Lower risk.

Common rhebok

Pelea capreolus

Rheboks are relatives of the wetland antelopes, such as the kob, waterbuck and lechwe. However, this species of antelope is unlike its relatives. In fact, with its wild woolly coat and odd-shaped head, it is unlike any other antelope. The rhebok lives in the mountains of South Africa. It occupies rocky alpine meadows and brush-covered areas.

The common rhebok is a browser. Unlike the grazers, which munch on mouthfuls of grass and leaves, this antelope picks the best leaves and buds from bushes and plucks the freshest shoots of grass. The rheboks feed in groups and one individual keeps watch for predators. If danger is near, the lookout animal warns the others in the group with a distinctive coughlike grunt.

Dominant male rheboks defend a harem of females, which typically contains about five females and their young. Most adult males have no harem or territory, however. These individuals are nomadic, and move through the territories of others, keeping watch for an opportunity to depose a dominant bull or sneak a mating with one of his females. During the rut before the autumn mating season, competition between males is fierce. Unusually for antelopes, fights to the death are not uncommon.

Rheboks are often mistaken for mountain goats because they have woolly coats, with hairs that are much longer than any other antelope. Only the males have horns.

Distribution: South Africa.
Habitat: Rocky mountainsides.
Food: Plucks leaves and buds from shrubs and also eats grass.
Size: 1.1–1.25m (3.5–4m); 25kg (55lb).
Maturity: 18 months.
Breeding: Calves born in November.
Life span: 8 years in the wild, although unusually these antelopes do not survive that long in captivity.
Status: Lower risk.

Springbok

Antidorcas marsupialis

Of all the gazelles, this species is perhaps the one most associated with "pronking". These are high and graceful leaps that are inserted at seemingly random intervals as the gazelle runs along. The legs are held straight and stiff during a pronk, with feet together and the head tucked toward the chest. The leaps are thought to be an evasion tactic when the gazelle is being chased by predators. The springbok's chief threats are lions and cheetahs, both of which generally attack from behind and can easily outrun the gazelle over short distances. The leaps make it harder for the predators to judge when to pounce. The antelope's odd posture might add to the hunter's confusion as well as moving the vulnerable hind legs to a less accessible position.

Springboks used to move, or trek, in herds of hundreds of thousands, possibly millions, across the grasslands of southern Africa. Treks of anything approaching this magnitude are almost unheard of now, although larger herds might form in remote parts of Botswana and Angola. Today, most springboks live in nature reserves. Breeding takes place in the dry season. Male-only herds migrate in search of mates.

Typically of a gazelle, the springbok has long, thin legs and a slender body. Both male and female springboks have horns, which are relatively short and more slender in the female.

Distribution: South-western Africa from northern Angola to Namibia and Cape Province of South Africa.
Habitat: Treeless savannahs often among the tall grass close to dry lake beds.
Food: Grass and other low-growing plants.
Size: 96–115cm (3.25–3.75ft); 33–46kg (72.75–101.5lb).
Maturity: Between 1 and 2 years.
Breeding: Females are pregnant for 5 months. A single calf is born at intervals of 2 years.
Life span: 7 years.
Status: Lower risk.

Dama gazelle

Gazella dama

Distribution: North-western Africa.
Habitat: Semi-desert.
Food: Grasses and leaves.
Size: 1.4–1.7m (4.5–5.5ft); 85kg (187.5lb).
Maturity: 1–2 years.
Breeding: Single calf born in September to November.
Life span: 10 years.
Status: Endangered.

The dama gazelle lives in the dry grasslands around the edge of the Sahara Desert. It is most common in the Sahel region, south of the desert in Mali, Chad and Niger, but it also extends to Mauritania and Sudan. This species is on the brink of extinction because it is a valuable source of meat in a region where food is scarce at the best of times. The gazelle's range has also been reduced by the encroaching desert.

Dama gazelles live in small herds of about 15 individuals comprising a more or less equal mix of the sexes. The gazelles are active during the day. When the rains come and pastures spring up along the edge of the desert, the gazelles migrate north. In the dry season the herds move south in search of food.

Female dama gazelles gestate for more than six months, which is a long time, even for a large gazelle of this kind. The calf is born highly developed, and within a week it is able to run as fast as the adults.

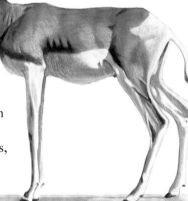

The dama gazelle is the largest gazelle of all. Even for a gazelle it has exceptionally long legs and a long neck. The S-shaped horns are short and thicker in the males. The red-coloured coat is darkest in western individuals.

Royal antelope (*Neotragus pygmaeus*): 50cm (19.75in); 2kg (4.5lb)
This is one of the smallest hoofed animals in the world, and is often found in forest clearings in parts of West Africa. It is well camouflaged, but will make huge bounds if spotted by predators, reportedly achieving leaps of up to 2.8m (9.25ft).

Thomson's gazelle (*Gazella thomsoni*): 0.8–1.7m (2.5–5.5ft); 12–85kg (26.5–187.5lb)
These attractive gazelles are found in the dry habitats of Sudan, Kenya and Tanzania. They have brown coats with a dark line running from the foreleg to the rump. This distinctive feature is not seen in other gazelles and may serve as a visual signal to help members of herds stay close together while moving at high speeds. Like several other antelopes, Thomson's gazelles have a behaviour called "stotting". When they spot predators stalking them, they make a series of curious jumps. This behaviour signals to the predators that they have been spotted and should not try to chase the obviously agile gazelles.

Dwarf antelope (*Neotragus batesi*): 50–57cm (20–22.5in); 2–3kg (4.5–6.5lb)
Also known as the pygmy antelope, this species lives in lowland tropical forests from southern Nigeria to Uganda. They are also common residents in orchards and plantations. Only male dwarf antelopes have horns. These are short and straight and project backward in line with the face. Dwarf antelopes are nocturnal and live on leaves, buds and fruits. Males defend an area of forest and attract groups of females into it during the mating season at the start of the rains.

Gerenuk

Litocranius walleri

The gerenuk is known for its unusual feeding behaviour. While other browsers are restricted to leaves growing at the bottom of a shrub, which are generally old and tough, the gerenuk can reach the young and tender leaves growing higher up. When the leaves are out of reach of even its long neck, the gazelle rears up on to its hind legs to reach that little bit higher.

Gerenuks are an East African species. They are now dependent on conservation for their survival and few live outside the reserves of Kenya and Tanzania.

Their unusual feeding habits have an impact on the gerenuk's social structure. Males are highly territorial and defend an area containing as many suitable feeding bushes as possible. Females band together and move through the males' territories. When a receptive female meets a male, she initiates courtship. Female calves are weaned for just one year, allowing the mother to give birth again the following year. However, bull calves are suckled for 18 months, presumably to help them grow to a dominant size.

Distribution: East Africa
Habitat: Grasslands with plenty of shrubs.
Food: Leaves.
Size: 1.4–1.6m (4.5–5.25ft); 43.5kg (96lb).
Maturity: 2 years.
Breeding: 1–2 calves born every 1–2 years.
Life span: 12 years.
Status: Lower risk.

The gerenuk's most distinctive feature is its exceptionally long neck, which allows it to reach the leaves of tall bushes. Females do not have horns.

Kirk's dik-dik

Madoqua kirkii

Kirk's dik-dik is a dwarf antelope. It lives in dry brushlands, where there are thick bushes to provide food and cover, seldom venturing out into open country. The species ranges across eastern Africa from southern Somalia to central Tanzania. From there its distribution extends into south-western Africa as far down as northern Namibia. For much of the year, the only moisture dik-diks get is the dew droplets on their plant food.

Dik-diks form breeding pairs that stay together for life. A male defends a large territory, which he shares with a single female. The pair produce young every six months or so. Most calves are born between November and December and then again between April and May. Breeding pairs mark their territory using their faeces. This is done in a ritualized manner, in which the male mixes his droppings and urine into his mate's so that their individual scents form a single odour for the pair.

These antelopes are shy, nocturnal creatures. They are easily spooked and will escape from danger by running in a confusing zigzag path, making a series of leaps as they do so. As it runs the antelope produces a "dik-dik" call, hence its common name.

Distribution: From the Horn of Africa across eastern Africa to northern Namibia in south-western Africa.
Habitat: Dry areas of brushland.
Food: Leaves, herbs and grasses.
Size: 52–67cm (20.5–26.5in); 3–6kg (6.5–13.25lb).
Maturity: Between 6 and 12 months.
Breeding: Single calves born twice a year.
Life span: 13 years.
Status: Common.

The most distinguishing feature of these little antelopes is the long, almost pointed, snout. This elongated snout is a mechanism for keeping cool, in that heat is lost through evaporation from the large, damp nasal membrane.

Klipspringer

Oreotragus oreotragus

Klipspringers are agile little antelopes that live on or around rocky outcrops in dry parts of eastern and southern Africa. They are commonly seen on cliffs and in rocky highland areas. However, the fragmented nature of their habitat means that they live in relatively small populations.

The name klipspringer means "rock jumper" in Afrikaans. The antelopes are well suited to life in steep habitats. Most antelopes have long, extended legs to allow them to run quickly across the open savannah. However, klipspringers' legs are short and robust compared to other antelopes, which makes them more sure-footed and able to withstand jumps on to hard surfaces.

The klipspringer's hair is unique among the antelopes and other bovine animals because it is hollow and only loosely connected to the skin. This makes it much more similar to the hair of deer and the unusual pronghorns of North America.

Klipspringers live in monogamous pairs, which defend a territory together, using their droppings and scent marks from a gland on their faces to advertise their claim to the land. The couple are seldom far from each other. Each year they produce a single calf after a gestation (pregnancy) of about five months. Only half the calves survive their first year.

Distribution: Eastern and southern Africa from southern Sudan and Ethiopia to Namibia and most of South Africa.
Habitat: Rocky terrain in dry areas.
Food: Leaves and fruits.
Size: 75–90cm (2.5–3ft); 10–15kg (22–33lb).
Maturity: 1 year. The young are forced out of their parent's territory at the age of 7 months.
Breeding: A single calf born each year. Twins are produced on rare occasions.
Life span: 14 years.
Status: Lower risk.

Male klipspringers have horns, which are short and spike-like. However, the females are slightly larger.

Oribi

Ourebia oureb

Distribution: Central and southern Africa.
Habitat: Grassland.
Food: Grass and leaves.
Size: 92–110cm (3–3.5ft); 12–24kg (26.5–53lb).
Maturity: 1 year.
Breeding: Most calves born in October or November.
Life span: 13 years.
Status: Lower risk.

Oribis are widespread antelopes, but despite their large distribution their populations are highly fragmented. The species is found in most parts of Africa south of the Sahara Desert except for the equatorial rainforests. Oribis live in flat areas of grasslands with a few bushes to provide food and cover. Today oribis are unlikely to survive in large numbers outside nature reserves.

The oribi is grouped in the dwarf antelope tribe. Along with its relatives, this species forms monogamous pairs, where a male and a female will mate for life. Occasionally, several individuals, including any young, gather into small herds. Females are smaller than males and achieve adult size as early as 10 months old. Males will take a few months longer to mature. Pairs mark their territories together, but the males have the dominant role. They rub secretions from the prominent preorbital gland on to landmarks such as tree trunks or stands of tall grass.

Oribis have large preorbital glands (modified tear ducts that produce scented liquids). The black glands form a teardrop-shaped mark below each eye. These antelopes also have tufts of long hair on their knees.

Salt's dik-dik (*Madoqua saltiana*): 52–67cm (20.5–26.25in); 4.25kg (9.25lb)
This dik-dik species lives in the dry mountains and stony semi-deserts of the Horn of Africa. They are the smallest of all dik-dik species. Like other dik-diks, this species forms lifelong breeding pairs. Each pair produces young twice a year, generally a single calf each time. As their name suggests, this species is also known for its "dik-dik" alarm call. At times of stress, the hairs on its forehead become erect.

Dibatag (*Ammodorcas clarkei*): 1.5–1.7m (5–5.5ft); 22–35kg (48.5–77.25lb)
Dibatags are beautiful antelopes that live in savannah habitats in Ethiopia and Somalia. They have very long, slender necks, which are used to reach the leaves on high branches. The antelopes have a long furry black tail, which is raised when they run. Their name comes from the Somali word for "erect tail". This species is now under threat of extinction due to poaching and war in the region.

Cape grysbok (*Raphicerus melanotis*): 61–75cm (2–2.5ft); 8–23kg (17.75–50.75lb)
The Cape grysbok is a rare antelope that lives only in the southern region of South Africa. It is similar in height to steenboks and other dwarf antelopes, but is considerably more stocky in build. Adults have reddish-brown fur, which helps them to blend into their woodland habitat. Grysboks are nocturnal. When they sense danger approaching, they lie down. If this tactic fails, the grysbok flees in the zigzag gallop that is typical of small antelopes.

Steenbok

Raphicerus campestris

Steenboks live in two distinct populations, one in East Africa and the other in the south of the continent. Steenboks are strictly grassland antelopes and never enter woodland areas. Between the great savannahs of East Africa and the velds (another name for grasslands) of southern Africa grows a belt of woodland. This woodland divides the steenbok population in two, and communication between the groups is extremely limited.

Steenboks live alone or in breeding pairs. The antelopes occupy a small territory, which they mark with piles of dung and enforce by chasing away intruders. Unlike most antelopes, the steenbok does not use scented secretions from glands on the face to mark their territory.

Breeding takes place all year round but most calves are born in the summer. They are weaned by 3 months and live independently by the end of their first year.

Distribution: South and East Africa.
Habitat: Grasslands with cover.
Food: Grasses and roots.
Size: 70–95cm (2.25–3ft); 7–16kg (15.5–35.25lb).
Maturity: 1 year.
Breeding: Calves born throughout year.
Life span: 12 years.
Status: Common.

Steenboks are small antelopes. Only the males have horns, which protrude directly up from the head. The steenboks have sharp hooves for digging roots and other foods out of the ground.

European bison

Bison bonasus

These large animals are now very rare, but, like their close relatives the American bison, they used to be very abundant. European bison disappeared from western Europe in the late Middle Ages, and became extinct in eastern Germany in the 18th century. The main reason for this decline was the loss of their habitat and an increase in hunting as human populations rose across northern Europe. By the early 20th century, European bison could only be found in Poland, and by 1925 both populations were extinct. Since then, new populations have been established in these places from captive European bison in zoos. In former times, European bison formed groups of hundreds of animals during migrations or in good feeding grounds. Nowadays groups are much smaller, consisting of a few related females and their young. During the mating season there is fierce competition over females, and males charge and clash heads.

European bison have less shaggy manes than those of American bison, but they have more powerfully built hindquarters.

Distribution: Originally found over large parts of Europe including England, but now restricted to eastern Europe.
Habitat: Forest and grasslands.
Food: Leaves, twigs, bark and grass.
Size: 2.1–3.5m (7–11.5ft); 350–1,000kg (770–2,200lb).
Maturity: 2–4 years.
Breeding: Single calf born every 1–2 years.
Life span: Up to around 20 years in the wild, and 40 years in captivity.
Status: Endangered.

African buffalo

Syncerus caffer

African buffaloes are formidable animals. They can be very aggressive, and have been known to inflict fatal injuries on lions. Accordingly, lions tend to be reluctant to tackle these large buffalo unless they are very hungry. African buffaloes form herds of between 50 and 500 individuals. These herds are most common in dry habitats, such as grasslands and woodland, and less so in dense rainforests.

Herds contain cows that are closely related to each other. Calves less than two years old stay with their mothers. Young bulls leave the herd after two years and join smaller, single-sexed, bachelor herds. There is a hierarchy of dominance within the bachelor herd, with rigorous competition for the top spots. This competition reaches its peak as the rainy season arrives, when the bulls join the main herd and compete for the cows. Cows take their time to select a mate, waiting to attract as high-ranking an individual as possible. Highly ranked bulls tend to be large and aggressive and will therefore produce large male offspring, which will grow up to become successful breeders themselves. In addition, any female offspring will also prefer to breed with large males.

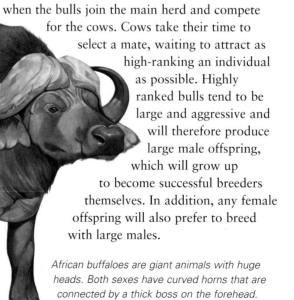

African buffaloes are giant animals with huge heads. Both sexes have curved horns that are connected by a thick boss on the forehead. This boss is most developed in the males to protect the head during fights.

Distribution: South of the Sahara Desert. Most common in eastern and southern Africa although they are found as far north as Sudan and west to Guinea.
Habitat: Grasslands and woodlands.
Food: Grasses and other low-growing plants.
Size: 2.1–3.4m (7–11.25ft); 300–900kg (660–1,985lb).
Maturity: Females able to produce young at 5 years; males start to breed at 8.
Breeding: Single calves born in rainy season after a gestation of about 11 months. Twins are very rare. Females typically produce young every two years.
Life span: 15 years.
Status: Lower risk.

Giant eland (*Taurotragus derbianus*): 2.1–3.4m (7–11.25ft); 330–1,000kg (730–2,200lb)

The giant eland is the largest antelope of all. They are woodland animals, while the slightly smaller common elands are associated with grasslands. They range from Senegal to southern Sudan. As a member of the spiral-horned antelopes this species is more closely related to cattle than the smaller grazing antelopes. Elands resemble cattle in many ways and as a result they are often hunted for their meat. Giant elands are now an endangered species because of this. Young and female giant elands have reddish coats, but this fades to grey in adult males. Both sexes grow horns, but the males' are twice the size of the females'. Giant elands live in small groups of about 25 individuals.

Mountain nyala (*Tragelaphus buxtoni*): 2.25m (7.5ft); 225kg (496lb)

Mountain nyalas are an endangered species. They live in the highlands of Ethiopia. During the intense rains that affect the region, the antelopes move to lower altitudes. Mountain nyalas are slightly larger than their lowland cousins. Both sexes have a grey coat, which grows shaggy during the winter.

Common eland

Taurotragus oryx

This is one of two species of eland, both of which occupy similar types of open savannah habitat. The eland is the largest of a number of related species, characterized by spiralling horns and vertical cream-coloured stripes along the flanks and haunches.

Elands occupy large home ranges, using different habitats at different times of the year, and can cover in excess of 220sq km (86sq miles) per year. Approximately 14,000 eland live in the Serengeti National Park in East Africa, where they form small herds, usually consisting of less than 25 animals.

Like many hoofed animals, eland males fight for dominance and the opportunity to mate with females. Competing males shove each other with locked horns, until one gives up and retreats. Elands are easily tamed and, due to their highly nutritious milk, tender meat and good-quality hides, people are trying to domesticate them on farms in Africa and Russia.

Male elands tend to be larger than females, but both sexes carry characteristic spiralling horns, which may be up to 1m (3.25ft) long.

Distribution: Southern and eastern Africa.
Habitat: Savannah and open woodland.
Food: Leaves and fruit.
Size: 1.8–3.4m (6–11.25ft); 400–1,000kg (880–2,200lb).
Maturity: Males 4 years; females 3 years.
Breeding: Single calf born.
Life span: 23 years.
Status: Conservation-dependent.

Nyala

Tragelaphus angasii

Distribution: South-eastern Africa.
Habitat: Damp areas of thick grasses.
Food: Leaves and grasses.
Size: 1.8–2.1m (6–7ft); 55–126kg (121–278lb).
Maturity: 2–4 years.
Breeding: Breeding peaks in spring and autumn.
Life span: 15 years.
Status: Lower risk.

Nyalas are seldom far from water in habitats where there are stands of thick grass and other cover. Nyalas are spiral-horned antelopes, and are therefore more closely related to cattle and bison than the grazing antelopes and gazelles.

They are nocturnal browsers, eating fresh leaves and buds. They resort to eating grasses and other low-quality foods only during dry periods. These antelopes live in small herds of about 20 individuals. Females tend to stay in the same herds throughout their lives, while males are more transitory, forming small, temporary, male-only herds that move between groups of females.

Both adult males and females have a crest of hair running along the back. This is often white in the males. During courtship, males raise the crest. This often engenders fighting among the males, and deaths and serious injuries are not uncommon due to the antelope's sharp horns.

There is a marked difference between male and female nyalas: females have the same colouring as the young (a red coat with thin stripes down the flanks) while males are larger and have a grey coat. Only males have horns.

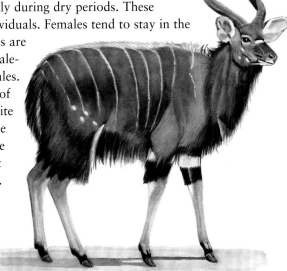

Greater kudu

Tragelaphus strepsiceros

The greater kudu is not the heaviest but it is one of the tallest antelopes, being up to 1.5m (5ft) at the shoulder. They also have the longest horns, at 1.2m (4ft), of any spiral-horned antelope. The sable and oryxes are the only antelopes to have longer horns.

Greater kudus live in southern and eastern Africa, being most common in the south of their range. They occupy a range of habitats that contain plenty of shrubs and areas of cover. During rainy periods the antelopes spend more time in woodlands while in droughts they migrate to river banks.

Members of the southern population of kudus are darker than those in the north. They are blue-grey, while northern kudus are more reddish. In common with their close relatives the nyalas, the males darken as they age.

The sexes are segregated. Adult males live in small herds of about five individuals, while a few adult females form their own herd, which also includes their offspring. The calves stay with their mothers until the age of about three.

The two types of herds occupy neighbouring territories and come together only during the breeding season. This takes place during the second half of the rainy season, which arrives between February and June. Males will mate with as many females as they can. Females give birth about eight months later.

Distribution: Southern and eastern Africa. The largest population live in Namibia and the Cape of South Africa. The eastern population is much more fragmented.
Habitat: Woodlands and areas of shrubs.
Food: Leaves, fruits, herbs and grasses.
Size: 1.9–2.5m (6.25–8.25ft); 120–315kg (264–694lb).
Maturity: 3 years. Males leave the herd after first year.
Breeding: Mating takes place at end of rainy season.
Life span: 20 years.
Status: Lower risk.

Bushbuck

Tragelaphus scriptus

Only male bushbucks have horns, which usually spiral once and are otherwise straight and parallel to one another. Females are a paler brown than the males.

Bushbucks live across Central Africa south of the Sahara Desert to the north of the Kalahari Desert. They are not found in the rainforest of the Congo but live in most other open habitats that have enough cover. They are browsers, picking leaves and fruits from bushes rather than eating grasses. They spend the day hidden among the woodlands and thickets that grow along river banks, but by night they emerge into more open areas to feed.

Bushbucks give birth at all times of year, although in drier areas they tend to wait until the rainy season. In wetter areas, there is enough food available for females to give birth two times each year. Newborn calves cannot outrun predators and so their mothers keep them hidden in the bushes for up to four months. The young calves have no distinctive odour to attract hunters, and their mothers move them to new hiding places regularly.

Unusually for antelopes, bushbucks are solitary creatures. They do not defend a territory and rarely get into disputes. In places with plenty of food, there may be several individuals living close together, though there is little social interaction.

Distribution: Central Africa as far south as northern Botswana. Not found in the Congo Basin.
Habitat: Woodlands and shrublands.
Food: Leaves, twigs and flowers.
Size: 1.2–1.5m (4–5ft); 24–75kg (53–165lb).
Maturity: 1–3 years.
Breeding: Calves born all year round but most commonly during rainy season. The gestation period is about 180 days.
Life span: 20 years.
Status: Common.

Bongo

Tragelaphus eurycerus

Distribution: West Africa, the Congo, northern Kenya and southern Sudan.
Habitat: Lowland tropical rainforests.
Food: Browses on leaves, fruits and flowers.
Size: 1.7–2.5m (5.5–8.25ft); 150–220kg (331–485lb).
Maturity: Between 1 and 3 years.
Breeding: Single calves born all year round. Twins are seen but only rarely. The gestation period is about 9 months.
Life span: 20 years.
Status: Lower risk, although at increasing risk of poaching.

Bongos are forest antelopes. They have shorter legs than other antelopes, which is a typical body form of forest herbivores. (Long legs are used for running quickly and this is not possible in dense jungle, whereas shorter legs make the bongos more sure-footed.) Bongos also have distinctive white markings on the legs and above the eyes. These may act as visual signals so that the antelopes can see each other among the dense foliage.

Most bongos live in lowland rainforest, although small populations also live in the highland regions in northern Congo and Kenya. Bongos are both grazers and browsers. They will eat a range of plant foods including leaves, flowers, twigs, thistles and grasses. They have long, flexible tongues, which they use to pluck the freshest leaves. The horns are also used to pull on or break high branches.

Most large forest animals live alone (the lack of space makes it hard for herds to stay together), but bongos do form small herds of around six individuals, containing an equal mix of the sexes.

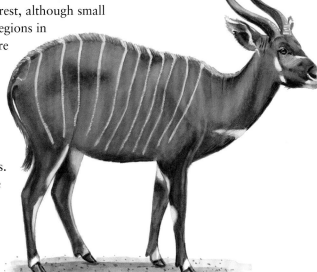

Along with the elands, the bongos are the only spiral-horned antelopes to have horns on both sexes. The horns of females are straighter than those of the males. Females and young are red but adult males are darker.

Sitatunga

Tragelaphus spekii

Distribution: Central Africa from Namibia and Botswana in the south to Gambia in the west and Ethiopia in the east.
Habitat: Swamps and marshes.
Food: Water plants.
Size: 1.1–1.7m (3.5–5.5ft); 50–125kg (110–275lb).
Maturity: Between 1 and 2 years old. Males mature a few months later than the females.
Breeding: Young born throughout year after a gestation of 8 months.
Life span: 20 years.
Status: Lower risk.

The sitatunga lives in swamps and marshy areas of Central Africa. It ranges from the forests of the Gambia to southern Ethiopia and then south to the Okovango Delta in Botswana. It is an excellent swimmer and often moves to deep water to avoid predators. It may submerge completely with just its nostrils emerging above the water, such as when seeking refuge from predators. In shallow water, the antelopes run in bounds, which would be ungainly and slow on land but is the most effective way of moving through, or rather over, water.

Male sitatungas are considerably larger than females. Only the males carry horns. Sitatungas are non-territorial and have only the most basic of social systems. Females form herds, which also contain the young of both sexes. As they approach maturity, males leave their mother's herd and adopt a solitary lifestyle.

Breeding occurs all year around. A male approaches a female and chases her through the water before mating Females produce a single young each year. Young are born in the water and hidden on a dry platform of reeds often surrounded by deep water.

The sitatunga is a semi-aquatic antelope that spends a great deal of time wading through water. Its hooves are elongated and widely splayed, and, like snowshoes, do not sink into soft wet ground.

Chamois

Rupicapra pyrenaica

Distribution: North-western Spain, Pyrenees and central Italy. *R. rupicapra* is more widespread from Europe to the Middle East.
Habitat: Alpine meadows.
Food: Herbs, flowers, lichen, moss and pine shoots.
Size: 0.9–1.3m (3–4.25ft); 24–50kg (53–110lb).
Maturity: 8–9 years.
Breeding: 1–3 young born in spring.
Life span: 22 years.
Status: Endangered.

There are two distinct species of chamois, both found in mountainous areas of Europe. They are both quite similar in appearance and behaviour, but this species – *Rupicapra pyrenaica* – has a more restricted distribution, is rarer than the other, and is now dependent on conservation efforts for its survival.

One of the reasons that chamois are rare is because they were hunted excessively for their meat – considered a delicacy in some regions – and for their hides, which were once made into high-quality leather for polishing glass and cars. Chamois are well adapted to living in mountainous habitats, and are very agile. When they are alarmed, they can bound up steep rocky slopes, and can leap almost 2m (6.5ft) straight up to get to inaccessible rocks.

Chamois live in small herds, usually consisting of females and their young. In autumn, males join the herds to compete for females, fighting each other with their sharp horns. Female herd members will often help one another. If a mother dies, other females will look after the young, and the animals are generally thought to take it in turns to stand guard while the rest of the herd feeds.

Chamois have long, thick fur to keep them warm in alpine conditions. Both males and females possess the distinctively slender, sharp horns, which are shaped like upside-down "J"s.

Barbary sheep

Ammotragus lervia

As their name suggests, barbary sheep originally came from the Barbary Coast – the old name for the Magreb region in north-western Africa. The sheep's local name is "aoudad". Today the species is rare in its homeland but has been introduced to Germany and Italy and has also become feral in the south-western United States. This last region shares many similarities with its natural habitats. In the wild, barbary sheep live on the rocky slopes of the Atlas Mountains as high as the snow line.

Barbary sheep are a desert species. The high mountains may often be cold but they are also very dry, and as a result barbary sheep must be able to survive without drinking for long periods.

Barbary sheep live in flocks with a strict dominance hierarchy. This ranking system runs through both the male and female lines. Even juvenile sheep have a rank, which goes a long way to establishing their future position in adult society. The hierarchy is enforced through frequent violent confrontation, where rivals butt heads and hook horns in twisting wrestling matches.

Most sheep mate between September and November. The gestation period is about 4 months, which means the lambs are born at the start of spring, when their chances of survival are best.

Barbary sheep are sexually dimorphic (the sexes look different). Males weigh up to twice as much as the females. Both sexes have horns, but those of the females are smaller.

Distribution: North-western Africa as far south as Chad and Sudan; introduced to Europe and North America.
Habitat: Deserts, canyons and mountains.
Food: Grasses and leaves.
Size: 1.5m (5ft); 65–145kg (143.25–319.75lb).
Maturity: 18 months to 2 years.
Breeding: Breeding season is in autumn with single lambs, or sometimes twins, born at the start of spring.
Life span: 10 years in the wild, but more in captivity.
Status: Vulnerable in natural range, although doing well in areas where introduced.

Ibex (*Capra ibex*): 1.1–1.7m (3.5–5.5ft); 35–150kg (77–330.75lb)
A relative of the domestic goat, the ibex lives in alpine regions of Europe, parts of the Middle East, north-eastern Africa and some mountainous regions of Asia. The ibex has massive, curved horns that can be over half the length of the animal's body in males. The coat is grey-brown. Older males have a small beard and a "mane" of longer hairs on the back of the neck. It is threatened with extinction in some parts of its range.

Walia ibex (*Capra walie*): 1.5m (5ft); 102kg (225lb)
This species of African goat is often regarded as a subspecies of the more cosmopolitan ibex. It is found only in the mountains of northern Ethiopia, where it lives a precarious existence in the canyons and gorges cut by the torrential rains that fall most years.

Spanish goat (*Capra pyrenaica*): 1.2m (4ft); 57.5kg (127lb)
The Spanish goat, also called an ibex, lives in the Pyrenees. It is darker than other ibexes and more closely related to *Capra aegragrus*, a largely Asian species that is the wild ancestor of domestic goats.

Musk ox

Ovibos moschatus

Although musk oxen look like large hairy cattle or bison, they are in fact relatives of goats and sheep. These animals live on the barren, windswept tundra that exists in the far north within the Arctic Circle. This habitat forms in places that are too cold and dry for trees to grow. It might seem odd that this icy land is too dry for trees, but plants need liquid water to grow, and there is only enough water available to sustain grasses and other hardy plants.

Both sexes have large hooked horns that cover most of the forehead. Male musk oxen are larger than females because they must fight other males to win and defend a harem of females. They butt each other with their horns in shows of strength. During the mating season the bulls produce a strong smell, which is what gives the species its name.

Distribution: Canadian Arctic and Greenland. Re-introduced to Norway and Russia.
Habitat: Tundra.
Food: Grass, moss and sedge.
Size: 1.9–2.3m (6.25–7.5ft); 200–410kg (440–904lb).
Maturity: 2–3 years.
Breeding: 1 or 2 young produced every 1–2 years in spring.
Life span: 18 years.
Status: Common.

The whole of a musk ox's body is covered in long fur except the area between its lips and nostrils. The hairs keep the animal warm but also defend against the huge numbers of biting insects that swarm across the tundra in the short summer.

European mouflon

Ovis musimon

Distribution: Sardinia and Corsica. Herds also introduced to middle Europe.
Habitat: Wooded areas on steep slopes.
Food: Grasses.
Size: 1–1.3m (3.25–4.25ft); 25–55kg (55–121lb).
Maturity: 1 year.
Breeding: Lambs born in autumn.
Life span: 10 years.
Status: Vulnerable.

Sheep were one of the earliest domestic animals. They are now classed as a separate species, *Ovis aries*, although crossbreeding with wild species is still possible. Most of today's domestic sheep are descended from the Asian mouflon, or urial (*Ovis orientalis*), although some breeds have ancestors that were European mouflons. The European mouflon's original wild range was western Asia, but it was introduced to Europe thousands of years ago and now some of the few places where this species lives wild are reserves on the Mediterranean islands of Corsica and Sardinia.

Mouflons live in flocks. In summer the rams stay away from the ewes and young. Fights are rare and flock members seldom wander far from each other. However, this herd instinct may be due to some selective breeding in the past.

Despite being the smallest wild sheep, European mouflons are sturdy animals, with a thickset neck and strong legs. Males are about 30 per cent larger than females. Adults have paler faces than the young and also grow paler with age.

SEALS

The coasts of Europe and Africa are home to pinnipeds – the group of mammals that includes seals, sea lions and walruses. The word pinniped means "fin footed". Unlike other sea mammals, these species are descended from carnivorous, terrestrial ancestors. Like whales and dolphins, pinnipeds have a layer of blubber under their skin, which keeps them warm in cold water.

Mediterranean monk seal

Monachus monachus

Distribution: Less than 20 sites around the Mediterranean and Black Sea and Atlantic coast of Mauritania.
Habitat: Subtropical coastline.
Food: Fish and cephalopods.
Size: 2.3–2.8m (7.5–9.25ft); 250–300kg (550–660lb).
Maturity: 3 years.
Breeding: 1 pup born every other year.
Life span: 24 years.
Status: Critically endangered.

This is the darkest seal of the region, uniformly dark brown except for a white patch on the belly.

The Mediterranean monk seal is possibly Europe's most endangered mammal, with only about 500 animals remaining in small, scattered groups around the Mediterranean and Black Sea. There is also a small isolated population off the Atlantic coast of Mauritania, in West Africa.

Monk seals are very intolerant of disturbance. If a pregnant female is distressed, she will abort her foetus, and mothers may desert their young. The increasing development of the Mediterranean and Black Sea coastlines has meant that there are fewer and fewer secluded spots left for these peaceful animals. They also suffer from hunting pressure and from becoming entangled in fishing nets. Being mammals, all seals have to breathe air; if they get caught in fishing nets and held underwater, they drown before too long.

Females give birth to their young in grottoes and sea caves. Those with underwater entrances are particularly favoured. Youngsters stay with their mothers for about three years, learning how to fish and interact with other seals before seeking their own territories.

Harp seal

Pagophilus groenlandicus

Harp seals are very social animals, congregating in huge numbers to give birth on ice floes in areas along the Arctic coastline. However, their sociality has led ultimately to their decline. The pups have very soft, thick fur, which is much sought after in some parts of the world. When the pups are gathered in large numbers, they are easy for hunters to find and club to death. Extensive hunting by humans reduced the total harp seal population from around ten million individuals to just two million by the early 1980s. However, once their plight was realized, hunting pressure was reduced and the population is now slowly recovering.

It will take a long time for harp seal numbers to reach their previous levels because the seals have a low rate of reproduction. Producing just one pup a year means that the population does not grow very quickly. When hunting, adult seals may dive to depths of 200m (666ft) in search of herring and cod, which make up the bulk of their diet.

Distribution: Arctic Ocean.
Habitat: Open sea for most of the year.
Food: Pelagic crustaceans and fish.
Size: 1.7–1.9m (5.5–6.25ft); 120–130kg (265–285lb).
Maturity: 5 years.
Breeding: 1 pup born every year.
Life span: 16–30 years.
Status: Vulnerable.

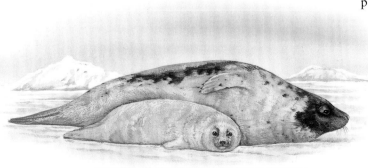

The luxuriant fur of the pups keeps them warm on the Arctic icepack.

Caspian seal (*Pusa caspica*):
1.3–1.5m (4.25–5ft);
55kg (121lb)

The Caspian seal lives in the Caspian Sea on the border of Europe and central Asia. It is one of only two seals to live in landlocked waters. Being a relatively small body of water, the Caspian Sea varies in temperature a great deal throughout the year. This variation impacts on the behaviour of the seals. In winter, when the northern part of the Caspian freezes, the seals live in large colonies on the ice. In summer, however, the ice melts and the seals migrate to the deeper water in the south, which remain cooler. Caspian seals eat fish and crabs. Water pollution has killed much of the seals' food supply as well as making many seals infertile. As a result, Caspian seals are vulnerable. Hunting has also been a problem for the seals. For centuries the people have relied on the seals for oils, skins and meat.

Common seal

Phoca vitulina

One of the two seal species found commonly in British waters, the common seal has a dog-like face. Its snout is much more rounded than the Roman-style nose which typifies the grey seal, Britain's other common seal.

It is difficult to get a good estimate of the common seal's population size because it lives in small, widely distributed groups, and is highly mobile.

Common seals have large, sensitive eyes with specialized retinas, which allow them to see well underwater. However, sometimes the water is too murky for seals to be able to hunt by sight. At these times common seals switch to another sense – touch. Their long whiskers are highly sensitive and allow the seals to feel for prey in the gloom.

Distribution: North Atlantic, Pacific and Arctic coastlines.
Habitat: Sheltered coastal waters.
Food: Fish, cephalopods and crustaceans.
Size: 1.2–2m (4–6.5ft); 45–130kg (99–285lb).
Maturity: Females 2 years; males 5 years.
Breeding: Single pup produced every year.
Life span: 26–32 years.
Status: Common.

From a distance, a seal's head poking above the waves can closely resemble that of a human. They are sometimes mistaken for swimmers in trouble. The common seal is also known as the harbour seal.

South African fur seal

Arctocephalus pusillus pusillus

Distribution: Coastline of southern Africa and Atlantic and Indian Oceans.
Habitat: Breeding colonies form on rocky islands and coastlines.
Food: Fish, squid and crabs.
Size: 1.8–2.3m (6–7.5ft); 120–360kg (264–794lb).
Maturity: 3–6 years.
Breeding: Mating season in October. Gestation lasts just under one year.
Life span: 20 years.
Status: Common.

South African fur seals are a subspecies of the Cape fur seal. Another subspecies, called the Australian fur seal, lives around the coast of southern Australia. The South African fur seal is slightly larger, but the two subgroups are otherwise very similar.

South African fur seals spend most of the year at sea. They rarely venture very far from the land, however, generally staying within 160km (100 miles) of the coast. The fur seals' main foods are free-swimming aquatic animals such as fish and squid. The seals dive to depths of about 40m (130ft) to find food and stay underwater for about 2 minutes. (Their Australian relatives must dive a great deal deeper and for longer to find their food.) South African fur seals also prey on animals living on the bottom of shallow coastal waters, including crabs and other crustaceans.

In spring, the males arrive on rocky islands and coastlines around southern Africa, where they set up territories. A few days later, the pregnant female seals arrive at the shore and choose a place on the beach to give birth. About a week after the calves are born, the males mate with the females in their territory. The products of these matings are born the following year.

Male South African fur seals are twice the size of the females. They are also grey-black in colour, while the females are browner. Males also have a thick mane that helps their necks to look larger and more powerful and also acts as protection during fights.

Grey seal

Halichoerus grypus

Grey seals live across the North Atlantic. As well as on the coast of Canada's maritime provinces, the grey seal is found from Iceland to the coast of northern Europe and in the Baltic Sea. A few colonies even exist as far south as northern Spain and Portugal.

Like most pinnipeds (the group of carnivores made up of seals, sea lions and the walrus), male grey seals are larger than the females. Despite the size difference, males reach their full adult size at 11 years old, which is four years earlier than the females.

Grey seals eat a range of fish and also a small amount of aquatic molluscs, such as squid, and crabs and other crustaceans. Grey seals hunt in open water but often return to the shore to rest. Breeding takes place on the coastline. Colonies form in early winter on beaches, rocky shores and in caves. Before breeding, the adults eat a great deal because they will fast while on shore. Females give birth on the beach to the pups conceived the year before, while the males fight for control of the mates. Mating takes place after the calves are weaned.

Distribution: Coastlines and islands of northern and western Europe and eastern Canada.
Habitat: Rocky coasts.
Food: Fish.
Size: 1.8–2.2m (6–7.25ft); 150–220kg (330–485lb).
Maturity: 3–6 years.
Breeding: Breeding season in winter. The males return to sea after mating. Calves are suckled by their mothers for 17 days. The mothers then leave calves on the beach. The calves follow after a few days.
Life span: 25 years.
Status: Common.

Both sexes of grey seal are grey, but the males are darker than the females. Females have dark spots on their paler skin, while males have pale spots on their darker bodies.

Bearded seal

Erignathus barbatus

Bearded seals are solitary animals. They live in the shallow water of the Arctic Ocean. They do come on to gravel beaches on islands and the northern coastlines of Eurasia and North America at times. They have even been seen on the coast of Scotland. However, bearded seals prefer areas covered in broken ice. They haul themselves on to the floes for a rest and then dive between the broken ice to feed. They also ram their heads through thin ice to create breathing holes for use while feeding.

Bearded seals find a lot of their food on the sea bed. Their highly sensitive whiskers detect the tiny water currents produced by the movements of their prey, which include crustaceans such as shrimp and crabs, shellfish such as clams and abalone, and fish.

The seals come together in large numbers only during the breeding season. The males sing a warbling song while underwater to attract the pregnant females to their floes. The calves that were conceived the previous years are then born on the ice. Like all seals, the mothers can only spare a few days to suckle their calves and feed them very fatty milk. After the calves are weaned, the females mate with the male in control of the floe. The resulting embryos lie dormant for several weeks before beginning to develop inside the mothers. This ensures that they are ready to be born during the next year's breeding season.

Distribution: Arctic coastlines and ice floes. A few individuals travel as far south as Scotland and Spain.
Habitat: Shallow water covered in thin ice.
Food: Shrimps, crabs, clams and fish.
Size: 2.4m (7.75ft); 288kg (635lb).
Maturity: Females at 3 years; males at 6 years but may take several more years before breeding successfully.
Breeding: Breeding season takes place in summer on beaches and ice floes.
Life span: 25 years.
Status: Common.

Bearded seals are named after the long white whiskers that grow on the snout. For at least part of the year they have very thick blubber, making the body rounded.

Crabeater seal

Lobodon carcinophagus

Distribution: Antarctica and surrounding landmasses including the southern Cape of Africa on rare occasions.
Habitat: Thick pack ice.
Food: Krill.
Size: 2–2.4m (6.5–7.75ft); 200–300kg (440–660lb).
Maturity: 3–4 years but males take many more years to breed successfully.
Breeding: A single pup born in spring after a gestation of 11.5 months.
Life span: Up to 25 year, although the males tend to die younger than the females.
Status: Common.

Crabeater seals are found mainly on the pack ice and barren islands that surround the continental landmass of Antarctica. They are also occasionally found farther north on ocean islands and on the coasts of southern Africa, South America and Australia. Crabeater seals are generally solitary and it is single seals that are spotted along the northern edge of its range. On the Antarctic ice, the seals may gather into large groups during the breeding season.

Despite its name, the crabeater seal never eats crabs. Instead it is a krill eater. It feeds by swimming through a school of krill with its mouth open. It sucks the small animals into its mouth from a distance of about 1m (3.25ft). Crabeater seals also eat small fish, choosing ones that are small enough to swallow whole. They are quite deep divers and get most of their food in the first 30m (100ft) of water.

Crabeater seals are generally solitary creatures but sometimes gather in large herds of more than 1,000 individuals. The largest aggregations occur during the calving and breeding season, which takes place on the pack ice in spring – October in Antarctica. Mating takes place after pups are weaned at the age of three weeks.

The fur of the crabeater seal changes from dark brown to blonde throughout the year. The winter coat is dark when it grows in autumn but becomes paler from then on. The species is also called the white Antarctic seal because of its pale fur.

Walrus

Odobenus rosmarus

Distribution: Coast of Arctic Ocean.
Habitat: Pack ice.
Food: Worms, shellfish and fish.
Size: 2.25–3.5m (7.5–11.5ft); 400–1,700kg (880–3,750lb).
Maturity: Females 6 years; males 10 years.
Breeding: Single young born once per year.
Life span: 40 years.
Status: Vulnerable.

Walruses live among the ice floes of the Arctic Ocean. These huge sea mammals are well known for their long tusks, which they use to stab opponents during fights. Walruses also use their tusks to "haul out", or pull themselves on to floating ice, and sometimes hook themselves to floes so that they can sleep while still in the water.

It was once thought that the tusks were also used to dislodge and dig out prey from the sea bed. However, we now know that walruses use their whiskered snouts to root out prey and blast away sediment with jets of water squirted from the mouth. They tackle shelled prey by holding them in their large lips and sucking out the soft bodies.

Walruses live in large herds, sometimes of many thousands. In winter they feed in areas of thin sea ice, avoiding thick, unbroken ice, which they cannot break through from beneath. In summer, when the ice recedes, they spend more time on land. Mating takes place in the water, and calves are born on the ice 11 months later. The young stay with their mothers for three years.

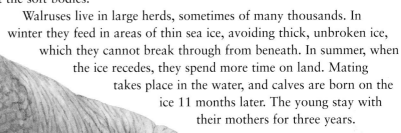

Walruses have long tusks growing out of their upper jaws. The males are twice the size of females and also have longer tusks. Their bodies are reddish-brown and sparsely covered in coarse hairs. Males have two air pouches inside their necks, which they use to amplify their mating calls.

DOLPHINS

The oceans around Europe and Africa are home to many species of dolphins. Dolphins are small members of the mammal order Cetacea, which also includes the whales. Most dolphins live far out in the ocean, but a few species come close to shore. Porpoises generally live in coastal waters, too. They are similar to dolphins, but tend to be smaller and have rounded snouts, rather than long beaks.

Atlantic humpback dolphin

Sousa teuszii

Atlantic humpbacks are shy dolphins, making them a difficult species for scientists to observe and study. Political instability in many West African countries along the coasts of which this dolphin lives has also compounded the problems of studying these animals. They inhabit tropical coastal waters, preferring to stay in shallow water. Typical school sizes range from between three and seven individuals, but groups of up to 25 have been observed. As these dolphins get older, they become more and more solitary, and eventually hardly ever associate with other individuals.

The humpback dolphin has a unique way of surfacing: the beak and head break the surface before the body arches tightly, making the dorsal fin more prominent. Orcas are a major threat to this species. They locate the dolphins by listening in to their calls. By staying close to land, the dolphins are able to disrupt their calls and thwart the killers.

The humpback dolphin gets its name from its distinctive method of surfacing and its slightly bulbous dorsal fin.

Distribution: Eastern Atlantic Ocean off West Africa.
Habitat: Tropical coastal waters, usually less than 20m (65ft) deep, and tidal zones of rivers.
Food: Fish.
Size: 1.2–2.5m (4–8.25ft); 75–150kg (165–330lb).
Maturity: Between 4 and 8 years.
Breeding: Single calf born every 1–2 years.
Life span: Not known.
Status: Declining because of habitat loss and entanglement in fishing nets.

White-beaked dolphin

Lagenorhynchus albirostris

Dolphins are notoriously difficult animals to study because they are small, and also very wide-ranging. Consequently, not much is known about their habits compared to those of most land-living mammals.

Like most cetaceans, white-beaked dolphins live in groups known as schools, which have complex social structures. Schools are usually made up of 2–20 dolphins, but occasionally lots of schools will come together to form large groups containing more than 1,000 individuals.

Dolphins are famed for a behaviour known as breaching, when they leap clear of the water, somersault and splash back down through the waves. Dolphins have also been observed playing games underwater, such as "chase the seaweed". White-beaked dolphins make annual migrations, moving between temperate and subpolar waters, tracking their prey, such as mackerel and herring.

The white-beaked dolphin's counter-shaded coloration helps to camouflage it from both above and below.

Distribution: Ranges widely through the North Atlantic and Arctic Oceans.
Habitat: Coastal waters.
Food: Medium-sized fish, squid and crustaceans form the bulk of the diet.
Size: 2.3–2.8m (7.5–9.25ft); 180kg (396lb).
Maturity: Not known.
Breeding: 1 calf born every year.
Life span: Not known.
Status: Common.

Common dolphin

Delphinus delphis

Distribution: Mediterranean Sea, Atlantic and Pacific Oceans.
Habitat: Ocean waters.
Food: Fish, squid and octopus.
Size: 1.5–2.4m (5–7.75ft); 100–136kg (220–300lb).
Maturity: 12–15 years.
Breeding: Single young born every 2–3 years.
Life span: 35 years.
Status: Common.

This dolphin is also called the short-beaked saddleback dolphin. It is especially common in European waters, including the Mediterranean Sea. The species also swims in the coastal areas of the Atlantic and Pacific Oceans, including along the coasts of the Americas.

Common dolphins are so-called coastal dolphins because they prefer to swim in warmer water near the surface. However, they are still found far out to sea though seldom dive into deep and colder water. They have many small, curved teeth, which are used for snatching small, slippery fish, such as herrings, from the water.

These mammals are one of the smallest dolphins. They live in small family groups called schools. There are reports that many schools sometimes group together, forming clans of up to 100,000 individuals. Most of the time they travel at 8kph (5mph) but can hit speeds of 46kph (29mph).

The common dolphin is one of the smallest dolphin species. They have a distinctive hourglass pattern of pale skin that connects the dark upper skin to the pale lower surface.

Atlantic spotted dolphin (*Stenella frontalis*): 1.6–2.3m (5.25–7.5ft); 90kg (198lb)

Adult members of this species have a spotted pattern. These spots are not present at birth but appear after weaning. This dolphin is found all around the warmer parts of the Atlantic Ocean. The dolphin rarely moves more than 350km (220 miles) from the coast and spends most of its time in shallow water over sand banks. Spotted dolphins are social animals and live in pods that range in size from a few individuals to groups of several thousand. Within large pods, dolphins of different sexes and stages of maturity are often segregated. The dolphins communicate using high-pitched whistles that are within the range of human hearing. Each individual dolphin has a unique call. Spotted dolphins feed on small fish, such as eels and herrings. They often track shoals, swimming above them just below the surface before diving down to attack as a group.

Spinner dolphin (*Stenella longirostris*): 1.8–2.1m (6–7ft); 55–75kg (121–165lb)

Spinner dolphins are oceanic animals. They roam through all the world's oceans, mainly staying in the warmer regions. They seldom come close to land and are only really seen from ships or around remote islands. Spinners track shoals of tuna, swimming at the surface above the fish. Tuna fishermen look out for spinners to lead them to the tuna. As a result, many dolphins get caught and drown in nets meant for the tuna. The spinner dolphins that live nearer to land are slightly different from those found out at sea. Biologists have detected at least four races, which have differently shaped dorsal fins.

Harbour porpoise

Phocoena phocoena

Harbour porpoises are relatively common in European waters and along the coast of North Africa, where they occupy shallow coastal waters. They are also able to withstand fresh water and often travel in the mouths of large rivers.

These porpoises, also known as common porpoises, are social, highly vocal cetaceans. They live in small groups of up to 15 members. They swim more slowly than dolphins and rarely jump out of the water. Instead they rise to the surface to breathe. Some groups migrate long distances, but most occupy a territory.

Harbour porpoises eat fish, such as herrings, sardines and pollack. They also eat squid and shrimp. Like other cetaceans, they use high-pitched clicking sounds to echolocate their prey. Many of the porpoise's prey are also commercially important species, and porpoises are sometimes caught up in fishing nets.

Distribution: Mediterranean Sea, Black Sea, North Atlantic and North Pacific.
Habitat: Shallow seas and coastal waters. Sometimes venture into estuaries.
Food: Fish and squid.
Size: 1.3–1.9m (4.25–6.25ft); 35–90kg (77–198lb).
Maturity: 5 years.
Breeding: Gives birth mainly in summer.
Life span: 20 years.
Status: Vulnerable.

Unlike their dolphin relatives, porpoises have blunt snouts without a beak. They also have fewer teeth, which tend to be less pointed and have a chisel-like biting edge. These teeth are suited to holding on to large struggling fish.

Risso's dolphin

Grampus griseus

Risso's dolphins live in small groups of about ten individuals. The groups move to warm tropical waters in winter and head back toward the poles in summer. The dolphins are often seen leaping out of the water as members of a school play with one another.

Risso's dolphins feed in deep water. They dive down to catch fast-swimming squid and fish. Like other dolphins, they probably use echolocation to locate their prey in the dark depths. They produce clicking noises that bounce off objects in the water. The dolphins can hear each other's clicks and echoes, and groups may work together to track down shoals of fish or squid. In areas where there is plenty of food, dolphin schools congregate, so that thousands of the leaping mammals may be seen together.

Not much is known about the breeding habits of this species. Most births take place in the warmer summer months.

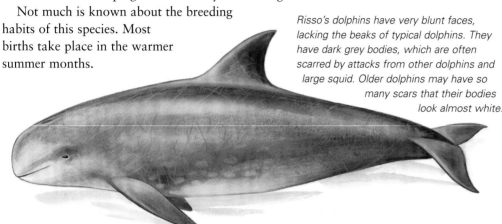

Risso's dolphins have very blunt faces, lacking the beaks of typical dolphins. They have dark grey bodies, which are often scarred by attacks from other dolphins and large squid. Older dolphins may have so many scars that their bodies look almost white.

Distribution: All tropical and temperate seas. Enters the Mediterranean and Red Seas, but is absent from the Black Sea. This species is not common in the South Atlantic.
Habitat: Deep ocean water.
Food: Fish and squid and occasionally octopus.
Size: 3.6–4m (11.75–13ft); 400–450kg (880–990lb).
Maturity: Unknown.
Breeding: Single young born once a year.
Life span: 30 years.
Status: Common.

Heaviside's dolphin

Cephalorhynchus heavisidii

Heaviside's dolphin is a relatively common species that can often be seen from the shore among the waves. However, it is found only off the remote coasts of Angola, Namibia and the Cape Province of South Africa, and therefore is not particularly well understood.

The dolphins swim from just beyond the breakers to about 80km (50 miles) off shore. They prefer water that is less than 180m (590ft) deep. Heaviside's dolphins prey mainly on fish and other animals, such as octopuses and lobsters, that live on or near to the sea floor. The long lower jaw may aid them in scooping prey from the bottom.

They are found mainly in pairs, probably a mother with her calf. Little is known about their reproductive habits, but most births occur in the summer months.

The dolphins often display by tail-flipping. This is a half somersault that ends in a splash with the tail. They are also often seen escorting boats. Heaviside's dolphins are thought to be common in their range, but there are reports that they are increasingly being hunted for their meat and killed by accident by fishing craft.

Heaviside's dolphin is a sturdy, rounded species. Its girth is about two-thirds of the total body length. It has a cone-shaped snout and lacks the beak of other dolphins. The lower jaw sticks out past the upper jaw. The back is is a dark blue with a grey "cape" over the head. A fork-shaped white mark runs along the belly.

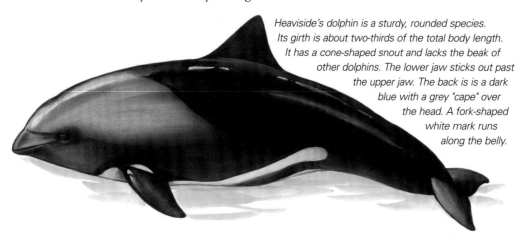

Distribution: South-western Africa.
Habitat: Shallow coastal waters. Often seen in the breaker zone.
Food: Fish and squid and other swimming animals, as well as octopus and other animals that live on the seabed.
Size: 1.7m (5.5ft); 70kg (154lb).
Maturity: Unknown.
Breeding: Young are born in summer and newborns are large, about half the length of adults.
Life span: Unknown.
Status: Common, although increasingly at risk.

Atlantic white-sided dolphin

Lagenorhynchus acutus

Distribution: Along the continental shelf of the British Isles, Norway and other North Atlantic coasts.
Habitat: Cold, open water.
Food: Shrimps and small fish.
Size: 3m (9.75ft); 250kg (550lb).
Maturity: 12 years.
Breeding: 1 calf born every 2–3 years.
Life span: 40 years.
Status: Common.

The Atlantic white-sided dolphin is seldom found near shore. It prefers instead to swim far out to sea in the clear water on the edge of the continental shelf, where the sea floor plunges to the great depths of the mid-ocean. It can dive to about 270m (885ft) and generally hunts at about 40m (130ft) below the surface. Down there it uses its long snout and many small teeth to snatch prey from the water. It targets shoaling prey, such as herrings, shrimps and even certain squid. The dolphin plunges into the shoal, snapping up food as it passes through.

Like many oceanic dolphins, this species is social and lives in family groups of about six individuals, although larger clans of more than a thousands dolphins do form. This species is nomadic (it has no distinct migration routes); instead the dolphins travel throughout their range in search of food.

Female Atlantic white-sided dolphins are considerably smaller than the males, weighing just 180kg (400lb). The dolphin's back is dark grey or black. This becomes paler on the sides and is white or cream on the underside. This coloration makes the animal hard to spot from both above and below.

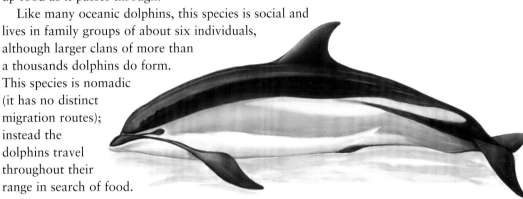

Long-finned pilot whale
(*Globicephala melas*): 5–6m (16.5–19.75ft); 3,000kg (6,600lb)
Grouped as one of the dolphins, this whale has a black body with a white belly. They do not have a beak but have a rather rounded head instead. This feature earns this species the alternative name of pothead whale. The heads of older males are especially bulbous. Long-finned pilot whales are found in cooler waters around the world. For example, they are common in European waters.

Cuvier's beaked whale
(*Ziphius cavirostris*): 6–7m (19.75–23ft); 3,000kg (6,600lb)
This species of whale lives in warmer waters. They stay in areas where the water is more than 10°C (50°F). They also prefer deep water and eat squid and fish. However, they are sometimes seen on African coasts. Males are smaller than females. The whales usually travel in small groups.

Bottlenosed dolphin

Tursiops truncatus

This is one of the most common and familiar dolphin species. It is found worldwide including along the Atlantic coasts of Africa and Europe.

Bottlenosed dolphins live in shallow water close to land and they are generally spotted breaking clear of the water in large bays. They often enter lagoons and the mouths of large rivers. They do not appear to migrate; instead they make a lifelong journey that may take them to all parts of the world. Since they prefer warmer waters, they tend to move between the Atlantic and Pacific Oceans around the Cape of Good Hope and via the Indian Ocean.

Bottlenosed dolphins travel at about 20kmh (12mph) and are rarely seen travelling alone. They hunt as a team, corralling shoals of fish and shrimp by circling around them and taking it in turns to dive through the shoal, snatching mouthfuls of food. They often follow fishing boats, snapping up the by-catch discarded over the side.

Distribution: Tropical and temperate coastal waters worldwide.
Habitat: Warm shallow water.
Food: Fish.
Size: 1.75–4m (5.75–13ft); 150–200 kg (330–440lb).
Maturity: 5–12 years.
Breeding: Single calf born every 2–3 years.
Life span: 40 years.
Status: Unknown.

This is the largest of the beaked dolphins, so called because of their short snouts, which are common in oceanic dolphins. River dolphins tend to have longer, slender snouts, while pilot whales and porpoises have no snout at all.

TOOTHED WHALES

Within the Cetacea order (which includes whales, dolphins and porpoises), there are 23 species of toothed whale. These cetaceans are hunting whales, and they include the world's largest predator, the sperm whale. Toothed whales live in family groups called pods. They hunt for food using echolocation – a sonar system that is focused through a fatty mass called the melon, which is located at the front of the head.

Narwhal

Monodon monoceros

Distribution: Parts of the Arctic Ocean near Greenland and the Barents Sea. Their range is patchy.
Habitat: Coastal Arctic waters.
Food: Cuttlefish, fish, crustaceans and squid.
Size: 4–5.5m (13–18ft); 800–1,600kg (1,760–3,520lb).
Maturity: Females 5–8 years; males 11–13 years.
Breeding: Single calf born every 2–3 years.
Life span: 50 years.
Status: Common.

Some people believe that the bizarre appearance of the narwhal first gave rise to the legend of the unicorn. The function of the male's long tusk is not properly known, but it may function as a hunting implement, or as a tool to break up ice and allow access to the air, so that the animals can breathe. However, the most favoured explanation is that the males joust with each other, fighting over access to females during the breeding season.

The narwhal's swollen forehead is known as its melon, a feature shared with other toothed whales, such as dolphins. The melon serves to focus the ultrasonic clicks that narwhals use, like other small cetaceans, to navigate and find their food. As in a sophisticated sonar system, narwhals listen as the high-frequency sounds they make rebound off objects nearby. So sensitive is this method of orientation that narwhals are able to tell not only what is food and what is not, but also how big, how distant and how quickly a potential prey item is moving.

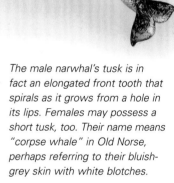

The male narwhal's tusk is in fact an elongated front tooth that spirals as it grows from a hole in its lips. Females may possess a short tusk, too. Their name means "corpse whale" in Old Norse, perhaps referring to their bluish-grey skin with white blotches.

Beluga

Delphinapterus leucas

Beluga means "white" in Russian, so these whales are sometimes called white whales. However, they should not be confused with white sturgeon – large fish that produce beluga caviar. Belugas also have a nickname of sea canaries because they call to each other with high-pitched trills.

Belugas live in the far north, where days are very short for much of the year. Some beluga pods spend all their time in one area of ocean while others are always on the move. The pods are ruled by large males, and all pods spend their winters away from areas of thick ice, which may mean being farther or nearer to land depending on where they are. In summer, they enter river estuaries and shallow bays, navigating with the sonar system. Calves are born in late summer, and their mothers will mate again in early summer a year or two later.

Distribution: Arctic Ocean, Scandinavia and Siberia.
Habitat: Deep coastal waters and mouths of large rivers.
Food: Fish, squid, octopuses, crabs and snails.
Size: 3.4–4.6m (11.25–15ft); 1.3–1.5 tonnes (2,850–3,300lb).
Maturity: Females 5 years; males 8 years.
Breeding: Single calf born every 2–3 years.
Life span: 25 years.
Status: Vulnerable.

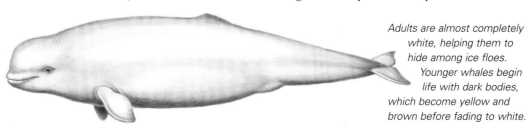

Adults are almost completely white, helping them to hide among ice floes. Younger whales begin life with dark bodies, which become yellow and brown before fading to white.

Orca

Orcinus orca

Distribution: Throughout the world's oceans.
Habitat: Most common in coastal waters.
Food: Seals, other dolphins, fish, squid, penguins and crustaceans.
Size: 8.5–9.8m (28–32.25ft); 5.5–9 tonnes (12,000–20,000lb).
Maturity: Females 6 years; males 12 years.
Breeding: Single young born generally in autumn every 3–4 years.
Life span: 60–90 years.
Status: Lower risk.

Orcas are also known as killer whales. They are expert hunters, being armed with up to 50 large, pointed teeth, and they catch prey in all areas of the ocean. Although orcas have been detected 1km (0.6 miles) below the surface, they prefer to hunt in shallow coastal waters and often swim into bays and mouths of rivers to snatch food near the shore.

Orcas typically live in pods of five or six individuals. Generally each pod is run by a large male, although larger groups have several adult males. Females and their young may split off into subgroups. Like other toothed whales and dolphins, orcas produce click sounds that are used for echolocation. The whales also communicate with each other using high-pitched screams and whistles. Orcas have several hunting techniques. They break pack ice from beneath, knocking their prey into the water, or they may rush into shallow water to grab prey from the shore. It is reported that they may crash on to the shore to drive prey into the surf, where other members of the pod pick them off. Orcas breed throughout the year, although most mate in the early summer and give birth in the autumn of the following year. Each pod has a single male, which mates with all the adult females.

Orcas have black upper bodies and white undersides. They also have grey patches behind their dorsal fins and white patches along their sides and above the eyes. These "whales" are really one of the largest members of the dolphin family.

False killer whale
(*Pseudorca crassidens*): 3.7–5.5m (12.25–18ft); 1.2–2 tonnes (2,650–4,400lb) Like its namesake the killer whale, the false killer whale is actually a member of the dolphin family. This is a wide-ranging species, which travels throughout the world's oceans. The false killer whale is able to reach speeds of up to 30 knots (30 nautical mph or 55kph) and is often encountered racing ships. It preys on smaller dolphins.

Southern bottlenose whale
(*Hyperoodon planifrons*): 6.5–7.5m (21.25–24.5ft); 5.4–7.25 tonnes (12,000–16,000lb) This large-toothed whale is found in the Antarctic Ocean and can be seen in the waters off South Africa. (A northern species is seen in the Arctic.) They move in small groups and feed on squid and fish. The whales dive to 1km (3,300ft). They locate food in the dark water by echolocation and also communicate with sound.

Sperm whale

Physeter catodon

The sperm whale is supremely well adapted to life in the deep oceans. These are the largest hunting predators in the world, with teeth up to 20cm (8in) long and the largest brain of any animal, weighing over 9kg (20lb). They prefer areas of ocean with cold upwellings at least 1km (3,300ft) deep where squid – their favourite food – are most abundant.

Sperm whales can dive to incredible depths to hunt, occasionally up to 2.5km (1.5 miles). They are social animals and live in groups of 20–40 females, juveniles and young. Sperm whales have been hunted for their oil since the mid-18th century, and, after serious population declines between the 1950s and 1980s, this species is now protected. In the north, sperm whales mate between January and August. In the south, they mate between July and March.

Distribution: Ranges throughout oceans and seas worldwide.
Habitat: Deep oceans.
Food: Mostly squid, including giant deep-sea squid, but also several species of fish and shark.
Size: 12–20m (39.5–65.5ft); 12–50 tonnes (26,500–110,000lb).
Maturity: Females 7–13 years; males 25 years.
Breeding: 1 calf born every 5–7 years.
Life span: 77 years.
Status: Vulnerable.

The box-like head of the sperm whale contains the spermaceti organ, which is filled with the fine oil that is so valued by whalers. The purpose of this organ is unclear but it may be to do with focusing sounds produced by the whale.

OTHER WHALES

The largest members of the Cetacea order are called baleen whales. There are about a dozen species of baleen whale and many of them pass the coasts of Africa and Europe as they make long migrations between the world's warm and cold waters each year. Instead of teeth, these whales have baleen plates – a thick curtain which hangs down from the upper jaw. This curtain sieves food items from the water.

Humpback whale

Megaptera novaeangliae

Humpbacks spend their summers feeding far from shore, in the cold waters near the poles. They feed by taking in huge mouthfuls of sea water, from which their baleen plates then strain out any fish or krill. Pairs of humpbacks also corral fish by blowing curtains of bubbles around them. The fish will not swim through the bubbles and they crowd together as the whales rush up from beneath with their mouths wide open.

In winter, the whales stop feeding and head to warmer, shallow waters near coasts to concentrate on reproduction. The males sing for days on end to attract receptive females that are not caring for calves that year, and also help rival males to keep away from each other. Pregnant females stay feeding for longer than the other whales, and arrive in the wintering grounds just in time to give birth.

Humpback whales are so called because of their dorsal fins, which may be swelled into humps by deposits of fat. Humpbacks have the longest pectoral (arm) fins of any whale – about a third as long as their bodies. These baleen whales have throat grooves, which expand to enlarge the throat size as the feeding whale gulps water.

Distribution: All oceans.
Habitat: Deep ocean water. They come closer to land to mate and calf.
Food: Small fish, shrimps and krill.
Size: 12.5–15m (41–49.25ft); 30 tonnes (66,000lb).
Maturity: 4–5 years.
Breeding: Single young born every 2–3 years. Mating takes place in winter. Gestation is 11 months.
Life span: 70 years.
Status: Vulnerable.

Bowhead whale

Balaena mysticetus

Bowhead whales, also known as Greenland right whales or Arctic whales, are among the largest animals in the world. They are named after the U-shape of the lower jaw, which is white. The rest of the body is black. The bowhead whale's mouth is the largest of any animal on Earth: it is large enough to swallow a van.

Bowhead whales live in the Arctic Ocean, where they live among ice floes. One of the many amazing things about this giant animal is its immense life span. Ivory and stone harpoon heads from the 19th century have been found in living specimens. Analysis of the whale's eye suggests that this species can live for 200 years, which makes it the longest-living mammal on Earth. However, hunting has made the bowhead one of the most endangered sea mammals. Biologists estimate that the population along the northern European coast is numbered in just the hundreds. Bowheads feed on tiny floating crustaceans, such as krill and copepods. They can eat 1.8 tonnes (4,000lb) in one day.

Distribution: Northern waters.
Habitat: Cold water.
Food: Plankton and krill.
Size: 11–20m (36–65.5ft); 50–60 tonnes (110,000–132,000lb).
Maturity: 20 years.
Breeding: Calves born in spring.
Life span: 200 years.
Status: Critically endangered.

SEA COWS

The sea cows are a small group of sea mammals that are not related to whales or seals. Instead, their closest relatives are elephants and hyraxes. Sea cows are thought to be the source of mermaid myths. Both remaining species of sea cows, the manatees and dugong, are tropical mammals. Steller's sea cow once lived in the Arctic but was hunted to extinction in the 18th century.

Dugong

Dugong dugon

Distribution: Coasts of eastern Africa, and southern Asia.
Habitat: Shallow water.
Food: Sea grass.
Size: 2.4–2.7m (7.75–8.75ft); 230–908kg (500–2,000lb).
Maturity: 9–15 years.
Breeding: 1–2 young born every 3–7 years.
Life span: 70 years.
Status: Vulnerable.

The dugong is a distant relative of the elephant, and is placed in the order Sirenia along with the manatees. Dugongs live in shallow coastal regions where the sea grass on which they feed is abundant. They rarely make long-distance migrations, though in some places they make daily movements from feeding areas to resting sites in deeper water.

Dugongs have unusually shaped mouths, with overhanging upper lips that are used for cropping sea grasses. They can swim at up to 20kph (12.5mph) if pursued.

The young are born underwater after one year's gestation. At first they ride on their mothers' backs, breathing when the females come to the surface. Sharks attack dugongs, but groups of dugongs will gang up on them and ram them with their heads. Orcas (killer whales) have also been known to attack dugongs, but by far their greatest enemy is human beings, who have hunted them extensively for their meat, hides and ivory.

Dugongs have thick, smooth hides, usually dull grey-brown in colour. Unlike the closely related manatees, which have rounded, paddle-shaped tails, dugongs have fluked tails like those of whales and dolphins.

African manatee

Trichechus senegalensis

Distribution: Western Africa.
Habitat: Coastal waters and freshwater river mouths.
Food: Water plants.
Size: 3.7–4.6m (12–15ft); 1.6 tonnes (3,500lb).
Maturity: 3 years.
Breeding: Calves born in late spring and summer.
Life span: 28 years.
Status: Vulnerable.

The African manatee is a plant-eating aquatic mammal. It lives between the mouths of the Senegal River (the border between Mauritania and Senegal) in the north and the Cuanza River in Angola. It occupies shallow coastal water and often swims in the mouths of rivers and swamps.

Manatees are plant eaters and consequently have long guts. Bacteria in the gut break down the tough plant food. Plant food also gradually wears down the teeth. To counter this, the manatees use the same system as their relatives, the elephants. As worn teeth become useless, they are pushed out at the front. New teeth are exposed at the back of the mouth, and gradually move to the front, pushed along by more teeth behind. The supply of teeth is not endless, but it is enough to last for a normal lifetime.

This species is very similar to the West Indian manatee, which lives in the Caribbean and Florida. It has large, flexible lips and thick bristles. Their tails are more rounded than those of the dugongs.

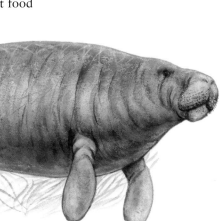

GLOSSARY

Aestivation A period of dormancy during hot and dry weather.

Amphibian One of a group of backboned animals that spend part of their lives on land, part in water, and are dependent on water to breed. Amphibians include frogs, toads, newts, salamanders and caecilians.

Anatomy The study of how bodies are constructed.

Animal A complex organism that collects food from its surroundings.

Arthropod A member of the large group of invertebrate animals, including insects, spiders, crustaceans and centipedes.

Bacterium A microscopic, usually single-celled organism. Many are parasitic and cause disease.

Baleen The horny plates found inside the mouths of some whales, which are used to strain the animal's food.

Biome A large area with a distinctive climate and community of wildlife.

Blubber A layer of fat found under the skin of many aquatic animals that live in cold environments. It provides insulation, helping the animal to retain body heat.

Caecilian A worm-like amphibian.

Camouflage The colour and patterns on an animal's skin that help it to blend in with its surroundings and so hide from predators or prey.

Canine A member of the dog family; or a long, pointed tooth.

Carnassial A type of tooth found in most large members of the Carnivora – the order of mammals that includes lions, dogs and hyenas. The four carnassial teeth are modified molars and premolars located in the middle of the jaw. They slide past each other and slice raw meat with a scissor action.

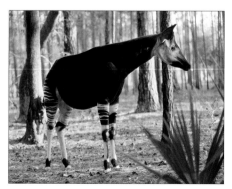

Okapi

Eastern black and white colobus monkey

Carnivore An animal that eats mainly meat, or a member of the group of mammals of the order Carnivora, most of which are carnivorous.

Cartilage A tough, gristly substance found in the skeletons of vertebrates. In fish such as sharks, almost the whole skeleton is composed of cartilage, not bone.

Cell One of the tiny units from which living things are made. Some living things consist of just one cell; others consist of millions of cells.

Circadian A lifestyle with a daily rhythm.

Colony A group of animals that live together and cooperate to find food and rear their young.

Continent A large landmass.

Crepuscular Active at dawn and dusk.

Diurnal Active during the daytime.

DNA A molecule found inside the cells of living organisms, which contains instructions to form the bodies of offspring when the organism reproduces. The instructions take the form of coded sequences called genes. DNA is short for deoxyribonucleic acid.

Drey A squirrel's nest.

Echolocation A technique that allows animals such as bats and dolphins to orientate themselves in darkness or murky water, and locate their prey. The animal emits a stream of high-pitched sounds and listens out for the echoes that bounce back off solid objects.

Egg The female reproductive cell; or the earliest stage of development for reptiles, amphibians and many other animals.

Embryo Any developing young animal in an egg or womb. In mammals, this is the stage before the unborn animal becomes a foetus.

Evolution The process by which living things gradually adapt in order to become better suited to their environment.

Extinction When all the individuals in a species die out, so that none is left.

Family In classification, a family is designated as a subgroup of an order.

Foetus A baby mammal developing in the womb, which is older than an embryo.

Fossil The remains or imprint of a once-living organism that has been preserved in stone.

Fungi A group of organisms that includes mushrooms, toadstools and yeasts.

Gene A section of DNA that carries the coded instructions for a particular trait in a living thing.

Genetics The study of heredity and variation.

Genus The second smallest division in taxonomy.

Gestation The period between mating and birth, during which young mammals develop inside their mother.

Gland A structure on the inside or outside of the body that secretes a chemical substance.

Habitat The external environment in which animals and other organisms live. Deserts and rainforests are examples of habitats.

Herbivore An animal that eats mainly plant matter.

Hibernation A period of dormancy that enables animals such as dormice to survive cold weather. During true hibernation the animal's body temperature, heart rate and breathing slow down, so that it appears to be dead.

Sifakas

Grey squirrel

Incisor One of the sharp chisel-shaped teeth found at the front of some mammals' jaws, which are used to gnaw or nibble food.

Invertebrate An animal without a backbone. Invertebrates make up about 95 per cent of the animal kingdom. This huge supergroup includes insects, crustaceans, molluscs, worms, jellyfish, sponges and starfish.

Kingdom In taxonomy, the initial and largest grouping into which living things are divided. All life on Earth is grouped within five kingdoms: animals, plants, fungi, protists and monerans, which include bacteria.

Larva An immature stage in an animal's lifecycle, e.g. in amphibians the larvae are tadpoles, which occur after hatching and before they become adults. The larvae differ greatly from the adult form.

Malagasy From Madagascar.

Mammal A vertebrate animal with hair on its body, which feeds its young on milk.

Marsupial One of a group of mammals whose young are born early and complete their development in their mother's pouch.

Migration A regular seasonal journey undertaken by an animal or group of animals to avoid adverse weather, to find food or a mate, or to reach a favourable site for raising offspring.

Monotreme One of a small group of unusual mammals that lay eggs instead of giving birth to live young.

Mutation A variation in the genetic code. Mutations occur naturally and may be harmful, beneficial or have no effect.

Natural selection The process by which unsuited organisms are weeded out, leaving only the strongest or most suitable to breed, thereby passing on their genes. Over time, natural selection helps to bring about evolution, resulting in organisms that are best adapted to the environment.

Nocturnal Active at night.

Organ A part of an animal's body with a distinct function, such as the heart, kidney or eye.

Organism A living thing, such as a plant, animal or fungus.

Parasite An animal that lives on or inside another animal, and feeds on its flesh or its food.

Permafrost The permanently frozen ground that lies beneath the topsoil in cold biomes.

Photosynthesis The process by which plants turn carbon dioxide and water into glucose, using the energy in sunlight.

Phylum The second-largest taxonomic division after kingdom.

Placenta A blood-rich organ that develops within the womb of a pregnant female mammal to nourish the unborn young.

Plankton Microscopic plants and animals that float near the surface of oceans and lakes, and provide food for many larger animals. Microscopic plants are known collectively as phytoplankton; microscopic animals are known as zooplankton.

Plant A complex organism that photosynthesizes.

Population The total number of individuals in a species, or the number in a group that is geographically separated from other groups of the same species.

Predator Any animal that catches other animals – its prey – for food.

Protein A complex chemical made up of chains of smaller units and used to construct the bodies of organisms.

Protist A single-celled organism.

Reflex A fast, involuntary muscular movement made in response to an external stimulus such as pain, involving nerve signals but not normally routed through an animal's brain.

Warthog

African buffalo

Reptile One of a group of scaly skinned vertebrate animals most of which breed by laying eggs. Reptiles include lizards, snakes, crocodiles, turtles and tuataras.

Retina The light-sensitive layer at the back of the eye.

Rodent One of a group of mammals with long front teeth called incisors. The group of rodents includes rats and mice.

Salinity Salt content.

Savannah A grassland or open woodland in Africa or Australia.

Scavenger An animal that feeds on decaying organic matter.

Social Living with others of the same kind in a cooperative group.

Solitary Living alone.

Species A particular kind of organism. Members of a species can interbreed to produce more of the same kind.

Spinal cord The main nerve in the body of vertebrates that runs down inside the backbone to link the brain with smaller nerves throughout the body.

Steppe A grassland in Europe or Asia.

Symbiosis A relationship between two different types of living things, from which both organisms benefit.

Taxonomy The scientific discipline of categorizing organisms.

Territory An area which an animal uses for feeding or breeding, and defends against others of its species.

Timberline The zone on a mountain beyond which the climate is too cold for trees to grow.

Toxin A chemical which is poisonous.

Tundra The barren, treeless lowlands of the far north.

Veldt A grassland in southern Africa.

Venom A cocktail of poisons made by a variety of animals to defend themselves or to kill or subdue prey.

Vertebrate An animal with a backbone.

INDEX

**PICTURE
ACKNOWLEDGEMENTS**
The publisher would like
to thank the following for
granting permission to use
their photographs in this book.
Key: l=left, r=right, t=top,
m=middle, b=bottom.
NHPA: 12bl, 20tr, 20b, 23tr, 24t,
24b, 25t, 25br, 26t, 27t, 27bl,
27br, 32t, 32b, 33tl, 35b, 36t, 38t,
39t, 39b, 41tl, 62b.
Tim Ellerby: 39m.

Illustration credits as follows:
Peter Barrett: 239b, 241b, 244b,
245t, 246t.
Jim Channell: 183t, 237b, 238,
239t, 240b, 241t, 242–3, 246b, 247.
Anthony Duke: all maps.
Rob Dyke: 67–8, 70–3, 120b,
125–7, 188b, 189b, 190b, 191–2.
John Francis: 113t, 116, 118t, 119t,
120t, 121, 124b, 128b, 157t, 220t.
Rob Highton: 130–1, 133,
135–7, 139, 142–3, 159–61,
223b, 225, 226t, 227t, 228, 229b,
231b, 232b, 233.
Stuart Jackson-Carter: 15, 42–61
(habitats), 129, 132, 134, 140–1,
144, 145b, 148b, 150, 156, 169, 172t,
174t, 175t, 212b, 213b, 215, 216b,
217–18, 220b, 222t, 230t, 231t, 234t,
236, 237t, 240t, 244t.
Paul Jones: 198b, 199t, 201,
202b, 205–6, 207b, 209.
Stephen Lings: 92t, 93t, 94, 112,
176–7, 196t, 197t, 198t, 200t.
The Magic Group: 89b, 90t, 95t,
96b, 98, 102b, 103t, 124t, 146t, 147,
148t, 149t, 153b, 154t, 157b, 158,
164, 165t, 166, 167t, 170b, 171,
173b, 187, 196b, 197b, 199b, 200b,
202t, 203, 204b, 208b.
Shane Marsh: 96t, 97, 104–5,
106t, 138.
Robert Morton: 66, 69, 74–87,
92b, 93b, 95b, 99, 102t, 106b,
107–9, 115t, 178–82, 183b,
184–5, 245b.
Fiona Osbaldstone: 103b, 128t,
162–3, 165b, 167b, 168, 172b,
173t, 174b, 175b, 189t, 190t,
194–5, 210b, 211, 212t, 213b,
214, 216t, 219, 221, 222b, 223t,
224, 226b, 227b, 229t, 230b,
232t, 234b, 235.
Mike Saunders: 88, 89t, 90b, 91,
100–1, 110–11, 113b, 114, 115b,
117, 118b, 119b, 122–3, 145t,
146b, 149b, 151–2, 153t, 154b,
155, 193b.
Sarah Smith: 170t, 186, 188t,
193t, 204t, 207t, 208t, 210t.